Popular Choice and Managed Democracy

POPULAR CHOICE AND MANAGED DEMOCRACY

The Russian Elections of 1999 and 2000

Timothy J. Colton

Michael McFaul

BROOKINGS INSTITUTION PRESS
Washington, D.C.

Copyright © 2003
THE BROOKINGS INSTITUTION
1775 Massachusetts Avenue, N.W., Washington, D.C. 20036
www.brookings.edu

Library of Congress Cataloging-in-Publication data

Colton, Timothy J., 1947–
  Popular choice and managed democracy : the Russian elections of 1999 and 2000 / Timothy J. Colton and Michael McFaul.
    p.   cm.
  Includes bibliographical references and index.
  ISBN 0-8157-1534-X (cloth : alk. paper) —
  ISBN 0-8157-1535-8 (pbk. : alk. paper)
  1. Elections—Russia (Federation) 2. Presidents—Russia (Federation)—Election—2000. 3. Russia (Federation). Federal'noe Sobranie. Gosudarstvennaëiìa Duma—Elections, 1999. 4. Political campaigns—Russia (Federation) 5. Political parties—Russia (Federation) 6. Russia (Federation)—Politics and government—1991– I. McFaul, Michael, 1963– II. Title.

JN6699.A5C645 2003
324.947'086—dc22   2003019080

9 8 7 6 5 4 3 2 1
The paper used in this publication meets minimum requirements of the American National Standard for Information Sciences—Permanence of Paper for Printed Library Materials: ANSI Z39.48-1992.

Typeset in Sabon

Composition by Betsy Kulamer
Washington, D.C.

Printed by R. R. Donnelley
Harrisonburg, Virginia

In memory of
Aleksandr Sobyanin and Michael Swafford

Contents

Acknowledgments

THIS BOOK WOULD NOT have been possible without generous contributions from institutions and individuals. The National Science Foundation and the National Council for Eurasian and East European Research funded the survey research. The Demoscope group at the Institute of Sociology of the Russian Academy of Sciences, headed by Polina Kozyreva and Mikhail Kosolapov, carried out the survey work with aplomb and precision, with Yelena Artamonova playing a key role. Michael Swafford helped greatly with all aspects of the project. We very much regret that he did not live to see it to fruition.

Michael McFaul would like to thank Tatyana Krasnopevtseva and Elizabeth Reisch for research assistance, Toula Papanicolas for administrative support, and the election team at the Moscow Carnegie Center, including especially Nikolai Petrov and Andrei Ryabov, for sharing their insights into Russian electoral politics. McFaul also thanks the Carnegie Endowment for International Peace, the Hoover Institution, the Bradley, Earhart, Mott, and Starr Foundations, and the Carnegie Corporation of New York for supporting his research and writing during the completion of this project.

Timothy Colton is grateful to Harvard University for the leave time necessary to write the book, to the Harvard Government Department and the Davis Center for Russian and Eurasian Studies for help with travel and other costs, and to the Carnegie Corporation for enabling him to observe the 1999 and 2000 campaigns. He is happy to thank Daniel Epstein and Maria Popova for their research assistance and

Melissa Griggs, Helen Grigoriev, Ann Sjostedt, and Maria Tarasova for administrative backup. At formative moments, Colton learned much about Russia's elections and the evolution of its political system from Yevgeniya Al'bats, Graham Allison, Sergei Grigoriev, Henry Hale, Fiona Hill, Stephen Holmes, Aleksandr Olson, Thomas Remington, and William Zimmerman.

We are indebted to the Brookings Institution for taking an interest in the book manuscript and seeing it through to publication so expeditiously. Strobe Talbott, Robert Faherty, Christopher Kelaher, Janet Walker, Susan Woollen, and Vicky Macintyre were marvelous to work with, and the three anonymous reviewers of the draft provided valuable feedback.

POPULAR CHOICE AND
MANAGED DEMOCRACY

1

Introduction: The Transition within the Transition

THIS BOOK IS A TALE of linked political events: a pair of recent elections in the heir to an extinct superpower, a troubled nation in whose stability, modernization, and openness to the global community the West still has a huge stake. A multitude of players jockeyed for advantage there. One particular group, to the amazement of most involved and the consternation of some, prevailed. We aim to explain how and why that happened and what difference it makes to the country, its postcommunist transition, and us on the outside.

Twice in the winter of 1999–2000, 75 million citizens of Russia flocked to their neighborhood voting stations. After a decade of rule by Boris Yeltsin, ordinary people had a say in who would lead them for the better part of the next decade. They scratched their ballots in an atmosphere crackling with uncertainty, rancor, and fear. Yeltsin's precarious health and erratic decisionmaking had marred his second term, begun in 1996. He was helpless in August 1998 to forestall a crippling financial crisis that saw the treasury default on its sovereign debt, the ruble shed four-fifths of its value, and dozens of banks shut their doors.[1] Although Russians had lived with hardship ever since marketization and privatization were launched in the early 1990s, this episode, as Yeltsin recounted later, was unique in the pain it inflicted on the winners in the reform process: "The worst of it was that it hit the barely born middle class . . . the property owners, businessmen, entrepreneurs, and professionals. . . . All this had been undertaken for their sake. These people were my main base of support."[2] Desperate to right the ship, Yeltsin fired one prime minister in March of 1998 as the fiasco loomed large, another when it was in full swing that summer, and a third the following spring, just as output indices rebounded.[3] Every dismissal triggered a confrontation with the State Duma, the paramount lower house of the Federal Assembly, over confirming a replacement. In May 1999 Yeltsin narrowly foiled a bill of impeachment in the Duma; a sign of the times was that one of the five counts was for "genocide against the Russian people." The North Atlantic Treaty Organization's (NATO's) air war against Serbia, protested but not averted by Russian diplomacy, struck another nerve. And on Russia's doorstep, the three-year-old truce in the North Caucasus hotspot of Chechnya crumbled amid recrimination, border raids, and abductions. In June 1999, Chechen gunmen, now hoisting the green banner of militant Islam, began infiltrating villages in Dagestan, an adjoining republic of the Russian Federation.

The anxiety quotient rose higher still on August 9, 1999, when Yeltsin axed a fourth prime minister and appointed a little-known Kremlin bureaucrat, Vladimir Putin, as acting premier, subject to ratification by the Duma, which it granted on August 16. To general incredulity, Yeltsin declared he wished Putin to succeed him as president in 2000, calling him "the person who is able to consolidate society and, drawing support from the broadest political forces, ensure the continuation of reforms in Russia."[4] In early September the violence in Chechnya and Dagestan spread into the heartland. Three hundred lives were snuffed out in nighttime terror bombings of apartment houses in Moscow and two southern towns; the Federal Security Service (FSB) claimed to have evidence incriminating pro-Chechen fanatics. Having limited itself to counterinsurgency in Dagestan, the Kremlin now decided to send tanks and tens of thousands of troops barreling into Chechnya to crush the resistance.

Against this ominous backdrop—with a national security emergency, cabinet instability, and burning memories of the 1998 financial crash overshadowing a whiff of economic recovery—Russians on December 19, 1999, voted for representatives to the 450-seat State Duma. They chose half of the members from lists of candidates served up by parties and equivalent organizations (in this volume we often employ "party" as shorthand for all these entities) and half in single-member territorial districts. The doom and gloom notwithstanding, antigovernment groups made no headway. Instead, a majority of the mandates went to lawmakers prepared to cooperate with the executive branch, a gift that had eluded the president since the election of the first post-Soviet Duma in December 1993. Yeltsin, alternately jubilant and tearful, took to the airwaves on December 31 to announce he was going into retirement six months in advance of schedule and was transferring interim power to Putin. On March 26, 2000, the dark horse who had scraped along at 2 percent in the polls in August was elected to a four-year presidential term.

Why Putin? For Yeltsin, it did not hurt that Putin was a hawk on Chechnya, had shepherded the army operation there, and was willing in a maiden decree as acting president to extend him immunity from criminal prosecution for acts in office.[5] The connection between patron and client ran deeper, however. A career foreign intelligence officer and the director of the FSB before being named premier, Putin was the latest in a string of military and security professionals to gain the favor of the patriarch. Their function in Yeltsin's eyes was to stem the centrifugal and disorderly forces in the governance of Russia that he, wearing the hat of crusader against Soviet tyranny, had earlier done the most to unleash. Revisiting private musings he had had in 1998, and skirting the ironies, Yeltsin says in his memoirs he "had been sensing for some while that the demand was growing in society for imparting a new quality to our state, a steel core, as it were, that would shore up the political structure of government." Needed at the helm was "a thinking, democratic, and innovative person, yet one who was firm in the military manner."[6] After a false start or two, Yeltsin found that metallic core in Putin.[7]

No sooner was the champagne downed at his inauguration on May 7 than President Putin set about nudging Russia's polity toward what his detractors and some of his admirers dubbed a "managed democracy" (*upravlyayemaya demokratiya*, in Russian).[8] From his opening gambit in Chechnya, Putin initiated change in domains as various as federalism, the secret services, the mass media, parliamentary procedures, government-business relations, and the party system. His moves did not always delight pensioner Yeltsin. Towering over all was a chief who fused the "military manner" Yeltsin fancied and the mien of "a manager of the Western type, a manager who calmly, without extra talk, solves problems."[9]

The elections, then, afforded Putin his golden opportunity to pull off a transition within the Russian transition. As Russia continued to make the tumultuous and protracted shift from communist rule to a different political and economic system, leadership of the process changed hands for the first time since it began, with a subsequent shift in course. Economically, the new leader set a more liberal agenda than his predecessor had: he buttressed private ownership, let capitalists be capitalists by whittling down the government's role, reduced taxes, balanced the budget, and improved the investment climate. Politically, Putin was more illiberal: favoring a more meddlesome, more coercive, and less accountable state, he worked to constrict flows of information and opinion and, when all is said and done, to reduce political competition and freedom. Complicating any Western reaction to these moves, the 1999–2000 elections also dealt Putin carte blanche to overhaul foreign policy, and he used it in ways that the United States and most Euro-Atlantic governments commended. The thaw in relations with Washington after September 11, 2001, would have been much harder to achieve without Putin in the Kremlin.

For Russians, the twin election campaigns in 1999 and 2000 commingled the expected and the unexpected. It was old hat when the Communist Party of the Russian Federation (KPRF) pocketed the most votes for the Duma, as it had four years before, and 20 million people backed its chairman, Gennadii Zyuganov, for president. Evening after evening from November 19 to December 17, 1999, television screens glowed with familiar faces—Zyuganov, for one, or Grigorii Yavlinskii of the Yabloko party, or Vladimir Zhirinovskii of the Liberal Democratic Party of Russia (LDPR)—mouthing well-rehearsed sales pitches. The elections featured a plethora of often-obscure warriors: twenty-six parties (and quasi parties) on the national ballot in December, eleven candidates for president in March. That, too, was a spectacle to which Russians were acclimated, as forty-three parties had vied for the Duma in 1995 and ten politicians for president in 1996. In 155 of the 224 local Duma districts—district 31, in Chechnya, was dormant because of the war—an incumbent stood for reelection.[10]

As eloquent a case could be made that the novel and the unforeseen defined the tenor of the elections. The glut of players was a constant; on the ballot slip, the bulk of the actual names were new. Among the national lists put up for the Duma, there were nineteen newcomers for the seven retreads from the 1995 campaign (the KPRF, Yabloko, the LDPR, and four smaller groups). Ninety-three percent of the single-mandate nominees had not represented districts in the previous Duma. The only survivors from 1996 among the presidential hopefuls were Zyuganov, Yavlinskii, and Zhirinovskii.[11]

The jarring surprise in 1999–2000 was not who was in the fray but who snatched victory. Virtually all pundits were caught unaware. Indicative of the unpreparedness is a sentence in a St. Petersburg political scientist's preview of the Duma campaign in September: "Judging by the initial lineup of candidates, the 1999 campaign does not look to hold any large surprises."[12] The surprises turned out to be large and plentiful.

Anticipation was well nigh unanimous that pro-government candidates would be drubbed and that the centrist bloc assembled by Yurii Luzhkov, the mayor of Moscow, would challenge the KPRF for primacy in the Duma. Luzhkov's electoral front stitched together the Fatherland movement he founded in 1998 with a grouping known as All Russia, the brainchild of some regional governors. In a crowning moment, he recruited the popular elder statesman Yevgenii Primakov, one of the four prime ministers Yeltsin sacked in 1998–99, to head the Fatherland–All Russia ticket (generally known by its Russian acronym, OVR, for Otechestvo–Vsya Rossiya). With its vague platform and its tentacles in officialdom and in business circles tied to it, OVR bore a more than passing resemblance to Our Home Is Russia (NDR, Nash Dom Rossiya), the party sired in 1995 by then prime minister Viktor Chernomyrdin. The shoe did not fit in one crucial regard: OVR was anathema to the president and his entourage, who accused Mayor Luzhkov of disloyalty and an indecent haste to shove Yeltsin aside. Being on the outs with the Kremlin did not necessarily dull OVR's luster. It was frequently held to be the trump card that, coupled with its image of competence, would equip OVR to sweep all before it. One article handicapping the forthcoming elections in September heralded Fatherland–All Russia as Russia's "new electoral powerhouse . . . the favorite to gain the largest number of seats in the Duma and to provide the winning presidential candidate in summer 2000." "Primakov's popularity, Fatherland's organization, and the governors' political machines are formidable assets. The bloc is also full of self-proclaimed 'proven managers' who can sell the . . . message that prudence and competence, not youth and economic theory, are the keys to Russian revival."[13] Another writer found the outlook so rosy that "the greatest uncertainty about OVR has to do with the bloc's activity beyond the elections rather than with balloting results."[14] It would have to decide, for instance, with whom to ally to form a controlling majority in the Duma and whether to propose Primakov or Luzhkov for president.

Only as nominations went down to the wire did OVR's nemesis make its debut. The pro-government slate going by the name of Unity was the newest and nimblest of the "parties of power" that have suited up in Russia's political wars since 1993. It was at the outset as much scoffed at as OVR was lionized. A report on business magnate Boris Berezovskii's tour of the Russian hinterland in August, to sound out his contacts on the feasibility of such a bloc, painted it as "one of the more comic episodes of the election season so far." The report was captioned "A Failed Bloc."[15] A respected political analyst and consultant, Igor Bunin of the Center for Political Technologies, predicted in early October, on the heels of Unity's founding congress and its selection of cabinet minister Sergei Shoigu as leader, that it would snag "1–2 percent, a maximum of 3 percent" of the vote.[16] Another article in early October, noting that Unity "violates almost every property of a political party" (true enough), said its one hope for seats in the Duma was to partner with Chernomyrdin's NDR. If it did, the tandem "will not be striving for first place, nor even for second place in the election race: those places are reserved for Fatherland–All Russia and the KPRF."[17] A published essay a month later took notice of a spike in Unity's ratings, only to brush it off as having "no chance of catching up with the current leaders."[18] Ten days before the election Bunin forecast "up to 8 percent" for the bloc, and Andrei Ryabov of the Moscow Carnegie Center 8 or 9 percent.[19] December 19 was to expose these ruminations, too, as wide of the mark.

The ultimate victor in 1999–2000 was, of course, Vladimir Putin, who at the age of forty-eight had never before campaigned for elective office, although he did have experience—severely distasteful to him—in election contests in St. Petersburg.[20] His meteoric rise coincided with the Duma campaign, which the Kremlin team and OVR alike viewed as the Russian version of a U.S. presidential primary. Unknown to all but inveterate Kremlin-watchers until Yeltsin appointed him premier, Putin had been ignored in the crystal ball–gazing about the succession.[21] His promotion in August left intact the suspicion that he was somehow not presidential timber. An American newsletter on Russian politics opined: "Few observers give this low-profile administrator, who once worked as a spy in East Germany, much chance of becoming president. Not only has he never proven himself as a major public figure, but Yeltsin's endorsement is widely seen as a kiss of political death."[22] Curiosity was piqued only in mid-autumn, when polls showed his star to be on the rapid ascent, mostly, it was felt, because of his handling of the Chechnya imbroglio. On October 11 Putin gave the Chechen leader, Aslan Maskhadov, an ultimatum to lay down arms and hand over fighters wanted by Moscow as terrorists, tacking on the slangy threat, "If need be, we will wipe them [the guerrillas] out in the toilet." Maskhadov balked, and Putin ordered the escalation of the war. "Literally overnight," one correspondent wrote, with some poetic license, "Putin became a serious pretender to the highest post in the state."[23] Putin during the last lap of the campaign voiced his support for the Unity bloc, "personally, as a citizen," after which his proxy surged to relative success in the vote. By year's end he was being treated in the domestic and foreign press—for good reason, our research confirms—as having the grand prize cinched. Putin's triumph in the March election, capping a desultory presidential campaign, has rightly been described as "a foregone conclusion."[24]

In dredging up mistaken prognostications from 1999, we do not mean to imply that we personally were prophets at the time. We were not.[25] Our point is rather that the electoral machinery was in high gear before even connoisseurs diagnosed where the test of wills was heading. The endgame is encapsulated in tables 1-1, 1-2, and 1-3.

Table 1-1 gives the results from the State Duma election by party and by what we call party "family," categorizing Russia's raft of parties and near parties by ideological orientation. We work with a sixfold template: *government* parties (or "parties of power") that start with defense of the status quo; *liberal* parties sworn to uphold, deepen, and humanize the economic and political reforms of the Yeltsin era (often referred to as "right-wing parties"); *centrist* parties that see merit in compromise and avoidance of extremes and passions; *nationalist* (or "patriotic") parties that glorify love of country, nostalgia for empire, and solidarity against internal and external enemies; *socialist* (or "leftist") parties that harken to the Marxist creed of the Soviet regime; and a dusting of *miscellaneous* parties defying classification. The taxonomy is not surgically clean, but there is agreement on where the big players belong.[26]

As can be seen, the socialistic KPRF led the parade in the nationwide popular vote and the districts, as it had in 1995, and lifted its fraction of the national vote by 2 percentage points. The shock was that the upstart government bloc, Unity, and not the centrist but anti-Kremlin OVR, pressed the communists for the lead. Unity's 23.79 percent finish on the party lists was but 1 point behind the KPRF and outshone all other par-

Table 1-1. Results of Election to the State Duma, December 19, 1999

Party[a]	Party family[b]	Party-list vote			District deputies elected	Total deputies elected
		Votes received[c]	Percentage of the vote[c]	Deputies elected		
Communist Party of the Russian Federation (KPRF)	Soc	16,196,024	24.78	67	46	113
Unity	Gov	15,549,182	23.79	64	9	73
Fatherland–All Russia (OVR)	Cen	8,886,753	13.59	37	31	68
Union of Right Forces (SPS)	Lib	5,677,247	8.68	24	5	29
Yabloko	Lib	3,955,611	6.05	16	4	20
Liberal Democratic Party of Russia (LDPR)[d]	Nat	3,990,038	6.10	17	0	17
Our Home Is Russia (NDR)	Gov	790,983	1.21	0	7	7
Communists and Toilers for the Soviet Union	Soc	1,481,890	2.27	0	0	0
Women of Russia	Cen	1,359,042	2.08	0	0	0
Pensioners Party	Mis	1,298,971	1.99	0	1	1
Party for the Defense of Women	Cen	536,022	0.82	0	0	0
Congress of Russian Communities–Boldyrev Movement	Nat	405,298	0.62	0	1	1
Stalinist Bloc for the USSR	Soc	404,274	0.62	0	0	0
Civic Dignity Movement	Lib	402,754	0.62	0	0	0
Movement in Support of the Army	Soc	384,404	0.59	0	2	2
Peace, Labor, May	Mis	383,332	0.59	0	0	0
Nikolayev and Fëdorov Bloc	Cen	371,938	0.57	0	1	1
Peace and Unity Party	Soc	247,041	0.38	0	0	0
Russian People's Union	Nat	245,266	0.38	0	2	2
Russian Socialist Party	Cen	156,709	0.24	0	1	1
Russian Cause	Nat	111,802	0.17	0	0	0
Conservative Movement of Russia	Nat	87,658	0.13	0	0	0
All-Russian Party of the People	Soc	69,695	0.11	0	0	0
Spiritual Heritage	Soc	67,417	0.10	0	1	1
Socialist Party of Russia	Cen	61,689	0.09	0	0	0
Social Democrats	Lib	50,948	0.08	0	0	0
Against all parties	n.a.	2,198,702	3.36	n.a.	n.a.	n.a.
Independent candidates (in districts)	n.a.	n.a.	n.a.	n.a.	105[e]	105[e]

Source: Tsentral'naya izbiratel'naya komissiya Rossiiskoi Federatsii, *Vybory deputatov Gosudarstvennoi Dumy Federal'nogo Sobranya Rossiiskoi Federatsii 1999: elektoral'naya statistika* (The 1999 election of deputies to the State Duma of the Russian Federation: electoral statistics) (Moscow: Ves' Mir, 2000), pp. 121–22, 230.

n.a. Not applicable.

a. Here, as is frequently the case in the book, we use the term "party" generically, as shorthand for any organization that put up lists of candidates in the party-list half of the Duma election.

b. Gov = Government, Lib = Liberal, Cen = Centrist, Nat = Nationalist, Soc = Socialist, Mis = Miscellaneous.

c. Omits spoiled ballots. Total valid ballots cast 65,370,690.

d. For procedural reasons, the LDPR was registered in 1999 as the Zhirinovski Bloc.

e. Does not include eight independents who were chosen in repeat elections in March 2000, in districts where votes against all candidates registered exceeded the votes received by the top candidate, or the independent candidate elected in a special election in Chechnya in August 2000.

ties and blocs, going back to the initiation of multiparty elections in 1993.[27] Shoigu and the Unity roster were at the top of the heap in thirty-two of the federation's eighty-nine regions, eight more than the KPRF had secured. The one sour note was in the districts, where no more than nine nominees of the bloc captured seats, although the Kremlin—independent of Unity—sponsored dozens of successful "independents" in these single-mandate races. Instantly, Unity's seventy-three deputies and the co-option of a tidy sum of the independents elected in the districts made it a blocking minority in the Duma, and before long the hub of a working majority.[28] OVR, meanwhile, languished at 13.59 percent of the popular vote, a half of what had been forecast. Thirty-one deputies in the local districts, second to the KPRF's forty-six, could not offset the shabby performance of the national slate. Defections were to trim OVR's ranks when the Duma convened in January; shortly afterward it opened merger talks with Unity. Three other political organizations cleared the 5 percent threshold for Duma representation. The liberal Yabloko and the nationalist LDPR parties, placing fifth and sixth, had sat in the chamber since 1993.[29] The Union of Right Forces (or SPS), which leapfrogged them to finish fourth, was a bloc melding several extant liberal associations. The lone entrant other than Unity for which Putin signaled sympathy, SPS had been given shaky odds of making the 5 percent cutoff when the campaign opened.[30] An assortment of minor parties, movements, and blocs that straggled well behind 5 percent in the party-list vote elected sixteen delegates in the districts.

Table 1-2 adds longitudinal perspective by tracing the popular vote attained by the six party families through the Duma elections of 1993, 1995, and 1999. One—the pro-government grouping consisting of the Unity bloc and the fast-fading Our Home Is Russia—made a quantum leap from 1995 to 1999, going from one vote in every ten tallied to one in four. The centrists inched up by about 2 percentage points and the miscellaneous parties by a fleck of 1 percent. The other party families sagged: the liberals by 1.40 points, the socialists by 4.00, and the nationalists by an egregious 12.64 points.

The presidential sequel in March (see table 1-3) was anticlimactic. The 53.44 percent vote for Putin absolved him of a runoff, as the law would have required if no one procured a majority in the qualifying round. He cruised in 25 percentage points ahead of Zyuganov and 48 ahead of Yavlinskii. A chastened OVR declined to file nomination papers and, along with SPS, joined the pro-Putin chorus. The Putin vote

Table 1-2. *Percentage of Party-List Vote Obtained by Party Families in the 1993, 1995, and 1999 Duma Elections*[a]

Family	1993	1995	1999
Government	15.51	10.33	25.00
Liberal	18.67	16.83	15.43
Centrist	18.29	14.59	17.40
Nationalist	22.29	20.04	7.40
Socialist	20.39	32.84	28.84
Miscellaneous	0.00	2.54	2.57

a. Families for 1993 and 1995 as given in Timothy J. Colton, *Transitional Citizens: Voters and What Influences Them in the New Russia* (Harvard University Press, 2000), p. 234. Families for 1999 follow table 1-1.

Table 1-3. *Results of Presidential Election, March 26, 2000*

Candidate	Nominated by	Votes received[a]	Percentage of the vote[a]
Vladimir Putin	Independent	39,740,434	53.44
Gennadii Zyuganov	KPRF	21,928,471	29.49
Grigorii Yavlinskii	Yabloko	4,351,452	5.85
Aman Tuleyev	Independent	2,217,361	2.98
Vladimir Zhirinovskii	LDPR	2,026,513	2.72
Konstantin Titov	Independent	1,107,269	1.49
Ella Pamfilova	Civic Dignity Movement	758,966	1.02
Stanislav Govorukhin	Independent	328,723	0.44
Yurii Skuratov	Independent	319,263	0.43
Aleksei Podberëzkin	Spiritual Heritage	98,175	0.13
Umar Dzhabrailov	Independent	78,498	0.11
Against all candidates	n.a.	1,414,648	1.90

Source: Tsentral'naya izbiratel'naya komissiya Rossiiskoi Federatsii, *Vybory prezidenta Rossiiskoi Federatsii 2000: elektoral'naya statistika* (The 2000 election of the president of the Russian Federation: electoral statistics) (Moscow: Ves' Mir, 2000), p. 191.

n.a. Not applicable.

a. Omits spoiled ballots. Total valid ballots cast 74,369,773.

was two and one-half times Unity's in December. It was 19 percentage points higher than Yeltsin's in the first round in 1996 and 1 point shy of Yeltsin's numbers in the two-man runoff in 1996. The cakewalk bears comparison with Russia's presidential election in the last year of Soviet power, 1991, when Yeltsin's popularity was at its zenith. The 57.20 percent Yeltsin attained that year in a field of six was not much above Putin's haul in a field of ten.

As with any historical occurrence, remote or proximate in time, it is tempting in hindsight to see the trajectory of the 1999–2000 elections as inevitable. Many Russians nowadays do exactly that. They are aware that an underpinning of Putin's managed democracy is the axiom that in the cruel world of the twenty-first century a depleted Russia has little scope for maneuver, so the gist of leadership is unsentimental adaptation to circumstances. The notion has two corollaries: realists forged, like Putin, in the crucible of government administration know best how to adapt; and a vital mission of these stewards of the state is to prevent actors who are not state based or who are the leaders of subnational governments from standing in the way of national salvation. Russian intellectuals, even when they find fault with the reasoning, sometimes accept aspects of it and project them backward to say that the elections in which Putin conquered power were an empty formality—and that no one should care which personality or clan carried the day. Boris Kagarlitsky, a gadfly researcher and columnist of a social-democratic bent, put the thesis provocatively in 2002:

> The very concept of a political alternative has disappeared during the past three years. The opposition at least made a show of battling with Yeltsin. Today the opposition doesn't hide the fact that the battle is only for second place. It makes no claim to an independent political role. . . . In the Yeltsin era, the public still believed that it elected the president. But in 1999–2000 this belief was revealed to be an illusion. The president arises in the bowels of the bureaucracy, the product of its secret laws. Elections have become nothing more than a gala before the inauguration. Talk about a changing of the guard now resembles discussions of climate change. The political elite are like bad weather; you can curse them all you like but you won't change a thing. If you don't like the climate or the government, move to another country.[31]

We share Kagarlitsky's concern about the sapping of democratic norms and practices under Putin, as outlined in chapter 8, but not his interpretation of recent history. If Russia and its rulers never changed, the hammer and sickle would still be flying over Moscow, Kiev, and Tashkent, and the likes of Kagarlitsky, a student dissident in the 1980s, would not be reading their words in the newspaper. Nor, in our view, can the elections that bridged the Yeltsin and Putin eras be written off as a hollow pretense or costume ball. The battle over power, position, and policy was real and suspenseful, as few eyewitnesses will fail to remember.

Any election in a democratic or semidemocratic setting is at once a contest at the level of the political elite and an act of choice by individual citizens at the level of the masses. Journalistic accounts of elections typically emphasize the former dimension and have a qualitative flavor. At their best in conveying the human drama and excitement of the campaign, they relate the stirring of political ambition, the forging of alliances, the articulation and dissemination of a political message, the cut-and-thrust with adversaries, and the like.[32] Scholarly accounts typically zero in on voting choice and are quantitative in method. They isolate and weigh influences on election-day decisions by sifting through sample surveys of the electorate and using the data to verify theories of political behavior.[33]

The present volume integrates these two methods of analysis. We devote real attention to analyzing qualitatively the *elections* per se. We offer a narrative that relays the motivations, calculations, and strategic choices of the elite-echelon actors in the drama. This strand of *Popular Choice and Managed Democracy* relies on print and Internet sources, on interviews with politicians and campaign personnel, and on personal observation of the electoral process.

At the same time, we rely on quantitative data to delve rigorously into microfoundations. Rank-and-file *voters* behind the curtains of the polling booth rendered the final verdict in the elections. To determine how their decisions were shaped, we and our Russian collaborators committed heavily to survey research (see appendix A for details). In the argot of the field, we did panel surveys; that is, we interviewed and reinterviewed the same respondents, shooting a crude motion picture of popular attitudes rather than a still photo. Our principal tool was a three-wave interrogation of nearly two thousand randomly chosen citizens between the autumn of 1999 and the spring of 2000. To uncover trends in the electorate, we did a follow-up interview in 2000 of surviving members of a preexisting panel, established to look into the national elections of 1995–96 and dormant since then.

We have constructed a multistage statistical model to decipher the 1999–2000 survey data (see appendix B for a rundown). The logit regressions in it sequentially incorporate indicators of voters' social characteristics, perceptions of national conditions, normative beliefs, partisanship, and assessments of incumbents, leadership character, and likely performance in power on issues such as Chechnya and economic revival. Numerical "total effects" estimate the effects of given variables on the vote, making allowance for other explanatory variables causally antecedent to or coeval with them, and computer simulations generate other quantities of interest. We keep the statistical model on the back burner, for our main goal is to explain the dynamics of the electoral fight as a whole and not to retrace exhaustively the behavior of individual voters. We further streamline the modeling and the narrative by going lightly on contestants who did not make a minimally respectable showing, for which our floor is 5 percent of the valid votes cast. Accordingly, we bear down in the Duma election on the KPRF, Unity, OVR, SPS, and Yabloko; for the most part, we skip over the LDPR, as an economizing measure and because it looked like a waning force at the end of this electoral cycle.[34] For the presidential election, we concentrate on Putin, Zyuganov, and Yavlinskii.

Our combined qualitative and quantitative analysis demonstrates that the best were much more proficient than the rest at operating in a transitional environment still distinguished by pervasive uncertainty and by underinstitutionalization, manifested here in the immaturity and partial reach of political parties. The Unity bloc and Vladimir Putin had formidable political arsenals and wielded their weapons in cutthroat, if not undemocratic, fashion. And yet, as of the kickoff of the Duma race, it was another participant also moored in the matrix of state organization, OVR, that was said to be the "powerhouse" with "formidable assets" up its sleeve, and it should not be forgotten that the precursors to Unity had wasted a not dissimilar bounty in earlier Russian elections. The communists and the liberals maintained an electoral market share by wooing well-defined social groups, piggybacking on discontent or contentment with current economic conditions, fostering affective ties, and catering to issue opinions. But the aggressive forces in 1999 and 2000 were those that, while doing some of these same things, also manipulated and mobilized the populace's short-term evaluations of the political actors: of the job done by current officeholders, of individual leaders' personal virtues, and of worthiness to handle the nation's pressing problems.

For the task of guiding voter attitudes toward the players, command over *the central apparatus of the state* was the pivotal resource. It had intrinsic value and could be leveraged to fetch other benefits—provided it was deployed effectively and enterprisingly, which it had not always been in the past. Unity, the hurriedly assembled and ideology-free party of power whose founders knew enough to hire skilled public relations experts, and Putin, lieutenant and then successor to Yeltsin and no less of a tyro at elections, utilized the resource brilliantly. OVR, a kind of wanna-be party of power captained by aging Moscow officials and risk-averse regional bosses, was unable to match Unity's energy or to counterpunch when attacked. Its humiliation and the withdrawal from presidential contention of the head of its Duma list, Primakov, left Putin with unimpeded passage to his goal. He proceeded remorselessly down that path.

Chapter 2 of our book sets the scene for the elections by reviewing the transition milieu in which they were waged, paying attention to electoral rules, the cast of players, and the mindset of the electorate, as displayed in attitudes and continuity/discontinuity in behavior. Chapters 3 through 7 form the core of the book. Each is organized around a particular electoral player or set of players, their objectives and strategies, their efforts to rally mass support, and the reasons for their ability or inability to entice voters, as revealed by our survey data. Chapter 3 presents a detailed account of the Unity bloc's breakthrough. Chapter 4 focuses on the hubristic Fatherland–All Russia, which was expected to coast to victory but fell by the wayside. Chapters 5 and 6 spotlight the communists and the liberals, opposites in ideology but akin in having a past that stood in the way of expanding their constituency, and contain compact sections on the Zyuganov and Yavlinskii presidential campaigns. Chapter 7 returns to the winners' circle, taking up the selling of manager-in-chief Putin, a saga intertwined with Unity's in some ways but separable from it in others. Chapter 8 recaps our findings and sketches implications for Russian politics and Russia's place in the world.

2

*Setting the
Scene*

THE TRANSITION PARADIGM has lately come under fire from scholars and policy specialists for "democratic teleology" that blurs the difference between the tearing down of failed authoritarian regimes and the building up of successful democratic ones.[1] Inasmuch as the paradigm rests on wishful thinking about unidirectional and irreversible progress, with a textbook liberal democracy as the blissful destination, a dose of skepticism is overdue. When it comes to Russia and Eurasia, optimism is in shorter supply today than ten or fifteen years ago, as nations travel at varying speeds and not infrequently along disparate paths. Some make strides toward Western models of rule; others spurn democratic politics and, for that matter, market economics. Freedom House, the well-known human-rights monitor, rates just three post-Soviet states (the Baltic countries Estonia, Latvia, and Lithuania, on the fast track for admission to the European Union and the North Atlantic Treaty Organization) as being governed in a "free" manner in 2001–02; it classifies six as "partly free" and six as "not free." Russia is in the middle of the pack, in the partly free category.[2]

To discard the concept of transitional politics, though, would be to throw out the baby with the bathwater. Glancing over the past decade or two, it still makes good sense to imagine Russia, if not all of the successor states, as absorbed in a meandering search for a political system to substitute for the one that folded in 1991. A plus of the transition metaphor is that it underscores the uncertainty that has been a cardinal feature of contemporary Russia's politics.[3] A transitional environment is

15

by its nature an in-between environment: old routines, perceptions, and loyalties have been uprooted, and new ones are slow to come forth; there is a lack of elite and mass consensus about the good life and a culture of mistrust in the public sphere; the institutions for resolving conflict are stunted. In 1999–2000, one decade into postcommunism, uncertainty in the Russian polity was excessive by the standards of a mature democracy, yet not boundless. In setting the scene for the elections, we refer repeatedly to uncertainty, to its limits, and to means of coping with it.

A corrective to glib use of the transitional paradigm must be, as Archie Brown puts it, that Russia's ride has been "extremely uneven" and it "has seen a transition from communism but not yet a transition to democracy."[4] Moreover, the attempt in Russia to dismantle one political regime and build another took place alongside two other great dramas, economic transformation and border redefinition, adding further complications and uncertainty to the political story.[5] Sad to say, Vladimir Putin's minitransition inside the transition is a regression away from some of the democratic gains of the 1980s and 1990s—a backtracking and not a mere stalling of forward motion. Victory in the elections of 1999–2000 was his opening to introduce the bundle of statist restrictions and controls that brought about what we term "managed democracy." The campaigns also provided some foretaste of what managed democracy would be like.

We begin this chapter by reviewing the rules that guided the electoral activity. They acted both to buffer uncertainty and to prolong and intensify it. Most were democratic in spirit and application; some were not. Next, we itemize the players in the elections. They are more numerous and less coordinated than their opposite numbers in the older democracies, since the great unifiers of electoral activity in the West—political parties—do not have hegemony over contests for public office in Russia. In a final section, we talk in a preliminary way about the electorate, taking its measure for anger, alienation, and volatility.

Rules in an Unruly Environment

Democracies evince substantive uncertainty and procedural certainty. Citizens do not know beforehand how an electoral or other competition will turn out. They should know beforehand that none of the competitors will dictate or subvert its terms. Rational planning is possible "because the probability of particular outcomes is determined jointly by the institutional framework and the resources that the different political forces bring to the competition."[6] In emerging democracies, the calculus is murkier.

Routinization and Lingering Uncertainty

The formal rules of the game for the Russian parliamentary and presidential elections of 1999–2000 were on the face of it well crafted, transparent, and stable. The upper house of parliament, the Federation Council, was not subject to popular election: it was filled ex officio by provincial governors, "presidents" of the minority republics, and legislative chairmen. The State Duma, the more influential body, was up for reelection under a two-tiered formula. Voters were to pick half of it by choosing one of the national lists of candidates groomed by parties and quasi parties; a proportional-representation (PR) formula would distribute seats to all obtaining 5 percent of the total votes. The second half was to be decided by plurality in single-member districts approximately equal in population, with the proviso that no federal region go without a Duma district. Whereas the parties had a stranglehold on the PR election, their participation was optional in the local districts, in which independents could also compete. The same was true in the presidential election.

The hybrid rules for electing the Duma were also very close to those in effect in 1993 and 1995 (we note a few minor changes as we go). The boundaries of the 225 territorial districts were unaltered from 1995. For the presidency, scarcely a comma had changed in the guidelines since 1996. None of several attempts to revise the rules for the one-sided advantage of one or another player had succeeded.[7]

An engine of suspense in the previous electoral cycle was absent this time. In March 1996 Boris Yeltsin, jittery about losing the pending presidential election to the communist opposition, was on the verge of canceling the vote, disbanding the newly elected Duma, and instituting emergency presidential rule. He says in his memoirs he had ordered his aides to pen an implementing decree, only to be talked back from the brink by his daughter Tat'yana D'yachenko and a trusted adviser, Anatolii Chubais.[8] There was no reprise in 1999 or 2000. Yeltsin and Putin abided by the letter of the constitution and seem never to have contemplated doing otherwise.[9]

Table 2-1. *Citizen Fears of Disastrous Consequences of the 1996 and 2000 Presidential Elections*[a]

Percent

Consequence	1996[b]	2000[c]
Civil war	45	24
Major economic deterioration	53	38
Jump in emigration	25	16
Loss of democratic freedoms	33	23
Radical worsening of relations with former Soviet republics	31	25
Radical worsening of relations with the West	32	27
Religious persecution	20	10

a. Question reads, "Please tell me if you were afraid that as a result of the presidential election there would be in our country . . ." Respondent answered "Yes" or "No" or was unable to say.

b. Postelection interview, in panel survey described in Timothy J. Colton, *Transitional Citizens: Voters and What Influences Them in the New Russia* (Harvard University Press, 2000). N = 2,472 weighted cases.

c. Postelection interview, 1999–2000 panel, wave 3 (N = 1,755 weighted cases).

If there was a tendency for electoral politics to settle down into a steadier mold, it would be wrong to exaggerate it. The broader environment was still rife with uncertainty. The army was raining fire on Chechnya, and anonymous terrorists were blowing up buildings in Moscow; social tensions were rampant; the economic situation was grim, despite advance signs of beneficial effects from the devaluation of 1998 and the rise in world petroleum prices. Picking up the vibrations, millions of citizens were nervous in 1999–2000 about imminent disaster and about the electoral process itself conspiring to exacerbate the peril. Table 2-1 summarizes responses to a survey question put to respondents in wave 3 of our 1999–2000 panel survey, in the spring of 2000, and responses to the same question in 1996, in an earlier election period. Citizens were asked if they had been afraid that "as a result of the presidential election" any of a litany of calamities could befall Russia. On all seven, people were less skittish in 2000 than four years before. The average decline was 11 percentage points; the steepest, consisting of 21 points, was for the blackest nightmare of all, a civil war. But the amount of fear still haunting the population and the willingness to connect it to political factors are disturbing. The pulse registered is not that of a society at peace with itself or with the capacity of state institutions to shield it from danger and discord. Sixty-seven percent responded in the affirmative in 1996 to one or more of the fear-of-catastrophe questions and 41 percent to three or more. In 2000, 51 percent gave at least one positive response and 27 percent at least three. Some 40 percent had fore-boding of an economic slump; about one-quarter of civil war, forfeiture of democratic freedoms, and troubles in foreign policy; and lesser amounts of flight from the country and religious persecution.

Mixed Effects of Rules and Procedures

The written and unwritten rules of political action in Russia brought uncertainty and its companion, arbitrariness, home to the interlocking election campaigns. Yeltsin's slick exit from the Kremlin, timed to reward his handpicked successor, illustrates this as well as anything. The one president of the United States ever to resign, Richard Nixon in 1974, did so involuntarily, and the last thing on his mind was to boost the career of Gerald Ford, his vice president. More binding, the fixed term in the U.S. Constitution barred Ford from seeking the electorate's validation during the honeymoon phase of his presidency. In Russia, Yeltsin trumpeted his desire to pass the baton to Putin at all costs, and the constitution written to his specifications in 1993 conveniently stipulated a presidential election within three months of the departure of an incumbent. Putin got to face the electorate with all the might of the state at his command and before there was a chance for negative fallout from Chechnya or any of his policies to accumulate.[10] Potential rivals, not legally protected and not privy to Yeltsin's intentions, got to decide about running and scrounging for resources at the peak of the Christmas and New Year's holidays.

The procedures for registering party lists and candidates constituted a fertile seedbed of uncertainty and were peremptory to boot. Would-be participants had to navigate a series of obstacles and accede in at times ad hoc and overbearing bureaucratic decisions. The overall impression conveyed was that running in a Russian election is a privilege granted by state officials, not a democratic right.

The federal law framing the Duma contest, signed only on June 20, 1999, allowed parties and quasi parties to apply for the national PR ballot by submitting (by no later than October 24) petitions signed by 200,000 eligible voters, the same quota as in 1995. No more than 7 percent of the signatories could have domicile in any one region, down from 15 percent in 1995. For the first time, the law offered the alternative of posting a cash deposit, equal to about $82,000, as a means to get on the ballot. Ten of the parties that registered (and five of the six winners) took the first route, fourteen the second, and two both. The Central Electoral Commission (CEC), a tribunal appointed in thirds by the president and the two houses of parliament, was supposed to be an impartial traffic cop in the nomination process but wound up wearing the robes of prosecuting attorney, judge, and jury. It ruled on credentials after verifying the signatures and passport data on the signature sheets and combing over the personal statements filed on all members of the putative slate for correct disclosure of income and property, evidence of a criminal background or foreign citizenship, and a host of other criteria—none of them constitutionally grounded. Fifteen percent's worth of defective signatures, or disqualification of any of the three leading candidates or of 25 percent of the entire list, would be fatal to the list. Prospective candidates in the districts threaded a similar labyrinth, delivering the signatures of 1 percent of the electorate (preferred by two-thirds of the applicants) or a ruble deposit worth about $3,300. For the presidential campaign, the ticket for admission (to be readied by February 13) was 500,000 signatures—halved from the usual 1 million owing to the compressed election calendar.

The CEC and its regional affiliates could and did use their discretion to restrict access to the ballot. In the countdown to the Duma election, the commission rebuffed five of the thirty-one slates that applied for registration.[11] It also banished 342 individuals from the party lists, in rulings that too often were capricious. For example, the commission removed the minister of federal and nationality affairs, Vyacheslav Mikhailov, from Yabloko's list because he omitted a Moscow parking space from his inventory of assets; days before, it let the Yabloko leader, Grigorii Yavlinskii, head the list after finding he had concealed $3,000 in income. Reviewing cases like these, the political consultant and analyst Vyacheslav Nikonov raised two objections: "First of all, the glaring inaccuracy of the internal revenue service and the evident lack of unbiased treatment in the Kremlin's . . . auditing agencies are no secret to anyone. The possibility of mistakes and number fudging is unlimited. Secondly, a whole realm of subjective treatment of 'substantiated' discrepancies opens up."[12] Flagrant favoritism tainted the judgments of the commission's local subsidiaries in some of the Duma districts.[13] In February two presidential candidates were ousted for signature irregularities.[14] The CEC's inquisitorial style under Chairman Aleksandr Veshnyakov is evident from its own précis of the registration of presidential candidates:

[The] candidates presented the Central Electoral Commission with 732 documents, as the law prescribed. In order to vouch for the authenticity of the information filed, the commission and its Control and Auditing Service prepared and sent off 162 official queries to the Ministry of Internal Affairs of the Russian Federation, the Ministry for Taxes and Levies, the Federal Security Service, the State Customs Committee, and the Tax Police. As data on the presence of undeclared income and property came to light, 23 additional checks were carried out on candidates. One hundred and eighty-five official replies were received from the indicated ministries and agencies. As a result of the checks conducted, the commission established 66 violations of legal requirements, in particular, the submission of incomplete information about property and income, cars, and shares in commercial firms.[15]

The area of campaign finance exhibited arbitrariness of a different sort. On paper, the scheme was squeaky clean. For the Duma election, the federal government doled out $10,000 from the budget to every active party or bloc and gave them leeway to solicit contributions from individuals and corporations up to a specified ceiling per donor. Monies were to be held in state-inspected bank accounts. The officially reported total for campaign expenditures in 1999 was $15 million, purportedly $1 million less than in 1995. By common admission, the tab was many times that. Just how many times cannot be said. According to a then high-placed official in Yabloko, the party spent $7 million on its parliamentary campaign and $15 million on the Yavlinskii presidential campaign. The CEC reported that Yabloko had spent 38.7 million rubles (about $1.5 million) on the first campaign and 23.8 million rubles (about $900,000) on the second. So for this one party the disparity between actual and reported spending may have been about 5:1 for the Duma campaign and nearly 20:1 for the presidential race. The Yabloko informant's counterpart in the Union of Right Forces (SPS) insisted that the Yabloko figure provided us was much too low—he thought the real number was close to $25 million—and disclosed that SPS's campaign cost in 1999 was "a little more" than the $25 million figure. We were not able to ferret out this information about other parties and candidates.[16]

In campaign financing, the admixture of unrealistic ordinances, whimsical enforcement above, and evasiveness below was for the honest participant confusing and demeaning. As one critic observed, the problem was not only the transgression of the funding rules "on a massive scale." More pernicious was that out of malice or neglect the legislation had been written "in a way that forces the overwhelming majority of the participants [in the] electoral process to . . . break it,"[17] and hence made everyone vulnerable to the state's discretion when enforcing these laws. Infractions in the presidential race, where spending was said to add up to $4.4 million, were less because the pace-setting Putin did not mount an expensive, advertising-rich campaign.[18]

Players

Since the nineteenth century, political parties in the industrial democracies of the West have been the arch coordinators of elections. They and individual politicians and groups nested in them control the nomination of candidates and campaigns on their behalf. In post-Soviet Russia, the parties are ill-developed, oppressively large in numbers, and forced to share the partisan space with quasi parties or near parties that are on the whole less well organized and less durable. Parties and partylike organizations have full control of but one of the trio of electoral contests that go on at the national level: the party-list half of the election of the State Duma. In the single-member Duma districts and the presidential arena, the actors are individuals for whom sponsorship by a party organization is a possibility, not a requirement. Many of those seeking to be elected as district representatives or president are either freelancers or get a lifeline from party substitutes such as gubernatorial political machines, big business, campaign consultants, and the Kremlin bureaucracy.[19]

Parties and Quasi Parties

The parties' ability to quarterback even some of the game is homage to the farsightedness of the drafters of the presidential edicts of September and October 1993 (later codified in laws) who believed proportional-representation rules would be conducive to swift construction of a multiparty system: "Just as creators of the electoral system had hoped, the PR system quickly established parties and electoral blocs as the central agents for structuring the electorate's voting choice" in the party-list half of parliamentary elections.[20] The new party system, though, was fragmented and shallow in its penetration of the governmental institutions that mattered—as some of its creators intended.[21] President Yeltsin was in favor of multiparty politics but wanted to have nothing to do with it himself, refused to staff the executive on a partisan basis, and refused to seek reelection in 1996 as a party nominee, a precedent Putin was to follow in 2000.[22] The putting of two-thirds of electoral activity outside the parties' exclusive purview was a body blow. And party proliferation was to go much further than most participants foresaw at the outset. Parties and quasi parties in the national PR race snowballed from thirteen in number in 1993 to forty-three in 1995, at a time when most voters wanted there to be two or three.[23]

To everyone's relief, there was some rationalization of the cast of characters in 1999. The number of parties and quasi parties in the hunt for Duma seats dropped from forty-three to twenty-six. They decreased in every category but the government parties, which doubled to two, and the socialist, which increased from four to seven. Liberal parties went from twelve to four, centrist parties from ten to six, nationalist parties from six to five, and miscellaneous parties from ten to two.

The change was propelled in part by better polling skills that honed realism about electoral prospects and in part by two deliberate efforts to augment professionalization and discourage fringe groups. First, a statute passed in 1997 required organizations intending to solicit votes in 1999 to have enrolled with the Ministry of Justice by one year before election day. In 1995 the waiting period had been six months; in 1993 there was none.[24] Second, new financial penalties were levied on parties and quasi parties receiving a minuscule vote. Any that qualified for the national ballot by making a cash deposit lost the surety if they took fewer than 3 percent of the PR votes. A party that got less than 2 percent was required to reimburse the government for the free television and radio time allotted during the campaign.[25]

Political scientists have known for years that the sheer quantity of parties is not the only indicator of fragmentation. The size of their popular constituencies is also of interest. A system with ten parties would look very different to the citizen and the analyst if the ten drew 10 percent of the vote each than if two giant parties polled 49 percent and eight midget parties fought over a couple of percent. The most discriminating quantitative measure, one that does correct for size, is the "effective number of parties."[26] Table 2-2 gives two versions of this index for the Russian Duma. A score of, say, 5.00 would correspond to the fractionalization symptomatic of a system of five equally strong

Table 2-2. *Effective Numbers of Parties in the 1993, 1995, and 1999 Duma Elections*[a]

Election	Elective parties	Legislative parties
1993		
Party lists	7.58	6.40
Districts	2.78	2.45
1995		
Party lists	10.68	3.32
Districts	5.53	4.88
1999		
Party lists	6.53	4.57
Districts	4.79	3.54

a. Indices for 1993 and 1995 from Robert G. Moser, "The Impact of Parliamentary Electoral Systems in Russia," in Archie Brown, ed., *Contemporary Russian Politics: A Reader* (Oxford University Press, 2001), p. 200. Indices for 1999 computed by the authors using the same formula.

parties. The first column in the table is for elective parties, or votes cast by the Russian electorate; the second is for legislative parties, or seats in the Duma.

The 1993 election epitomized fragmentation of the party-list vote in the electorate and in the 50 percent of the Duma chosen by PR. The district vote was less dispersed, but this is to some degree an artifact of the convention of classifying independents as a unitary group when computing the effective number of parties. Atomization worsened in 1995 in every respect but one: the deputies returned on the party lists. That contingent was more homogeneous than in 1993 as a consequence of the unwieldy number of parties entered, most of which fell prey to the 5 percent barrier. In the 1999 election there was a conspicuous abatement in the effective number of elective parties and a more ambiguous trend for legislative parties. The electorate's votes were less splintered in the district and especially the PR settings. Among deputies elected in the districts, fragmentation receded about halfway toward the 1993 level. For those elected on the party lists, the trend was toward heterogeneity, chiefly because of the inclusiveness associated with diminution of the "wasted vote."[27] Wasted votes, cast for a party that did not make it into the legislature or against all the parties, soared from 12.94 percent of all party-list votes in 1993 to 48.52 percent in 1995, then subsided to a more tolerable 17.00 percent in 1999. And, unlike 1995, those that failed to cross the 5 percent threshold really failed; none of these parties garnered much more than 2 percent of the national vote.

If one looks beyond vote share to political orientation, Russia's deluge of parties and quasi parties taxes the analyst's inventiveness and the voter's patience. Thinking of them as belonging to ideological families (see tables 1-1 and 1-2) imposes some order, but terminological and conceptual fuzziness abounds. One source of dissonance is the parties' self-selected nametags. For instance, the oldest nationalist party, the Liberal Democratic Party of Russia (LDPR), styles itself a "liberal democratic" organization. The primary centrist player in 1999, Fatherland–All Russia (OVR), enshrined the nationalist buzzword "fatherland" in its title. The two parties with a "socialist" label were, by our lights, best pigeonholed as centrist. The second-ranking liberal party, Yabloko, bears the name of a fruit (*yabloko* is the word for "apple") and features shiny apples in its promotional material.[28]

Nor were the politicians bashful about making appeals to the beliefs and symbols saluted in other party families. The best specimen of cross-pollination is the nearly universal evocation of nationalist values. Although the vote share of overtly nationalist parties and leaders plummeted, patriotic rhetoric billowed in every quarter. When Sergei Shoigu of Unity rattled off some nationalistic clichés in a press interview in December 1999, the journalist objected, "everybody who is on the ball is now arming himself with patriotic slogans." Shoigu had to concede that "resonant phrases" about nation and fatherland were a dime a dozen.[29] The language of consolidation and compromise—sometimes but not always turning on the word "centrist"—was also common currency in 1999–2000.[30] Almost no one wanted to look like a radical outlier or an agent of political destabilization.

Multiple Organizational Forms

There was another uncertainty-linked complication with the dramatis personae, namely, the multiplicity of organizational forms. Russian law as of 1999 assigned nomination rights to any registered organization whose bylaws authorized it to engage in political activity. The 139 organizations satisfying these criteria came in two strains: political parties as such, having the sole announced objective of partaking in elections and lawmaking and empowered to sign up dues-paying members; and more unstructured "civic movements" with a variety of objectives.[31]

In the 1999 Duma election (see table 2-3), twelve of the freestanding organizations in the party-list vote were political parties and five were

Table 2-3. *Organizational Types in the 1999 Duma Election*

Political parties	Civic movements	Electoral blocs
Communist Party of the Russian Federation (KPRF)	Civic Dignity Movement	Unity
Yabloko	Movement in Support of the Army	Fatherland–All Russia (OVR)
Liberal Democratic Party of Russia (LDPR)[a]	Russian People's Union	Union of Right Forces (SPS)
Our Home Is Russia (NDR)	Conservative Movement of Russia	Communists and Toilers for the Soviet Union
Women of Russia	Spiritual Heritage	Congress of Russian Communities–Boldyrev Movement
Pensioners Party		Stalinist Bloc for the USSR
Party for the Defense of Women		Peace, Labor, May
Peace and Unity Party		Nikolayev and Fëdorov Bloc
Russian Socialist Party		Russian Cause
All-Russian Party of the People		
Socialist Party of Russia		
Social Democrats		

a. For procedural reasons, the LDPR was registered in 1999 as the Zhirinovskii Bloc.

civic movements. The popular vote accruing to the parties dwarfed that of the movements by 43.92 percent to 1.82 percent, but four-fifths of all the party votes were snared by the Communist Party of the Russian Federation (KPRF), Yabloko, and the LDPR. In isolation, the civic movements and the borderline parties were forgettable extras on the set. In context, they gained significance because of a procedural loophole on the books since 1993. Neither movements nor parties were required to go into an election on their own steam. The alternative was to band together in an electoral alliance or "bloc" (*izbiratel'nyi blok*). Blocs wanting to enter the 1999 Duma contest had the same deadline as parties or movements to get their papers to the CEC. Member organizations, like individual politicians, were entitled to withdraw from a bloc until six days before the vote.

For the politicians, the green light to blocs served a threefold purpose. One was to gratify "the elementary wish to insure oneself" against mishap, and most of all against trouble at the CEC.[32] An incident involving the LDPR, the party that ranked second in the 1995 election and first in 1993, showed the utility of this safety hatch. On October 11 the CEC withheld registration from the LDPR after resolving that the second and third members of its candidates' list, below Vladimir Zhirinovskii (Anatolii Bykov and Mikhail Musatov), were gangsters and contravened its disclosure requirements. Forty-eight hours later two LDPR offshoots skippered by family and friends of the leader-for-life (the Party of Spiritual Rebirth of Russia and the Russian League of Free Youth, a civic movement) met in a Moscow auditorium to form the "Zhirinovskii Bloc." The CEC registered it, after taking a monetary deposit and verifying a truncated and sanitized candidates' list, on November 2.[33]

A second function of the blocs was to widen politicians' organizational options. A party required a modicum of agreement on goals, presentation of self, future trajectory, and the like. Blocs, which could be assembled from several or many organizations, were a device of almost infinite tactical flexibility and were not necessarily predicated on any moral or ideological consensus. The OVR alliance, for instance, set its sights on electing Yurii Luzhkov or Yevgenii Primakov president and saw the winning of seats in the Duma as a means to this end, pure and simple. The Unity bloc was at root a response to OVR. When OVR failed to realize its immediate aims, its days were numbered, while the Unity bloc, vindicated, was to be reconfigured as a political party. The Union of Right Forces and the Zhirinovskii Bloc, finishing third and fifth in the party-list voting, experienced different fates. SPS, a coming together of liberal groups and movements, upgraded itself, like Unity, into a regular party, while the Zhirinovskii Bloc vacated the stage in favor of its progenitor, the LDPR.

The third use of the electoral bloc was to augment the value of the civic movements and microparties that crowded the political landscape. With the possibility of forming and reforming blocs ever alive, ownership of a boutique party or movement brought with it a license to sell the organization for pecuniary or other compensation or, were those in control so inclined, "to participate in the political bargaining with the idea of worming your way into one of the main participants" in the show.[34]

Parties, movements, and political middlemen struck deals in this Russian election bazaar as early as January 1999. The next seven or eight months are strewn with the bones of ephemeral blocs that were solemnly agreed to and then went belly up: Popular Front, Patriots of Russia, Voice of Russia, Rebirth and Unity, Russian House, Right Cause, and so on. The pacts that survived bracketed from two to seven signatory organizations. Counting the Zhirinovskii Bloc as a surrogate for the LDPR, three of the six contenders to surmount 5 percent in December were late-blooming electoral blocs—Unity, OVR, and SPS—

which harvested more than 30 million votes, 46.07 percent of the total. All told, the nine blocs accounted for 50.90 percent of the popular vote for the Duma, or more than parties and civic movements combined. By giving elite participants an excuse to shop for deals until the last possible moment, the blocs, which acted in part as a bulwark against uncertainty, simultaneously heightened politically useful uncertainty.

The Districts

For rank-and-file voters, to whom all this was a spectator sport, the whirlwind of intergroup wrangling and eleventh-hour deals was bound to compound uncertainty in the party-list contest. But it was nothing beside the convolutions of the district portion of the election.

As with the parties and quasi parties, there was a trend toward a reduction in the numbers of candidates in the single-member districts. Having averaged 11.7 per district in 1995 (and 6.8 in 1993), they tapered off to 9.9 per district in 1999. One reason was a new provision requiring security deposits to be confiscated for candidates receiving less than 5 percent of the votes.

In every other way, the district races remained as difficult as ever to sort out. Although they overlapped with the countrywide party-list campaign, the bond was loose in key respects. Unlike the two-tiered electoral system found in Germany and some other countries in Western Europe, the local and national elements of Russian Duma elections are not yoked by a provision for compensatory seats. The partisan affiliations of candidates who happen to be nominated by parties have been emblazoned on the ballot since 1995, but this alone does not tie a neat knot. The parties have "experienced drastically different levels of success under the different systems."[35] Local partisans of all ideological hues are often more loyal to local patrons than to the national party headquarters.

The parties' own behavior has contributed to the disparity. Strapped for resources, national party committees were selective in their district nominations in 1999, as they had been all along. Only the KPRF, Yabloko, and the socialist Spiritual Heritage movement found candidates in as many as 100 districts. The citizen, therefore, was often denied the possibility of voting a straight ticket. Under Article 39 of the electoral law, any candidate on a nationwide party list could simultaneously run in a local district. One and the same politician could seek voters' favor under the two rubrics, and there was no roadmap indicating to the unwitting electors who was doing what. Although new fine print in the electoral law cut down on the practice, it was still not unheard-of for a national campaign to do little more than cook up publicity for a party leader seeking to be elected to a district seat.[36]

The most serious issue was the continued presence of hundreds of independent candidates, at liberty to bid for votes without so much as a nod at the PR half of the election. The 1,134 independents in the 1999 election, 52.29 percent of all the candidates, took 48.61 percent of the district seats and so made up one-quarter of the new Duma.[37] Dashing hopes that the parties would gain ground, *more* independents were winners than in 1995 (when they were victorious in 34.67 percent of the districts). Only in 1993, when the parties were in their infancy, had Russians elected more nonparty deputies (61.10 percent) than in 1999. Although it was tenable in table 2-2, when calculating the effective number of parties, to lump independents into a uniform category, on concrete issues they were a motley crew. There were few mechanisms for coordinating their campaigns either across or within districts.

Presidential Simplicity

Compared with the intricate mosaic of the Duma election, the presidential election was the picture of simplicity. The rules were straightforward and precluded multicornered alliances. Neither vote-counting nor representation had a territorial component. In the gallery of nominees in 2000, only three were truly asterisk candidates: a Moscow businessman (Umar Dzhabrailov), a former cabinet minister and head of a civic movement (Ella Pamfilova), and a university professor and founder of Spiritual Heritage (Aleksei Podberëzkin).[38] The rest were known commodities to most of the electorate: Russia's interim president (Vladimir Putin), three party leaders (Grigorii Yavlinskii, Vladimir Zhirinovskii, and Gennadii Zyuganov), two provincial governors (Konstantin Titov and Aman Tuleyev), a famous movie director (Stanislav Govorukhin), and a scandalmongering former procurator-general (Yurii Skuratov).

There were about a third as many candidates for president in 2000 as there were parties in the run for the Duma in 1999. Citizens were less inclined to scatter their votes in the presidential than in the parliamentary election. One can calculate an index analogous to the effective number of parties for the vote fractions of the various presidential candidates in 1996 and 2000.[39] In the first round of the 1996 election, the "number of effective elective candidates" was 3.67. In 2000 it was 2.55—not far off the moderate fractionalization in the U.S. presidential election of 1992, when Bill Clinton defeated George H. W. Bush and Ross Perot.

In comparative perspective, the crucial characteristic of Russian presidential elections is the limited role of political parties. The winner, Putin, and five of the remaining candidates ran in 2000 as independents (see table 1-3). Parties and quasi parties that took 62.35 percent of the popular votes in December had no nominee in March, although many of them endorsed one of the nonpartisan candidates (usually Putin). If one accepts that party labels and the process of acquiring them would normally provide useful information to voters, it follows that Russians were not as well informed about their presidential candidates as they would have been in a party-dominated system.

They did, nonetheless, find it less of a chore to make decisions about the presidential election. A convenient barometer of public uncertainty about parties and candidates is the timing of electoral choices. Waves 2 and 3 of our 1999–2000 panel survey, replicating questions administered in the mid-1990s, inquired when it was that participating voters nailed down their decisions. Hesitancy ebbed between 1995 and 1999, although at a more leisurely pace than between 1993 and 1995 (see table 2-4). As before, Russians found it easiest to come to closure in the presidential election, not so easy in the PR voting, and hardest in the Duma districts. Seventy-nine percent said they finalized their presidential decision by one month prior to the 2000 election. Sixty-eight percent decided that early about a party list in 1999, and 55 percent in their local district. These subjective assessments jibe with the objective evidence about the complexness of the respective campaigns.

In the Wings

Players in the wings, and not only the politicians at center stage—and assuredly not only politicians in the parties—were an integral part of the 1999–2000 election story. We show them in action in chapters 3 to 7. Introductions are in order.

It is helpful to bear in mind Pippa Norris's tripartite typology of campaign styles. In the "premodern" campaign, the norm in the Euro-Atlantic democracies until the 1950s, political organization "is based upon direct forms of interpersonal communications between candidates and citizens at the local level, with short-term, ad-hoc planning by the

Table 2-4. *Timing of Voting Decisions Recalled in Postelection Surveys*
Percent

Timing	Party lists			Districts			Presidential	
	1993[a]	1995[a]	1999[b]	1993[a]	1995[a]	1999[c]	1996 (1st round)[a]	2000[d]
More than one month before election	18	44	48	9	23	27	64	62
One month before election	13	19	20	10	14	28	14	17
Two weeks before election	16	11	12	19	15	19	7	8
Final days of campaign	39	18	16	42	28	14	9	10
Election day	12	6	3	18	17	8	3	2
Don't know	2	3	1	3	3	3	3	1

a. From Colton, *Transitional Citizens*, p. 12.
b. From 1999–2000 panel, wave 2 (N = 1,403 weighted cases).
c. From 1999–2000 panel, wave 2 (N = 1,168 weighted cases).

party leadership." It puts a bounty on "relatively demanding political activities like rallies, doorstep canvassing, and party meetings." In a "modern" campaign, the effort is "coordinated more closely at a central level by leaders, advised by external professional consultants like opinion pollsters," and with "national television [as] the principal forum for campaign events." The nub of a "postmodern" campaign, Norris writes, is feedback from citizens through the Internet and other interactive channels. "The new technology allows for forms of political communication that can be located schematically somewhere between the local activism of the premodern campaign . . . and the national-passive forms of communication characteristic of the modern television campaign."[40]

For Russians, one can more or less forget for the moment about postmodern campaigning. Internet access in 1999–2000 was insufficient to sustain it except for small numbers of young and well-educated citizens in metropolitan areas.[41] Russia has a mix of the other two campaign types, the modern without question being ascendant.

Premodern Campaigners

Premodern activities based on printed materials packaged in advance are quite common in Russian elections, and party organizations by now have tons of experience in managing them. Fifty-eight percent of citizens reported receiving party campaign literature in their mailboxes in 1999; 56 percent encountered party leaflets or posters on the street. Party activists often do the bulk mailings and the legwork of distributing leaflets and pasting up posters, but this labor is easily outsourced to businesses and can be performed at the behest of political players who are not connected with parties. Exposure to literature, handouts, and visual materials was slightly higher for candidates in the Duma district races in 1999 than for the national parties, and roughly half of all those candidates were independents not nominated by parties.[42] In the 2000 presidential election, premodern campaigning was less intense than in the parliamentary election. The leading candidate, Putin, had no patience with it, and the parties were markedly less active.[43]

The more the premodern activity relies on extensive grass-roots networks and on a willingness to take part in formal events outside the home and occupational setting, the more Russians tend to resist it. A trifling 6 percent in 1999, and 5 percent in 2000, were canvassed during the campaign in person or by telephone. Citizens seldom participated in official campaign events: 2 percent in both 1999 and 2000 volunteered to work for a party or presidential candidate; 6 percent in 1999 and 4 percent in 2000 attended a public rally. Unofficial settings where the citizen, in effect, is the campaigner, were much livelier. Ninety percent said they had conversed about the Duma campaign with relatives, friends, neighbors, or workmates (and 92 percent about the presidential campaign); 19 percent in 1999 and 21 percent in 2000 had tried to persuade someone else how to vote.[44]

The Media and the Modern Campaign

Campaign-related information in 1999–2000 flowed by and large through the archetypal modern conduit, the mass media, and in particular through television. Some facts and figures on the media and the parliamentary and presidential campaigns are compiled in appendix C. Suffice it to say here that television use is all but universal in Russia. When asked in our voter survey which communications medium was their basic supplier of political information, 89 percent of our respondents replied it was television. The average adult in 1999 spent three and a half hours a day in front of the small screen, usually tuned in to one of the major national networks: ORT, 51 percent state owned but, practically speaking, controlled by a consortium of tycoons headed by Boris Berezovskii; the wholly state-owned RTR; and NTV, Russia's pioneering commercial network. TV-Tsentr, controlled by the city of Moscow, and TV-6, a private venture of Berezovskii, catered to more circumscribed audiences, and most consumers had access to local or cable outlets. About 90 percent of Russians in 1999 watched evening news programs. Eighty percent were fans of the freewheeling and opinionated weekend newsmagazines. These shows' anchormen—principally Sergei Dorenko on ORT, Nikolai Svanidze on RTR, and Yevgenii Kiselëv on NTV—were household names. They inserted themselves with gusto into the struggle for votes.

Campaign Professionals

For a price, Russian politicians by the late 1990s had at their disposal an ever more refined toolkit for formulating and executing campaign game plans. Parties were able to contract for use of these tools, as in any country, but so could the nonpartisan politicians, intent on avoiding contact with parties, who were thick on the ground in the Duma districts and the presidential race. In the party-list campaign, which is legally reserved to parties and quasi parties, party organizations for the most part retain their centrality. But in contests in the single-member districts and for president of Russia, the firms embodying campaign skills have gained ground at a time when the political parties have been in somewhat of a morass.

Commercial public relations firms have sprouted by the hundreds in Russia. A review of the industry by the polling agency ROMIR in 2000 counted forty-eight public relations companies with subdivisions for "political consulting and electoral technology."[45] Nikkolo M (Igor Mintusov and Yekaterina Yegorova) and Image-Kontakt (Aleksei Sitnikov) have been the market leaders in recent years. ROMIR's top ten listed them first and second, followed by the Foundation for Effective Politics, the Politika Foundation, NOVOKOM, PR-Tsentr, the Center for Political Technologies, R.I.M., Publicity-PR, and the International Press Club. Based in Moscow, they all have associates in the provinces and in some cases in other post-Soviet countries.[46] The Unity project in 1999 and Putin's presidential campaign catapulted several of them—the Kremlin-connected Foundation for Effective Politics (headed by Gleb Pavlovskii and the operator of several online publications prized by Russian political cognoscenti), R.I.M., and PR-Tsentr, as well as individual guns for hire such as the late Yuliya Rusova—into prominence.[47]

These firms deploy techniques that rival their Western counterparts in sophistication. Many of their founders are alumni of campaign-training programs in the West.[48] After several electoral cycles in which they adapted Western techniques to Russian circumstances, they are no longer dependent upon foreign assistance and have the financial means to send their employees to professional courses abroad. In addition to the standard repertoire—strategic planning, message development through polling and focus group research, targeting of swing voters, and so on—they have developed some distinctive methods. Perhaps because many of the builders of the big firms were educated as psychologists, they often focus on the cognitive and emotional psychology of voters.[49] They have developed computerized programs to record and analyze reactions to a candidate's speech rhythm, dress, and facial expressions. Typically, these professionals are called not campaign *konsul'tanty* but *imidzh-meikery*.[50]

The work of the political consulting firms is supplemented by maturing commercial sectors in public relations and polling. While a few consulting firms have acquired some expertise in television advertising and focus groups, most contracted this work out to others during the 1999–2000 elections. One company, Video International, headed lately by Maksim Boiko, a protégé of Anatolii Chubais, has dominated the market. It produced all the major publicity—clips as well as canned "news" reports—for Yeltsin's 1996 presidential campaign and Putin's 2000 drive. Other successful media companies, including R.I.M., Mikhailov and Partners, Imageland Edelman, NOVOKOM, and Maxima, offer individual candidates a wide choice of agents when selecting a campaign team.

Two entities have had the pick of the polling business during elections: FOM (the Public Opinion Foundation), headed by Aleksandr Oslon, which has collaborated closely with the Kremlin since 1996; and VTsIOM (the All-Russian Center for the Study of Public Opinion), an older agency directed by Yurii Levada that has contracted with liberal parties, government-backed candidates, and individual campaigns and continues to work with Russian and foreign academics. The 1999–2000 electoral cycle was no different, although other firms with good reputations, such as ROMIR and ARPI, also thrived. Most of them began operations to service political campaigns. The more profitable now emphasize marketing research; ROMIR is the authorized Russian representative of the Gallup organization and ARPI does Nielsen-type ratings for television. In the Duma districts, regional firms, usually with a commercial profile, played a large part in the campaigns of those candidates able to afford their services.

Big Business

Economic elites played a more indirect role in electoral politics, yet hardly an inconsequential one. Just recovering from the 1998 default and devaluation, they were beginning to look to a less apocalyptic future than had seemed likely then, one in which the government might provide not only indemnity against extinction and not only the insider deals that flourished in the Yeltsin years, but opportunities for unobtrusive accretion of profits and wealth. Whatever the positive incentives, the negative incentives generated by a high-uncertainty environment were compelling—political inaction could be bad for business and even for survival. As we discuss in subsequent chapters, a number of the Russian "oligarchs" were active in the 1999 and 2000 elections. They helped underwrite the campaigns of Unity—in whose creation Boris Berezovskii took a personal hand—but also Fatherland–All Russia, the Union of Right Forces, and to some extent Yabloko.[51] If they participated less in Putin's presidential campaign, that was due to his reluctance to take their money and not to any lack of desire or ability on their part to help.

Not as noticeable as business's intervention in the up-front party-list and presidential campaigns was its participation in the election of Duma deputies from local districts. Many corporations proposed and financed candidates, most but not all of whom were unaffiliated with a party and thus are not a main object of our study. As one example, Gazprom, Russia's giant gas utility, is said to have made payments to candidates in about 100 district races and to have retained Nikkolo M to run about seventy campaigns. Fifty candidates to whom they gave some aid were victorious, creating de facto a Gazprom lobby on energy issues within parliament.[52] Oil and metal-exporting companies adopted a similar strategy on a smaller scale, calculating that it was a sounder investment to fund candidates in single-mandate races than to back political parties in the nationwide campaign or to take the dicey step of supporting a candidate for president. Dozens of agricultural, food-processing, and other corporations competing in regional markets threw their weight unobtrusively behind district candidates.

The State

It has become commonplace to observe that Russia has a "weak state." Putin—who came into high politics from the "bowels of the bureaucracy," in Boris Kagarlitsky's words—made this critique himself and had in mind to rectify some of the pathologies commented on by domestic and foreign observers: the decay of infrastructural functions such as revenue collection and maintenance of order, inability to deliver basic public goods to citizens, lack of internal cohesion. That being said, government agencies and individual officeholders are very influential in Russian electoral politics. Indeed, over and over again we find them to be the *most* powerful actors on the scene.

Boris Yeltsin, the president of the country, made a huge difference with his decisions to make Putin prime minister and then acting president. In the Duma campaign, departments of the federal government provided candidates to whom they were partial all manner of organizational advantages known as "administrative resources" in Russia— such as free office space, telephone lines, printing equipment, and staff time. State officials cooperated with business interests, many of which had recently emerged from the public sector through government-led privatization. Gazprom, for example, straddled the public-private boundary, and many of the private oil companies that funded campaigns were highly politicized. Most vital, as discussed in chapters 3 and 4, state-run and state-loyal electronic media carried out partisan missions in support of the Unity bloc and against Fatherland–All Russia and introduced a level of personal invective never before witnessed in a Russian campaign. In the 2000 presidential campaign, the politicization was less overt, as we show in chapter 7. Putin could afford it to be so, since the discrediting of alternatives to him had been so brutally accomplished by December. Leaders at the regional plateau of Russia's federal structure also figured in electoral events. The contender the Kremlin feared the most in 1999, the OVR bloc, was the creation of the mayor of Moscow and a group of regional governors and republic presidents. Lending nuance to the regional leaders' role is that they were quite diverse in their political preferences and were cautious not to "put all their eggs in one basket" even when publicly committed to one side in a contest.[53]

The Mood of the Electorate

All electoral players were cognizant that the road to success lay through the hearts and minds of the voters. The voters of Russia were a restless lot. Mundane daily experience and news fare confirmed that the country was wallowing in crisis. Many people did not know where to turn. Uncertainty haunted most.

As a prelude to chapters 3 to 7, we touch here on three aspects of the popular mood especially pertinent to politics and electoral activity. The first, anger/contentment, captures the intensity of the dissatisfaction with the status quo and the eagerness to change it. The second, alienation/engagement, refers to how much citizens discerned politics and elections to be relevant to their concerns. The third dimension is volatility/stability, or the extent of attachment to precedent and habit. On all three scores, the question in 1999–2000 was not whether the popular mood was angry, alienated, and volatile but to what degree it was, and with what repercussions.

How Angry?

Our survey work confirms what any casual conversation about public issues suggested at the time—that Russians were unhappy with the state of the nation and the performance of their public institutions and systems. Asked about the health of the economy around the time of the State Duma election, 76 percent said it was bad or very bad; 18 percent called it neither good nor bad; one-half of 1 percent said it was good; nary a soul was willing to describe it as very good. Seventy percent of citizens in another interview said that the financial crash of August 1998 had hurt their family. A fair number of Russians did see hints of a favorable trend in the economy: early recognition of the healing effects of the currency devaluation and higher oil prices. Twenty-five percent in the winter of 1999–2000 thought the economy had improved some over the past year and 42 percent expected it to improve a little over the next year (2 percent thought it would improve a lot). While still negative in tenor, economic evaluations were a bit more positive than in the mid-1990s.[54]

Table 2-5. *Citizen Preferences for General Course of Government Action to Be Followed after Duma and Presidential Elections*[a]

Course of government action	Percent
No change ("essentially continue the current course")	6
Gradual change ("change the present course, but gradually")	60
Radical change ("make a sharp change in the present course")	25
Don't know	9

a. From 1999–2000 panel, wave 1 (N = 1,919 weighted cases). Preamble reads, "There soon will be elections to the State Duma and after that an election of the president of Russia. Would you want the new government to . . . ?"

The political misery index was not much different from the economic one. When asked to evaluate "how democracy is developing in Russia," 79 percent of informants answered that they were dissatisfied or completely dissatisfied, 11 percent that they were satisfied, and one-half of 1 percent that they were fully satisfied. Most Russians in our sample did not regard their country as a democracy at all. Pushed to say what they made of the statement, "The political system that exists in Russia today is a democracy," 51 percent expressed moderate or strong disagreement, 19 percent were indifferent, and 19 percent agreed or strongly agreed.[55] Counter to the mildly optimistic trend in economic evaluations, political evaluations in 1999–2000 were more pessimistic than in the mid-1990s.[56]

What was to come of this ocean of anger? In 1917 the Russians took the path of violent revolution, overturning all their society had inherited and trying to build a paradise on earth. Their descendants at the end of the twentieth century, now that the communist utopia had been renounced, had little stomach for another revolution. We asked citizens on the eve of the Duma election what general course they wanted their new government to follow after parliament and president had been voted in (see table 2-5). While there was negligible sentiment for perpetuating present policies, a radical break with the status quo had minority appeal. The preferred option for a majority, 60 percent, was gradual change.

The remarkable thing about this preference was that it reigned in all swaths of the population: old and young, college-educated and barely literate, rich and poor, villagers and urbanites, women and men. Going slowly one step at a time had acceptance in every opinion niche, even where the flame of discontent was hottest. Gradualists had the upper hand over radicals by 56 percent to 28 percent among persons who thought the economy was in very bad shape, by 62 to 26 percent among those whose families had suffered from August 1998, by 57 to 30 percent among those who thought the economy had worsened over the past year and by 55 to 33 percent among those who thought it would over the next year, and by 54 percent to 34 percent among individuals who strongly disputed that Russia was a democracy. Stunningly, 55 percent of the citizens who disapproved most heartily of Yeltsin's work as president were gradualists, as against 33 percent radicals.[57]

How Alienated?

Most Russians in 1999–2000 deemed their government to be unresponsive, impenetrable, and indifferent to their plight. This alienation was severe by cross-national standards and perceptibly worse than it was midway through the Yeltsin era. Fifty-six percent of our survey respondents agreed or strongly agreed with the statement, "People like me have no say in what the government does" (an increase of 10 percentage points over 1995–96). Seventy-eight percent (8 points higher than in 1995–96) went along with the statement, "Sometimes the activity of the government looks so complicated that people like me cannot understand what is going on." And 83 percent (5 points more than in 1995–96) concurred in the assertion, "It seems to me government officials do not especially care what people like me think."[58]

The silver lining is that these feelings of abandonment were not accompanied by wholesale disengagement from politics and the electoral mechanism. On the contrary, most Russians continued to think it matters who holds political office, had faith in competitive elections, and felt obliged to participate in them. As can be seen in table 2-6, there was greater unanimity on the first point than on the second. Survey respondents thought it makes a difference who is in power in the country (taking positions 1 and 2 as indicating agreement) at a rate of more than 80 percent; 20 percent fewer thought voting makes a difference (positions 4 and 5 on the second question). When it comes to individual responsibility, however, an overwhelming 86 percent considered voting a civic duty and a scant 6 percent did not. It is presumably this sense of obligation that lies behind the turnout of about two-thirds of the citizenry in the two elections.[59]

How Volatile?

Citizen volatility, too, was part and parcel of the mass politics of 1999–2000 and is an important background factor for analysis of the

Table 2-6. *Attitudes in 1999–2000 toward Control of Government Office, Competitive Elections, and Obligation to Vote*

Survey question and responses	Percent
Does it make a difference who is in power? (5-point scale)[a]	
1–It makes a difference who is in power	69
2	14
3	6
4	3
5–It doesn't make a difference who is in power	5
Don't know	3
Does it matter who people vote for? (5-point scale)[b]	
1–Voting does not make a difference for the country	12
2	9
3	14
4	19
5–Voting does make a difference for the country	40
Don't know	5
It is the duty of each citizen to vote in elections[c]	
Completely disagree	1
Disagree	5
Indifferent	7
Agree	46
Fully agree	40
Don't know	1

a. From 1999–2000 panel, wave 2 (N = 1,846 weighted cases). Question reads, "Some people say it makes a difference who is in power. Others say that it doesn't make a difference who is in power. Using the scale on this card, where 1 means that it makes a difference in power and 5 means that it doesn't make a difference who is in power, where would you place yourself?"

b. From 1999–2000 panel, wave 2 (N = 1,846 weighted cases). Question reads, "Some people say that no matter who people vote for, it won't make any difference to what happens. Others say that who people vote for can make a difference to what happens. Using the scale on this card, where 1 means that voting won't make a difference to what happens and 5 means that voting can make a difference, where would you place yourself?"

c. From 1999–2000 panel, wave 1 (N = 1,919 weighted cases).

electoral actors. Like anger and alienation, it had its limits and did not paralyze electoral activity or reduce it to mere random thrashing.

Volatility in *voting* behavior is of the greatest analytical interest. Erroneous recall makes it difficult to gauge voting turnover at the individual level in cross-sectional surveys. The availability of panel data spanning the years 1995 to 2000 circumvents this minefield for Russia (see appendix D for details). The clearest measure ought to be for the Duma party lists, since this is the electoral segment structured wholly around political organizations and not personalities. Table 2-7 estimates the flow of the PR vote between the elections of 1995 and 1999. Less than one-quarter of 1999 party-list voters were "loyalists" who voted for the same party in 1999 and 1995. "Converts" who absconded to another party were

Table 2-7. *Flow of Party-List Vote between the 1995 and the 1999 Duma Elections*[a]

Behavioral category	Percent[b]
Loyalist	23
Convert	
Same party family	12
Different party family	47
Ex-dropout	12
Novice	5

a. From augmented 1995–2000 panel, waves 2 and 4 (N = 1,110 weighted cases). See appendix D for method. Terms explained in the text. The cells in this table are the same as in appendix table D-5, except that here we split the converts into two subgroups.

b. Denominator includes respondents who reported voting in the 1999 election and voting for one of the party lists (that is, excluding voters who voted against all the parties).

Table 2-8. *Flow of Party-List Vote 1995 to 1999, by Availability on 1999 Ballot of Party for Which Individual Voted in 1995*[a]

Percent

Behavioral category	A 1995 party available	
	No	Yes
Loyalist	0	35
Convert		
Same party family	31	11
Different party family	69	54

almost 60 percent of the electorate. Of them, 12 percent had changed within the same party family and four times as many to a party in a different family. Twelve percent in 1999 were "ex-dropouts," by which we mean voters who had either abstained in 1995 or voted against all the parties. Five percent were "novices," individuals born after December 1977 and thus ineligible to vote in the 1995 election.

An electorate in which no more than 23 percent choose as they had in the preceding election is surely fickle. But several factors mitigate the electoral volatility somewhat. The one convert in five who switched within the same party family did not undergo as thorough a conversion as migrants to another political family. Furthermore, a certain number of voters were not free to stand pat, because the party they chose in 1995 washed out and was not on the 1999 ballot. Twenty-one percent of our 1995–2000 panel falls into this category. Table 2-8 compares those forced converts with individuals who had the opportunity to vote in line with their 1995 preference. The share of loyalists among individuals whose 1995 party was intact rises to 35 percent, and loyalists and within-family converts rise to 46 percent. None of the forced converts could have been loyalists, but one-third of them had done their vote switching within the same party family as before.

Partisanship, or the psychic bond with a political party, is a second area calling for measures of continuity and change. Partisan identification of American or West European vintage, whereby citizens affiliate with a party indefinitely or for life and transmit that affinity to their children, has not had the time to solidify in Russia, except perhaps among communist voters whose attachments date back to Soviet times. It is defensible, all the same, to speak of "protopartisanship" or "transitional partisanship," inclinations of limited shelf life that may affect behavior in the near and middle term.[60] In wave 1 and again in wave 3 of our 1999–2000 election survey, we asked a battery of questions designed to elicit this subliminal attitude. The responses allow us to construct an ordinal scale comprising "strong partisans," "moderate partisans," "weak partisans," and "nonpartisans."[61]

By this touchstone, 42 percent of citizens qualified as partisans in 1999 and 48 percent in 2000 (see table 2-9). This represented neither an improvement nor a deterioration in the reach of partisanship within the electorate: it was essentially frozen at its level of the mid-1990s.[62] Two-fifths of all declared partisans championed the most retrograde of Russian parties, the KPRF. Moreover, there continues to be great flux from one reading of partisanship to the next. Most pronounced in table 2-9 are the downturn in the number of OVR partisans after the Duma elections and the upturn in the number of Unity partisans, trends that mirror those parties' changing fortunes in the Moscow power struggle.

Our 1995–2000 panel opens a wider window. Table 2-10 traces fluctuations in partisanship for citizens first interviewed in 1995, over intervals of less than one year and a half decade. In gross outline, the changes between 1995 and 1996 and between 1995 and 2000 are very similar. Thirty-five to 40 percent of our informants are consistently nonpartisan in both time frames. A slim 10 percent are consistent partisans, devotees of the same party during successive interviews.[63] Another several percent swap parties within the ambit of the same party family. Individuals who change party families in 1995–96 are about half the group who stay in the family but match them as a proportion of the whole in 1995–2000.

Table 2-9. *Partisanship in the Electorate, 1999 and 2000*

Percent

Measure	Fall 1999[a]	Spring 2000[b]
Strength of partisanship		
Strong	13	14
Moderate	10	14
Weak	18	20
Nonpartisan	58	52
Distribution of partisans by party		
KPRF	40	46
Yabloko	14	10
OVR	11	4
Unity	9	21
LDPR	6	3
SPS	5	9
Women of Russia	3	2
Our Home Is Russia	3	1
Pensioners Party	2	1
Other parties	6	3
Distribution of partisans by party family		
Government	11	22
Liberal	19	20
Centrist	16	6
Nationalist	8	4
Socialist	43	46
Miscellaneous	3	2

a. From 1999–2000 panel, wave 1 (N = 1,919 weighted cases for strength of partisanship, 823 weighted cases for distribution of partisans).

b. From 1999–2000 panel, wave 3 (N = 1,755 weighted cases for strength of partisanship, 860 weighted cases for distribution of partisans).

Table 2-10. *Continuity and Change in Partisanship, 1995–96 and 1995–2000*

Percent

Pattern	1995–96[a]	1995–2000[b]
Nonpartisan both years	40	34
Nonpartisan first year, partisan second year	11	16
Partisan first year, nonpartisan second year	29	26
Partisan both years		
Same party	9	9
Different party, same party family	4	3
Different party family	7	12

a. From 1995–2000 panel, waves 1 and 3 (N = 2,472 weighted cases).
b. From 1995–2000 panel, waves 1 and 4 (N = 1,612 weighted cases).

One conclusion table 2-10 drives home, apart from the ubiquity of change, is that the prototypical civic response to partisan uncertainty in Russia after communism is to move into and out of detachment, and not to roam aimlessly from one party or party family to another. The challenge for the politicians in 1999–2000 was less to lure voters from other partisan camps than to arouse them from equidistance from all parties. A conclusion hidden behind the table is that the hardiness of partisan allegiances varies enormously from party to party and party family to family. Only two of the six party families show above-average retention of adherents from 1995 to 2000: socialists (at 37 percent) and liberals (at 17 percent). Three 1995 parties beat the average: the socialist KPRF (45 percent) and the liberal Russia's Democratic Choice (a forerunner of SPS, at 32 percent) and Yabloko (at 30 percent). Socialists and liberals are weak poles of the nascent Russian party system, but poles nonetheless.

A third task for the analyst is to fathom how labile *issue opinions* were. One must take care not to measure Russian attitudes against an ideal type of unblemished stability. Students of American public opinion have long known about, and endeavored to explain, large displacements in issue attitudes over time—changes that respond to long-term social trends but also to short-term events and to the influences of elected officials and private interests.[64] Our 1995–2000 panel permits us to ascertain how quickly Russians' opinions change, just as it did for partisanship. Table 2-11 reports on responses to six question items about economic and social policy that were put to respondents in 1995 and repeated word for word and in the same order in the 1996 and 2000 reinterviews. They asked the subject to agree strongly, agree, indicate indifference, disagree, or strongly disagree with statements about policy read out by the interviewer.

There is intriguing evidence here of a more stable equilibrium on issue opinions than exists on transitional Russians' voting behavior or partisanship. The results for the 1995–96 and the 1995–2000 interludes are very nearly interchangeable. Be it over one year or over five, citizens rarely bolted from one side of the question to the other (13 percent did so from 1995 to 1996 and 15 percent from 1995 to 2000). Forty-two percent in both 1996 and 2000, or triple the number of waverers, gave the very same answer to the question as they had in 1995. One-quarter changed the intensity of their answers (going from strong to moderate agreement, for example). And one-fifth seesawed into or out of the non-

Table 2-11. *Comparison of Panel Responses to Six Survey Questions about Economic and Social Policy, 1995–96 and 1995–2000*
Percent

Question and interval	Same response	Changed direction	Changed intensity	Into or out of indifference
1995 wave compared with 1996[a]				
Guaranteed jobs[c]	54	4	37	4
Trade protection[d]	41	12	28	18
Set food prices[e]	43	12	28	18
Foreign investment[f]	37	18	14	30
Private land[g]	38	18	18	26
Income controls[h]	39	16	23	22
Average	42	13	25	20
1995 wave compared with 2000[b]				
Guaranteed jobs[c]	60	5	32	3
Trade protection[d]	40	15	29	16
Set food prices[e]	44	10	33	12
Foreign investment[f]	35	21	14	30
Private land[g]	33	23	16	28
Income controls[h]	38	16	23	23
Average	42	15	25	19

a. From 1995–2000 panel, waves 1 and 3. Excludes "Don't know" responses. N = 1,923 to 2,398 weighted cases, depending on the question.

b. From 1995–2000 panel, waves 1 and 4. Excludes "Don't know" responses. N = 1,310 to 1,595 weighted cases, depending on the question.

c. Statement reads, "The government ought to guarantee a job to everyone who needs one."

d. Statement reads, "We must protect our industry against competition from foreign firms that are out to seize the Russian market."

e. Statement reads, "The state should set food prices."

f. Statement reads, "Russia should attract foreign investment in its economy."

g. Statement reads, "Private property in land should exist in our country."

h. Statement reads, "The state should limit the incomes of the rich."

committal position of neither agreeing nor disagreeing with the proposition. All of this goes to say, as John R. Zaller found for the political attitudes of Americans, that individuals vacillate in their responses to survey questions and in their inner beliefs, "but only within a certain, systematically determined range."[65]

Conclusions

There was no shortage of reminders of Russia's unsettled condition in the setting of the elections of 1999–2000. One year after the financial meltdown of 1998 and weeks after terrorist attacks against Russian citizens and the armed reoccupation of Chechnya, stress and fear of catastrophe were omnipresent in the social environment of politics. The rules of the contest, at least for the Duma, were bafflingly complex and their implementation tangled in red tape. The separate components of the electoral game, loosely connected, engendered diverse outcomes. The party system was ramshackle. Largely for that reason, there was a zoo of individual and collective players, and the latter changed face and shape as the game wore on. The electorate, meantime, was angry, alienated, and volatile.

But there were more encouraging straws in the wind as well. There was no talk in the corridors of power, as there had been in the mid-1990s, of abrogating elections and governing by executive fiat. The prolixity of the rules and the nontransparent and high-handed way they were administered did not dissuade several dozen parties and quasi parties, several thousand district nominees, and eleven presidential candidates from throwing their hat in the ring. The clutter of parties was reduced, and with it the fragmentation of votes and of the representation of interests in parliament. Angry, alienated, and volatile though rank-and-file voters were, they preferred gradual amelioration to revolution, felt duty-bound to vote, and entered the electoral cycle with a stockpile of opinions and, less frequently, partisan sentiments that went some way toward cushioning the uncertainty engulfing them.

3

The Party
of Power

THE RELATIVELY SERENE transitions from communism to democracy in East Central Europe reflect a common electoral sequence. Democratic insurgents rout the communist old guard in the first competitive elections and set in motion economic reforms. Soon their policies antagonize voters and drive wedges in the reformers' own ranks. The first-round victors tend to lose in second-round elections to reconfigured communist and social-democratic parties. This "pendulum effect," elegantly modeled by Adam Przeworski, has also been visible in some noncommunist transitions. Third-round elections in the region vary greatly. By then, though, power has usually changed hands twice, and politicians have begun to cultivate partisan identification as a means of cementing their positions.[1]

Russia deviates from the pattern. Its communist party dug in its heels and did not repudiate its socialist and authoritarian birthright. The anticommunist reformers rode into office on the coattails of Boris Yeltsin, who was elected president in 1991, before the Soviet regime broke down, and did so without first gaining a majority in the Congress of People's Deputies. In the inaugural multiparty election, for the Duma in December 1993, the already vulnerable reformers suffered severe setbacks. These went from bad to worse in the 1995 Duma election, which saw the unrepentant Communist Party of the Russian Federation (KPRF) corral the most votes and seats. In 1993 and 1995 political commentators classified the one party or quasi party most intimately associated with Yeltsin and the Kremlin administration as "the party of power" (*partiya vlasti*).[2] Yegor Gaidar's Russia's Choice movement in 1993 was a vehicle for Westernizing liberals determined to accelerate the country's transformation. Its replacement as the new party of power two years later, Our Home Is Russia (NDR), was more of a calming force. Its main objective was to ensure continuity in state personnel and policy. The founder of the party, at the directive of the president, was Prime Minister Viktor Chernomyrdin, a consummate product of the communist-era bureaucracy and the originator of Gazprom, the natural gas monopoly that was one of the first subdivisions of the state-owned economy to go commercial.[3] The stolid Chernomyrdin, as Yeltsin phrased it in his memoirs, embodied "a compromise between market relations and the Soviet corps of factory directors."[4] While Yeltsin desisted from campaigning actively for either party, copious state resources were put at their disposal. ORT and RTR, the television networks owned principally by the federal government, lavished attention on them. Their electoral slates bristled with senior officials. Moscow and regional bureaucrats, especially in 1995, uncomplainingly lent a helping hand. In 1995 a number of Russia's new business tycoons were also in NDR's corner. A popular quip taunted it and Chernomyrdin for their coziness with Gazprom, christening the party "Nash Dom Gazprom" (Our Home Is Gazprom).

Despite their tremendous resources, the electoral successes of these parties of power were second-rate: Russia's Choice was held to 15.51 percent of the popular vote in 1993 (second, behind the Liberal Democratic Party of Russia, LDPR) and NDR to 10.33 percent in 1995 (third, behind the KPRF and the LDPR). This popularity deficit was cushioned by the constitutional preeminence of the executive branch and of the president at its apex, who could be elected and reelected without recourse to a party label. Yeltsin escaped electoral punishment in 1996 for his shelling of the parliament in 1993, his ill-fated war in Chechnya, and the painful economic and social consequences of his reforms. He handily won the presidential vote by framing it as a referendum on communism and not a decision about how he had governed since 1991.[5] While not formally linked to any party, Yeltsin was frequently described as presiding informally over a more amorphous "party of power," something politically attuned Russians think of rather the way Westerners think of "the establishment." It is striking that this broader group had as of the late 1990s never ceded power. Many analysts suspected after 1996 that the syndrome had run its course and that Russians, given another chance, would mimic East Central Europe by evicting those they held responsible for hard times.

The party of power, narrowly and broadly construed, was in dire straits as the political temperature rose in 1999. Opinion polls showed only a few percent planning to vote for NDR. Yeltsin had ousted its leader, Chernomyrdin, from the premiership in March 1998 and failed in an attempt to reinstate him after the financial meltdown that August. Chernomyrdin talked of a presidential bid, but few took the possibility seriously. As approval ratings of Yeltsin, constitutionally barred from serving a third term, hovered in the single digits, the government seemed rudderless and overmatched by Russia's mountain of problems. Vladimir Putin, who took the oath of office in August 1999 after a procession of short-term prime ministers, was a hitherto unnoticed officer from the state-security apparatus bereft of electoral experience.

The outlook did not perceptibly brighten when a fledgling pro-Kremlin bloc, Unity, was rolled out in September 1999. Few pundits, as noted in chapter 1, gave Unity a shot at success. As it transpired, the electoral outcome was a stunning departure from the past and from the forecasts. The question one has to ask is why *this* party of power broke the mold in Russia.

Most analysis has dwelt on the resources marshaled by the state and economic elite. Without question, this largesse was necessary for a new government party to rise up and seek out support. But it is not a sufficient explanation, since Russia's Choice and NDR enjoyed an embarrassment of riches in their day without a commensurate electoral bonanza. The eclectic message Unity communicated with the aid of this wherewithal, and that message's resonance with millions of anxious voters, must come into the reckoning. Not content to imitate their predecessors, the architects of Unity reinvented the party of power and deftly turned several factors to their advantage. Among them were a mobilization strategy keyed to unattached voters and overlooked social constituencies; an ability to look "new" and to bring fresh faces before the voters; an acting out of feelings of national pride; a signature issue, the second war in Chechnya, and skill at projecting capacity on other issues; a marketable party leader, Sergei Shoigu; and a devastatingly effective Kremlin patron, Putin.

Creating Unity

As late as midsummer of 1999, Our Home Is Russia was the closest thing on the horizon to a party of power in the bloodline of Russia's Choice in 1993 and itself in 1995. Vladimir Ryzhkov, the thirty-three-year-old chairman of its caucus in the Duma, wanted the party to have a more Western-style conservative stamp. With Chernomyrdin preoccupied by palace politics, Ryzhkov revamped NDR's program and tried to enlist younger candidates for the forthcoming campaign and to reopen communication with regional leaders.[6] The platform, adopted at a convention in April 1999, rededicated NDR to "the development of Russia on the basis of tradition."[7] A hurdle it could not overcome was the cooling of Yeltsin's attitude. Fond as he was of Chernomyrdin, the president was adamant that NDR was wedded to a top-down approach and there could be no repeat of the mistakes of 1995.[8]

Trial Balloons

As NDR floundered, rivals tested the vacuum. One alternative was the regionally grounded Voice of Russia coalition founded in January 1999 by Konstantin Titov, the governor of Samara region. Titov, an administrator of liberal views (and until then a vice chairman of NDR), signed up twenty provincial governors to a letter of intent, lined up financing from the Siberian Aluminum company, and expressly kept Yeltsin informed. His bid to have Voice of Russia serve as the core of a resuscitated party of power fizzled when again the president's office balked, and, intimidated, other governors dragged their feet.[9] Titov then joined forces with a group of ambitious liberal politicians, some of them involved years before in Russia's Choice, to create the Union of Right Forces, or SPS. SPS kept aloof from the Kremlin and insisted it was an opposition movement, not a potential government party.

A goad to action was the presence of a shadow party of power in the guise of the Fatherland–All Russia (OVR) bloc. Current and recent officials from the executive branch, national and regional, held the reins in OVR, and former prime minister Yevgenii Primakov stood at the head of its national list. Most in OVR took for granted its run for the Duma would flourish and would give Primakov a launching pad for the presidency. They and the journalists on the campaign beat likened it to a U.S.-style presidential primary, which would winnow the options down to two or three. Despite the bloc's elite cast, Yeltsin and his political menage loathed it and its sparkplug, Mayor Yurii Luzhkov of Moscow. The well-connected financier Boris Berezovskii was exceptionally concerned as, recalling Primakov's hostility toward him as premier in 1998–99, he believed that Primakov would assail his economic and political interests should he become president. Berezovskii was impatient to preempt Primakov in the parliamentary campaign.

Berezovskii floated a trial balloon for a refashioned pro-Kremlin bloc in the late summer of 1999. He broached the subject with receptive provincial leaders who had not yet sworn themselves to OVR or another faction. Some neutrals gave their approval, some switched sides, and some tipped their support without repudiating prior commitments. Governors Eduard Rossel of Sverdlovsk, Aleksandr Lebed of Krasnoyarsk, Yevgenii Nazdratenko of Primor'e, and Viktor Ishayev of Khabarovsk were the first to respond. Thirty-nine regional leaders in all gave their blessing to a nebulous letter of sympathy, "For Clean and Honorable Elections," released to the press on September 20. The chairman of the Federation Council and governor of Orël province, Yegor Stroyev, and the former vice president of Russia and now governor in Kursk, Aleksandr Rutskoi, dutifully signed. Even several communist-affiliated governors (Aman Tuleyev of Kemerovo, Aleksandr Chernogorov of Stavropol, and Vasilii Starodubtsev of Tula) affixed their names.

Berezovskii first labeled the budding coalition Muzhiki (Fellas), in reference to the vigorous and virile regional leaders behind it. The governors relished the sobriquet Medved—Bear in Russian and also a catchy abbreviation of the formal name settled on for the bloc, Mezhregional'noye Dvizheniye Yedinstvo, or "Interregional Unity Movement." Throughout the campaign, the designations Yedinstvo and Medved were used interchangeably.

From a Regional to a National Blueprint

Unity's initial intent was to undercut OVR by fighting it in individual regions. The plan had to be scrapped after most of the governors who signed the letter of accord, unsure which way the wind was blowing, backed off.[10] In contrast to 1995, when thirty-six governors were members of NDR's list, which allowed NDR to crack the whip with little difficulty, the governors in 1999 were popularly elected, no longer appointed by the president, and sat in the Federation Council. They were much less amenable than before to political projects not in their self-interest.[11] When Unity registered its national slate of candidates with the Central Electoral Commission, the only governor on it was Vladimir Platov of Tver. Six ran for OVR, six for NDR, and two for the KPRF—parties that had been in full combat mode for a year.

Owing partly to the regional barons' hedging and partly to growing interest in the initiative in Moscow, Unity speedily morphed into a capital city–based organization under the thumb of Kremlin insiders and hired consultants and bankrolled by friends of the government.[12] Igor Shabdurasulov, the first deputy head of the presidential administration, and Vladislav Surkov, a deputy head, were pivotal to recruiting members and acquiring resources, while Aleksei Golovkov, the general director of Russia's biggest insurance company, Rosgosstrakh, took responsibility for strategy.[13] Golovkov brought on board Yuliya Rusova, an adroit campaign manager who with him had orchestrated Aleksandr Lebed's third-place finish in the 1996 presidential vote; Sergei Popov, an aide to Yeltsin in 1996 who took charge of day-to-day operations; and younger and lesser-known experts such as Vladimir Ruga of the Public Relations Center and Aleksei Chesnakov of the Russian Center for Political Marketing. Aleksei Sitnikov and the big public relations firm Image-Kontakt were given a contract—paid for by Berezovskii—to work out tactics and create Unity cells at the regional level.

Unity, paradoxically, was a campaign first and an electoral bloc and party-in-the-making second. Preparations for selecting candidates were in train when its "initiating group" was set up on September 24 and its founding congress was held in Moscow on October 3 and 6, 1999. A portentous step was the overture to Sergei Shoigu, the Russian minister of emergency situations since 1991, to lead the venture.[14] Shoigu had briefly taken part in All Russia (which became one of the pillars of OVR) and was then attracted to a grand coalition in which NDR would have a part. After arm-twisting by Kremlin functionaries, he finally agreed to spearhead Unity in time for the convocation of the initiating group. The exclusion of NDR, part of the compact, was made official on October 1. NDR went on to run a separate campaign, finishing in seventh place with just over 1 percent of the popular vote.[15]

The Campaign

To comply with legal niceties, Unity had to be concocted from a handful of preexisting entities. The only precursor of note was the National Patriotic Party, an association of veterans of the Soviet war in Afghanistan that was part of Russia's Choice in 1993 and in the 1995 election participated in a bantam centrist bloc called For the Motherland. The other six partners were "essentially fictitious."[16] Unity held its charter congress only two and a half months before December 19. Most novice parties would not have had a prayer of showing up on the electorate's radar in so short a period of time. Most also would have thought the electoral goal its organizers set for themselves—10 percent of the popular vote, which proved to be an underestimate—overambitious.[17]

If almost every other player claimed to be in political opposition in some respect, Unity from the outset underlined its loyalty. "The policy of the current government," as Shoigu expressed the mantra, "is worthy of support. This is all the more so now that, under the leadership of Vladimir Putin, policy has come to be so decisive and purposive."[18] But Unity went beyond defending the Kremlin and the status quo. Golovkov, Rusova, and Popov had all toiled on the NDR campaign in 1995 and were aware from bitter experience that being a party of power—and spending money like one—were not enough. A winner, they were convinced, needed to have a message of improvement and deliverance of the nation to sell with its resources.

A New Wave

The first message Unity punched home was that, unlike the stodgy NDR before it, it was an insurgent and youth-oriented movement.[19] Sergei Shoigu stressed in unfurling plans for its congress that Unity was "a totally new bloc" and would "bring new, fresh people to the Duma."[20] Shoigu himself, an energetic forty-four-year-old, had never once stood for political office. The second and third slots on the list were occupied by Aleksandr Karelin (age thirty-two), a three-time Olympic medalist in Greco-Roman wrestling, and Aleksandr Gurov (age fifty-four), the former head of the organized crime section of the USSR police ministry, long touted as an incorruptible fighter of crime and graft. Karelin, like Shoigu, was an electoral rookie; Gurov had been a backbench member of parliament from 1990 to 1993 and coheaded an unsuccessful electoral slate in 1995.

In putting neophytes atop its list, Unity planners conveyed that they wanted to attract first-time and apolitical voters more than go head-to-head with parties like the KPRF and Yabloko for the affections of politicized citizens. They also hoped to reach out to individuals of various views, without antagonizing any group irretrievably. The assumption was that, even after two parliamentary elections, a majority of the electorate still did not identify with any political party and were weary of the veteran politicians who ruled the roost in the entrenched parties and the OVR bloc. Unity spokesmen castigated OVR and ultranationalist groups, but not the citizens who supported them. They went light on the communists and lighter still on liberal parties and voters. The enemy, as Shoigu put it, was the petty politicians who had steered the Duma since 1993:

> Our voters are tired of endless political chirping, of public intrigues, and of one politician scheming ad hominem against the other. . . . The fractions [Duma caucuses] live in a virtual world they created for themselves alone. They are driven by political sloganeering and programs and care only for their own image. We are driven by a sense of responsibility, which we feel almost in our bones. It is political theater that agitates them. It is the rebirth of Russia that agitates us.[21]

In a crowd-baiting riff on the theme, Shoigu demanded a law levying fines on Duma deputies who missed plenary sessions.[22]

As a showpiece of its novel look, Unity underscored that as an "interregional movement" it had its roots in the Russian periphery. "We have united," Shoigu expostulated shortly after the formation of the coalition, "in order to change the face of power and to give it to the people, to the real representatives of Russia's regions," and "to sweep away Moscow-dwelling politicians of whom people will remember nothing" at the end of the day.[23] When asked what stirred up Unity's founders, Aleksei Golovkov replied, "They do not like Moscow."[24] While most blocs had from ten to the maximum of eighteen names on the federal portion of their party list, Unity was the only one to have the minimum of three names, flaunting its regional pedigree: "Our remaining candidates have been put forward by the regions themselves. No one threw down these names in a long row from Moscow."[25] Unity literature reminded voters that Shoigu (from Tuva, on the Mongolian border) and Karelin (from Novosibirsk) were Siberians. Shoigu hailed the bloc as a progeny of the *glubinka*—a word literally translated as "remote places" but not far in chemistry from the American epithets "the backwoods" or "the sticks." Unity, then, was different from earlier parties of power in that its leaders did not blindly defend status quo policies and did not hale from the capital.

In a twist on the newness theme, Unity was to pump up enthusiasm in the campaign homestretch with the argument that it was a late-breaking phenomenon and an antidote to tired faces and slogans. After Putin's endorsement and polls showed its popularity swelling, Unity's television commercials sought to wrap it in an air of momentum and excitement and to invite voters to climb on the bandwagon. Several pro-Unity videos broadcast during free airtime on national television contained no words at all, only footage of the bloc's three leaders and the sound of music working up to a crescendo.

The Use and Manipulation of Resources

Unity was blessed with abundant funding, support networks at the regional level, and privileged access to the mass media—all prerequisites of the modern campaign it meant to mount. The financially flush Gazprom, while continuing to subsidize NDR, decided in October to shell out for Unity, too. After flirting with other blocs, Russia's major oil company, Lukoil, gave money to Unity, as did Sibneft, the petroleum concern owned by Boris Berezovskii and Roman Abramovich.[26] Central Electoral Commission data put Unity's campaign fund at 46.5 million rubles (about $1.9 million), a close second to the LDPR, but the actual total was much higher than that.[27] Investigative journalists several times raised questions about where Unity got its money, and in exchange for what. Tension mounted over the participation of Berezovskii, who was for most Russians an odious figure. Having accepted his handouts since its inception, the Unity hierarchy pushed him away from the table during the closing weeks of the campaign. Aleksandr Karelin openly accused him of trying to purchase votes in the single-mandate district where he was seeking a seat. Sergei Shoigu then cast aspersions on a Chechnya peace plan Berezovskii had bruited and stated that if Berezovskii wanted to be active in politics he should "choose a more clean way than being an adviser about all and everything."[28] Fortunately for Unity, its schizophrenia on Berezovskii attracted little attention.

In the government structure, Deputy Prime Minister Nikolai Aksë-nenko, a Siberian, was assigned to coordinate administrative backup to Unity.[29] His Ministry of the Railways and Golovkov's Rosgosstrakh provided appreciable monetary and logistical aid. Shoigu took an official leave of absence from his ministry in late September but used its extensive local offices and transportation assets as infrastructure for his campaign. Putin ceremoniously recalled him to active duty in mid-November, citing exigencies in Chechnya, whereupon Shoigu claimed he was "a government minister during working hours and the leader of Unity only after 5 P.M." A KPRF complaint to the Central Electoral Commission was rejected.[30]

Unity's most enviable resource was the extensive and positive television coverage of its every move on ORT and RTR; there was also red-carpet treatment on TV-6, a smaller private channel mostly under Berezovskii's control. Sarah Oates, a British-based scholar who examined news programming during the campaign using data from the European Institute for the Media, found that ORT expended 42 percent of its story time on stories playing up Putin and 19 percent on Shoigu stories; on RTR, Unity was mentioned in 24 percent of the reports, although other parties got more attention than they did on ORT.[31] Unity leaders kept away from media outlets that might compel them to grapple with precise issues, boycotting candidates' debates and rarely giving on-camera interviews. They funneled half of their advertising budget through regional television stations, tailoring the content to local conditions.[32] Pain was taken to beam some TV ads at farm dwellers, shooting scenes in villages and having agrarian folk speak into the microphone.

In addition to the sweetheart coverage of Unity, state-owned television expended vast tracts of airtime on attacking its opponents. The urgent task was to discredit OVR, the original favorite in the race. The weekend newsmagazines hosted by Sergei Dorenko on ORT and Nikolai Svanidze on RTR were the most scathing, although stories on OVR's misdeeds also burgeoned in the daily news, along with brief "analytical" features such as Mikhail Leont'ev's "Odnako" ("However") piece on ORT. The most popular weekend show, Dorenko's Sunday evening program, boosted the Unity cause in broadcast after broadcast. Dorenko was a personal associate of Berezovskii, the guiding force behind ORT's news programming and one of the instigators of the bloc.[33]

Another resource cited by organizers and analysts we debriefed was the cooperation of regional executives. Most provincial leaders were willing to assist Unity with introductions, access to television studios, permits for rallies, and the like. To be sure, Unity staff said they discounted the governors' courtesies and did not go out of their way to cash in on them. As Sergei Popov, Unity's deputy campaign manager, stated in an interview shortly before the election, they preferred an "air war" they could guide from Moscow to getting bogged down in a "ground war" where they would be hostage to governors with dubious electoral skills and ambiguous loyalties.[34] Besides Platov in Tver, the elected heads of seven lightly populated provinces—Chukotka, Kalin-ingrad, Kursk, Omsk, Primor'e, and the republics of Kalmykiya and Tuva—made statements of support in October and November. Courte-sies were provided even by some governors who on paper adhered to other electoral blocs. In a surreal touch, the most avid proponent was the mercurial Aman Tuleyev in Kemerovo, in western Siberia, the fourth-ranked candidate on the national list of the KPRF! Hosting Karelin in November, Governor Tuleyev beseeched residents to vote for the party of power as an act of hard-nosed realism: "He spoke of the need to support Unity, since it is power (*vlast'*) and one has to coexist with it."[35]

Yet another weapon Unity's leaders brandished was public spending and more generally the state's influence over the national economy. As luck would have it, ballooning world oil prices, the stimulating effects of the 1998 ruble devaluation, and fiscal belt tightening were reviving eco-nomic growth and easing budgetary stringency. In a nakedly political move, Putin on November 9 announced he was hiking old-age and vet-erans' pensions and that January pensions would be paid out in Decem-ber. The federal authorities also redoubled efforts to defuse the chronic problem of wage arrears owed to teachers and other public sector work-ers. Unity missed few opportunities to point out that Russia's economy was at last in a hearty recovery from the nadir of 1998. Putin gave Shoigu ammunition with reports such as his statement to the Duma in November that industrial output had increased 7.5 percent over the pre-vious year, profits were up five times, and there were "positive changes in the financial, monetary, and credit spheres."[36]

Stability, Patriotism, and Strength

Unity on the stump conveyed an attitude more than a solid program. It published a booklet of policy ideas only two months after the election. Campaign-period materials were sparse. They included a question-and-answer brochure, a set of "Theses for a Platform for the Unity Electoral Bloc" splashed on a single page of *Nezavisimaya gazeta* (a newspaper owned by Berezovskii) on December 12, and remarks, sometimes cryptic and slapdash, by Shoigu and his running mates.[37]

Unity insisted that it eschewed ideology and put no credence in such abstractions as socialism or capitalism. "We do not bind ourselves to any narrow ideological direction," averred Shoigu. "We are not 'centrists,' 'rightists,' or 'leftists.' We are a party of consolidation of all healthy forces in society, free of ideological bias." The bloc, he continued, was against "extremism" of all stripes and for "political stability," but it was also against miring Russia in a "swamp" or the "stagnation" of the late Soviet period. It was necessary, Shoigu said, to face up to "decisive measures" and "to place things in order . . . in Chechnya . . . in the economy, in the social sphere, in the defense sphere." In economic policy, the Unity approach was mostly liberal and pro–private property. It was opposed to "a new division of property" and any reconsideration of privatization and favored free sale and purchase of land and policies "to develop the middle class and support entrepreneurs who are capable of quickly saturating the domestic market with Russian goods and services." Liberal rhetoric was interlarded with populist verbiage about a clampdown on corruption and the "social responsibilities" of the new bourgeoisie.[38]

A constant refrain in Unity's campaign was veneration of Russia's territorial integrity and national greatness. "Only on the basis of patriotism," Shoigu intoned, "is it possible to form not a narrow party ideology but a national ideology. It is impossible to respect oneself without respecting one's country." Foreigners would honor Russia once it demanded to be heard. "We have no reason to frighten the whole world, but we should force them to take us into account. Then they will take notice of us and speak with us as equals."[39]

On the visceral issue tattooed in the headlines, the war in Chechnya and the North Caucasus, Unity's stance was vociferously nationalistic. Shoigu commended the soldiers battling the guerrillas and lashed out at dissenters as disloyal. In an aside, he lamented the demise of the Soviet Union, saying that someday Mikhail Gorbachev "will be judged for the collapse of the USSR."[40] Unity hewed to civic Russian (*rossiiskii*) rather than ethnic Russian (*russkii*) patriotism, appropriately for a bloc in which ethnic non-Russians were prominent (Shoigu is a Tuvian and the eminence grise behind Unity, Berezovskii, a Jew). But its stand on Chechnya and national unity earned Unity kind words in *Zavtra,* the shrilly Russophile newspaper that in past elections had always sided with the communists.

In television clips and handouts, Unity chose as its self-image a stylized drawing of a bear. In Russian popular culture, the bear is a monument to primordial strength, custom, and practicality. Hibernating in frigid weather, the lord of the woods awakens when its habitat is threatened, much as Unity professed its clarion call would perk up Russia's long-suffering people. One of its thirty-second TV ads was a cartoon evoking a native fairy tale about a forest cottage. Animals standing for other parties and social forces—one of them a sharp-toothed wolf, an evil trope in Russian folklore—invade the house and wreak havoc in it. Finally a brown bear—wearing a cutaway wrestler's suit, in an allusion to Karelin—gallumps up and growls, "It's time for repairs." "He pulls the other animals out of the house, fixes the broken window, and puts the weathervane back on the roof. At the end of the commercial, Unity's emblem . . . appears at the top of the screen, next to the number 14, its line on the ballot."[41] The Unity campaign was the first in Russia's short electoral history to rely so heavily on a symbol and on a unified cartoon image, rather than on disparate images and on the speeches of its leaders.

Marquee Names

All three marquee names on the Unity slate were featured in its campaign propaganda. General Gurov was lauded for his intrepid attacks on racketeers and the muscular Karelin for his athletic prowess. But the limelight was on Sergei Shoigu, the bloc's superstar. His diverse résumé and current duties were great fodder for Unity's sales team. Shoigu, the son of a communist party apparatchik, had come to Moscow in the 1980s as the protégé of a conservative Siberian official, Oleg Shenin, and had many ties to the Soviet nomenklatura. His education as a construction engineer and his long service in the Council of Ministers, where he was untouched by scandal, gave him an aura of professionalism and quiet competence.[42] As head of the uniformed federal agency responsible for civil defense, Shoigu was a junior *silovik,* a "power minister" of the kind Putin was at ease with, and had been a member of Russia's Security Council since 1993. His ministry's specialization in cleaning up after earthquakes, bomb blasts, and other natural and manmade disasters—which, of course, are legion in contemporary Russia— enabled image consultants to package Shoigu as blending strength, selfless devotion to duty, and compassion. The Chechnya operation, with its refugees and civilian casualties, was a green field of opportunities for getting this across. Shoigu toured the republic and adjacent territories in the weeks before the election, trailed by camera crews and dispensing comfort to all and sundry.

Connecting with Putin, Disconnecting from Yeltsin

In keeping with its pro-government position, Unity stated its belief in continuation of Russia as a "presidential republic" and its determination, once seated in the legislature, to facilitate collaboration with the executive branch and to defer to presidential and prime ministerial leadership. More and more, beginning around November 1, this pro-government line was rendered as support for Putin personally. The pledge was resoundingly reciprocated on November 24 when the prime minister spoke to a luncheon at the Ministry of Emergency Situations—with dozens of governors seated before him, on the pretense that they were there to discuss civil defense policy. A beaming Shoigu at his elbow, Putin uttered two lapidary sentences to a gaggle of television reporters: "As concerns Unity, I will not define my political preference, since I am the chairman of the government. But personally, as a citizen, I will vote for Unity." The garbled aside about his government position was instantly forgotten; the sentence that stuck was the second. A Unity bulletin released on December 1, 1999, stated the understanding explicitly: "Our goal is to create a pro-Putin majority in the State Duma," because "Unity supports Putin, and Putin leans on Unity."[43]

Unity organizers came to believe, not unreasonably, that the photo op of November 24 padded their vote total by a dozen percentage points.[44] Had it come a few months before, it would have meant little. In August 1999, shortly after Putin became premier, 1 or 2 percent of citizens in national polls planned to vote for him as president in 2000. By the first week in December, that figure was up to almost 50 percent. Members of the Russian elite were deeply impressed by Putin's support and the concomitant ascent of Unity in the polls.

A prickly issue for the Unity brain trust, in terms of the mutual embrace with Putin and of their portrayal of themselves as innovators, was what to do with President Yeltsin. Most of the time, Unity finessed the problem by maintaining a stony silence. Yeltsin for his part, wary of giving Unity a kiss of death, abstained from public comment. After sitting in on some of the deliberations about forming the bloc, he wrote later, "I soon ceased to have anything to do with this work." "From the beginning it was clear to me that this party of 'social optimism' should not be associated in the consciousness of the voters with my name or by the same token with the name of any other well-known politician of the previous generation. The peculiarity of the new movement . . . lay in its absolute freshness and the apolitical nature of its participants."[45] Unlike

Gaidar in 1993 and Chernomyrdin in 1995, who were aggrieved by Yeltsin's unwillingness to take up cudgels on their behalf, Shoigu and his colleagues were relieved. Answering a reporter's questions about Yeltsin in December, Shoigu referred to him as "a figure of historical scale" whose place in Russian history would be clear only "generations from now." Appraisal of Yeltsin, in other words, was best left to the historians. Shoigu also tried ingeniously to make hay from Unity's indirect connection, through Putin, with Yeltsin. Noting that other parties, the KPRF among them, were in agreement with Putin's Chechnya policy, he accused them of deceit for rounding on Yeltsin: "We relate to Yeltsin as the incumbent president who appointed the government we support. We are not communists. We cannot support the government appointed by the president and be in opposition to the president. That would be political hypocrisy."[46]

The Districts

The only blot on Unity's record in 1999 was its woeful results in the single-mandate districts. Its election of nine deputies in districts, versus sixty-four returned on the nationwide list, is one of the anomalies of the entire Duma election. It is strange when one considers the premium the bloc placed on regions. Doubly strange is that the Unity leadership advocated wholesale reorganization of the electoral system on the territorial principle. All Duma deputies, its platform "theses" said, should be elected by majority in districts, with runoffs between the top two finishers and "absolutely equal conditions of struggle."[47]

Earlier incarnations of the party of power had waged aggressive district campaigns, and Our Home Is Russia had with Yeltsin's assent tried to tilt the electoral law against proportional representation. Russia's Choice ran 105 district candidates in 1993, the most of any party, and elected 26 of them, also the most. NDR had 103 nominees in 1995 (third) and elected a deflating 10 (fourth, far behind the KPRF's 58) in a botched campaign mortgaged to local notables it could not discipline.[48] Russia's Choice and NDR favored district elections on pragmatic grounds. They calculated that, with regional elites bulldozing the road, candidates of the party of power would be more successful than those of almost any party.

Unity's district campaign got off on the wrong foot when it nominated only 30 district candidates—a pittance compared with the number put forth by the KPRF (129), Yabloko (113), OVR (91), and even the wounded NDR (90). Ten parties and blocs registered candidates in more districts than Unity. Having 30 entrants in 224 geographically dispersed races (225 districts minus the 1 district in Chechnya), the best it could aspire to was also-ran status.

The reasons for Unity's torpor were more practical than philosophical. Prime among them was tardiness. Its adversaries had been beating the bushes for district candidates since the spring of 1999. Rusova, Popov, and Sitnikov had only a few weeks in October to counter. The window of opportunity for putting up district candidates coincided with the time in which the Unity steering group was shelving its reliance on governors for a national, media-centered campaign. Forced to concentrate on the higher-priority undertaking, it gave short shrift to the district nominations. Since Unity had so few horses in the local races, tending to the stable was no higher a priority after registrations closed than before. Nonpartisan candidates who might be induced to play along with the government if elected were of much more interest to Unity's Kremlin sponsors. In fact, under the supervision of a deputy head of the presidential administration, Vladislav Surkov, the Kremlin selected and coordinated assistance to friendly candidates in the districts in an operation that was entirely independent of the Unity campaign. One-third of the nominations the Unity bloc did make were in regions where it had, or thought it had, dependable support from the governor. But the governors willing to extend themselves for district candidates were few.[49] In some regions, pro-Unity leaders were themselves embattled politically. Platov in Tver, for example, had limited support in the local bureaucracy and media and nearly lost his own reelection race in December 1999. It was clear early on that "the level of administrative control in those regions on which Unity is counting is as a rule not great, and in many districts there are already favorites who have no connection to the movement."[50]

The Voters

What was the impact of this multibarreled strategy on the electorate? Our survey data allow us to map Unity's mass support with some precision, an exercise we repeat in chapters 4 to 7 for OVR, the communists, the liberals, and Putin. We make recurrent reference to the multistage model of the voting decision derived from the data (consult appendix B), as well as to other information coming out of the survey work. The burden of the evidence is that the 1999 rendition of Russia's party of power matched many if not all of the expectations of its makers.

Fresh Faces

Unity aspired to attract first-time and alienated voters and persons from a wide range of electoral biographies. It excelled at these missions. Our 1995–2000 survey panel reveals that 7 percent of Unity's supporters were novices (who had not been of voting age in 1995) and 13 percent were ex-dropouts (who abstained or voted against all parties in 1995). Eighty percent were converts from other parties. Unity led all parties entered in the election in *every* continuity category but one (loyalists, or repeat voters, of which it had none). It attracted 40 percent of all novice voters, 34 percent of all ex-dropouts, and 41 percent of all interparty converts, among them 44 percent of all converts from a different party family. A tribute to its catholicity was the political cross section from which it landed its electors. The largest subgroup among Unity's converts was the 31 percent who had voted socialist in 1995, trailed by erstwhile supporters of centrist parties (19 percent), nationalist parties (18 percent), the 1995 government party, NDR (16 percent), and liberal parties (15 percent); 1 percent had voted for miscellaneous parties in 1995.[51]

Unity's new-wave advertising strategy clicked with many electors. Of survey respondents in our 1999–2000 panel who said they "especially liked" the advertising clips of one or more parties in the Duma campaign, 44 percent singled out Unity's ads, twice as many as the next party.[52] Called upon to say in their own words what they liked about its promotions, they summoned up some of the bloc's pet themes. Here is a sampling:

These are all young people, with progressive intentions. . . .

I like the fact that the people in the Unity bloc are young and that their motto is, "Let us renew Russia." The name "Bear" is a symbol of might. . . .

These young people will lead the country in a completely different way. It is high time to get rid of the old people. . . .

I see decisiveness here, not only in words but in deeds. These are young and new people who are capable of doing something for the country. . . .

Table 3-1. *Vote for Our Home Is Russia in 1995 and Unity in 1999, by Community Size and Age*
Percent

Social category	Our Home Is Russia, 1995[a]	Unity, 1999[b]
Community size		
Bottom quintile	9	34
2	8	26
3	12	26
4	12	27
Top quintile	20	13
Age		
Under 30	16	37
30s	12	33
40s	13	26
50s	7	21
60s	13	21
Over 69	12	15

a. From panel survey described in Timothy J. Colton, *Transitional Citizens: Voters and What Influences Them in the New Russia* (Harvard University Press, 2000). N = 2,159 weighted cases.
b. From 1999–2000 panel, wave 2 (N = 1,439 weighted cases). The demographic information was collected in wave 1.

With them you feel the fresh wind of change. You get the hope that things will improve in Russia. . . .

These are young lads, and maybe this is our future. It looks as if they too are thinking about how to improve the life of humble people.

Unity made deep inroads into two demographic constituencies—denizens of smaller communities and younger people—that it targeted in its campaign planning and that had been inhospitable in the past to parties of power. Table 3-1 crosses the Unity vote in 1999 and the NDR vote in 1995 against urban-rural location and age. NDR's support was hardest in 1995 in the big cities and softest in the villages and small towns. Unity ran against the grain in 1999, garnering about triple the votes in the smallest communities that it did in metropolitan areas and faring wretchedly in Moscow, the Russian capital against which it let fly so many barbs.[53] NDR's support had been relatively flat across the age gradient. Unity fared slightly better among older voters in 1999 than NDR had but much better among young adults, scooping up the votes of almost 40 percent of all under the age of thirty. Its principal competition for the rural and small-town vote was the KPRF and the socialists; for the youth vote, it was the liberals.[54]

Our multivariate statistical model, which controls for the effect of overlapping variables, provides more fine-grained measures of the electoral effects of sociodemographic factors. The "total effects" on the Unity vote estimated in the model (see appendix table B-1) punctuate the selfsame social influences as the bivariate analysis. Holding all other social coordinates constant at their median values, the probability of a citizen living in one of the smallest communities voting for Unity in December 1999 was .13 (13 percentage points) higher than if he or she resided in one of the largest communities, and there was a separate deficit of .21 (21 percentage points) for residents of Moscow. Ceteris paribus, the probability that an individual less than thirty years old would have voted Unity was .14 (or 14 percentage points) higher than if that person had been age seventy or older.[55] Since the multivariate technique purges the estimates of the confounding effects of other social attributes, the differences in proportions are smaller than the raw numbers in table 3-1, especially for age group. But they point in the same direction, are nontrivial in size, and clear the conventional threshold for statistical significance of a relationship ($p \leq .05$). No other social attributes wield significant influence over the Unity vote.

Finally, Unity's political consultants tried to exploit the bloc's newness to incite a bandwagon effect in the campaign windup. Here again they were rewarded with considerable success. Seventy-nine percent of Unity voters said they made up their minds one month before election day or later; the mean for all non-Unity voters was 43 percent, and for KPRF voters it was 27 percent. Forty-nine percent of Unity voters came to a decision in the last two weeks of the campaign, as opposed to 18 percent of the voters for other parties. Since they decided late, Unity voters converted later from other parties, modifying preference during the course of the campaign. Thirty-eight percent of Unity voters said when interviewed after the election that they at one time had intended to vote otherwise. Interestingly, the largest group among the in-campaign switchers to Unity consisted of former KPRF supporters (36 percent); 14 percent said they had switched from OVR, a result at odds with Unity's fixation on OVR.

Payoff to Resources

The party of power's cornucopia of resources paid off handsomely in name recognition and the dissemination of favorable information.

Eighty-three percent of our 1999–2000 survey respondents, questioned in wave 2 (the postelection interview), recognized Unity and were able to evaluate it on a numbered scale, an awesome achievement for an organization incubated only months before. As is the norm in Russian campaigns, Unity did better at getting printed materials and visual aids in front of the voters than at making human contact with them. Twenty percent of our respondents said they had observed its posters and leaflets on the street frequently during the campaign and 15 percent that they received its materials frequently in their mailboxes; 0.8 percent had been canvassed by a Unity representative. Unity's organization, though real, was hardly a steamroller. It finished ahead of all other parties in mailings, yet was slightly inferior to OVR in posters and leaflets and fell just behind three others (the KPRF, Yabloko, and OVR) in canvassing.[56]

The blanket coverage of Unity in the mass media afforded dividends. Supplementing our basic model of the party-list vote, constructed mostly out of attitudinal variables, we have put together a second model using media-consumption indicators as predictors. As can be seen in appendix table C-6, the total effect of having *any* exposure to Russian television was a .17 hike in the probability of voting for Unity. What with Unity's advertising budget and the fulsome support of state media outlets, watching television seemed to bring about the effect no matter what the citizen's taste in content. Daily news viewing was not significantly associated with the Unity vote, but exposure to the strident weekend newsmagazines decidedly was. Specifically, individuals who watched the pro-Kremlin Sergei Dorenko show on ORT three to four times a month had a .16 higher probability of voting for Unity than individuals who did not watch it. Frequent viewers of Yevgenii Kiselëv's "Itogi" ("Summing Up") on NTV were .08 less likely than nonviewers to vote for Unity. Frequent exposure to Nikolai Svanidze's "Zerkalo" ("Mirror") on state-owned RTR, perhaps surprisingly, tamped down the likelihood of voting for Unity by .11. RTR disparaged Unity's main antagonist, OVR, but not as vitriolically as Dorenko and ORT, and tugged anti-OVR voters toward liberal parties, not toward the government party.

Gubernatorial guardianship was mildly helpful but not a potent determinant of the Unity vote. In six of the nine regions where the local establishment was supportive, Unity's share of the popular vote did exceed 30 percent—and in Tuva it almost broke 70 percent. Since these regions were small in average population, the Unity vote in the nine constituted but 7.58 percent of its votes Russia-wide.[57] The percentage of the total Unity vote accounted for by its five most successful regions— 16.31 percent—was second from the bottom of the six big parties and blocs (higher than only the LDPR). In just one banner region, Kemerovo, did the governor support the bloc.

As for public spending and the gravy from economic growth, there are also certain signs of a payoff. Our core model of the party-list vote (see appendix table B-3) shows Unity voters to be governed by current economic and political conditions (pro and con) at about the average for the parties that cleared the 5 percent threshold. As far as particular conditions are concerned (see appendix table B-1), there was no significant relationship in the overall electorate between a decision to vote for Unity and material success in the reform period, pocketbook-level economic assessments of family welfare during the preceding twelve months, or assessments of political conditions. But there was a robust association with sociotropic-level economic assessments bearing on the health of the economy rather than of the individual and household.[58] The total effect of sociotropic economic assessments on the Unity vote in 1999 was .18. That is to say, the citizen who had the most upbeat possible appraisal of the trend in the national economy over the preceding twelve months was 18 percentage points more likely to vote for Unity than the citizen who was most downbeat. The effect of detecting that the economy was on the right track was especially large among rural and small-town voters.[59]

Partisanship and Issue Opinions

Our multistage model of the party-list vote (appendix table B-1) assigns partisanship for Unity a total effect of .37 on the vote for the bloc. Although this is the lowest partisanship effect recorded for any first-tier party, it does suggest a sizable impact. Controlling for antecedent and collateral variables, a citizen who saw Unity as "my party" was 37 percentage points more likely to vote for the Unity slate than a neutral person.

The association between partisanship and the Unity vote does contain some useful information, but two large caveats are in order. The first is about newness. Sincere though survey respondents may have been in telling interviewers that Unity was "their" party, the object of their affection was barely out of the cradle at the time, meaning that the psychic link cannot have had the power and persistence of identification with a decades-old party in a mature democracy. The second qualification is about the size of the partisan group. The total-effect statistic conveys how big an effect partisanship exerted on an individual who shared that partisan sentiment; it contains no information about the incidence of the sentiment. Unity partisans in the autumn of 1999, as we define them, came to 9 percent of all partisans and a piffling 4 percent of the electorate. Eighty-one percent of those ostensible Unity partisans voted for the Unity list, but Unity partisans came to only 14 percent of all Unity voters. For the balance, other considerations must have been decisive.[60]

Normative issue opinions are causally concurrent with partisanship in our model of the voting decision. We tested for the electoral impact of seven issue opinions: a left-right scale and attitudes toward economic reform, Chechnya, regime type, the constitutional division of powers, federalism, and the need for "a strong leader who does not have to bother with parliament and elections." As appendix table B-3 shows, Unity's chances are more colored by issue preferences than any of the party lists except the KPRF's. As with partisanship, this judgment needs to be qualified.

The heftiest total effects on the likelihood of voting for Unity are those posted for the left-right scale (.30) and the preference for a more democratic over a Soviet-type regime (.26). The tendency to place Unity toward the right of the ideological spectrum and to associate it with a less authoritarian regime type testifies to the bloc's effective dissociation in the public mind from the Soviet and communist past. But Unity did not campaign directly on either of these meta-issues. The same applies to the prospect of rule by a strongman; it may have been implicit in some of the more slavish comments about Putin but was not an explicit goal in the Unity credo. One might include economic reform under the same rubric; Unity was in favor of a capitalist economy but, unlike the liberal parties, offered no concrete recipes for market reform. On these two issues, citizen opinion had no bearing on the odds for voting for Unity.

Shoigu and the bloc did campaign on three of the seven issues. On only one of them—support of presidential over parliamentary prerogatives—was there a major (.11) and statistically significant effect. On regional autonomy in the federation, the observed effect was of major magnitude (.10) and in the expected direction, yet was not statistically significant. The stunning lacuna is the absence of effect from opinion

Table 3-2. *Evaluations of the Records of President Yeltsin and Prime Minister Putin, Winter of 1999–2000*[a]
Percent

Evaluation	Yeltsin	Putin
Completely disapprove	22	1
Disapprove	37	2
Approve some, disapprove some	33	23
Approve	5	45
Completely approve	1	19
Don't know	2	10

a. From 1999–2000 panel, wave 2 (N = 1,846 weighted cases).

about the neuralgic issue of Chechnya. Although the war and its spillover were central in elite debate, at the mass level it did not matter whether a person was a hawk or a dove—opinion on solutions had no demonstrable bearing on the vote for Unity or for any political party.[61]

Evaluations of Political Players

Mass evaluations of elite-level players in the electoral game—of officeholders, of party leaders, and of parties' potential for performing well in elective office—are more manipulable in the short term than issue opinions or partisanship in the Western sense. They had direct and potent consequences for voting choice in 1999. Unity was no exception to this rule.

Attitudes toward incumbent officeholders had more of an effect on the propensity to vote for Unity than for anyone else in the election (see appendix table B-3). We asked five-point approval questions about the record of Russia's heads of state and government. As they had been since the mid-1990s, President Yeltsin's ratings were dismal (see table 3-2). About 60 percent of respondents moderately or strongly disapproved of his work as president, ten times as many as approved. The situation for Prime Minister Putin was an almost perfect mirror image: 64 percent approving, 3 percent disapproving.

Unity's strategy was to couple its image to Putin's and uncouple it from Yeltsin's. That it did both superbly is evident from our statistical model of the vote (see appendix table B-1). All relevant variables taken into account, the total effect of evaluations of Yeltsin on the Unity vote was negligible in magnitude (.05) and statistically not significantly different from zero. It was as if the Unity campaign, with Yeltsin's aid, had

Table 3-3. *Unity Vote and Evaluations of the Yeltsin and Putin Records*

Evaluation	Predicted probability of voting for Unity[a]
Yeltsin	
Completely disapprove	.30
Disapprove	.32
Approve some, disapprove some	.33
Approve	.35
Completely approve	.35
Putin	
Completely disapprove	.07
Disapprove	.12
Approve some, disapprove some	.21
Approve	.32
Completely approve	.45

a. Computed from multistage statistical model, holding causally prior and simultaneous variables constant at their medians. Sample N = 1,414; $p \leq .01$ for all cells in the column.

managed to coat itself in political Teflon where the president was concerned. The total effect of evaluations of Putin was statistically significant and large in magnitude (.38). Table 3-3 gives the probabilities of voting Unity predicted by the model for successive levels of approval of president and prime minister. For Yeltsin, evaluation of the incumbent is orthogonal to the voting choice.[62] For Putin, there is a close relationship. For a median voter, the predicted probability of voting for Unity swelled from .07 if the voter strongly disapproved of Putin's performance as prime minister, through .21 if he or she gave it a mixed review, to .45 if the voter strongly approved of Putin's work.[63] To think of it a different way, had Putin's ratings been as low in 1999 as the median rating for Yeltsin, the probability of the median voter supporting Unity would have been .12. Under this assumption, the predicted probability of that typical Russian voting for Fatherland–All Russia, Unity's prime challenger, would have been .18. Such an eventuality would have dropped Unity's vote share below OVR's and cast the election in a qualitatively different light.

Evaluations of party leaders, not only of incumbents, affected the 1999 election result. It was no coincidence that Unity, like all the other parties and blocs in the race, strained to promote the individual at the head of its national candidates' list. Sergei Shoigu, never before thought of as casting a national shadow, rocketed to a level of popularity eclipsed only by Putin himself. Asked to evaluate the main party leaders in wave 2 of our 1999–2000 panel survey, respondents indicated Shoigu

Table 3-4. *Evaluations of Sergei Shoigu's Character Traits*[a]

	Rating (percent)			
Trait	Yes/ probably yes	No/ probably no	Net yes/probably yes over no/ probably no	Ranking of net rating among 6 party leaders
Intelligent and knowledge- able person	73	5	68	2
Strong leader	65	10	55	1
Honest and trustworthy person	63	7	56	1
Really cares about people like you	54	13	41	1

a. From 1999–2000 panel, wave 2 (N = 1,846 weighted cases). "Don't know" responses included in the denominator but not shown here.

had the lowest recognition of all, 85 percent, but this was far above where it would have stood months before. On a scale of 0 to 10, where 0 connotes strong dislike and 10 a strong liking, our informants gave Shoigu the best overall evaluation of any party leader. His mean score of 6.40 was the only one above the midpoint of the scale (Putin's was 7.50).

We also probed for specific character traits, reasoning that they would go more squarely to the leadership function and would be less compromised by feedback from the voting decision. The four desirable traits selected were intelligence, strength, honesty, and empathy with ordinary people. Assessments of Unity's leader are summarized in table 3-4. Of those heading the six major lists, Shoigu had the most positive evaluations on a four-point scale on every criterion but intelligence, where he was tied for fourth with Sergei Kiriyenko of SPS (behind Primakov, Zyuganov, and Yavlinskii). Owing, one guesses, to his recent arrival on the scene, Shoigu had the fewest negative evaluations on all four criteria. His net ranking was first on strength, honesty, and empathy and second on intelligence.

The election-day payoff is apparent from the predicted probabilities in table 3-5. Other influences being constant, someone whose mean rating of Shoigu's qualities on the four-point index was in the bottom category had almost no chance (.02) of voting for Unity. At the upper end, the probability of voting Unity was .58. The difference between the two quantities is .56, which equals the estimated total effect of evaluations of Shoigu's character (see appendix table B-1). This was the largest differential computed for any party leader in 1999. Not only did Shoigu

Table 3-5. *Unity Vote and Evaluations of Shoigu's Character*

Mean evaluation of four traits	Citizen opinion (percent)[a]	Predicted probability of voting for Unity[b]
Does not have the positive trait	2	.02
Probably does not have the positive trait	7	.07
Probably has the positive trait	64	.25
Has the positive trait	28	.58

a. N = 1,846 weighted cases. Missing data coded at the mean of the distribution for the specific trait.

b. Computed from multistage statistical model, holding causally prior and simultaneous variables constant at their medians. Sample N = 1,414; $p \leq .01$ for all cells in the column.

Table 3-6. *Unity Vote, as Conditioned by Evaluations of Putin's Record and Shoigu's Character*[a]
Predicted probabilities

Mean evaluation of four traits for Shoigu	Evaluation of Putin's record				
	Completely disapprove	Disapprove	Approve some, disapprove some	Approve	Completely approve
Does not have the positive trait	.00	.01	.01	.02	.03
Probably does not have the positive trait	.01	.02	.04	.07	.12
Probably has the positive trait	.05	.09	.16	.25	.37
Has the positive trait	.18	.29	.43	.58	.70

a. Computed from multistage statistical model, holding causally prior and simultaneous variables constant at their medians. Sample N = 1,414; $p \leq .01$ for all cells in the table.

have flattering evaluations; the Unity campaign was an effective mechanism for converting them into votes.

Does it follow that Unity's winning suit was Sergei Shoigu and not Vladimir Putin? There is no denying Shoigu's contribution to victory, but looking at it out of context masks the interdependence between his and his mentor's reputations. As table 3-6 attests, the influence of the Shoigu factor was conditioned by the esteem in which the voter held *Putin*. For citizens who rated Putin lowest, going from low to high in regard for Shoigu raised the probability of voting for Unity by .18; if they held Putin's work in the highest regard, the predicted probability of voting for Unity leapt up by .67. The better the voters thought of Putin, the more what they thought of Shoigu told on their electoral behavior.

A final aspect of voter motivation concerns political players' expected performance in office. Some major actors in 1999—the communists and

Table 3-7. *Prospective Evaluations of Unity's Issue Competence*[a]

	Say Unity is best prepared		
Issue	Percent	Percent of those who named a party	Ranking
Social security	17	25	2
Economy	17	25	2
Human rights	16	27	2
Chechnya	34	52	1
Foreign policy	17	28	2
Crime and corruption	25	39	1

a. From 1999–2000 panel, wave 2 (N = 1,846 weighted cases).

the liberals—waged idea-based campaigns and peddled substantive responses to Russia's problems. Unity took an atmospheric approach and shunned detailed policy prescriptions. It sought the public's approbation less for what it would do about the issues than for its qualifications to do *something* about them. We asked our survey informants which party they thought could best handle six discrete policy problems: social security, the economy, human rights, Chechnya, foreign policy, and crime and corruption. On two keynote issues, Chechnya and crime and corruption, a plurality of Russians in 1999 judged Unity best prepared to cope; on the remaining four, it came in second to the KPRF (see table 3-7). On Chechnya, one in two survey respondents who named a party as best on the issue named Unity; on crime and corruption, two in five named Unity. Forty-two percent of all respondents were sanguine about Unity as the most competent party or bloc on at least one issue—10 percentage points more than about the next, the KPRF.

It is impossible to bundle issue-specific measures into our comprehensive analysis of the vote without overloading it. We employ instead an additive issue-competency index for each party, with values from 0 to 6. Our statistical model (see appendix table B-1) shows the Unity vote to be sensitive to the index, although not especially so compared with the other leading parties. The total effect of the combined issue-competency score is .72—which is high, if somewhat less than for the other large parties and blocs. Table 3-8 tracks predicted probabilities of voting Unity across ascending scores on the competence question; they stretch from a .21 chance of voting Unity for persons who were at the median on other indicators and saw it as tops on none of the issues, all the way to .93 for those median voters who rated it best at handling all six issues. At a score of two issues, the chances of voting for Unity go over fifty-fifty. If one manipulates other parties' scores as well as Unity's

Table 3-8. *Unity Vote and Prospective Evaluations of Its Issue Competence*

Number of issues Unity can handle best	Citizen opinion (percent)[a]	Predicted probability of voting for Unity[b]
0	58	.21
1	13	.35
2	10	.52
3	4	.68
4	3	.80
5	3	.88
6	9	.93

a. N = 1,846 weighted cases.

b. Computed from multistage statistical model, holding causally prior and simultaneous variables constant at their medians. Sample N = 1,414; $p \leq .01$ for all cells in the column.

within common limits (see appendix table B-3), Unity comes out at the lower end of the range. More trenchant perhaps, Unity from scratch instilled in millions of voters the conviction that it had what it takes to remedy Russia's problems.[64]

The District Vote

The party of power reaped what it sowed in the other half of the Duma campaign. Superintending campaigns in the far-flung single-member districts was of secondary concern to Unity's Moscow-based image-makers. The nomination of thirty candidates automatically set a ceiling. The KPRF, Unity, and OVR all elected approximately one district deputy for every three candidates nominated. Extrapolating, Unity would have returned about twenty more deputies if it had put up as many nominees as OVR and about thirty-five more if it had as many as the KPRF.

The aggregate results of the election hint at other shortcomings. Three of Unity's nine winners were native sons (one of Shoigu's deputy ministers in his birthplace of Tuva and Aleksandr Karelin and another candidate in Karelin's home region of Novosibirsk); two were clients of Governor Tuleyev in Kemerovo; and one apiece was elected in Kalmykiya and Primor'e, where the local elite was pro-Unity.[65] Unity was one of four national parties and quasi parties for which the vote share obtained by its local designees lagged behind its party-list vote in the districts where it did field candidates. The gap, some 11 percent, was larger than the gaps for the other three (the KPRF, SPS, and the LDPR)

Table 3-9. *Electoral Consistency between District and Party-List Votes,*
Unity Voters and All Voters
Percent

Candidate voted for in the district	All districts		Districts where a nominee registered	
	Unity voters[a]	All voters[b]	Unity voters[c]	All voters[d]
Nominee of party supported in the party-list vote	2	17	16	40
Nominee of a different party	28	24	30	26
Independent candidate	52	45	32	24
Votes against all candidates	18	14	23	10

a. N = 344 weighted cases.
b. Excluding persons who voted against all parties in the party-list vote. N = 1,318 weighted cases.
c. N = 44 weighted cases.
d. Excluding persons who voted against all parties in the party-list vote. N = 566 weighted cases.

combined. Unity, it would seem, had unusual trouble converting its strength in the PR contest into votes for its district candidates even when it succeeded in getting them on the ballot.[66] The typical Unity winner was "a rather major economic manager or a bureaucrat supported by the regional authorities."[67] Nominees without these qualities were lost in the shuffle.

Our individual-level data shed further light on Unity's problem. Nationwide, about one-sixth of Russian voters picked a district candidate nominated by the party or bloc whose list they had supported. For Unity voters, as table 3-9 sets forth, that proportion was a microscopic 2 percent. Much of this shortfall stems from its patchy nominations work. Only 13 percent of the Unity voters among survey respondents had the chance to vote for a Unity-nominated candidate in their local district (this is very close to the ratio in the actual election); 87 percent had no such opportunity. Beyond that, only 16 percent of Unity voters in districts where there was a Unity candidate voted the straight ticket— far below the average of 40 percent for all parties.

A determinant of this curious result was voters' knowledge about their options, and that in turn was shaped by the flow of information. When not thwarted by the nomination process, the default setting for well-informed Russians in 1999 was to vote consistently across the party-list and district segments of the election. As is seen in columns 3 and 4 of table 3-10, Unity voters were much like other voters in this regard. Seventy-five percent of Unity constituents who resided in districts where the bloc had presented a candidate and were aware of who

Table 3-10. *Electoral Consistency and Voter Knowledge, Unity Voters and All Voters, in Districts Where a Nominee of Party Supported in Party-List Vote Is Registered*[a]

	Percent		Percent of category who vote straight ticket	
Position	Unity voters[b]	All voters[c]	Unity voters[b]	All voters[c]
Knows there is a nominee and can identify the nominee	12	41	75	80
Knows there is a nominee and cannot identify the nominee	24	10	0	10
Thinks there is no nominee	26	24	22	21
Does not know if there is a nominee	38	25	8	24

a. Excludes persons who voted against all candidates in the district.
b. N = 34 weighted cases.
c. N = 509 weighted cases.

that candidate was voted the straight ticket; the average for all parties was 80 percent. Unity's real handicap is evident in columns 1 and 2, namely, that so few of its party-list voters in these districts—12 percent of them, or 29 percentage points less than average—had knowledge of the candidate. The efforts of the bloc on behalf of its depleted corps of candidates were lackadaisical. Unity's thirty district candidates received 1,393,780 votes, or 8.97 percent of its total on the national party list. Most were cast by individuals who had *not* rallied to the national campaign. In our survey sample—in which, admittedly, the number of persons who supported Unity candidates in the districts is very small—37 percent of those individuals had voted for Unity on the party list and 63 percent for other parties. The ratio for all parties and quasi parties was 42 percent to 58 percent.

This small yield on the formal level is not the only indicator of performance by pro-government forces in the districts. Kremlin officials, and Vladislav Surkov in particular, used informal avenues to influence events. Separate from the Unity effort, they arrived at understandings with several dozen nonpartisan candidates, trading promises of campaign funding and assistance from governors and regional television studios for cooperation if elected. Gennadii Raikov from the oil-rich Tyumen region coordinated the conversations with these politicos, who later formed the core of the People's Deputy faction in the Duma.[68] Pro-government business oligarchs and corporations such as Gazprom also worked directly with candidates in some districts. In addition, high officials reached out to a few single-mandate candidates running under other party banners beside Unity. Dmitrii Rogozin, for instance, was the number two on the Russia-wide list of a minor nationalist bloc that had earlier been allied with Yurii Luzhkov (the Congress of Russian Communities–Boldyrev Movement), but in district 74 in Voronezh province he sought and received Kremlin help. Well-financed and unopposed by a Unity candidate, he defeated eight others, including KPRF and OVR nominees, to take the seat. It was no coincidence that Rogozin quickly joined People's Deputy after the election and was awarded the prestigious chairmanship of the Duma's foreign affairs committee.[69]

Conclusions

It was the national half of the election, not the unprepossessing outcome in the districts, that let the new party of power make its mark. The party-list vote weighed heaviest in the public relations war, made Unity the fulcrum of the new Duma, and was an invaluable stepping-stone for its champion in high places, Vladimir Putin. On January 18, 2000, Unity reached an accord with the KPRF to divvy up the main leadership positions and committee chairs in the Duma. On February 27, with the presidential campaign under way, Unity held its founding congress as a self-standing political movement. On May 27, three weeks after Putin's inauguration, several thousand delegates in the Kremlin Palace of Congresses were to vote to register it as a "centrist" political party, confirm Sergei Shoigu as its leader, and incorporate the remnants of Our Home Is Russia, which had voted itself out of existence the day before.

One cannot imagine Unity pulling this off without the financial, media, and administrative resources tossed its way by the central government, the governors, and some of the business elite. And yet Unity made far more entrepreneurial use of those resources than earlier versions of the party of power. From its beginnings as a loose-knit coalition of provincial politicians, it quickly became a Kremlin-led operation conducted by campaign professionals. Their mission was to preserve the post-Soviet status quo, but its leaders found nontraditional ways of fulfilling it. They enlarged their social base of support beyond the pockets reached by NDR in 1995 and Russia's Choice in 1993. By stacking its ticket with political newcomers and shrewdly contriving a media message, Unity avoided being tarred with the failures of the Yeltsin years and built bridges to apolitical voters and to individuals with a wide smattering of prior political commitments. It gained credibility on some salient issues of the day without, in most instances, articulating a plan of action on them. In Shoigu, it made a cagey choice of senior leader. And fortune smiled on it in that it sallied forth at the very moment that a capable prime minister, Putin, was seizing the initiative on Chechnya and staking his claim to primacy. Putin's endorsement, as the Unity publicity machine drove home relentlessly, gave citizens the cue that a vote for Unity would be a vote of confidence in him. The party of power and Russia's new man of power fed off one another.

4 *The Party of Hubris*

FATHERLAND–ALL RUSSIA was in certain respects
Unity's twin. Like Unity, it was a by-product of the political disarray
that gripped Russia's elite in the late 1990s, as economic and social
problems piled up and Boris Yeltsin's authority waned. Both blocs were
plugged into the state apparatus, at the national and regional levels, and
aimed to use it to move into positions of control. Both took the parliamentary election to be a preliminary round to the more important duel
over the presidency in 2000. Thus it was for credible reasons that analysts at first affixed the same label to OVR that they had to Russia's
Choice and Our Home Is Russia, calling it "in essence . . . a new 'party
of power' . . . a party that [can] contend for victory not only in the parliamentary elections but also in the presidential ones."[1] The advent of
Unity muddied the waters, but for some time observers were content to
view OVR as a "shadow party of power," the "alternative party of
power," the "party of future power," a "party-of-power-in-waiting,"
and so on. In style and personnel, OVR was if anything a closer facsim-
ile of earlier parties of power than Unity.

For all their similarities, OVR differed from Unity in two fundamental ways. First, in terms of the immediate struggle, OVR was a political
movement in opposition to the Kremlin. Unlike Russia's Choice, Our
Home Is Russia, and Unity, it was neither instituted nor nurtured by
those in power in the executive branch of government. Even as analysts
underscored the organization's ties to the establishment and that it
"essentially represents a broad coalition of pro-regime elites," they had

to admit that for the first time "such a coalition is taking shape from below, without the 'benediction' of the 'narrow regime,' that is, the team of the outgoing president, and over its resistance."[2] OVR leaders occupied the most powerful positions in regional government structures but did not hold senior positions in the federal government.

Second, OVR differed in its electoral trajectory. Unity was like the late entrant in a marathon who pulls from behind in the last lap to win the race. OVR was the immediate front-runner, well-trained and fleet-footed, who loses the lead with the finish tape in sight. And what a long lead it was. A national poll in July 1999 by the trusted VTsIOM (All-Russian Center for the Study of Public Opinion) showed 28 percent of all eligible voters intending to cast ballots for Fatherland (its election compact with All Russia had not yet been consummated). OVR was riding high well into the autumn. A poll at the beginning of October pegged its support at 26 percent, which was 8 points ahead of the KPRF and 22 points ahead of Unity. As late as mid-November, before Vladimir Putin began plugging Unity, OVR was at nearly 20 percent and Unity at 7 percent.[3] OVR spokespeople spun the early reports into gushing forecasts: the bloc, one boasted, would win 266 Duma seats and form a government accountable to its caucus.[4] The outlook for OVR as the electioneering started was undeniably bullish.

What, then, dashed these hopes? How did a bloc expected to pull in 25 to 30 percent of the popular vote in the summer come away with 13.59 percent in December? Why 68 deputies and not 266? The defeat was so resounding that in the New Year OVR leaders Yevgenii Primakov and Yurii Luzhkov both decided to back out of the presidential election and, grimmer still, to acquiesce in a merger with Unity.

In one sense, OVR succumbed to the blows of the Yeltsin government, Prime Minister Putin, their accomplices in Unity, and the mass media. It is no exaggeration to call the counteroffensive against it a smear campaign whose scale was unprecedented in Russian electoral history. In another sense, OVR was a victim of its own strategy and of its own hype. It was always more a flag of convenience for disparate officeholders and notables than a cohesive movement, and it placed excessive faith in regional governors. Its electoral message was murky, even by the lax standards of post-Soviet politics. Owing to these failings, the bloc did not draw in a well-bounded social constituency. Most lethal, the giddy advance reviews lulled it into complacency. When its adversaries pounded at it in the name of patriotism, renewal, and clean government, it had no effective response. OVR aspired to be the party of power. Yet, in overplaying its hand and not anticipating the damage that the real party of power could do, it went down in history as a party of hubris.

A Hyphenated Bloc

Fatherland–All Russia was the only prime participant in the 1999 election bearing a hyphenated title. The fact that it joined several entities without subsuming them under a plain appellation speaks volumes about the process that brought it forth.

Luzhkov and Fatherland

The linchpin of the effort was Yurii Luzhkov, the mayor of Moscow.[5] A chemical engineer and executive in the Soviet plastics industry, Luzhkov was brought into city government in the mid-1980s by Yeltsin, then the first secretary of the local communist party. He was elected vice mayor in 1991 and inherited the mayor's position in 1992 when his running mate, Gavriil Popov, resigned. Luzhkov blossomed into an accomplished and hard-fisted manager of local services and capital works, the man who had the last word on matters large and small. Everyday amenities in the capital improved in the 1990s while deteriorating elsewhere. Two-thirds of foreign investment in Russia streamed into it. Muscovites showed their appreciation by reelecting Luzhkov in 1996 by a lopsided majority.

Luzhkov was a stout ally of Yeltsin's in the 1991 Soviet putsch, the 1993 constitutional confrontation, and the 1996 presidential election, but their relationship had its ups and downs. While styling himself a "practitioner" (*praktik*), Luzhkov had heartfelt political views and did not mince words. He crossed swords with radical economic reformers like Yegor Gaidar and Anatolii Chubais, especially on the issue of privatization. He irked Yeltsin by striking an alliance with Vladimir Gusinskii, one of the first of the Russian oligarchs and the proprietor of NTV, Russia's only private television station with a national audience and an editorial slant often critical of Kremlin policies. Wrapping himself in the flag, Luzhkov cultivated ties with the patriarch of the Orthodox Church (he provided funding from the Moscow budget for reconstruction of the Cathedral of Christ the Savior, a landmark dynamited by Joseph Stalin in the 1930s) and denounced Russian acquiescence in Ukrainian sovereignty over the disputed Crimea peninsula. Relations with the president went downhill after Luzhkov in 1997 became one of the first politicians to say Yeltsin might not be physically capable of carrying out his duties. At the time of the 1998 economic panic, he urged Duma deputies to torpedo the bid to restore Viktor Chernomyrdin as premier. Yeltsin retaliated by firing his national security adviser, Andrei Kokoshin, and his press secretary, Sergei Yastrzhembskii, for pushing Luzhkov's candidacy. Luzhkov freely sponsored reports that the president was captive to a venal and irresponsible "Family" coterie, arrayed around Yeltsin's daughter Tat'yana D'yachenko, his onetime chief of staff (and her future husband) Valentin Yumashev, and business tycoon Boris Berezovskii. The last straw was when pro-Luzhkov members of parliament voted for Yeltsin's impeachment in May 1999. "No politician at the federal level," says Yeltsin, "had ever violated my personal rights so crudely and brazenly."[6]

The Moscow government's purchase in 1997 of TV-Tsentr, a television station with regional affiliates, was the tip-off that Luzhkov was climbing onto the national political stage. His growing reputation encouraged others to see in him a potential patron and leader. Two main groups extended feelers. The first was of a social-democratic bent and was centered on the Russian Movement for New Socialism, formed in 1997 with the intent of drafting Luzhkov as its head. Kindred organizations included Arkadii Vol'skii's Russian United Industrial Party, the Employees' Self-Management Party of Svyatoslav Fëdorov, and the ecological party KEDR. The head of the second group, General Andrei Nikolayev, a former commander of the border guards, was primarily a "statist" (*gosudarstvennik*), alarmed by the weakness of the state at home and the diminution of Russian influence abroad. Nikolayev and his confederates were instrumental in blocking Chernomyrdin's comeback in August 1998.

These two groups coalesced with Luzhkov and his city hall team in November 1998 to form the Fatherland (Otechestvo) movement. Their objective was to contest the 1999 parliamentary election and after that to elect Luzhkov president of Russia. Fatherland's founding congress was held on December 19, precisely one year before the scheduled Duma election (it rushed to file its sheaf of papers with the Ministry of Justice that very same day). Luzhkov, unanimously elected its chairman, bragged that it would be "the mightiest organization in the country."[7]

Fatherland was an umbrella for social democrats, moderate and not-so-moderate nationalists and statists, centrists, and political opportunists. From the left and center-left came the Federation of Independent Trade Unions of Russia, chaired by Mikhail Shmakov, an admirer of Luzhkov; the federation's political wing, the Union of Labor, and its leader, Andrei Isayev;[8] Vladimir Lysenko, leader of the Republican Party of Russia; and Alevtina Fedulova of Women of Russia, a party occupied mostly with social-welfare issues. High-profile "patriots" to sign on included Duma deputies Konstantin Zatulin, Stepan Sulakshin, and Dmitrii Rogozin (the head of the Congress of Russian Communities); the entertainer Iosif Kobzon; retired general Boris Gromov of the My Fatherland movement; Aleksandr Rutskoi, the governor of Kursk region and former vice president; and Viktor Mishin (of My Fatherland) and Boris Pastukhov (a deputy foreign minister), two past heads of the Komsomol, the Soviet youth league. Former members of Yeltsin's government rounded out the group, conspicuously, Anatolii Kulikov, a former minister of the interior; Georgii Boos, once the minister of taxation; Gennadii Kulik, former minister of agriculture; Kokoshin, who became first deputy chairman of Fatherland; and Yastrzhembskii, who became its spokesman. Staffing arrangements were loose. Luzhkov dropped the idea of imposing Mishin as chief of staff and assigned most organizational work and fund-raising to Vladimir Yevtushenkov and his Sistema organization, a Moscow holding company with interests in telecommunications, real estate, oil trading, and manufacturing.

All Russia

Regional executives were much more activist in 1999 than in previous elections and, as noted in chapter 3, more resistant to instructions from above. Some wanted no more than power at home and to ensure that Duma deputies elected from the districts on their turf met with their approval. Others had grander notions. Luzhkov had presidential ambitions, as did Konstantin Titov, the Samara governor and founder of the short-lived Voice of Russia coalition. The most vigorous attempt to get the governors to act in concert was that of the All Russia bloc.

The initiator of All Russia was Mintimer Shaimiyev, the "president" (governor) of the republic of Tatarstan. Shaimiyev sought to use the bloc to promote decentralization within a stable federation, and at a minimum to foreclose any rollback of the concessions the governors had wrested from Moscow in the 1990s. The organizing board, which met on April 22, 1999, had as members two other presidents of minority homelands, Murtaza Rakhimov of Bashkortostan and Ruslan Aushev of Ingushetiya, and the mayor of St. Petersburg (or governor, as he was officially called in Russia's second city), Vladimir Yakovlev. By its first congress in St. Petersburg in late May, its committee comprised ten governors and presidents, seven speakers of regional legislatures, and nineteen Duma deputies. Many of them had been associated until then with Our Home Is Russia or Voice of Russia.[9] All Russia was committed to "principled polycentrism," with unanimous consent for all decisions, and stated that it would have neither an official leader nor a presidential candidate in 2000. Shaimiyev and Rakhimov, whose republics had big oil and gas deposits and refineries, persuaded Lukoil, Gazprom, and Tatneft, flagships of the Russian petroleum industry, to provide funds and even to express public enthusiasm. Yeltsin let it be known that he deemed All Russia a destabilizing element and in particular that he frowned upon Shaimiyev's participation.[10]

Shaimiyev from the outset favored an entente with Luzhkov and drafted Oleg Morozov, the chairman of the Regions of Russia caucus in the Duma—and the deputy from district 23 in Tatarstan—as an intermediary. After months of haggling, Fatherland and All Russia hooked up on August 3, 1999, to form the Fatherland–All Russia bloc. Mayor Luzhkov and Governor Yakovlev cochaired a thirteen-member governing council; Morozov acted as secretary.[11]

Primakov and the Noah's Ark Effect

When negotiations with All Russia opened, Luzhkov was regarded as the rightful leader of the shadow party of power and had every intention of standing for president.[12] It was Yeltsin, though not by design, who upended his plans. By peremptorily dismissing his prime minister, Yevgenii Primakov, on May 12, 1999, the president instantaneously created a magnet for opposition sentiment. Primakov had been Russia's foreign minister and spymaster and in Soviet days had directed research institutes, chaired one of the houses of parliament, and sat on the ruling Politburo. He had "a knack for not making enemies, an unusual quality in Russia."[13] In his eight months as premier, Primakov had helped restore a semblance of calm to financial markets and comported himself with dignity. His Politburo past, his comfort with public ownership, and his appointment of a communist, Yurii Maslyukov, as first deputy premier gave him an inside with leftist voters. Unlike Chernomyrdin and Sergei Kiriyenko, the two heads of government Yeltsin ousted in 1998, Primakov maintained his popularity after leaving and was besieged by suitors from parties and blocs revving up for the campaign. On August 17, Luzhkov landed him for Fatherland–All Russia. Luzhkov probably had little choice but to try to recruit Primakov, since his loss to another bloc would have been perceived by Fatherland's leaders as a ravaging blow to their electoral prospects. Primakov was to occupy first spot on the national list, flanked by Luzhkov and Yakovlev. His cocksure statement at the press conference, one editorialist wrote tartly, "resembled a presidential state-of-the-nation address" and intimated that he "is not inclined to underestimate either the allure of his personality or the degree of his influence on the outcome of parliamentary or presidential elections."[14] Primakov seemed the perfect complement to Luzhkov. He had the intellectual depth and national experience that Luzhkov lacked, and his jowls and basso profundo voice radiated solidity without the mayor's menacing tone.

As recently as June, national polls gave Luzhkov a leg up on every potential candidate for president but Gennadii Zyuganov. By late summer, though, Primakov had outstripped Luzhkov and Zyuganov. A Public Opinion Foundation poll at the end of August showed 22 percent of all intended voters in Primakov's corner, with 16 percent behind Zyuganov and 8 percent for Luzhkov.[15] According to his staffers, Primakov accepted OVR's solicitation on the understanding that the Duma election would serve as the springboard for his presidential campaign.[16] Luzhkov explicitly said on August 23 he would root for Primakov if Primakov were to run. Some Fatherland organizers continued to hope that future conditions (such as a breakup of OVR after the Duma election) would free Luzhkov to welsh on the deal. Barring that, there was inconclusive discussion of Luzhkov serving as Primakov's prime minister or, if the constitution could be amended, as his vice president.[17]

The enlistment of Primakov inspired others to come calling. The most welcome was the leftist Agrarian Party of Russia (APR), which, running independently, had cleared the 5 percent barrier in 1993 and barely missed it in 1995. It had a small caucus in the Duma of 1995–99, brought up to strength by deputies "loaned" to it by the KPRF, and the minister of agriculture was customarily appointed from its ranks. The APR acceded to the OVR coalition on August 20. Chairman Mikhail

Lapshin specifically cited Primakov and his stint in government: "We will run with a politician whose deeds, not words, as head of government showed that Russia can revive if its rulers are changed. Yevgenii Maksimovich [Primakov] demonstrated very convincingly that even a prime minister can bring about positive changes. He extended his hand to the Russian peasants." Lapshin contrasted Primakov's practicality with the languor of his former comrades in the KPRF, who merely chattered about Russia's problems.[18]

The leavening did not stop with the Agrarians. Admitting groups of almost every political hue, the bloc became a veritable Noah's Ark in September.[19] Six of the eight organizations that formed Titov's Voice of Russia flocked to it. So also did Regions of Russia from the Duma, Aushev's Equal Rights and Justice movement, the Union of Christian Democrats of Russia, and Spiritual Heritage. Each partner fixed a quota in OVR's 261-person national candidates' list: 65 for Fatherland, 27 each for the APR and Regions of Russia, 12 for Equal Rights and Justice, 8 for the Union of Labor, and 22 for thirteen sundry organizations. Six governors were on the list (Luzhkov, Yakovlev, and their peers from the Kirov and Moscow regions and the republics of Kareliya and Mordoviya). In good party-of-power tradition, OVR also nabbed celebrities as individual candidates, among them a renowned armaments designer (Mikhail Kalashnikov), a female astronaut (Yelena Kondrakova), a nationalist filmmaker (Stanislav Govorukhin), a prize-winning figure skater (Aleksandr Gorshkov), an Arctic explorer and deputy speaker of the Duma (Artur Chilingarov), and a bemedaled Soviet marshal who commanded the Warsaw Pact in the 1980s (Viktor Kulikov).

Padding the masthead had its uses, but it bred problems, too. Many individuals "gave their assent to inclusion on the list, knowing that they would not make it into the Duma in this election but counting on Fatherland's support in their future career."[20] They had little stake in the campaign and little patience for sacrifices in its name. The triumvirate atop the federal list set a poor example by announcing that, if elected, they would not fill their Duma seats (Primakov later relented). "The first three names on the list," Luzhkov said, "are mainly symbols" for the electorate, and he underlined the point by scheduling a Moscow mayoral election in which he was again a candidate for December 19.[21] The three republic presidents who took the initiative in forming All Russia (Shaimiyev, Rakhimov, and Aushev) declined to have their names on the list. With organizational partners increasing, commitments multiplied, and it was not always possible to honor them. Dmitrii Rogozin and the Congress of Russian Communities walked out of Fatherland in June 1999 because they were opposed to trucking with All Russia and were upset with their limited allotments on the national party list. They campaigned separately, and Rogozin, elected in a district seat with Kremlin support, was to be a staunch ally of the government after December. Governor Rutskoi and his Great Power movement also broke with OVR. Also dissatisfied with their meager quotas on the party list and their limited influence, Spiritual Heritage, Women of Russia, and the Republican Party bailed out in September. The Agrarians were promised a separate caucus in the Duma, but that was not enough to avert a schism. Most of the party's regional bosses followed Lapshin and Gennadii Kulik into OVR. A rump group headed by Nikolai Kharitonov, chairman of the faction in the outgoing Duma, threw in with the KPRF. Of the district deputies who constituted the majority of the Agrarians' Duma caucus, only one was to contest a seat for OVR.[22]

The Campaign

The campaign opened auspiciously when on September 21 Fatherland–All Russia was the first party or quasi party to collect the signatures required to qualify for the ballot. Primakov's and Luzhkov's every statement created a buzz. Thanks to its bevy of regional leaders, OVR had a presence in the provinces well before any contender save the KPRF. Come December, though, it was locked in a rearguard action against its opponents, salient among them a party of power, Unity, which did not exist when Luzhkov cobbled OVR together. In three months of campaigning, it lost a good half of its foothold among the electorate and, contrary to expectations, found itself fighting for survival.

Organization

In the spring of 1999, Russian businessman Vladimir Yevtushenkov and his associates at Sistema surrendered control of Luzhkov's emerging election drive to the Fatherland organization. Key roles there were played by Aleksandr Vladislavlev and Vasilii Lipitskii of the Union of Industrialists and Entrepreneurs, a heavy-industry lobby founded by Arkadii Vol'skii. Once OVR was in business, Fatherland provided head offices, the chairman of the national campaign (Georgii Boos), and its chief spokesman (Sergei Yastrzhembskii), and members of Fatherland (as distinct from persons chosen by it) seem to have made up more than 60 percent of the OVR national list.[23] A coordinating council of delegates from Fatherland, All Russia, and the Agrarian Party was charged with integrating their efforts. Vladimir Medvedev of All Russia was deputy chairman of the campaign, while Artur Chilingarov headed the department responsible for liaison with the regions. Fund-raising was run directly from Luzhkov's office.

OVR, in contrast to Unity, did not hire professional public relations firms to run the campaign. Rather, it relied on political figures already in their coalition who had some election expertise. Most had participated in Yeltsin's 1996 presidential campaign. Topping the list was Vyacheslav Nikonov, president of the public relations and consulting firm Politika, who had worked on publicity for the Yeltsin campaign and was disappointed not to have been assigned to an attractive post afterward. Igor Malashenko, the president of NTV and a key adviser in Yeltsin's 1996 reelection effort, provided strategic advice. Other strategists included Boos, Yastrzhembskii, Sergei Karaganov of the Council on Foreign and Defense Policy, and Sergei Mndoyants, as Primakov's representative at the bloc's campaign headquarters. From the outside, Igor Bunin's Center for Political Technologies provided occasional analytical reports, while the firm PRopaganda helped with organization of the press center.[24] Professional campaign consultants were generally unimpressed with the OVR lineup, pointing out that most of these campaign strategists had little campaign experience.[25]

The resources at OVR's fingertips were evidently second only to Unity's.[26] Large financial donors included Sistema, Gazprom, and Lukoil.[27] The bloc succeeded in recruiting 380,000 individual members by the end of September, chiefly through other organizations. In the media realm, the Moscow government's TV-Tsentr station enjoyed a much smaller share of the national television audience than the big three of ORT, RTR, and NTV (see appendix C), but it was unflinchingly loyal to the Luzhkov cause and gave him and his running mates constant and worshipful coverage. NTV and the Media-Most media empire, controlled by Vladimir Gusinskii, also adopted a benign attitude in the early part of the campaign. Gusinskii was feuding at the time with Boris Berezovskii, and this prompted him all the more to thumb his nose at the Unity bloc.[28] Several leading newspapers were sympathetic to OVR: Media-Most's *Segodnya*, *Izvestiya* (controlled by Lukoil), *Moskovskii komsomolets* (a gossipy tabloid subsidized by the city of Moscow), and *Komsomol'skaya pravda.*

OVR leaned most heavily on "administrative resources" at the regional level. In areas where they were in power, OVR members and well-wishers helped with free airtime on regional television networks, the use of printing presses and office space, and other indirect costs that could be hidden within the local budget. Provincial financial and industrial groups also backed the bloc in such places. In some regions where the regional administration was neutral or backed another party, OVR dealt with the mayor of the regional capital.[29]

Luzhkov's style as mayor of Moscow was to delegate responsibility to trusted lieutenants, obtain maximum publicity for the leader, and occasionally exercise mayoral intercession. In the context of an electoral coalition, this approach had its shortcomings. With its emphasis on power over principle, Fatherland and then OVR had no common purpose beyond winning the election and sharing the spoils. "The molding of the political feelings of the Moscow mayor," the columnist Andrei Kolesnikov noted in early 1999, "is being undertaken simultaneously by several teams with absolutely different mentalities and political views."[30] The incorporation of other associations intensified the problem. Luzhkov acted largely through Fatherland, but it, All Russia, and the APR maintained separate budgets. Primakov, the head of the ticket, controlled few campaign resources. As the campaign proceeded, his aides working in OVR headquarters complained of being shunted aside.[31]

Believe Only in Deeds

OVR's strategists reasoned that the election was its to lose, and that to seal the bargain the bloc had to communicate moderate, nonideological positions and emphasize that it had the experience to govern responsibly and effectively. Its public stance on economic and socioeconomic issues was a notch left of center. Primakov and Luzhkov had worked with communists in government and found ways to indicate that they would be open to cooperation after the election. On their own, the two probably would have moved OVR more decisively to the left, but polling commissioned by Vyacheslav Nikonov persuaded them they could not compete with the communists on this terrain and were better off keeping to the center. Over time, its programmatic statements soft-pedaled leftist themes.[32]

OVR championed a market economy with a "social orientation" (code words for a large public sector and welfare programs) and gave precedence to the "real" industrial economy over paper profits in banking and finance. On a campaign jaunt in November, Primakov hinted that he was not against renationalization under the right circumstances: "If a privatized enterprise is stagnating, its resources are being stolen by new proprietors, and the workers are being dismissed or if some other bad things are going on, and together with this it is found out that privatization was illegal, then we will review it retrospectively."[33] OVR also spouted statist rhetoric, saying it would fortify the national government and reclaim Russia's rightful place in international relations, the latter a theme pushed by Primakov for years during his service in the Foreign Ministry. Primakov pushed constitutional amendments that, he claimed, would strengthen state authority, such as reestablishment of the office of vice president, clarification of the role of the Security Council, and protections for retired presidents.

At the same time, OVR did not attach any ideological label to its program—socialist, social-democratic, or otherwise. "We are not on the left, we are not on the right, we are pragmatists," Georgii Boos explained in December, in words lifted straight out of Unity's playbook.[34] Primakov and Luzhkov were portrayed as wise and sober technocrats who had the authority and bureaucratic skills to make things happen. Television clips featured Primakov at the negotiating table with foreign statesmen and Luzhkov in a hardhat, paving a street or walking a factory floor. Their age—Primakov turned seventy in 1999, and the three men at the top of the OVR ticket were on average sixty-four, or twenty-one years older than the Unity troika—was presented as a plus, not a minus.

Fatherland–All Russia published several electoral pamphlets, mostly collections of pithy slogans, and circulated "One Hundred Laws for Russia," a list of pieces of legislation it would adopt once installed in the Duma. The closest thing to a formal platform was the untitled manifesto the bloc put out on November 5, totaling all of 575 words.[35] It was a mishmash of watery generalities and good wishes, describing OVR as "a union of patriotic and democratic forces . . . people of action, people of honor and conscience, who are capable of taking responsibility for the fate of the Motherland." "We are," it said, "all for providing decent living conditions to every Russian family, women, children, the elderly. Our principle of vital importance is to concentrate on

concrete actions in the name of Russia and her people." On some divi-
sive macro-issues, the document straddled the fence—vowing to build
an "indivisible" Russia but also to retain it as a federative and multieth-
nic country, for example; or to foster "the best conditions for active, talented people who take the initiative" but also "help those who need
support"; or to sanctify private property but also "not tolerate unfair
enrichment that goes against the interests of society"; or to "maintain
the rights of [minority] nationalities" but also observe "uniform standards for citizens' rights over the whole territory of the country." The
only specific policy pledges were to invest more in agriculture, beef up
the armed forces, and "revive the traditions of free education and health
care." There was little here that any party would have objected to, and
no word on where the resources would come from.

The motto that resounded in OVR's rhetoric converted programmatic
vagueness into a virtue: "Believe Only in Deeds," fasten on what politicians do rather than what they say. Years of government experience, in
fact, was the most distinct feature of OVR's leadership. Its first burst of
advertisements highlighted the achievements of the bloc's candidates,
but in time they shifted to the projects that others had undertaken and
cheated on. As described by Radio Free Europe/Radio Liberty,

> One 30-second advertisement depicts Yevgenii Primakov as a man
> who delivered where others failed. The clip begins with footage of
> a clearly agitated and discontented man reading a newspaper. A
> voice-over says, "They promised us a land flowing with milk and
> honey, but instead they put the country on the brink of economic
> catastrophe. [The video shows footage from various antigovern-
> ment protests.] Today we need the one who has already proven in
> difficult times that he will do the main thing: preserve stability in
> the state and accord in society." [The video shows Primakov
> addressing the Duma during his tenure as prime minister.] The
> camera goes back to the man shown at the beginning of the com-
> mercial, who says, "I believe only in deeds."

Ten-second ads in the same vein depicted ordinary people—a mother, a
university student, a physician—cogitating as a voice-over mentions
some politician or other's perfidy.[36]

Tensions within the bloc contributed to the blandness and evasiveness
of OVR's programmatic statements. For instance, Vladislavlev objected

to Primakov's pinkish pronouncements on the economy, preferring a more pro-market, pro-business approach.[37] There was also a marked fissure on the issue of Russia's federal system. Fatherland generally linked the strengthening of the state to recentralization of control in Moscow. Luzhkov, personally associated with the capital city and its bureaucratic class, had spoken out in the past against what he termed the unjustifiable privileges of the minority republics, and Primakov, while prime minister, had attempted to rein in the governors. Republic leaders like Shaimiyev, Rakhimov, and Aushev, meanwhile, loudly advocated reconstituting the state from the ground up and leaving regional and republic rights alone. As Vladimir Gel'man said, quoting a Russian proverb, OVR's attempt to find language to accommodate these diverse positions was like trying "to climb a fir tree without pricking yourself."[38] The spectacle failed to solidify OVR's reputation as the party that would put the state's house in order and enabled Sergei Shoigu and the Unity bloc to forecast that OVR's Duma caucus would fracture after the December election.[39]

Slinging Mud and Twisting Arms

For OVR, the signal campaign event was the unexpected media barrage directed *against* it. The campaign commercials of partisan rivals were of secondary importance. The heavy guns were the news broadcasts, analytical reports, and newsmagazines of the ORT and RTR television networks. Through them, the Kremlin launched, as a Radio Free Europe/Radio Liberty report detailed in December, "an 'information war' of staggering proportions against Fatherland–All Russia."[40] The themes were many: OVR leaders were unfit to govern (much was made of Primakov's age and his recent hip surgery); they were closet communists who would cave in to the KPRF after December; they were incompetent and corrupt, siphoning off budget funds, enriching Luzhkov's wife through government contracts, and building Luzhkov a country mansion; Luzhkov had not secured the capital before the September house bombings; OVR was linked to organized crime, religious cults, and fascist organizations; its candidates had condoned the murder of political and business rivals; they had wasted millions on vanity projects like the Cathedral of Christ the Savior; they were unprincipled, secretive, and ugly to boot (Sergei Dorenko characterized Luzhkov as a "political pygmy" and made fun of his bald pate); they were conniving with Western governments to sabotage loans to Russia and unseat Vladimir Putin. "Some allegations," wrote RFE/RL's analyst, "are highly plausible—but it is notable that they were never brought to the public's attention when the OVR leaders supported the Kremlin. Other reports may contain a grain of truth but are exaggerated. Still others are fabricated."[41] Governor Yakovlev, who had terrible personal relations with Putin, going back to Putin's years in city government in St. Petersburg (see chapter 7), was skewered for fishy financial dealings and allowing his city to become Russia's "criminal capital." By early December, Mayor Luzhkov ranked behind only Yeltsin and Putin as most mentioned politician in the country, with the negative commentaries outnumbering the positive by five to one.[42]

Reinforcing the propaganda blitz was an attempt to lure defectors from the bloc. By the account of OVR campaign officials, Kremlin agents offered bribes to more than fifty people, winning over four party-list candidates (two from All Russia and two from the APR). They worked hard, though unsuccessfully, to get Vladimir Yakovlev to leave the bloc, a departure that would have jeopardized OVR's legal status since he was one of the top three names on the party list.[43] Allegedly, senior officials also ordered policemen and tax inspectors to harass OVR leaders and made physical threats against the families of candidates.[44] Seeing the government's ill will and OVR's slide in the polls, Lukoil, a generous benefactor, ceased its cash contributions in November.

Some regional elites also proved to be fair-weather friends. In the latter stages of the campaign, governors and republic presidents who had allied with OVR thought the better of it or tried to cut deals. As Primakov wrote later, "Certain governors, who not long before had extolled OVR and said its success was a sure thing, now averted their eyes in meetings with representatives of our movement or threw up their hands. 'You see,' they said, 'we are dependent on financial transfers from the center.' Others said nothing, but we understood very well that they did not want to fall out with law-enforcement agencies."[45] President Shaimiyev publicly called for cooperation between OVR and Unity. Privately, he is said to have promised Sergei Shoigu that Unity would get 10 percent of the votes cast in Tatarstan, no matter what.[46]

The onslaught caught the OVR team flat-footed. In sketching their campaign plan in September, they were so sure of the irrelevancy of Kremlin loyalists that they did not consider how to fend them off. Their main foe, they erroneously supposed, would be the communists. OVR, therefore, directed its first advertising broadside against the KPRF. While OVR kept its focus on the KPRF in the single-member districts, in the national race it gradually shifted emphasis to Yeltsin and his political clan.[47] But such a posture rang hollow in an election in which Yeltsin was not a candidate and the government party, Unity, was also distancing itself from the president. The prime minister might in normal times have presented an inviting target, but as overseer of a popular war, he was untouchable. Because Putin was so new in the job, OVR also could not blame him for Russia's economic and social woes. Although the pro-OVR press portrayed Putin as a puppet in the hands of the Yeltsin family and insinuated that the war in Chechnya was a ploy to boost his and Unity's popularity, the OVR campaign did not repeat these charges. Primakov and Luzhkov explicitly voiced approval of the crusade against Chechen "bandits," with some caution sounded on the pace of the offensive. Taking on Putin was dangerous because of his opinion ratings and the growing likelihood that he would be president. As two shrewd observers noted at the time: "None of the major political actors can afford to act against the overwhelming sentiments of public opinion. Therefore, they will find it difficult to criticize the government not only on its Chechen policy, but on any significant topic. . . . Such a situation presents a strong disadvantage for opposition political parties as they wage their electoral campaign."[48]

Mudslinging was in the end not a tactic easily embraced by the bureaucrats and men of "deeds, not words" in Fatherland–All Russia. Some considered the campaign against them so ridiculous that such distortions could not possibly influence the electorate. In American elections, seasoned politicians consider it absolutely necessary to respond promptly and aggressively to negative material—as did the celebrated "reaction team" in Bill Clinton's 1992 campaign. The leaders of the OVR bloc were psychologically unprepared for the trench warfare in the media. Primakov in particular was a campaign novice who felt that his vital contribution to the parliamentary race was merely deciding to run. OVR officials cried foul, tried to sue ORT, and called Dorenko a latter-day Goebbels, all to no avail.[49] Their main practical adaptation at the end of the campaign was to downplay Luzhkov, the butt of the most venomous attacks, and pin their television advertising on Primakov. Luzhkov obliged by busying himself more with the Moscow mayor's race—which he was to win with 70 percent of the votes, or 30 points more than OVR drew in the city—and less with the Duma vote.

The Districts

OVR, unlike Unity, did not neglect the district half of the election. It deployed candidates in 91 of the 224 districts in play. Part of the division of labor in the bloc sprang from the understanding that All Russia and the governors would take the lead in selecting candidates for districts in their regions. This decentralized arrangement was necessary, given the speed with which candidates had to be picked, and efficient, since it invested regional leaders in the electoral process at the place where they could be most effective. OVR gave priority to regions where its leaders were in charge.[50] Thirty-four of its nominations were in the nine regions where the governor was on the OVR national list or (in Bashkortostan, Ingushetiya, and Tatarstan) had helped set up the bloc. Candidates with ties to OVR bigwigs sometimes ran as independents. This was the norm with incumbents from the Regions of Russia caucus, who had established a political reputation before the birth of OVR.[51] In two regions where the election of a governor was timed to coincide with the Duma election (Moscow province and Tver), OVR linked the gubernatorial and Duma campaigns. The hasty fusion of dissimilar organizations and interests inevitably sparked local skirmishes. Strong executives such as Shaimiyev and Luzhkov settled them quickly; less dominant figures such as Governor Yakovlev in St. Petersburg had a harder time. In the regions with gubernatorial contests, local leadership was slack, and OVR ended up expressing support for more than one candidate: two in Moscow region and three in Tver.[52]

The reliance on established leaders was testimony to the well of resources OVR had to tap. But there was nothing like a sufficient number of strong leaders in the OVR camp to blanket the country. The typical governor had either never backed OVR or trimmed his sails at the insistence of the central authorities. Another problem had to do with willingness and ability to fulfill promises. When unable to coax local dignitaries to hazard it, pro-OVR governors typically moved a "lost generation" of once prominent politicians into the district nominations—here a former federal minister, there a retired vice governor or speaker of the regional assembly, somewhere else a failed gubernatorial candidate or a member of the 1993–95 Duma—or else dragooned an unsung academic or businessman.[53] In quite a few regions where the governor sympathized with the bloc, there was no OVR nominee in some or all of the region's districts. In some regions where the OVR-affiliated governor or president was powerful, the local head of administration chose to support independents rather than OVR candidates, calculating that these independents would be more loyal to a local patron than to a national party after the vote. Furthermore, as Makarenko observed during the campaign, the governor's capacity for helping out was a function of his control of the regional political scene, and that varied from place to place. "Whereas the executive authorities in Moscow and many ethnic republics, and for APR deputies in the rural districts, will be able to extend effective assistance, in St. Petersburg and many other regions with a high level of political pluralism it will turn out to be clearly insufficient."[54] The unevenness in resources and political will would weigh on the prospects of the national list as well as the district races.

The Voters

Shifting gears from campaign activity to voter choice, it is necessary to bear in mind the volatility of popular regard for Fatherland–All Russia. Had the election been held in October or early November, it would have come out ahead of Unity and perhaps nipped at the heels of the KPRF. Forty-seven percent of our survey respondents who stated in the preelection interview an intent to vote for OVR, and who cast a vote on December 19, ended up in another party's column or voted against all parties. Only Yabloko had a higher campaign-time defection rate. OVR campaign personnel told us on the eve of the election that media reports of the swing in momentum away from them had propelled undecided voters in droves to join Unity's bandwagon. Our task, nonetheless, is to understand what swayed voting choices, and not to trace their prehistory. Here we can put together a reasonably clear portrait of correlates of the OVR vote.

Payoff to Resources

If nothing else, its deep pockets and famous names made OVR familiar to most Russian voters. Eighty-eight percent of our survey informants recognized the bloc and appraised it on an eleven-point scale, a better outcome than for the Kremlin-coddled Unity. Twenty-one percent noticed OVR billboards, posters, and leaflets frequently in the campaign, and 14 percent received its printed materials frequently through the mail. On the first score, OVR had more exposure than any other party, and on the second a tad less than Unity. Its canvassing effort, like that of all parties, was lame; it touched 1 percent of all voters, marginally less then the KPRF and Yabloko.[55]

In the media domain, however, OVR could not hold its own. The backing of three or four daily newspapers helped with some voters, chiefly in the large cities, but the result hinged on television. [56] Here, the politely positive coverage on NTV and the fervent advocacy on TV-Tsentr were overpowered by the torrent of vituperation on ORT and RTR. As a glimpse at appendix table C-6 confirms, recurrent exposure to Yevgenii Kiselëv's Sunday-evening "Itogi" show fattened the chances of voting for OVR, but the effect was mild and was counterbalanced by the ORT daily news and, to a slight extent, Sergei Dorenko's muckraking exposés on Sunday night. Watching TV-Tsentr, Mayor Luzhkov's city-owned television station, had no meaningful impact on the OVR vote. Content aside, Fatherland–All Russia was hobbled by the restricted audience share of its media allies. About half as many citizens tuned in to the evening news practically every day on NTV as on ORT and about one-tenth as many saw it on TV-Tsentr. The Dorenko weekend show had almost double the audience of Kiselëv's and about thirty times the viewers of Vladislav Flyarkovskii's "Nedelya" ("Week") offering on TV-Tsentr.

OVR's plum campaign resource was the cooperation of a claque of subnational leaders. It was vividly reflected in the geographic structure of the voting. The strength of the OVR national list was much more concentrated in space than that of any other party or bloc. Of all its votes, 52.72 percent were tallied in *five* banner regions: the city of Moscow, Moscow province, Tatarstan, Bashkortostan, and St. Petersburg. Moscow alone, with fewer than 7 percent of Russia's electors, accounted for 21.25 percent of OVR's vote.[57] The bloc's vote share exceeded 30 percent in three of these territories: Tatarstan (41.90 percent), Moscow city (41.58 percent), and Bashkortostan (36.04 percent). By way of comparison, OVR's share of the popular vote in the remaining eighty-odd regions of the federation was 8.15 percent, which was less than the national vote share of the fourth-running SPS bloc. In each of the five pace-setting regions, the local leadership was a major player in the formation of OVR; in Moscow, Moscow province, and St. Petersburg, the governor was on the OVR list. OVR also received in excess of 30 percent in two other federal regions where the regional boss was onside: it captured 33.62 percent in Mordoviya, where the president was on the OVR list, and a mind-boggling 89.38 percent in Ingushetiya, where the president was not on the list but a fervent OVR supporter nonetheless.[58] Although the stuffing of ballot boxes and other forms of electoral fraud may have contributed to the outcome, they were icing on the cake in most OVR strongholds.[59]

It goes without saying that the patronage of the regional establishment boosted OVR's performance in these areas. But it did so unevenly. If almost everyone on the rolls in Ingushetiya took guidance from President Aushev, in Kirov region, where Governor Vladimir Sergeyenkov was a charter member of OVR and was on its national slate, turnout for OVR was a mere 5.10 percent.[60] And though Mayor Luzhkov raked in more than 40 percent of the vote for OVR in Moscow, St. Petersburg's Governor Yakovlev could manage only 15.88 percent, which put OVR behind Unity and SPS. Results also differed by subarea in some of OVR's high-performance regions.[61]

Although a nationwide voters' survey and a standardized model of the vote can only go so far in uncovering localized effects on mass behavior, we can say that the degree of "political pluralism" (as Boris Makarenko conjectured) and, more broadly, the pro-OVR governor's authority within the region set limits on his electoral clout, as was the case for all the principal parties and blocs. Few OVR fans at the mass level considered gubernatorial preferences as such to have been an important factor in their vote, making them not very different from their fellow citizens in this connection.[62] Whatever impact the governors had would by and large have been mediated by other political attitudes, such as assessments of the parties' leaders or issue competence—and these attitudes, in principle, should have been picked up by the panel survey and so be available for examination in our model of the voting decision.

Demographics and Current Conditions

OVR's electorate was shaped mostly by smallish influences from a miscellany of social factors (see appendix table B-1). Of the ten sociodemographic variables in our voting model, only one—residence in the capital city—had a major total effect on the OVR vote, that is, a statistically significant effect with a magnitude of at least .10. The Moscow effect is gigantic—the measure is .44, or 44 percentage points—and is the largest observed for any social characteristic and any party or bloc in 1999. We would in all likelihood be able to show sizable effects for residency in Bashkortostan or Tatarstan had we done extensive survey work in those regions.[63] After that, the most notable social influences stem from higher levels of education and from non-Russian ethnicity, a mark, no doubt, of the backing of republic leaders like Shaimiyev, Rakhimov, and Aushev. OVR also enjoyed a tiny edge among the residents of the western parts of the country.

From this social base, our modeling shows OVR picking up little of the protest vote against current conditions in the country, drawing in only one-half to one-third of the KPRF tally in this regard (see table B-3). Its best card was "sociotropic" discontent with the state of the national economy, where the total effect of $-.08$ was half that displayed by the KPRF. Economic attainment in the 1990s, pocketbook economic trends, and assessments of political conditions had no effect to speak of on the Fatherland–All Russia vote.

Partisanship and Issue Opinions

Like Unity, OVR, as a newly instituted electoral alliance, did not have the benefit of a reservoir of political loyalists. Twenty percent of its voters were ex-dropouts (who abstained in the 1995 Duma election or voted against all parties), the highest such figure for any party in the election. Eight percent were novices (too young to vote in 1995). Seventy-two percent were converts from other parties. Of these voters, the largest batch (29 percent) had voted socialist in 1995, and the second largest group (21 percent, which put them 5 percentage points above the representation of former NDR voters in the Unity electorate) had voted for the pro-government Our Home Is Russia.[64]

According to the attitudinal criteria employed elsewhere in this study, some electors in 1999 may be considered recently recruited "partisans" of Fatherland–All Russia. The statistical total effect of OVR partisanship on the probability of voting for the bloc was .50 (50 percentage points), or roughly the mean for all parties (see appendix table B-1). As with Unity, OVR partisans were by definition fresh to the role, and the incidence of OVR partisanship was small in relation to the OVR vote. Sixty-two percent of putative OVR partisans voted for the bloc; OVR partisans came to 29 percent of all OVR voters.[65]

Consonant with OVR's light-on-the-issues campaign, its voters were little swayed by ideas and policy opinions. On only one of the seven issue yardsticks used in our voter survey—the summary left-right scale—was there any statistically meaningful correlation with the chances of voting for Fatherland–All Russia. The total effect of left-right self-placement was in the expected direction (left-leaning citizens were more apt to vote OVR than right-leaning citizens) and was passably large (.10), which meant it had about one-third the effect of the same attitudinal variable on the KPRF and Unity votes. That was all. Preferences with regard to economic reform, Chechnya, the political regime, and constitutional issues had no discernible bearing on the OVR vote. Looking at the seven issues as a whole (using the test of simultaneous, moderately large changes in all variables in the bloc of putative causes; see appendix table B-3), OVR is the only party or quasi party in the 1999 election for which no causal effects of opinions could be established. Where citizens stood on the issues of the day literally made no difference to the chances of voting for OVR.

Evaluations of Political Players

OVR's anemic partisan base and its dearth of proprietary issues put all the more onus on its organizers to connect with Russians' short-term evaluations of players in the electoral game. That was the gist of the "Believe Only in Deeds" shibboleth and of the personalized campaign the bloc prosecuted from the beginning. Its success in coupling political assessments to voting choice was mixed.

On the first potential point of engagement—evaluations of political incumbents—OVR struck out completely. With Yeltsin divorced from the current scene, Putin, the new prime minister, was the incumbent who mattered. Unity thrived on the flood of admiration for Putin's performance in office, and the communists on the backlash against him. OVR got traction from neither opinion.

On the other hand, OVR did get some mileage from citizen evaluations of the personal qualities of its own leadership. Yevgenii Primakov cut an imposing figure in 1999, which is why the bloc's organizers worked assiduously to recruit him. Positive evaluations of Primakov outnumbered negative evaluations on all four character traits about which we interrogated our survey panel (see table 4-1). Among the six major party leaders, he was second to Sergei Shoigu on strength, honesty and trustworthiness, and empathy and first on intelligence and knowledge. To be sure, the responses do hint at some vulnerability—the

Table 4-1. *Evaluations of Yevgenii Primakov's Character Traits*[a]

	Rating (percent)			
Trait	Yes/ probably yes	No/ probably no	Net yes/probably yes over no/ probably no	Ranking of net rating among 6 party leaders
Intelligent and knowledge-able person	88	6	82	1
Strong leader	62	26	36	2
Honest and trustworthy person	61	22	39	2
Really cares about people like you	48	33	14	2

a. From 1999–2000 panel, wave 2 (N = 1,846 weighted cases). "Don't know" responses included in the denominator but not shown here.

upshot, one guesses, of the anti-OVR propaganda war. Primakov's negatives are several times more numerous on strength, honesty, and in particular on empathy with ordinary people than they are for Shoigu. On the summary evaluation, using a scale of 0 to 10, he trailed only Shoigu, but his score (4.94) was below the midpoint of the scale.

For each of the six parties, we made the simplifying assumption of including a single leadership indicator in our multistage model of the vote. We thus do not test systematically for second and third members of the collective leadership of blocs such as OVR and SPS, which were composites of preexisting organizations, all with their founding fathers. For OVR, Yurii Luzhkov obviously played a seminal role, first in creating Fatherland and then in marrying it to All Russia and assembling the national candidates' list. Table 4-2 sets forth citizen evaluations of the mayor, using the same touchstones as for the six ascendant leaders but omitting the ranking. On the strength criterion, Luzhkov's net rating (+58) was in fact superior to all of the top leaders, Primakov included. On intelligence, Luzhkov falls behind Primakov and Shoigu but still has a safely positive balance. On integrity and empathy—the very attributes silhouetted in the relentless media bombardment—Luzhkov's net score is sharply negative, with about twice as many citizens saying he lacked the leadership attribute as those who said he possessed it. The only party leader to have worse ratings for integrity and empathy, and to have a more ogrelike image overall, was Vladimir Zhirinovskii, whose LDPR bagged about 6 percent of the popular vote.[66] What with the intensity of Luzhkov's association with Fatherland and OVR, one has to suspect that some of his negatives rubbed off on the bloc.

Table 4-2. *Evaluations of Yurii Luzhkov's Character Traits*[a]

	Rating (percent)		
Trait	*Yes/ probably yes*	*No/ probably no*	*Net yes/probably yes over no/probably no*
Intelligent and knowledgeable person	74	15	59
Strong leader	72	15	58
Honest and trustworthy person	26	52	−26
Really cares about people like you	30	51	−21

a. From 1999–2000 panel, wave 2 (N = 1,846 weighted cases). "Don't know" responses included in the denominator but not shown here.

Table 4-3. *OVR Vote and Evaluations of Primakov's Character*

Mean evaluation of four traits	*Citizen opinion (percent)*[a]	*Predicted probability of voting for OVR*[b]
Does not have the positive trait	3	.00
Probably does not have the positive trait	19	.02
Probably has the positive trait	55	.10
Has the positive trait	24	.42

a. N = 1,846 weighted cases. Missing data coded at the mean of the distribution for the specific trait.

b. Computed from multistage statistical model, holding causally prior and simultaneous variables constant at their medians. Sample N = 1,414; $p \leq .01$ for all cells in the column.

While citizens who had a favorable impression of Primakov were far from certain to vote for the bloc he headed, multivariate analysis shows that persons who had a strongly unfavorable impression of him would vote against it. Stripping away the influence of other variables, the median voter who felt on average that Primakov definitely lacked the positive character traits had a mathematically zero chance of voting for OVR (see table 4-3). If her or his assessment was at the positive pole, our model estimates a rise in the probability of voting for OVR to .42. Hence the Primakov factor had a total effect of .42 on the OVR vote.[67]

The OVR vote, we have argued, was not governed by popular opinions about issues. It was strongly affected, nonetheless, by prospective evaluations of issue competence. We asked survey respondents to indicate which party could best tackle six concrete policy problems. Among citizens who named a party, those who identified OVR as the best ranged from 8 percent to 26 percent (see table 4-4). OVR ranked third in perceived competence for all half-dozen issues. It rated worst on the Chechnya issue—which is where Unity rated best. Only 8 percent

Table 4-4. *Prospective Evaluations of OVR's Issue Competence*[a]

| | Say OVR is best prepared | | |
Issue	Percent	Percent of those who named a party	Ranking
Social security	8	12	3
Economy	10	14	3
Human rights	7	11	3
Chechnya	5	8	3
Foreign policy	16	26	3
Crime and corruption	7	11	3

a. From 1999–2000 panel, wave 2 (N = 1,846 weighted cases).

Table 4-5. *OVR Vote and Prospective Evaluations of Its Issue Competence*

Number of issues OVR can handle best	Citizen opinion (percent)[a]	Predicted probability of voting for OVR[b]
0	79	.14
1	10	.46
2	4	.80
3	2	.94
4	2	.98
5	1	.99
6	3	1.00

a. N = 1,846 weighted cases.

b. Computed from multistage statistical model, holding causally prior and simultaneous variables constant at their medians. Sample N = 1,414; $p \leq .01$ for all cells in the column.

thought OVR the party best qualified to deal with Chechnya, whereas 52 percent said Unity was best. OVR's attractiveness was at its height on the issue where Primakov's pedigree was most outstanding—foreign policy—but the number of favorable mentions here (26 percent) was a shade lower than it was for Unity and the KPRF.

The total effect on the OVR vote of the index of prospective issue evaluations was .85 (see appendix table B-1), which is on a par with the other major parties. Predicted probabilities for successive competency scores are given in table 4-5. Notice how quickly the likelihood of a favorable electoral choice cumulates. The probability of the median voter who believes OVR can best handle two policy issues voting for the bloc is .80: the highest for any first-tier party or quasi party, and much higher than the quantity for Unity (.52) or the KPRF (.46). This suggests that Fatherland–All Russia's motto, "Believe only in deeds," did get through to many voters. What set a cap on its electoral performance was the number of Russians who felt OVR's deeds the most likely to deal effectively with the issues. Twenty-one percent of our survey respondents put OVR first on one or more issues; this left it far behind Unity (42 percent) and the KPRF (32 percent). There may also have been a mismatch between the subject area of OVR's perceived competence and citizen priorities. OVR's forté, foreign policy, seems to have been least pertinent to electoral decisions. About half of those who rated it supreme in this issue area voted against it. On the other five issues, where OVR's reputation was thinner, that ratio was 20 to 25 percent.

The District Vote

OVR seated nearly as many deputies from the single-mandate districts (thirty-one) as from the national party list (thirty-seven). It outperformed every party in the districts except the KPRF. This is not to say it was an unadulterated success—there were bold forecasts in the summer that it would return fifty to eighty district members—but it foiled expectations less here than in the PR race.

OVR's accomplishments in the districts were even more geographically concentrated than in the nationwide ballot. No less than twenty-two of its thirty-one winners were from six federal units where the governor was either on the OVR candidates' list or otherwise enmeshed in the cause: the city of Moscow (nine deputies elected), Moscow region (four), Bashkortostan and Tatarstan (three each), St. Petersburg (two), and Mordoviya (one).[68] That left only nine other winners for the rest of Russia. Four were incumbents, and all had "high elite positions."[69]

The bloc achieved about average consistency between the two halves of the Duma vote. Approximately one OVR voter in six supported an OVR nominee in the local district (see table 4-6). Many times, no such nominee was in place.[70] When there was one on the ballot, the frequency of voting for the candidate nominated by OVR grew to 32 percent, which was almost 10 percentage points less than average.

OVR was hard pressed to let its supporters know who the district candidates nominated by the bloc actually were. Although not as inept as Unity, it did far worse at transmitting this information than the communists and the liberals. In districts where an OVR candidate was on the district ballot, only about every third OVR voter was cognizant of that and could identify the nominee in the post-election wave of our survey (see table 4-7). No less of a problem was how to lure party-list sup-

Table 4-6. *Electoral Consistency between District and Party-List Votes, OVR Voters and All Voters*
Percent

Candidate voted for in the district	All districts		Districts where a nominee registered	
	OVR voters[a]	All voters[b]	OVR voters[c]	All voters[d]
Nominee of party supported in the party-list vote	16	17	32	40
Nominee of a different party	28	24	32	26
Independent candidate	46	45	23	24
Votes against all candidates	11	14	12	10

a. N = 167 weighted cases.
b. Excluding persons who voted against all parties in the party-list vote. N = 1,318 weighted cases.
c. N = 81 weighted cases.
d. Excluding persons who voted against all parties in the party-list vote. N = 566 weighted cases.

Table 4-7. *Electoral Consistency and Voter Knowledge, OVR Voters and All Voters, in Districts Where a Nominee of Party Supported in Party-List Vote Is Registered*[a]

Position	Percent		Percent of category who vote straight ticket	
	OVR voters[b]	All voters[c]	OVR voters[b]	All voters[c]
Knows there is a nominee and can identify the nominee	30	41	53	80
Knows there is a nominee and cannot identify the nominee	13	10	37	10
Thinks there is no nominee	27	24	40	21
Does not know if there is a nominee	31	25	20	24

a. Excludes persons who voted against all candidates in the district.
b. N = 71 weighted cases.
c. N = 509 weighted cases.

porters who were aware of the bloc's standard-bearer. A bare majority (53 percent) of these knowledgeable OVR supporters voted the straight ticket, or substantially less than the all-party mean of 80 percent. Consistency levels were not drastically lower for OVR voters who knew there was an OVR nominee but could not identify him (37 percent of whom voted the straight ticket without realizing what they were doing) or who misguidedly thought there was no OVR nominee in the district (40 percent of whom voted the straight ticket in ignorance).

Conclusions

One might say that Fatherland–All Russia had nothing to be ashamed of once the returns were in. It had vaulted the 5 percent barrier, amassed a greater percentage of the popular vote than all but three parties and quasi parties before it, and won a few dozen seats in the districts. [71] Its failure was not absolute but relative to the objectives its founders had set for it, which were nothing less than to prevail in December and march from there to take the presidency. OVR did not sweep the board: it did not win the Duma election, and it was not to field a candidate in the presidential election. Primakov, who inexplicably chose December 17, forty-eight hours before the Duma vote, to announce his candidacy for president, was left high and dry by the results. In the first week of the New Year, the regional bosses Shaimiyev, Rakhimov, and Yakovlev of All Russia and Oleg Morozov of Regions of Russia abandoned ship and declared their support for Putin as president. Luzhkov pulled out of contention the next week and Primakov embarrassedly on February 4. Luzhkov eventually gave Putin a qualified endorsement at a Fatherland meeting ten days before the election and was then filmed smiling wanly at the acting president at a construction site in the Moscow subway. Mikhail Lapshin and the Agrarian Party of Russia chimed in with another endorsement in March. The film director and OVR deputy, Stanislav Govorukhin, running without reference to the bloc, polled about 300,000 votes in a campaign distinguished by his irreverent political jokes.

To the ingenuity and ruthlessness of its enemies must go much of the credit for OVR's defeat. Once awakened to the threat, its foes activated the panoply of resources available to the postcommunist state and to the private and semiprivate actors under its wing. But OVR and its leaders cannot be absolved. The commentators who saw in them a new party of power recognized that by instinct they operated within and through public institutions. Their phalanx of candidates, stocked with graying, high-ranking officials and luminaries, resembled nothing more than Viktor Chernomyrdin's Our Home Is Russia in 1995, and their media voice was a municipally owned television station. OVR's stance was that of a group "that announced it would 'receive' the power they thought was falling out of the hands of the Kremlin team."[72] The hole in the strategy was that it overlooked the competition from within the state's own household and the presence of new and more grasping hands there. In propaganda terms, Unity pulled the trick of defending things as they were while promising their renewal through the infusion of restless and talented newcomers from the provinces. OVR vowed essentially to substitute one set of veteran officeholders for another and dangled no vision of rebirth. When it tried to sell this message in the electoral marketplace, the strategy proved far more fallible than its inventors realized. The regional bosses who helped bring OVR into being were too few in number and too dependent on the center to carry the campaign on their shoulders. The bloc grew through mechanical addition of factions and individual entrepreneurs to the original core, giving scarcely a thought to working out a common approach to governing. It was taken aback by and overmatched in the televised information war. Its threadbare program having occasioned no response, the only clay its image-makers had to work with was short-term perceptions of personalities and administrative competence. In the greater scheme of things, Fatherland–All Russia imitated both a proponent and an opponent of the status quo, never quite becoming either.

5

The Communists

IF THE 1999–2000 ELECTIONS were about opportunities blown as much as opportunities seized, it was arguably the Communist Party of the Russian Federation (KPRF) and not Fatherland–All Russia that squandered the main chance. The economic woes that culminated in the debacle of August 1998 seemed to a good many Russians to be smoothing the way for a communist resurgence. Boris Yeltsin himself, reeling from the crash of the ruble, felt compelled to propose secretly in 1998 that a KPRF front-bencher, Yurii Maslyukov—once the chairman of Gosplan, the USSR's industrial planning agency—become prime minister.[1] When Maslyukov demurred and his former Politburo colleague Yevgenii Primakov took the post, Primakov made Maslyukov his first deputy. The KPRF looked ripe to feast electorally on the swing to the left.

The KPRF could lay plans secure in its possession of the strongest organizational backbone and the largest mass base of any party. Originating in 1990 as the Russian section of the Communist Party of the Soviet Union, it was banned in November 1991, reconstituted after judicial rulings in February of 1993, banned again that October, and then legalized a second time weeks later. Jumping belatedly into the 1993 Duma campaign, it came in third in party-list vote (12.40 percent) and deputies elected (48). In the 1995 Duma election, two years of regrouping bore fruit in a plurality of the nationwide vote (22.73 percent) and legislative seats (157) and installation of a communist and erstwhile editor of *Pravda*, Gennadii Seleznëv, as speaker of the house. In the 1996 presidential election, the chairman of the KPRF central committee, Gennadii Zyuganov, gave Yeltsin a fierce fight, garnering almost one-third of the ballots and forcing a runoff in which he took upward of 40 percent.

In December 1999 the KPRF was confined to minor gains in the popular vote (24.78 percent). That, the arcana of the PR formula, and less luck in the single-mandate districts whittled its caucus down to 113 deputies.[2] Although Seleznëv hung in as speaker, he did so with Kremlin backing, and more and more the Duma was to dance to the Kremlin's tune. Back in the running for president in 2000, Zyuganov watched his support skid three points from 1996 (to 29.49 percent) and could not push Vladimir Putin into a second round. The dawn of the Putin era thus found the communists a protest movement becalmed. Fraternal parties in Poland, Hungary, and Lithuania revamped themselves and marched back to power as social democrats in the second or third electoral cycle after the demise of single-party rule, but Russia's communists did not. Why? The bottom line was an unwillingness to shake off ideas and methods formed in a different age.

Defining the Left

The Russian left has never been the monolith that the Soviet communist party was before *perestroika*. Parties and sects have abounded, and the KPRF has by turns competed and cooperated with them. Its organizational choices have been linked to the evolution of its broader goals.

Socialism and Nationalism

The most doctrinaire leftists, such as Viktor Anpilov's Working Russia and Aleksei Prigarin's Union of Communists, boycotted the 1993 Duma campaign and chided Zyuganov for taking part. Mostly as insurance against disqualification, a number of communist politicians formed the Agrarian Party of Russia (APR) around the rural infrastructure of the old ruling party. The APR grabbed 7.99 percent of the popular vote in 1993, electing twenty-one deputies on its list and twelve in the districts. Several ranking communists from the defunct deputies' congress, including Ivan Rybkin and Vladimir Isakov, won on its ticket, and Rybkin was to be speaker of the Duma from 1993 to 1995.

Three socialistic slates other than the KPRF's campaigned for the Duma in 1995. The APR did not make the 5 percent cutoff this time, but twenty Agrarians prevailed in the districts. The Power to the People movement of Nikolai Ryzhkov, a former Soviet prime minister, and nationalist Sergei Baburin polled nearly 2 percent, with nine nominees elected in district seats. Communists and Toilers for the Soviet Union, a diehard faction chaired by Anpilov and Viktor Tyul'kin, fell just shy of 5 percent and returned one district deputy. The Agrarians and Power to the People managed to form Duma factions, bulking up to the quota of members by inducting deputies elected on the KPRF ticket.

Zyuganov's solution to the fragmentation and containment of the left was apparent in his first presidential campaign. This died-in-the-wool apparatchik had made his name in the party in 1990–91 as a composer and signatory of ringing nationalist proclamations and a broker of what Russian liberals call "red-brown" coalitions.[3] Throwing down the gauntlet to Yeltsin in 1996, he had himself nominated by a makeshift Bloc of Popular and Patriotic Forces—spanning 126 groups, among them the KPRF's rivals on the left and a slew of nationalist associations. The bloc reorganized itself in August 1996 as the Popular-Patriotic Union of Russia, chaired by Zyuganov but with five cochairmen from outside the KPRF. It gave logistical support and know-how to leftist candidates in gubernatorial elections in 1996–97. Aleksei Podberëzkin, the founder of the small Spiritual Heritage movement and a principal adviser to Zyuganov in 1996, lobbied publicly for having it supersede the KPRF as Russia's leading opposition force. Seleznëv, Viktor Zorkal'tsev, a senior communist politico, and several Zyuganov staffers aligned with Podberëzkin, while the party's second in command, Valentin Kuptsov, defended the vanguard role of the KPRF. Zyuganov equivocated.[4]

Flying Solo

On November 1, 1998, the KPRF central committee resolved to go it alone in the impending elections, waiving a renewed attempt to gather up all socialist and nationalistic groups under one roof. It did so partly out of exasperation with the disputatiousness of the left and partly out of the self-assurance bred by Yeltsin's retreats and Prime Minister Primakov's deference to it. Another imperative was to erect a dike against ultrana-tionalists like General Al'bert Makashov, a communist member of the Duma emboldened by the financial crisis to vent xenophobic and rabidly anti-Semitic views. Makashov caused a firestorm in October when he demanded quotas on Jews in political office and the deportation of the "yids," "shylocks," and "bloodsuckers" who, he said, had wrecked Russia's economy. Zyuganov wanted to muzzle Makashov, although, tellingly, he refused to censure him or banish him from the caucus and intimated that the issue had been inflamed by foreign powers.[5]

In the months to come, the KPRF brass wavered. They toyed in the winter of 1998–99 with a "three-column" scheme whereby the party would foal separate "orthodox," "enlightened nationalist," and "radical nationalist" blocs. After some bickering, they upheld unilateralism. Titling their electoral slate "For Victory," they were blunt about it being the creature of the party and registered it as the KPRF's list. Some previously autonomous politicians agreed to these conditions. Others took their leave, firing off parting shots and, in Podberëzkin's case, being expelled from the Duma faction. The minor leftist parties and quasi parties in the hunt for votes leapt to six: Podberëzkin's Spiritual Heritage, whose outlook was relatively inclusive Russian nationalism; Communists and Toilers for the Soviet Union (led by Tyul'kin); the Stalinist Bloc for the USSR (headed by Anpilov, with Joseph Stalin's grandson Yevgenii Dzhugashvili high on its list), which touted Marxism and restoration of the Soviet Union; the Peace and Unity Party (Sazhi Umalatova) and the All-Russian Party of the People (Anzori Aksent'ev-Kikalishvili), groups for cultural nationalists of non-Russian ethnicity (Umalatova is Chechen and Aksent'ev-Kikalishvili Georgian); and the Movement in Support of the Army (under Viktor Ilyukhin, a KPRF stalwart, Duma committee chairman, and comrade-in-arms of Makashov).[6] The Power to the People movement ceased activity; the APR, split between pro-KPRF and pro-OVR wings, did not submit a list.

The posing and skirmishing in the party's home neighborhood was a distraction. The Makashov affair betrayed some awareness that the petty politics of the leftist camp, and the invective spewing from it, could be encumbrances further afield. But still, communist decisionmakers idled away the year between the 1998 economic panic and the buildup to the Duma campaign under the illusion that success would fall into their lap. The only partners they saw as worth courting were nationalists. No visionary stepped forward to advocate the agonizing step of recreating the party as a social-democratic movement. The returns in December 1999 were to attest to the limitations of playing it safe. While the KPRF did gain a step or two on its leftist brethren, the aggregate vote share of the socialist family of parties was to fall 4 percentage points, from almost 33 percent for four parties in 1995 to less than 29 percent for seven in 1999 (see table 1-2).

Short of a root-and-branch reform of the KPRF, it could latch onto electoral allies closer to the political center. The ostensibly best bet, and the most admired public figure in Russia in mid-1999, was Yevgenii Primakov. Weeks after Yeltsin ousted him as prime minister in May, Zyuganov voiced support for assigning Primakov first spot on the KPRF list. The offer, either naive or insincere, was a nonstarter. Primakov was entranced by government, not opposition, and said later he would only have warmed to stewardship "of a centrist or left-center movement which amalgamated a number of organizations."[7] Primakov's being of Jewish descent, Makashov's bigotry, and the party's wishy-washy line on it, could not have been a selling point. By August Primakov had signed up with the OVR bloc.

Submergence of the KPRF campaign in a center-left alliance would have obliged it to compromise on cherished policies. Zyuganov would have had to make way for Primakov in the presidential election and likely to step down as leader, sooner or later. But a repositioning also would have been a godsend in the Duma contest. Some polls in July and August showed that for Primakov to throw in with the communists would add 6 to 13 percentage points to its popular vote.[8] A member of the KPRF secretariat, Viktor Peshkov, said in September that Primakov's absence would all but preclude the party transcending its core electorate.[9]

In mulling their options, the communists factored out the tectonic changes taking shape in Russian politics. The emergence of Vladimir Putin found them at their most myopic. Having fought tooth and nail in 1998 against reinstatement of the colorless Viktor Chernomyrdin as prime minister, in 1999 they did not try to halt the Yeltsin acolyte who was about to hit it off with the populace—with nationalist sentiment, trained on Chechnya, as the catalyst. Perhaps because Putin was an alumnus of the KGB, still revered by communist traditionalists, the Duma caucus took no position on his confirmation, and individual communist deputies supplied his margin of victory.[10]

The Duma Campaign

The communists had, in the Russian context, a well-oiled campaign machine. The program it put across was mostly tried and true, though with some refinements and tactical adjustments.

Well-Tested Methods

The fact that the KPRF's coffers were no match for establishment-based and business-friendly groups like Unity and OVR was less disconcerting than one might guess.[11] It was an article of faith among communists that a national election campaign should be labor-intensive, low-cost, and low-tech. The belief harkens back to the agitprop style of the Soviet party, developed in an undemocratic context but sharing much with what Pippa Norris calls the premodern campaigns prevalent in Western democracies before television (see chapter 2).

The conduit for spreading the word was a rank-and-file membership the KPRF claimed to number 530,000 in 1999.[12] Volunteers rang doorbells and telephones and patrolled street corners and subway stops. Some compiled registers of names and addresses of known supporters, canvassing them first. All card carriers were exhorted to press family and neighbors to vote for communist candidates. The party required Duma deputies and nominees to attend old-fashioned factory and town hall meetings in their home districts and be on call for barnstorming elsewhere.[13] Zyuganov logged more kilometers than anyone else.

The KPRF also put stock in "red governors" and left-leaning legislators in the provinces. Spokesmen estimated that up to one-third of the regional governments were under its sway, but this is more a guess than a precise measure, and the depth of commitment varied.[14] The governors who consented to be on its national list were just two: Vasilii Starodubtsev of Tula, in third place on the list, and Aman Tuleyev of Kemerovo, in fourth. Governors from the Altai, Krasnodar, Ryazan, Smolensk, Stavropol, Vladimir, and Volgograd regions signed a pro-KPRF appeal.[15] In a sign of how easily relationships can come undone in a transitional polity, Tuleyev, the best known, turned coat in November. In an open letter to Zyuganov, with whom he had been feuding since 1997, he accused his own party of accepting "dirty money" from MIKOM, a metallurgical company with interests in his home region. Several weeks afterward, in the presence of a touring Aleksandr Karelin, the number two on the Unity national list, he summoned Kemerovo voters to mark their ballots for Unity. The astonishing thing is that Tuleyev executed this pirouette without withdrawing from the KPRF's candidates list.[16] Tuleyev, with help from the Kremlin and the courts, was to have MIKOM stripped of its Kemerovo assets in early 2000.[17]

The premodern communications medium of choice was the commu-
nist-oriented press. Three national newspapers had stable readerships of
party loyalists and sympathizers: *Pravda* (with a circulation of 40,000
copies), *Sovetskaya Rossiya* (allegedly printing 300,000 copies daily),
and *Zavtra* (claiming a circulation of 100,000). Four hundred and seventy local newspapers were either party property or friendly to the
cause.[18] Unlike other Russian parties, the KPRF owned the presses that
printed its campaign materials and allied newspapers.

The KPRF did dabble in modern techniques in 1999, unlike 1995,
when it spent pennies on television advertising. It sank funds into four
national television ads and thirty regionalized clips, commissioned focus
groups and opinion polls, and availed itself of the unpaid TV and radio
time afforded all parties and candidates.[19]

Compared with other prime players, these ventures in electronic campaigning were timid. The KPRF restricted itself to in-house campaign
expertise and hired few outsiders as consultants or pollsters. Nor did it
get the backhand publicity it had during the 1996 presidential race,
when Yeltsin's fusillades against Zyuganov accentuated the KPRF's
stature as the premier opposition party. Zyuganov expected a repeat in
1999, predicting a "total attack from all television networks . . . an avalanche of mud and slander." "We cannot count on receiving during
these three months a decent place in the country's information space. . . .
Therefore, our arsenal retains the well-tested methods of agitation: from
house to house, from person to person, from heart to heart."[20] As it
happened, the avalanche of mud from state television fell on OVR's
head, not the KPRF's, while NTV and TV-Tsentr targeted the Kremlin
and Unity. National news outlets barely reported on the KPRF one way
or the other. Communist officials construed the dearth of criticism as a
detriment, as it implied no one cared what they said or did.[21] A televised
offensive by the KPRF might have sparked a response from its opponents. None was in the cards, and through inertia the party stayed with
its "well-tested methods."

Words of Hope

The KPRF beat the drums for a decidedly evangelical campaign
gospel. It sought to hold onto the affections of loyal communists and to
proselytize in demographic groups where it knew it had lagged behind
in 1995–96, especially in more urbanized areas and younger age categories. It updated some political imagery, spotlighting Gennadii

Zyuganov as an avuncular personality who made outsiders feel at home in the party. In one well-circulated leaflet, Zyuganov was photographed in a colorful urban setting with a group of Russian youths, beneath the slogan, "With Zyuganov life will be set on the right track."

The KPRF was true to form in cranking out elaborate statements of its positions on public issues. Its keynote document was a screed with the arresting title "Stand Up, Giant Land!" Zyuganov and his aides released a procession of bulletins and interview transcripts.

On economic questions, the party significantly moderated its stance. Sergei Glaz'ev, a thirty-nine-year-old economist who generally favored market reforms and had served in Yegor Gaidar's liberal cabinet, had Zyuganov's ear and was listed eighth on the KPRF's roster of candidates, while the most dogmatic Marxists were excluded from the list. The party was praiseful of the hardheaded anticrisis measures taken after the 1998 economic crunch by Primakov and Maslyukov. Most eye-catching, it affirmed the importance of property rights:

> In one of the most dramatic turnarounds since 1995, the CPRF [KPRF] is now talking about how to enforce property rights and provide effective protection of the private property which was acquired "honestly." The CPRF explicitly accepts that where competition exists, private property should be the dominant form of ownership. Although the CPRF continues to support collective ownership, it now defines this term as it is defined in Western economies, meaning private, employee-owned firms, [and] supports state ownership only for natural monopolies and enterprises in need of long-term restructuring.[22]

One observer, perusing leaflets urging tax relief for small business, quipped that the communists were beginning to imitate U.S. Republicans.[23]

And yet, it was hardly true that the KPRF had sheared its state-socialist roots. Its slate, even stripped of the most zealous elements, still contained older communists who had qualms about the rapprochement with capitalism.[24] The approbation of private property and markets was qualified by an abiding conservatism on hot-button issues such as the privatization of urban utilities and farmland. Populism was a constant motif, as the party called for compulsory reductions in the price of foodstuffs, industrial commodities, energy, and transport.[25] The sweetly reasonable verbiage on economic theory faded out when the topic turned to the practice of the transition to the market. Revisiting the 1996 presidential campaign, KPRF literature slammed Yeltsin, his administration, and the business elite for causing the economic and social degeneration of Russia. "Thieving oligarchs" had propped up a "criminal dictatorship" whose policies produced "millions of unemployed, poor, homeless, and destitute" people. One pamphlet swore to "return property stolen by 'reformists' to the people" and to "put strategically important sectors under state control."[26]

The party subordinated this economic jumble to positions taken on a welter of noneconomic issues that had cultural resonance with KPRF cadres and candidates—issues of national identity, integrity, and self-assertion. The "Stand Up, Giant Land!" proclamation was subtitled "An Appeal to the Patriots of Russia," not to its communists, leftists, or proletariat. The historical antecedent elicited was the Great Patriotic War (World War II), not the Bolshevik Revolution. The cover page was imprinted with Joseph Stalin's famous salutation after the Nazi invasion of 1941: "Comrades! Brothers and Sisters!" The insignia on the ballot next to the party's name depicted the star-shaped Order of Victory pinned on the chests of war heroes rather than the KPRF's trademark hammer, sickle, and book. In flyers and other campaign information the party harped on "five words of hope": *spravedlivost'* (fairness or justice), *derzhavnost'* (statehood), *narodovlastiye* (people's power), *dukhovnost'* (spirituality), and *patriotizm* (patriotism). None are of Marxist or Leninist provenance, and the last three terms are unabashedly nationalistic. Although the communists pledged to protect ethnic minorities, they gave the ethnic Russian (*russkii*) majority pride of place. "Enemies of Russia," went one pamphlet, "are trying . . . to annihilate our culture. We shall put an end to the russophobic practice of the regime. The Russian (*russkii*) man, now humiliated and [lied to] . . . shall claim the place that he deserves."[27] In an odd pose for a former "scientific atheist," Zyuganov also wooed Russian Orthodox believers, saying the creed and the clergy deserved a role in Russia's revival.

Mining the same vein, the KPRF tirelessly enunciated standard anti-American and anti-NATO slogans, commending closer ties with Iran, Iraq, and Libya and offering to "remove all obstacles to the unification of Russia, Belarus, and Ukraine."[28] Several texts portrayed the Western powers as co-conspirators in Russia's degradation. Noting the influx of food imports, one leaflet concluded darkly, "It is not just coincidence that the International Monetary Fund, the World Bank, the U.S.A.,

Germany, and other states all impose on us, in an increasingly ultima-tum-like form, their schemes for undertaking reforms in the interests of foreign capital."[29]

When it came to motivating voters, the nationalistic wordplay came up short in three ways. Its escapist quality and remoteness from day-to-day concerns was the first. Adulteration of the party's mellowed economic message was the second. From one side of its mouth, the KPRF said it would work within the post-Soviet economic and social frame-work. From the other, it railed against global institutions and aid pro-grams and condemned the soft leftist Primakov as an "accomplice" to the "team of traitors and gravediggers of the Soviet state" and as having ignored the "fifth column" which was out to subvert the nation.[30] Although Zyuganov retracted the welcome mat for extremists such as Ilyukhin and the noxious Makashov, he confessed that they were work-ing toward the same ends as the KPRF and would be its soul mates in the Duma.[31] A third source of friction was the party's inability to formu-late a distinct position on the one nationalist issue, and the one shooting war, at the hub of the political agenda in 1999–2000: Chechnya. Rage as it might at Yeltsin and his minions, the KPRF agreed with the Putin government's war effort, stood by the military and the FSB, and rejected Chechen independence.

The Districts

The KPRF nominated 129 candidates in the districts. This was more than any other party or quasi party, yet amounted to no change from 1995 and hence to a sluggish effort.[32] The selection process was decen-tralized. First secretaries of the party at the regional level could if they wished take the best district in the region and had the final word on nominations. The national party congress in September ratified the selections as a formality. Moscow headquarters did, nonetheless, make decisions about whom to support with the party's scarce financial resources. Zyuganov and Second Secretary Kuptsov often disagreed on the priorities. Zyuganov resorted to finding donors who would make payments directly to his favored candidates, a practice that infuriated Kuptsov and other KPRF leaders.[33] From time to time, players from out-side the party—an example being Arkadii Vol'skii of the Union of Indus-trialists and Entrepreneurs, a member of the OVR national slate—also subsidized communist or pro-communist candidates.[34]

In those regions with "red" administrations, the governors had a predictably heavy say in nominations. KPRF incumbents generally got their endorsement. Lacking an incumbent, the governor proposed the communist candidate or, in some instances, backed a nonpartisan. In the nine regions where the governor was on the KPRF slate or signed the pro-KPRF appeal a month before the election, twenty-one communist candidates were nominated in thirty-two seats, freeing up eleven districts for leftist but officially nonpartisan favorites of the governor. For example, in Krasnodar, on the Black Sea coast, Governor Nikolai Kondratenko plumped for KPRF candidates in four districts and for independents (unopposed by the KPRF) in two, staying neutral in a seventh district. In Kemerovo, one incumbent, Teimuraz Avaliani, was deposed as chairman of the regional KPRF committee in 1998 during infighting between Zyuganov and Governor Tuleyev and was barred from the ballot by a pro-Tuleyev electoral commission in 1999. No communist was nominated and Tuleyev worked on behalf of a nonpartisan client.[35]

The KPRF acted almost without regard for other leftist factions, as had been true in 1993 and 1995. The exception to this rule was the kid-gloves treatment of incumbents from APR and Power to the People, the two non-KPRF socialist factions represented in the last Duma. Eleven of the twenty Agrarians elected in districts in 1995 ran in 1999: four were awarded the KPRF nomination in the district (one of them was Nikolai Kharitonov, who led the rebellion against the defection of the APR to OVR); two were put on the KPRF's national list; and five competed as independents, four of them not opposed by a KPRF candidate. Of the nine leftists elected as Power to the People nominees in 1995, two (one of them Nikolai Ryzhkov) ran as independents and four on the list of Sergei Baburin's nationalistic Russian People's Union. The KPRF registered a candidate against only one of the six (Baburin, in the Siberian region of Omsk).

The other courtesy granted was to KPRF incumbents. Most who found it convenient had the opportunity to run as an independent or, in unusual cases, for another socialist party—unimpeded by an authorized KPRF candidate. Sitting members in thirteen districts did not contest their seats as KPRF nominees in 1999. Seven sought reelection as independents. Two (one of them Viktor Ilyukhin) accepted nomination by the Movement in Support of the Army. Four vacated the scene and no KPRF candidate was to appear in the district; one of the four was General Makashov, whom a local electoral commission in Samara region removed from the ballot on a technicality.

Table 5-1. *Registration of KPRF Candidates in the Districts in 1999, by Presence of a KPRF Candidate in 1995 and KPRF's Share of the Party-List Vote in 1995*

Percent

KPRF's share of party-list vote in 1995	A KPRF candidate in 1995	
	No[a]	Yes[b]
< 20	33	56
20 to 29.99	47	76
≥ 30	70	79

a. N = 94 districts.
b. N = 130 districts.

Despite the devolution of the nomination process, the KPRF's district nominations were made strategically, in the sense of directing resources to places where the prospects of victory were best. The communists proposed candidates in about 70 percent of the 130 districts where they had a nominee in 1995 and in about 40 percent of the districts where they did not.[36] In both categories, and especially the second, the chances of a nomination being made rose steadily with the party's political strength in the district, as indicated by the percentage of the party-list vote cast for the KPRF in the 1995 election (see table 5-1). Where its 1995 vote share was less than 20 percent, the KPRF fielded candidates 33 percent of the time if it had not been represented in the 1995 campaign and 56 percent of the time if it had. Where its 1995 vote share was over 30 percent, those figures rose to 70 percent and 79 percent.

The Voters in 1999

The modalities through which communist supporters engaged with the campaign did not depart much from other parties, whatever the assumptions of KPRF planners. The determinants of their electoral behavior, however, were distinctive. Although heedful of leadership and other short-term evaluations, communist voters were the most likely to have unfaltering loyalties to their party, had the best-etched demographic attributes, were the most outraged about current Russian realities, and were most swayed by issue opinions.

Premodern and Modern Conduits

While KPRF leaders presupposed that their constituents were uniquely accessible through premodern campaigning methods, the fact is that communist voters in 1999 seldom indulged in old-style activities of an active nature and did so more frequently than other citizens in only one narrow respect: attending public rallies. All in all, a mere 12 percent of all our survey respondents who voted for the KPRF national list reported visiting a rally or meeting, 24 percent tried to steer someone else's vote, and 2 percent agitated for the party; for voters for other parties, these levels were 5, 22, and 2 percent, respectively.[37] In passive mode, only 6 percent of communist voters were contacted by canvassers for any party (versus 7 percent for the supporters of other parties) and 1 percent by a representative of the KPRF. Twelve percent received KPRF materials in the mail (versus 16 percent for persons who voted for other parties), 17 percent came across KPRF leaflets and posters on the streets (versus 15 percent for others), and 30 percent were approached by an acquaintance seeking to influence their vote (versus 37 percent for others). The party's effort was not well targeted, either, as KPRF voters were two and one-half to three and one-half times more likely to have been canvassed or exposed to materials by parties *other than* the KPRF. Not one KPRF party member in our survey sample recalled being canvassed by the KPRF during the campaign.

Red governors surely did deliver some votes to the KPRF, if not a huge number, to judge from the regional vote totals. In all nine regions with pro-KPRF governors (counting Kemerovo's Tuleyev for these purposes as pro-KPRF), the party's vote share surpassed its national mean, as had happened in seven of those same regions in 1995.[38] But the vote for the KPRF in its five most productive regions, 19.38 percent of its total nationwide, put it in fourth place on that indicator among the six leading parties. In only one top-notch region, Krasnodar, did the local leader side with the communists; in three (Moscow, Moscow region, and Bashkortostan), he was a backer of OVR.[39]

As for the vaunted pro-communist press, it got through to a minute slice of its intended audience. When questioned about media intake in the preelection interview, 29 percent of our respondents who ultimately decided in favor of the KPRF said they had read a national newspaper during the preceding week; this was 9 points less than indicated by the supporters of other parties. A mere 4 percent had dipped into *Pravda, Sovetskaya Rossiya,* or *Zavtra.*[40]

Where, then, did communist voters procure their campaign-relevant information? In truth, they were as addicted as other Russians to modern broadcast communication. Their exposure to electronic electioneering occurred at almost precisely the mean levels for the electorate. Ninety-two percent of KPRF voters watched the daily television news once or more during the week of the campaign in which they were interviewed (55 percent watched it each day of that week), and 89 percent considered television their basic medium for political information. About 80 percent viewed weekly television newsmagazines on television and recalled seeing ads during the Duma campaign. About 70 percent watched the television news quite or very attentively.

The KPRF's own forays into the television world brought modest results. Of members of our survey panel who reported especially liking some party's clips, 20 percent mentioned the KPRF (tying it with OVR for third place, far below the 44 percent who mentioned Unity). Only 13 percent of KPRF voters volunteered that they liked its clips, equal to the number who savored the ads of other parties. If Unity and to a lesser extent OVR had slanted news broadcasts to take up the slack, the KPRF did not. Neither was it the recipient of withering attacks such as those visited upon OVR at the hands of the ORT and RTR networks. Our regression of the December vote on media variables (see appendix table C-6) shows only frequent exposure to Yevgenii Kiselëv's weekend "Itogi" program to have depressed the odds of voting KPRF. Most news coverage did not materially affect the KPRF vote.[41]

The Tried and the True

The KPRF led all parties and quasi parties in continuity of voting behavior. Fully half of communist voters in 1999 were loyalists who had voted for the party four years before (and three-quarters of all loyalists in the electorate were communist voters). Another 12 percent had voted in 1995 for some other socialist party, usually the Agrarians. In other behavioral categories, the KPRF was underrepresented: its electors comprised fewer converts from different party families (28 percent), fewer ex-dropouts (9 percent), and fewer electoral novices (2 percent) than any major party or bloc. The biggest pool for its out-of-family defectors was nationalist voters from 1995 (36 percent of the subtotal).[42] KPRF voters decided early: nearly 85 percent resolved which party to support by one month before election day. Other indicators of stability of intent say the same.[43] All of which is to say that Secretary Peshkov's glum forecast—that the KPRF would conserve but not enlarge its traditional electorate—was borne out with a vengeance.

Table 5-2. *KPRF Vote in 1995 and 1999, by Community Size and Year of Birth*

Percent

Social category	1995[a]	1999[b]
Community size		
Bottom quintile	39	41
2	37	39
3	24	31
4	29	26
Top quintile	16	17
Year of birth		
Before 1930	45	49
1930s	42	46
1940s	31	34
1950s	22	29
1960s	20	15
1970s and 1980s	18	13
Mean for entire sample	29	31

a. Total N = 2,114 weighted cases. Data from panel survey described in Timothy J. Colton, *Transitional Citizens: Voters and What Influences Them in the New Russia* (Harvard University Press, 2000).

b. Total N = 1,403 weighted cases.

Nor was support up in social groups where the communists had drawn poorly before. The 1995 and 1999 survey interviews referred to in table 5-2 somewhat exaggerate the KPRF vote, but by equal amounts (6 or 7 percentage points), which ought to make comparisons reasonably accurate. Among urban voters, we found a slight backsliding, with the KPRF posting a 7-point increase in third-quintile communities and lesser increases in the smallest and second-smallest quintiles. Age-wise, Russians born after 1959 were about 5 percentage points less likely to vote for the KPRF in 1999 than in 1995; in all older age ranges, citizens were more likely to vote KPRF in 1999 than in 1995, by margins running from 3 points to 7 points. The average KPRF voter in December 1995, born in 1944, was fifty-one years of age; in December 1999 the average KPRF voter had been born in 1943 and was fifty-six years old. On the rural-urban and more so on the generational continuum, the KPRF was headed stubbornly in the direction opposite to where its leaders and organizers wanted to go.

Demographics and Current Conditions

Our multivariate statistical model of the vote confirms the discrete effects of urbanization and age, as well as of a series of other demographic variables (see appendix table B-1). The KPRF had without question the most crisply defined electorate in the 1999 election. Altogether, it can be characterized as the party of the have-nots. Its supporters were significantly more likely to be villagers or small-town dwellers, poorly educated, middle-aged or elderly, sometime members of the disbanded CPSU, low in economic well-being, and residents of southern regions. For all these variables, the effects are of major size, that is, ≥ .10 (10 percentage points or higher). On almost every score, they are consistent in direction and approximate magnitude with the KPRF vote in the 1995 election.[44]

The left-wing KPRF was also one of the two parties (along with the right-wing Union of Right Forces) whose vote was most alive to mass perceptions of current conditions in the country—in this case, critical perceptions (see appendix tables B-1 and B-3). Communist voters were not moved by short-term pocketbook considerations, although they did react to a sense that they had been left behind during the economic reforms of the 1990s. The sharpest effects came from negative evaluations of the nation's economy and political system. All other things being equal, citizens who took the most unforgiving view of the economic situation were .16 more likely to vote communist than those who took the most favorable view, and individuals who took the blackest view of the course of democratization were .21 more likely to vote for the KPRF than those who took the most favorable view.

Partisanship and Issue Opinions

The apparent total effect of KPRF partisanship on the probability of voting for the party in 1999 was .45, which was average for the major parties. Unique to the communists was not partisanship's manifest effect but its high incidence and durability. Two in every five Russians to identify with a political party in 1999 were partisans of the KPRF (see table 2-10). Of self-reported KPRF partisans, 80 percent voted communist in December, and these partisans made up 54 percent of the communist electorate—a stark contrast with the transient Unity and OVR blocs. We have already commented on the persistence in communists' voting behavior across elections. For a hefty minority, a similar stickiness is evident in matters of partisanship. Thirty-nine percent of year 2000 partisans of the KPRF in our 1995–2000 panel (which excludes persons too young to vote in 1995) had been KPRF partisans in 1995. The stronger the partisanship, the more continuity was the likely outcome. Where 24 percent of weak KPRF partisans in 2000 had been attached to the party five years before, 33 percent of moderate partisans had been and 56 percent of strong partisans had been.

Issue cleavages also had an impact on communist voters in 1999, as in earlier Russian elections—and much more emphatically than on any other section of the electorate (see appendix tables B-1 and B-3). These effects were variegated by issue. Statistically significant and high-magnitude (≥ .10) total effects on the KPRF vote are found for positions on three of the seven issues we tested: leftness on the left-right scale, preference for a Soviet-type political regime, and, more feebly, preference for a parliamentary over a presidential republic. On all three, the effect is in the expected direction. On four of the seven issues, though, there is no demonstrable issue effect. The KPRF's attempts to muffle its negativity on privatization and the market may explain the absence of an effect for opinions on the pace and direction of economic reform. It remains disconcerting from the point of view of democratic theory that there was no connection whatever between the vote for the communists, the main opposition force, and citizen opinions on the Chechnya conflict that overshadowed all other issues of the day.[45]

The two issues where normative opinions most affected the KPRF vote were left-right orientation and preference for political regime. Had the KPRF successfully moderated its image, citizens should have imputed nonextreme positions to the party, and it should have attracted support from center-tending voters. Neither was really the case in 1999, as can be gleaned from table 5-3. On the ideological scale, 20 percent of survey informants placed themselves to the left of center, but 63 percent placed the KPRF there, and almost 40 percent put it in the most leftist category. Controlling statistically for other determinants, the predicted probability of voting KPRF tumbles about twice as rapidly when citizens move from the far left of the scale to the center point than when they move from the center to the far right (a displacement of .22 versus one of .12). Concerning system of government, about one-quarter of all citizens preferred an unreformed Soviet system, as against nearly 60 percent who thought the KPRF stood for such a change. Again, the largest difference in the probability of voting communist is the result of relocation from the most retrograde position (an unreformed Soviet regime) to the next (a democratized socialism). The probability of supporting the KPRF declines .22 across those two positions and by about half that amount across the rest of the issue scale.

Table 5-3. *Citizen Opinions, Issue Positions Imputed to KPRF, and the KPRF Vote*

Issue and position	Citizen opinion (percent)[a]	Position imputed to KPRF (percent)[b]	Predicted probability of voting for KPRF[c]
Left-right scale			
0 (left)	7	37	.38
1	3	12	.34
2	3	8	.28
3	4	5	.24
4	3	1	.20
5	23	4	.16
6	4	1	.13
7	7	1	.10
8	6	1	.08
9	3	2	.06
10 (right)	6	4	.04
Don't know	32	25	.15
Preferred political system			
Soviet system we had before perestroika	25	57	.37
Reformed Soviet system	41	24	.15
Current political system	13	3	.05
Democracy of the Western type	9	0.3	.02
Don't know	12	15	.15

a. From 1999–2000 panel, wave 2 (N = 1,846 weighted cases). First question reads, "In politics people sometimes talk of left and right. Imagine a scale from 0 to 10 where 0 means the left and 10 means the right. Where would you place yourself on this scale?" Body of the second question reads, "What kind of political system, in your opinion, would be most appropriate for Russia?"

b. From 1999–2000 panel, wave 2 (N = 1,846 weighted cases).

c. Computed from multistage statistical model, holding causally prior and simultaneous variables constant at their medians. Sample N = 1,414; $p \leq .01$ for all cells in the column.

Evaluations of Political Players

Compared with Unity and especially OVR—for whom social constituencies were fuzzily demarcated, partisanship shallow, and issue opinions relatively inconsequential—the KPRF campaign revolved less around short-term evaluations of political players. In absolute terms, however, such considerations did matter as much for the communists as for the other contenders.

KPRF supporters were more disparaging than others about incumbents. Evaluations of Boris Yeltsin had no autonomous effect on the likelihood of voting communist, proof yet again of the skill of his handlers in keeping him under wraps (see appendix table B-1). For approval

Table 5-4. *Evaluations of Gennadii Zyuganov's Character Traits*[a]

Trait	Rating (percent)			Ranking of net rating among 6 party leaders
	Yes/ probably yes	No/ probably no	Net yes/probably yes over no/ probably no	
Intelligent and knowledge- able person	77	14	62	3
Strong leader	60	27	33	3
Honest and trustworthy person	49	30	20	3
Really cares about people like you	46	35	12	3

a. From 1999–2000 panel, wave 2 (N = 1,846 weighted cases). "Don't know" responses included in the denominator but not shown here.

of Prime Minister Putin, there was a demonstrable negative effect. Making allowance for other variables, the citizen best disposed toward Putin's work in office was 25 percentage points less likely to cast a ballot for the KPRF than the most ill disposed.

A common misconception about the communists of Russia is that their party-mindedness, interest in issues, and principled opposition to the status quo nix the leadership factor. Nothing could be farther from the truth. In 1999 appraisals of the personal attributes of Gennadii Zyuganov weighed on the KPRF vote as much as parallel attitudes did for the other parties.

Zyuganov ranked third of the six principal party leaders in summary evaluation (after Shoigu and Primakov) and third on all four traits probed for in our voters' survey (see table 5-4).[46] His net rating was solidest on intelligence and knowledge and most anemic on empathy with ordinary people; traits of strength and integrity were assessed in between those extremes. We estimate the total effect of assessments of Zyuganov's character on the KPRF vote to be .50, well within the normal range (appendix table B-1). Median voters who on average judged Zyuganov to be intelligent, strong, honorable, and empathetic were 50 percentage points more likely to vote for the KPRF than if they were sure Zyuganov did not possess those virtues.[47] The predicted probabilities in table 5-5, mounting from .01 to .50, trace the effect through successive readings of the leadership measure.

The total-effect measure is for the average voter. What about subsets of the electorate? An especially interesting question concerns partisanship, which was more widespread for communist voters than anywhere

Table 5-5. *KPRF Vote and Evaluations of Zyuganov's Character*

Mean evaluation of four traits	Citizen opinion (percent)[a]	Predicted probability of voting for KPRF[b]
Does not have the positive trait	6	.01
Probably does not have the positive trait	24	.04
Probably has the positive trait	48	.18
Has the positive trait	22	.50

a. N = 1,846 weighted cases. Missing data coded at the mean of the distribution for the specific trait.

b. Computed from multistage statistical model, holding causally prior and simultaneous variables constant at their medians. Sample N = 1,414; $p \le .01$ for all cells in the column.

Table 5-6. *KPRF Vote and Evaluations of Zyuganov's Character, by Partisanship*

Mean evaluation of four traits	KPRF partisans		Yabloko partisans		Unity partisans	
	Citizen opinion (percent)[a]	Predicted probability of voting for KPRF[b]	Citizen opinion (percent)[a]	Predicted probability of voting for KPRF[b]	Citizen opinion (percent)[a]	Predicted probability of voting for KPRF[b]
Does not have the positive trait	0.3	.04	16	.00	15	.00
Probably does not have the positive trait	6	.17	22	.02	32	.01
Probably has the positive trait	37	.51	56	.09	45	.03
Has the positive trait	57	.82	6	.31	8	.13

a. N = 1,846 weighted cases. Missing data coded at the mean of the distribution for the specific trait.

b. Computed from multistage statistical model, holding causally prior and simultaneous variables constant at their medians. Sample N = 1,414; $p \le .01$ for all cells in the column.

else in the system. Would citizens with a psychic attachment to the KPRF qua organization be more or less affected than others by their attitudes toward that organization's leader? How about the devotees of other political parties?

Table 5-6 provides some answers. It recites the simulated probability of voting communist for partisans of the three parties and quasi parties that had the most numerous followings in 1999: the KPRF, Yabloko, and Unity. There is convincing evidence of a two-step relationship. First, KPRF partisans were much more inclined to give favorable impressions of the character of the KPRF's chairman than identifiers with other parties (or than the nonpartisans in table 5-5).[48] Fifty-seven percent of

Table 5-7. *Prospective Evaluations of KPRF's Issue Competence*[a]

| | Say KPRF is best prepared | | |
Issue	Percent	Percent of those who named a party	Ranking
Social security	25	38	1
Economy	22	32	1
Human rights	19	31	1
Chechnya	15	23	2
Foreign policy	17	28	1
Crime and corruption	20	31	2

a. From 1999–2000 panel, wave 2 (N = 1,846 weighted cases).

KPRF partisans thought on average that Zyuganov fully possessed the virtues about which we asked; for Yabloko partisans it was 6 percent and for Unity partisans 8 percent. Second, and equally important, each level of assessment of Zyuganov's character was a lot more likely to translate into propitious odds of voting KPRF if the citizen was a communist partisan. Individuals who graded Zyuganov highest had a .82 chance of voting KPRF if they were KPRF partisans, a .31 chance if they were Yabloko partisans, and a .13 chance if they were Unity partisans.

Finally, the vote for the KPRF's national list was responsive to prospective evaluations of its capacity to govern. On the six specific policy problems where we asked survey informants to name the party in the best shape to handle the issue (see table 5-7), the communists came out first on four (social security, the economy, human rights, and foreign policy) and second to Unity on a pair (Chechnya and crime and corruption). Thirty-two percent of citizens rated the KPRF best on at least one issue. The total effect on the KPRF vote of our additive index of issue competence was .83. The probabilities of the median voter voting communist predicted by degree of enthusiasm about the KPRF's issue competence are laid out in table 5-8. The likelihood was better than fifty-fifty once the citizen expected the party to do the best job in three issue areas. There were only small differences in relationship to the voting decision across issues.

The District Vote

Forty-six communists made it into the Duma through the districts. A dozen fewer than the seats in 1995, this was still almost as many as all other leading parties combined elected in 1999. There was some connec-

Table 5-8. *KPRF Vote and Prospective Evaluations of Its Issue Competence*

Number of issues KPRF can handle best	Citizen opinion (percent)[a]	Predicted probability of voting for KPRF[b]
0	68	.12
1	7	.26
2	4	.46
3	4	.66
4	3	.81
5	3	.89
6	11	.94

a. N = 1,846 weighted cases.

b. Computed from multistage statistical model, holding causally prior and simultaneous variables constant at their medians. Sample N = 1,414; $p \leq .01$ for all cells in the column.

tion with past performance: twenty-seven winners, or about three in five, were in districts where the KPRF had been victorious in 1995. There was a connection, too, to tutelage by the regional elite: fifteen of the districts with winning candidates, or one in three, were located in regions like Krasnodar or Tula where the governor openly promoted the cause.

For OVR and Unity, we have noted the parties' failure to denominate candidates in the majority of Duma districts, their imperfect success at informing supporters about the representatives they did nominate, and partly as a result the frequent disconnect between district and party-list voting behavior. On all these dimensions, the communists demonstrated greater consistency in 1999.

Having made nominations in more districts than any rival, the KPRF fostered an expectation that district and party-list voting choices would be linked. One-third of the KPRF supporters in our survey sample, or double the average, voted for a KPRF nominee in their district of residence (see table 5-9). In districts where the party did have a candidate on the ballot, that proportion was one-half. KPRF supporters knew more frequently than most voters who their party's local nominee was and, where this was so, more frequently voted the straight ticket (see table 5-10). Forty-eight percent of the KPRF's party-list supporters who were presented with a KPRF candidate in their local district knew there was such a candidate and were able to identify him in the postelection interview. Of them, 82 percent voted the straight ticket.

Table 5-10 actually understates consistency, in that it does not reckon with the party's implicit endorsement of nominally independent candi-

Table 5-9. *Electoral Consistency between District and Party-List Votes,*
KPRF Voters and All Voters

Percent

Candidate voted for in the district	All districts		Districts where a nominee registered	
	KPRF voters[a]	All voters[b]	KPRF voters[c]	All voters[d]
Nominee of party supported in the party-list vote	33	17	50	40
Nominee of a different party	17	24	22	26
Independent candidate	42	45	22	24
Votes against all candidates	7	14	6	10

a. N = 415 weighted cases.
b. Excluding persons who voted against all parties in the party-list vote. N = 1,318 weighted cases.
c. N = 278 weighted cases.
d. Excluding persons who voted against all parties in the party-list vote. N = 566 weighted cases.

Table 5-10. *Electoral Consistency and Voter Knowledge, KPRF Voters*
and All Voters, in Districts Where a Nominee of the Party Supported in
the Party-List Vote Is Registered[a]

Position	Percent		Percent of category who vote straight ticket	
	KPRF voters[b]	All voters[c]	KPRF voters[b]	All voters[c]
Knows there is a nominee and can identify the nominee	48	41	82	80
Knows there is a nominee and cannot identify the nominee	8	10	9	10
Thinks there is no nominee	22	24	23	21
Does not know if there is a nominee	22	25	36	24

a. Excludes persons who voted against all candidates in the district.
b. N = 262 weighted cases.
c. N = 509 weighted cases.

dates and, more rarely, of the designees of other socialist or nationalist
parties and quasi parties. As discussed earlier, the KPRF declined to register its own candidates in a total of eighteen districts being contested by
deputies elected in 1995 on the KPRF, Agrarian, and Power to the People tickets. Were the pro-KPRF incumbents in such districts to be
counted as tantamount to official KPRF nominees, the level of consistency with the party-list decision would be some percentage points
higher. Eleven of the eighteen proxy communists—conspicuously Nikolai Ryzhkov and Viktor Ilyukhin—won pluralities in their districts and

were to be seated in the Duma in either the KPRF caucus or its satellite Agroindustrial group.[49]

Presidential Postscript

When Gennadii Zyuganov began his first pass at the presidency the winter of 1995–96, he was out front in the polls and would see his lead evaporate only the month before the vote. In 1999–2000, advisers understood hours after the Duma ballots were tallied that the possibility of victory was remote. The soaring popularity of Putin, the Unity breakthrough, and the KPRF's electoral stagnation made the prime minister the prohibitive favorite. When Yeltsin resigned without warning on December 31, elevating Putin to acting president and advancing the election date from June to March, the writing was on the wall.

The bleakness of the communists' predicament shines through unmistakably in our survey data. In wave 2 of the 1999–2000 panel survey, conducted between late December and late January (with a median date for the interview of January 8), our interviewers asked how respondents would vote if a presidential election were held the next day, reading out the names of six hypothetical candidates (Zyuganov, Sergei Kiriyenko of the Union of Right Forces, Yurii Luzhkov, Primakov, Putin, and Grigorii Yavlinskii) and allowing them to volunteer others. Sixty-four percent of decided voters chose Putin, 19 percent Zyuganov, and 8 percent Primakov; no one else got over 1 percent. We also asked whom people would prefer in two-man runoffs pitting Putin against Zyuganov and Primakov. Zyuganov was favored by 21 percent, a bare 2 percent more than in the six-candidate race, to Putin's 75 percent. Primakov earned 16 percent to 79 percent for Putin.[50]

For a few days around New Year's, the KPRF batted around alternatives to a Zyuganov run. Some figures in the party suggested a boycott of the election, especially after the Yeltsin resignation truncated the campaign. Others wanted to draft Primakov as the presidential nominee of a socialist-nationalist alliance and cast Zyuganov as prime minister-designate, perhaps beginning with election of Primakov as speaker of the Duma. The first idea foundered on the fear of political isolation and the second on the hostility of the protagonists—Primakov did not care to run and Zyuganov did not care to step aside—and on Kremlin machinations. The KPRF-Unity deal on leadership positions in the Duma, reached on January 18, kept Primakov from becoming speaker of the house and opened up a gulf between him and the KPRF.[51] With other routes blocked, Zyuganov's candidacy came about by default.

The campaign had three quite limited goals: to reaffirm the communist party as the leading voice in the opposition; to protect Zyuganov from internal rivals; and, more optimistically, to force a runoff that would weaken Putin's mandate and lay the groundwork for a KPRF comeback.[52] Zyuganov was to achieve the first and second goals yet not the third. If he outran some observers' expectations, that was mainly because they were so low. His raw vote total of nearly 22 million was about 5 million fewer than he commanded in 1996 and not enough to deny Putin his first-round majority. Zyuganov carried forty-three regions in the first round against Yeltsin in 1996 and twenty-five in the second. In 2000 he carried four.

A Defensive Campaign

The KPRF's defensive strategy was reflective of its electoral goals, the long odds against defeating Putin, and several additional realities.[53] One constraint was disunity among socialists and their recent allies of nationalist stripe. Although the Popular-Patriotic Union of Russia remained on the books, Zyuganov did not go through the motions of seeking its nomination and submitted his papers through a faceless "initiative group." Some backers of his from 1996 defected outright to Putin, including the leadership of the Agrarian Party of Russia (which had run with OVR in 1999) and even the secretary of the communists' youth league.[54] Former allies in other quarters saw the campaign as an opportunity for personal vindication and aggrandizement. Zyuganov was joined on the campaign trail by three socialistic candidates—Aleksei Podberëzkin (the enthusiast of the Popular-Patriotic Union), Yurii Skuratov (Russia's procurator-general from 1995 to 1999), and Aman Tuleyev (the erratic governor of Kemerovo region)—and two nationalists: Stanislav Govorukhin (an OVR deputy in the Duma) and Vladimir Zhirinovskii (the perennial presidential hopeful). Tuleyev, the in-house dissident of the autumn, got in his usual digs at the KPRF hierarchy; Podberëzkin announced ten days before voting day he found Putin a "worthy" candidate and would support him in a runoff; and Zhirinovskii trained his guns on Zyuganov.[55] The Kremlin tacitly supported the entry of these interlopers as a way to sow discord and drain votes from Zyuganov, which they probably did in trace quantities.[56]

The pro-KPRF governors who had put themselves out in 1999 sat on their hands in 2000, not wishing to expend political capital on a doomed project. Supporting candidates for a multiparty Duma could be a shrewd investment in assuring representation. In a winner-take-all presidential contest, there was much more pressure to go along with the victor. In a number of "red" regions, the governors indirectly supported Putin, which "led to a perceptible rise in tension in relations between the governors and the local party organizations."[57] The one governor to make an unqualified endorsement of Zyuganov was Vasilii Starodubtsev in Tula, and he did so as a leader of the Agrarian Party of Russia as much as a regional boss.

The communists' own actions after December also rendered a super-aggressive electoral strategy problematic. The realpolitik of sharing leadership positions in the Duma with Unity in mid-January 2000, securing Seleznëv a second term as speaker, preempted any attempt to present Zyuganov as a radical alternative to Putin. As Vyacheslav Nikonov put it, the Kremlin had "strangled the communists with an embrace."[58] The Putin "noncampaign" in February and March (see chapter 7) extended the embrace by desisting from frontal attacks on Zyuganov.

What with the circumscribed objectives of the Zyuganov campaign, his advisers saw no sense in a special program and recycled topics from the fall. As before, they had a television presence, mostly in the monologues presented free of charge, but kept their focus on KPRF activists. "Thousands of our supporters," Zyuganov told reporters in February, "will go door to door, from the most remote rural town to the highest village in the mountains. Only we have the power to bring our ideology and goals to every Russian family."[59] True to his word, Zyuganov did step up direct mailings considerably, and canvassing less so, from the fall campaign.[60]

Zyuganov on the stump continued to ascribe Russia's woes to a rogue's gallery of liberal politicians and rapacious businessmen. They may not have had a serious candidate in the race, but Zyuganov insisted—not inaccurately, as it turned out—that Putin would forge ahead with the economic and social reforms they and Yeltsin had broached. "Although Yeltsin has resigned," he stated, "his epoch has not ended."[61] One oft-played Zyuganov video pictured a shell game being worked by a "new Russian" swindler, a fine gold watch on his wrist. As the con man moves the cups around the tabletop, images of unsavory aspects of the Yeltsin period flicker on a screen behind him. The video then segues to the same World War II emblem used during the Duma campaign and the same soothing slogan. "Part of a patriotic Soviet-era song begins to play and a picture of a smiling Zyuganov appears, with a view of the Kremlin and the Order of Victory in the background. The voice-over says, 'Vote for victory! For peace! For prosperity! With Zyuganov, life will be set on the right track.'"[62] The "on the right track" jingle sounded over and over in the television and radio ads. Zyuganov the peppery opposition orator took a back seat to Zyuganov the amiable family man, posing amid small children, simple laboring folk, balloons, books, and the like. The purpose, as Viktor Peshkov phrased it—damning with faint praise—was to put him across as "if not an engaging character, then at least capable of inspiring some interest."[63]

Zyuganov's concrete proposals were variations on arguments aired in 1999. He said he would appoint moderate communists like Sergei Glaz'ev, Yurii Maslyukov, and Ivan Mel'nikov to his cabinet, if elected. He called for a state-led but marketized model of development, borrowing from the New Economic Policy of the Soviet 1920s, the New Deal, the Japanese miracle, and China's current reforms. He demanded tax cuts while pledging a clutch of economic improvements—higher pensions and wages for government workers, controls over the price of food and basic services, restoration of savings accounts depleted by inflation or bank insolvency, relief for the armaments industry. "If the current policy course is continued," he harrumphed, "a new collapse of the Russian economy will occur at the beginning of this summer." As in the Duma campaign, he advocated constitutional changes to strengthen parliament and the government at the expense of the presidency: "I do not want the unchecked power that Yeltsin secured and which his heir is intending to preserve."[64] Zyuganov's rhetoric was also replete with the patriotic themes that had become a staple of communist campaigns and under somewhat different cover were now being hawked by Putin. In one of the few sharp contrasts with the front-runner, Zyuganov again gave them an ethnic coloration. Proclaiming ethnic Russians "the most oppressed people in their own country," he won a battle with the Central Election Commission allowing him to list his Russian nationality on the campaign poster that would hang in polling stations.[65]

Homing Instinct

Where did the votes for the chairman of the KPRF come from? If we compare ballots cast on March 26 with citizen intentions in early winter,

Table 5-11. *Zyuganov Vote and 1999 Party-List Vote,*
by Presidential Voting Intention after Duma Election[a]
Percent

	Voting intention after Duma election		
Party-list vote in 1999	Vote for Zyuganov	Abstain, vote against all, or undecided	Vote for another candidate
Voted for KPRF	84	65	47
Abstained or voted against all	56	25	11
Voted for another party	40	13	8

a. N = 1,470 weighted cases. Party-list vote and presidential voting intention ascertained in wave 2 of 1999–2000 panel and presidential vote in wave 3.

in the afterglow of the Duma election, the Zyuganov vote appears quite dynamic. A smidgeon fewer than one-half of his eventual March voters had plans to vote for him in December and January, and one-third to vote for another candidate, mostly Putin.[66] If, however, we compare the presidential vote with behavior in the Duma election, the impression is of a more static electorate. Two-thirds of Zyuganov voters in 2000 had voted for the KPRF on the party list three months earlier. Eighty-nine percent had decided how they would vote by one month in advance of election day.[67]

These two perspectives can be reconciled if we recognize the political homing instinct in the minds of many KPRF supporters from 1999. Following the Duma ballot, these voters at one point found their affections wandering—usually toward Vladimir Putin—but subsequently returned to the fold. As can be seen in table 5-11, citizens who intended after December 19 to vote for Zyuganov and had already voted for the KPRF list followed through on that intention at a rate of 84 percent. Forty-seven percent of persons who declared the intent to vote for some other presidential candidate but who had voted for the KPRF in December ended up voting for Zyuganov, that is, going back on their initial presidential voting intention. That was slightly higher than the proportion of non-KPRF voters who indicated an intent to vote for Zyuganov (40 percent of them followed through on this intent). Vacillating KPRF voters—persons who voted for the party in December and were not inclined initially to support Zyuganov's presidential bid—accounted for one-quarter of his electorate come March 26. When presidential concerns and past involvement with the KPRF pushed in the same direction, the result was either a near-certainty of voting for Zyuganov or, in the bottom right of the table, a near-certainty of voting for another candidate (a mere 8 percent of citizens who voted non-KPRF in December and preferred another presidential candidate after the Duma election cast their ballots for Zyuganov in March). In between these poles, the probabilities were mixed. Communist voters who flirted with Putin and then came back to the KPRF nominee were among those who pushed pollsters' estimates of the intended vote for Putin over the 60 percent level in January, after which his support dropped steadily until the March vote.

Zyuganov's Electorate

Given the overlap between Zyuganov supporters in 1999 and KPRF supporters in 2000, it is no wonder that our statistical modeling (see appendix tables B-2 and B-4) shows a fundamental convergence in the microfoundations of the vote. Zyuganov voters, like KPRF voters, tended to be more rural, less educated, older, former members of the CPSU, poorer, and more remote from Moscow. The one demographic influence to moderate appreciably is that of age. Its total effect contracts from .25 for the Duma election to .15 for the presidential election, the result of a small increase in support among younger voters and a larger decrease among the elderly.

From 1999 to 2000, there is little change in the contribution to the communist vote of perceptions of current national conditions, KPRF partisanship, normative issue opinions, assessments of Zyuganov's leadership qualities, and prospective evaluations of issue competence. There is a change in the impact of evaluations of incumbents—a mark of the ability of a presidential election in an executive-centered polity to concentrate citizens' attention on the performance of rulers. The total effect of evaluations of Putin's record on the communist vote is about half again as large as in 1999 (−.39 versus −.25); the effect of evaluations of Yeltsin goes from a statistically insignificant figure to −.14.

The Zyuganov campaign did its utmost to gild his personal image and popular understandings of his capability to govern wisely. So far as leader personality goes, the needle of public opinion essentially stuck in place.[68] So far as issue competence goes, there was a marked change for the worse. Comparing table 5-12 with table 5-7, we detect a pronounced deterioration in competence ratings since the Duma campaign. If the KPRF in December 1999 was judged best prepared to handle four of six key issues, in March 2000 Zyuganov was inferior to Putin on all six. The fraction of the electorate considering Zyuganov to be proficient

Table 5-12. *Prospective Evaluations of Zyuganov's Issue Competence*[a]

| | | Say Zyuganov is best prepared | |
Issue	Percent	Percent of those who named a candidate	Ranking
Social security	20	26	2
Economy	17	22	2
Human rights	17	24	2
Chechnya	10	13	2
Foreign policy	14	19	2
Crime and corruption	14	18	2

a. From 1999–2000 panel, wave 3 (N = 1,755 weighted cases).

Table 5-13. *Zyuganov Vote and Prospective Evaluations of His Issue Competence*

Number of issues Zyuganov can handle best	Citizen opinion (percent)[a]	Predicted probability of voting for Zyuganov[b]
0	73	.09
1	8	.14
2	4	.21
3	3	.30
4	2	.40
5	1	.51
6	8	.61

a. N = 1,755 weighted cases.

b. Computed from multistage statistical model, holding causally prior and simultaneous variables constant at their medians. Sample N = 1,481; $p \leq .01$ for all cells in the column.

on one issue or another in 2000 was about one-third smaller than for the KPRF in 1999. Not only that, it took more respect for the communists' issue proficiency to induce a citizen to vote for Zyuganov than it had for the KPRF Duma slate. Compare the simulation in table 5-13 with table 5-8: the probability of voting KPRF in 1999 went over the breakeven point (.50) for the person who thought the party most competent on three issues; for Zyuganov in 2000, recognition on five issues was required.[69]

Conclusions

For the Communist Party of the Russian Federation, the elections of 1999–2000 confirmed that the party was still a fixture of the national political scene but no longer, if it ever was, an insurgent force, shaping and defining it. The resting point is all the more striking when one bears in mind the extraordinary economic crisis that beset Russia's regime at the end of the 1990s.

One reason the communists' electoral machine stalled was that those in the driver's seat misjudged the far left's electoral strength as well as the appeal of nationalists who shared their anti-Western animus. They consequently put too little effort into building bridges toward centrist coalition partners and havens of support. Although the party did purge its candidates' list and dilute some of its issue stands, it cleaved to orthodox positions on certain specific issues and frequently spoke in a voice evocative of the fire-breathing campaigns of days gone by. Sticking with a doctrine that in totality most Russians perceived as out of date and divorced from their daily concerns, it convinced few citizens other than communist loyalists that it could be trusted to deal with the foremost challenges facing Russian society. To make matters worse, it clung to premodern campaigning methods in which it did not have nearly the superiority its leaders thought it did, bypassing the modern, television-based techniques to which its supporters were just about as thoroughly exposed as other citizens were.

The KPRF's chances of governing do not look bright. To discard its Leninist style and symbols (including its name), acquire a more progressive animating vision, adopt modern political technologies, and bring in alienated social and political groups would require the rupture with the past that most Soviet-bloc communist parties underwent at the end of the 1980s and that the KPRF has always frowned upon. Finding enough communists willing to pay the price, and in the process to accept the inevitability of the angry exodus of many of the party's most dedicated members, might not be enough, since other forces will not necessarily play along. At the top, the ongoing presence of a big, inert, and non-threatening communist party is a fillip for Russia's second president and his design for a managed democracy. He has every reason to throw the KPRF just enough crumbs to freeze it as it is, thereby assisting him in maintaining equilibrium in the wider political order.

6

The Liberals

MODERN RUSSIAN LIBERALISM is a child of the country's unfinished democratic and capitalist revolution and exemplifies the complexities and contradictions of the transition. Its primary authors, hitching their star to a charismatic rebel from the Soviet nomenklatura, Boris Yeltsin, outdid their wildest dreams in dynamiting the old order and then using the state apparatus to launch radical economic reforms. No sooner was that done than the pact with Yeltsin frayed and the liberals scattered into antagonistic factions. In the first post-Soviet election, in 1993, the Russia's Choice movement was simultaneously the tribune of liberal reform and the party of power. By 1995 the parties and quasi parties on the right had mushroomed from four to twelve and all considered themselves part of the opposition. The combination of disunity and a slump in popularity left Yabloko as the only one to cross the Duma's 5 percent threshold. While Yabloko was to afford the liberals their only consistent presence in the legislature during Yeltsin's second term, presidential patronage kept them in the thick of things in the executive branch. Liberal fortunes peaked in March 1998 when Yeltsin chose a thirty-six-year-old cabinet minister and banker from Nizhnii Novgorod, Sergei Kiriyenko, to replace Viktor Chernomyrdin as premier. The collapse of Kiriyenko's government during the August financial crash seemed to mark a fatal reversal, as many laid it at the right's door.

The outlook for the liberal parties as the curtain lifted on the 1999–2000 elections was profoundly uncertain. Some astute observers thought their chronic sectarianism symptomatic of a deeper malaise. Steven Fish wrote as early as 1996 that the liberals' basic problem was "not their lack of unity but rather their lack of public support."[1] The executive-branch liberals mitigated the fragmentation if not the unpopularity in 1999 by coalescing into a new electoral bloc, the Union of Right Forces (SPS). Beside it and Yabloko, only two micro-parties of liberal bent (Civic Dignity and the Social Democrats) were to climb into the ring. Hardly any observer gave SPS, its list headed up by Kiriyenko, the proverbial snowball's chance in the election. Few parties and blocs on the ballot, Laura Belin said in November, "have image problems as serious as those afflicting the Union of Right Forces." Its lineup of candidates "include[s] former government officials who are widely blamed for Russia's economic problems" and for the excesses of shock therapy and privatization.[2] Opinion polls in September gauged support for the bloc at 2 percent, and it fluttered at or below the 5 percent limit well into the campaign.[3] For Yabloko, which had stayed out of government, the omens were better. Grigorii Yavlinskii, Yabloko's leader, believed the 1998 financial disaster to have permanently disgraced liberals who had collaborated with Yeltsin and that the beneficiary at the ballot box would be his party, the only tenable "democratic opposition" in Russia.[4] Polls in late summer appeared to back him up, portending a turnout for the party of 12 to 15 percent. One journalist predicted Yabloko could seize 25 percent of the seats in the new Duma.[5]

Election day 1999 confuted the fine points of these prognoses. Yabloko went down in the party-list vote from 7.02 percent in 1995 to 6.05 percent, or from fourth place to sixth, and had its Duma caucus halved from 45 members to 20. SPS surpassed expectations by taking in 8.68 percent of the national vote and electing 29 deputies. Jointly, the right-wing parties slid from 63 seats to 49, and in the popular vote from 16.83 to 15.43 percent. In turbulent times, this was not the shabbiest outcome, and it came but months after pundits had read out the liberals' obituary. The right, however, proved irrelevant to the 2000 presidential election. Yavlinskii was the sole liberal of stature to be nominated. He undershot his 1996 vote share by almost 2 percentage points and did worse than Yabloko had in the Duma race. The experience of the liberals in 1999–2000, then, is one of resiliency, of tottering steps toward cooperation, of upsets of the pecking order among the parties, and of being sidelined in the main event, the selection of a president.

The Union of Right Forces

SPS grew out of attempts to erect a grand coalition of liberal and right-center politicians. The political has-beens it pulled together seemed so lacking in prospects that an analyst dubbed it a "coalition of the lonely."[6] Once assembled, it proved to be capable of waging an effective campaign, regardless of its makers' liabilities.

Forming the Bloc

The nucleus of SPS consisted of survivors from the glory days of Russia's democratic movement. The all-embracing association they created in 1990, Democratic Russia (DR), lost its hegemony among reformers within a year or two.[7] DR activists, in league with agents of economic transformation like Yegor Gaidar and Anatolii Chubais, parented Russia's Choice in 1993.[8] Renamed Russia's Democratic Choice (DVR) in 1994, the party was battered by disputes over Chechnya and Yeltsin's leadership and missed the 5 percent cutoff in the 1995 election.[9] Outside of Yabloko, the only liberals to make it into the Duma won seats in districts.

By the year before the 1999 election, prominent liberals were calling for a truce. Fourteen of them struck up an Organizational Committee of Rightist and Centrist Forces in December 1998. Perversely, signs of cooperation stimulated organizational proliferation, as politicians sought out bargaining chips for the negotiations on a joint electoral vehicle. Sergei Kiriyenko established a New Force movement in late 1998 and hired one of Russia's best public relations firms. Nikkolo M. Boris Nemtsov, the former governor of Nizhnii Novgorod who served as first deputy premier in 1997–98, ginned up his own virtual organization, Young Russia. As nonstop talks opened in the spring, cellphone-toting envoys shuttled between DVR, which had maintained a skeleton organization and was sponsor of an umbrella group, Right Cause; Voice of Russia, the governors' outfit headed by Konstantin Titov; older boutique parties such as Irina Khakamada's Common Cause, Boris Fëdorov's Forward Russia, and Konstantin Borovoi's Party of Economic Freedom; and even the fallen party of power, Our Home Is Russia (NDR), which was in the throes of an identity crisis. Yabloko was the only major liberal organization not at all interested in exploring the possibilities of a grand right-of-center alliance. Ego clashes were largely at the root of the liberals' divisions, but issues of principle did flare. For example, Kiriyenko, who had businessmen and managers in his entourage, steered clear of Chubais, fearing he was tarred by the failings of privatization.[10] DVR leaders and Nemtsov resisted collaboration with Chernomyrdin, reliving animosities from their days in government, and Chernomyrdin faced a youth faction within NDR that preferred a philosophically conservative course.[11] Holdovers from Democratic Russia distrusted anyone who did not imbibe in their passion for human rights causes.

Hope swelled in the summer of 1999 that a consensus figure could reconcile the cacophonous liberals. The candidate for savior was Sergei Stepashin, the second-to-last of Yeltsin's prime ministers, who was suddenly available for reassignment when the president supplanted him in early August with Vladimir Putin. As Nemtsov remarked, "Everyone, including our most ambitious politicians, agree that Sergei Stepashin should lead the right-wing bloc."[12] Stepashin had held major cabinet portfolios, was considered a Yeltsin confidant, took pro-market positions on the economy, and, like Putin and Sergei Shoigu, was a *silovik*, a product of the Russian security services. Imported as a mediator, he swiftly grew frustrated and was unable to get agreement on his personal role or the Kremlin's attitude. On August 21 he declared he would run for the Duma as a nonpartisan district candidate in his hometown of St. Petersburg. Two days later he said he would be on the Yabloko slate.

Stepashin's huffy departure brought the players back to the table. Within days, Kiriyenko and Governor Titov announced the formation of the SPS electoral bloc. The much maligned but immensely influential Chubais pulled the strings behind the scenes to close the gap with the "old liberals" in DVR and Democratic Russia.[13] SPS had its founding congress on August 29 and filed a list of candidates on September 4. The top positions were delicately allocated—Kiriyenko first, Nemtsov second, Khakamada third—and hard bargaining ensued for the remaining slots.[14] As a consolation prize, Titov chaired the board. Gaidar, the founder of DVR, the most capable of SPS's precursors, swallowed his pride and accepted a spot on the Moscow sublist.[15] The odd liberal, aside from the perpetually standoffish Yabloko, refrained from joining, but the birth of SPS presented the right as finally putting collective above personal interests.[16]

Organization

Anatolii Chubais, the dealmaker in August 1999 and the coordinator of Yeltsin's reelection campaign in 1996, was appointed chairman of the campaign committee. At first, distracted by his duties as CEO of Unified Energy System, Russia's electricity monopoly, he held back from the campaign. The absence of a strong executive hand at SPS's campaign headquarters produced what one participant called utter chaos (*bardak*).[17] Fierce competition for control erupted between the old hands from Russia's Democratic Choice and the new faces that Sergei Kiriyenko invited into the coalition.[18] Only when Chubais engaged full-time in running the campaign did the SPS effort gain coherency. Chubais functioned as energizer, supreme arbiter of conflicts, and fund-raiser. He pried money from Russia's most prosperous companies, private and public. Big donors included the Transneft pipeline firm, Alpha Bank, Unified Energy System itself, and Siberian Aluminum, whose president, Oleg Deripaska, had bankrolled Voice of Russia and one of whose officers, Konstantin Remchukov, was to be placed high on the SPS candidates' list.[19] Chubais squirreled away funds for an advertising blitz in the stretch drive of the campaign, recalling how Vladimir Zhirinovskii and the LDPR had surged to victory over Russia's Choice in the weeks before the 1993 election.

Chubais's trusted political adviser, Leonid Gozman, served as chief strategist and de facto day-to-day manager of the campaign and worked closely with a cadre of seasoned organizers reporting to the SPS executive committee. They had cut their teeth politically in the anticommunist movement ten years before. Gozman also tapped the creative talents of journalists, artists, and campaign advisers such as Daniil Dondurei, Maksim Sokolov, and Murat Gel'man, who together with others constituted the "Creative Council" of the SPS coalition after the election was over. The multiheaded SPS leadership and the prima donna propensities of its members were a recurrent worry. Kiriyenko fouled up the time and financial budget by persevering with an eccentric project begun in the spring of 1999—running for mayor of Moscow against the invincible Yurii Luzhkov. He refused pleas to pull out, even as colleagues pointed out he might dissuade Muscovites from voting SPS and would do more for the cause campaigning in his native Nizhnii Novgorod and the Volga area.[20]

A modern media-centered campaign came naturally to SPS. They aimed at a younger, well-educated, and urban crowd and understood that such people ingest their political information from television. The bloc allocated most of its communications budget to television, reserving paid spots for general themes and unpaid time for individual candidates. The most attractive SPS leaders were delegated to perform regularly on news and talk shows, even when a payment had to be made for their appearance. To cultivate the youth audience, SPS hosted a series of rock concerts called "Ty prav!" ("You Are Right"). In Moscow and the metropolitan areas, it put up splashy billboards, shooting for voters who commuted to work by car, not subway. Bloc planners contracted professional pollsters and focus group moderators to conduct voluminous research. Armed with the data, they focused first on a dozen big cities, pinpointing loyal and prospective voters and pelting them with direct mail and door-to-door contact. Some voters in Moscow were canvassed several times.[21]

A windfall for the SPS campaign was gracious coverage in the national media. The most congenial outlet was RTR, the state-owned television network; its president, Mikhail Shvydkoi, and urbane weekend anchorman, Nikolai Svanidze, were stalwart liberals who thought well of the bloc. Media Minister Mikhail Lesin, RTR's protector within the government, is the founder of Video International, Russia's leading advertising agency, and it was to Video International that Chubais turned to produce his campaign videos. ORT and NTV also aired on occasion sympathetic stories on SPS, although their principals, Boris Berezovskii and Vladimir Gusinskii, were sworn enemies of Chubais.

Representatives of Russian Democracy

The Union of Right Forces staked out the liberal pole in the election. A double entendre in its name accentuated the point: the Russian adjective for "right" or "right-wing" (pravoye) also connotes "correct" or "righteous."[22] The big guns in SPS had occupied high government positions in the Yeltsin decade—Gaidar and Kiriyenko as prime minister and Chubais and Nemtsov as first deputy prime minister—and had pursued policies consistent with their values. Voters who backed SPS should have done so with their eyes open. SPS's approach was to target not the typical voter but the select minority who shared the bloc's vision, and to hope it was greater than 5 percent of the electorate. Its leaders were preoccupied with the Duma and had no intention of being players in the presidential election.

Not a few planks in the SPS platform harkened back to Russia's Choice in 1993 and Russia's Democratic Choice in 1995. The bloc described itself as "the representative of Russian democracy" and referred contentedly to the liberal reforms it had helped promulgate:

"Communist Russia was a country without a future. Today [as a result of the reforms], Russia has a future."[23] Its pro-Westernism was unapologetic:

> Citizens of Russia should live no worse than those in Europe, no worse than Germans or Swedes. Let's stop looking for a special way. A special way means poverty and illegality. It's a path to a dead end like North Korea and Colombia. . . . The Russian state needs a *Yevroremont* [a European-style remodeling, as might be done to an apartment]. This is the task of educated and powerful professionals, who share convictions and the values of a free society and who protect the interests of individuals, not the state. This is the cause of the Union of Right Forces. Vote for a Russian Euro-standard! Vote for the Union of Right Forces![24]

Regarding the economy, SPS called for trimmed government spending, a balanced federal budget, and a flat income tax of 12 percent, among other unalloyed liberal reforms. Following up on the priorities of Chubais, Nemtsov, and Kiriyenko in government in 1997–98, it cast the oligarchs as parasites who had to be bridled in the interests of Russia's "new middle class."

In the political area, SPS took its distance from its architects' former idol, Boris Yeltsin. Kiriyenko recommended that Yeltsin retire; Nemtsov made it less personal by saying Russia should bid farewell to "elderly and ill" leaders. The bloc deplored the democratic deficit it said had accumulated on both the executive and the legislative side of the constitutional aisle, promising an end to "our superfluous dependence on the president . . . and the huge destructive force of the anti-reformist parliament."[25] On Chechnya, SPS renounced the antiwar stance DVR had taken in 1995, during the first war. It supported the military strike, saying the second war was thrust on Russia by the Chechen incursion into Dagestan and the terrorist bombings in Moscow. Chubais, emoting on the topic, helicoptered around Chechnya to "turn on the lights" as towns and villages passed into army hands. Some in the bloc's human rights wing, such as Duma member Sergei Kovalëv (formerly a prisoner of conscience in a Soviet labor camp), dissented, yet could not derail the policy. Kovalëv, given a place on the SPS national slate, never showed up in ads or promotional materials. Those steering the bloc felt that romantic and revolutionary gestures had had their day in Russian politics and the residual constituency animated by humanist concerns could safely be forfeited to Yabloko.[26]

A gimmick SPS adroitly used to underline its issue commitments was to collect signatures in favor of a national referendum on four questions: legal guarantees for private property; rescinding Duma deputies' immunity from criminal prosecution; military reform and the elimination of conscription; and a constitutional amendment to limit the president's right to dismiss the government. The referendum was aborted, but the petition assisted in identifying SPS with these causes and dampening its elitist image.[27]

Like Unity, and unlike the KPRF and OVR, SPS added a strong generational element to its campaign. Its leaflets printed the age of its troika of leaders (Kiriyenko, thirty-seven; Nemtsov, forty; Khakamada, forty-four), and other materials divulged that its candidates averaged forty years of age, all but three had university degrees, and the majority were "lawyers or economists."[28] Unlike Unity, though, SPS crowed that its team knew the folkways of power and had a wealth of practical experience: "The Union of Right Forces today is youthfulness and experience. . . . We know exactly what needs to be done. We know which laws need to be passed. . . . Our laws were prepared long ago." To skeptics who held that its experience was with failed policies, SPS retorted defiantly: "We have made mistakes, but we have never lied. And we have also accomplished much."[29]

The Putin Card

As Putin built a reputation separate from Yeltsin's, SPS strategists sensed an opportunity to ingratiate themselves with a winner. Liberal publicists began making glowing references to Putin. With the vote a few days away, Chubais—who knew Putin from St. Petersburg and from their time in government in 1997–98—persuaded Putin to meet with Kiriyenko in the Kremlin to accept a copy of SPS's recommendations for economic reform. On December 13 Kiriyenko handed a Bible-sized tome to the prime minister. Television cameras whirring, Putin plunked it down on his desk and stated he was pleased by SPS's willingness to bring "young and energetic" people into the government.[30] The morning after, SPS billboards and leaflets exclaimed "Putin for President, Kiriyenko into the Duma!" Its television clips for the balance of the campaign rolled footage from the meeting.

The Districts

The single-mandate districts were barren soil for SPS. It nominated sixty-six candidates. National headquarters calculated that only a handful were competitive and perforce skimped on resources, tasking DVR's decaying outposts in the regions with supervision of the effort.[31] The provincial elite were not a bulwark for the bloc. Even in Samara, with Titov in the governor's chair, the bloc had an official nominee in only one of five districts. The most that can be said is that few governors actively impeded SPS, an honor they did not necessarily extend to other parties such as Yabloko and OVR.[32] SPS negotiated fitfully with Yabloko over local agreements to ward off fratricide between the two big liberal parties. Their candidates ended up competing against one another in thirty-three districts.

Yabloko

Russia's second large liberal aggregation, the Yabloko party, has been as much a mainstay of post-Soviet Russian politics as the KPRF. It went into the 1999 election with a profile barely altered from four years before and confident that at last its fidelity to principle would bear fruit.

Yabloko originated in 1993 as an electoral bloc dominated by intellectuals and dedicated to liberalism with a difference. Its leader, Grigorii Yavlinskii, had celebrated the difference since becoming a public figure in 1990. An economist by training, he had coauthored a famous reform project, the "Five Hundred Days Plan," which Mikhail Gorbachev and Boris Yeltsin considered implementing but then scrapped. Yeltsin in 1991 put the initiation of radical reform in the hands of another young economist, Yegor Gaidar, instead of Yavlinskii. The Gaidar-Yavlinskii relationship was fraught from that moment, and each was regularly to cast aspersions on the other's professional abilities.[33] For Yabloko, the reform course initiated by Gaidar was reckless and inhumane, although pointing in the correct general direction. Its economic program, beginning with the 1993 Duma campaign, had social-democratic as well as free-market overtones.[34] The party lit into Yeltsin for sacrificing popular welfare and often voted against the government's austerity budgets. It also "paid special attention . . . to protection-of-rights, humanitarian, and institutional subjects," which it asserted had been sold short by executive-branch liberals who would pay any price to share in power.[35] Yabloko hotly opposed the first Chechen war, agitated for a downsizing of presidential powers, and castigated the antidemocratic drift under Yeltsin. More than anything, the hallmark of its liberalism was independence—of government and of entangling alliances, even with fellow liberals. Yavlinskii insisted on standing for president in 1996 and spurned almost yearly offers to join the cabinet of ministers, posing impossible conditions.[36] In 1995 he vetoed a proposal by Gaidar to form a common Yabloko-DVR candidates' list. Yavlinskii's prickliness did not exempt members of his own party, a steady stream of whom left in exasperation.[37] So implacable was he against unification of the right-wing players that there were no sustained negotiations with him in 1999.[38]

Reorganizing for Success

Stability in leadership and worldview did not keep Yabloko from making several innovations. To broaden its appeal and counteract its insular reputation, it looked outside its walls for star candidates for the first time since 1993. The former prime minister, Sergei Stepashin, having jilted SPS, accepted the second spot on the national party slate. Also recruited were Nikolai Travkin, the founder of the Democratic Party of Russia; Mikhail Zadornov, a former finance minister who had earlier resigned from the party; the Russian minister for federal and nationality affairs, Vyacheslav Mikhailov; and an outspoken former press secretary of Yeltsin's, Pavel Voshchanov.[39] New blood notwithstanding, Yabloko's was the most stable of all the national lists, and it was dominated by members of the party.[40]

Yabloko complemented the roster changes with a revised organizational look. Vyacheslav Igrunov, deputy chairman of the party, had been building regional chapters since 1995—they now numbered fifty-seven—and training cadres at a party school outside Moscow. Taking over as campaign chairman at the September party conference, he relied heavily on the revitalized provincial base. In the 1995 and 1996 campaigns, Yabloko had paid commercial firms to work out strategy and produce campaign materials, which were often frivolous and cartoonish, incongruent with the party's somber demeanor. This time around, Igrunov and the party's activists were in command and outside consultants did no more than shoot television clips for Yavlinskii. Yabloko allegedly raised some $7 million in campaign financing, securing fat donations from Gazprom, the head of the Media-Most media empire (Vladimir Gusinskii), and the president of Russia's number two oil producer at the time, Yukos (Mikhail Khodorkovskii).[41] The RTR and especially NTV television networks reported respectfully on Yabloko. In addition to outlays on modern-mode television advertising, the party took premodern activities more seriously than anyone except the KPRF. Yavlinskii barnstormed through thirty regions of the country between October and December, addressing pep rallies and giving press conferences. Yabloko spent freely on printed materials and souvenirs, summoning its members to dispense them and talk them up.

Party of the Future

The party's research shop early on sketched a composite Yabloko voter—attracted to the organization, pro-reform but disillusioned with its practice in Russia. He or she would be youngish, better educated than average, urban, and in white-collar employ, but adapting poorly to Russia's new economic conditions—for instance, a civil servant or army officer, a scientist, or an engineer. To connect with such people, Yabloko expatiated on issues and policy and transmitted its pronouncements through all media, including a highbrow website. It underscored its status as a party with permanence, contrasting that to passing electoral alliances like Unity, OVR, and SPS: "We have existed since 1993 and, in distinction from the electoral blocs, we will exist after the election. You will be able to put questions to us about what we have done and why we have taken this or that decision. The blocs of bosses, which are just after more and more power, will fall apart right after the election and there will be no one there to ask."[42]

The Yabloko electoral program styled it "the party of the future," "the party of hope," and "the party of clean hands" best qualified to lead Russia to better days. In the political domain, it recapitulated its call for constitutional reforms to curb presidential prerogatives and tossed in new suggestions for popular election of the Federation Council and a ban on government ownership of media outlets. Despite previous social-democratic overtures, the nub of its economic program in 1999 was resolutely liberal, as it pledged tax reductions (to a 10 percent levy on income and 20 percent on profits), legalization of the "shadow economy," and production-sharing agreements and free trade zones to woo foreign capital. Not noting the possible contradiction, Yabloko swore that its economic approach would be "oriented toward the social sphere" and would quickly raise living standards, its "most important aim." Immediate priorities were hikes in pensions, social security benefits, soldier pay, and student stipends; increasing the minimum wage to the poverty level; more money for science; and renegotiation of Russia's external debt.

Some in Yabloko's brain trust wanted to package these statements, which often verged on the platitudinous, in a glossy visual envelope and to frame the party historically. Vyacheslav Igrunov believed Russia to have moved into a period of "thermidor," as the final, waning phase of its latest revolution, and saw Yavlinskii as the perfect figure for tying such an era in with the Soviet and Russian past. The Yabloko standard bearer was a proponent of new economic and political arrangements, yet had not been corrupted by office and had never favored the dissolution of the USSR. To convey the notion, Igrunov commissioned a short film. Shot in black and white to invoke nostalgia, it featured selected achievements of the Soviet period (such as the launch of *Sputnik* in 1957) and ended with Yavlinskii vowing to build upon what earlier generations had accomplished. Yavlinskii hated the film and yanked it from circulation. Short-circuiting Igrunov, he had another production team do simple and more populist commercials, reiterating Yabloko's integrity and desire for kinder, gentler reforms that would assuage the pain Russia endured in the 1990s.[43] Yavlinskii flaunted his inflexibility as a virtue. A TV clip broadcast during the final week of the campaign depicted him in the company of acolytes, asking, "If a person says for ten years that two times two equals four, is he stupid or principled—what do you think?" He would never cheat on the arithmetic to curry public favor, even if his detractors complain he is "saying the same old thing again."[44]

The Enemy Next Door

Although Yabloko officials first viewed Fatherland–All Russia as their main competition,[45] their campaign program also flayed "radicalism of any type" and equated the misguided reforms of Yeltsin's governments with revolutionary Bolshevism.[46] From a subsidiary theme, swipes at their rightist kin burgeoned into a master theme. By the tail end of the campaign, Yabloko was attributing no achievements to the Kremlin-friendly liberals and bent over backward to counterpose its policy positions to SPS's. The anti-SPS rhetoric could take on hyperventilating proportions. For instance, when asked why Yabloko did not support Kiriyenko, SPS's nominee for mayor of Moscow, Yavlinskii responded in the following way: "During the course of the campaign, they [SPS] positioned themselves not as a right-liberal party that defends human rights but as a party that defends, in words, anyway, the principles of private, burgher [sic] property. A party that defends private property but does not defend human rights is a party that traditionally falls into the category of totalitarian and pro-fascist."[47]

There was more to this bombast than trolling for votes. One concrete issue—the renewed fighting in Chechnya—struck a nerve and brought the simmering rivalry between the liberal factions to a boil. SPS, as discussed, dropped its predecessors' opposition to a military solution to the conflict. Yabloko was of two minds on the issue, and discerned from polls that the electorate was torn, too. Its September conference approved limited military action against "terrorist aggression"; Stepashin voiced solidarity with the security choices made by Putin and the government he had led until the escalation of violence that summer.[48] In a speech in early November, Yavlinskii, without input from Stepashin, demanded a halt to the Russian troops' advance at the Terek River and the opening of negotiations with the Chechen president, Aslan Maskhadov. He was promptly arraigned in the media as a traitor. Anatolii Chubais branded his statement a knife in the army's back, and on November 25 the two squared off in a prime-time debate on NTV. While accepting the armed response to guerrilla attacks as just and necessary, Yavlinskii said it was "impossible to install peace by force." Chubais retorted by asking sarcastically if Yavlinskii would have recommended a cease-fire and political settlement with Adolph Hitler, the last person to order an invasion of Russia.[49] The exchange delighted SPS leaders, who were angling to glue themselves politically to Putin. It marked Yabloko as out of step with the majority of the populace. Campaign chairman Igrunov was furious with Yavlinskii, saying his pacifism was not only bad electoral politics but violated the position the party officially adopted in September. He was later to claim it cost Yabloko half of its supporters.[50] In an awkward aside, Stepashin discreetly backed away from his adopted party. In the closing weeks of the campaign, he seldom spoke on Yabloko's behalf and put his time into winning his single-mandate seat in St. Petersburg.[51]

The Districts

Yabloko fielded 113 district candidates, and its local branches endorsed a few more. Yavlinskii channeled money to the 15 to 20 he thought had a serious chance of winning and left the rest to fend for themselves. In some places there were tussles over nominations between a local old guard, regional leaders Igrunov had imposed, and cronies of Yavlinskii, whose financial control gave him the final say.[52] Igrunov consulted with the early favorite, OVR, and eventually with SPS to avoid head-butting with Yabloko nominees that would fracture the non-KPRF, non-Unity vote. There was some accommodation with SPS but far less with OVR: Yabloko faced SPS opposition in 33 of 113 districts and OVR opposition in 60.[53]

In trying to build regional wrinkles into the campaign, Yabloko was hamstrung by having to go without gubernatorial patronage. As Yavlinskii's antigovernment rhetoric became shriller, for many governors Yabloko "was no less oppositionist than the communists."[54] The party had somewhat more cachet among mayors and municipal councilors. In the Yaroslavl region's two districts, it tried for synergy with the campaign for governor of its nominee, Sergei Vakhrukov, the chairman of the regional legislature. In its regional stronghold in 1995, St. Petersburg, it showcased Stepashin and the campaign of former vice governor Igor Artem'ev for governor against Vladimir Yakovlev. Yabloko nominated seven candidates in the city's eight districts; they faced six opponents there from OVR and four from SPS. In Moscow, there were seven Yabloko nominees in fifteen Duma districts, arrayed in those districts against five OVR designees and three from SPS.

The Voters in 1999

We review the mass response to the liberals' campaigns in a single analytical sweep. It reveals both differences and underlying commonalities.

Keeping and Earning Support

In the immediate context of 1999, Russian voters diverged in the routes they took to the two primary liberal parties. As befits a regular on the stage, 65 percent of Yabloko's voters recalled making up their minds by earlier than one month before election day. For the newly minted Union of Right Forces, that proportion was 36 percent; the average in the electorate was 48 percent. As befits a party that lost altitude in the polls, numerous intended Yabloko voters strayed to another party. Fifty-one percent of those planning to vote for Yabloko (as of when we quizzed them during the campaign) did so, as against 49 percent who reneged—the highest fraction of any party or quasi party elected to the Duma. Sixty-six percent of would-be SPS voters delivered on the intent.[55]

In the longer time frame, SPS and Yabloko were not so unalike. Across parliamentary elections, their electors displayed more continuity than any peer group except communists. By testimony of our 1995–2000 survey panel, 28 percent of 1999's Yabloko voters were loyalists who had voted for it four years before; the mean for all parties was 23 percent and for all parties other than the KPRF, 9 percent. Twenty-two percent of SPS voters were loyalists (taking that to mean 1995 voters for a precursor organization, mostly Russia's Democratic Choice). Yabloko and SPS also had unusually large minorities of converts from within the same family of parties, pushing the total of loyalists and in-family converts to 40 percent for each of them. That being said, there were subtle differences between them on two fronts. First, SPS had more novices, first-time voters, among its supporters (15 percent) than Yabloko or any other party or bloc. Second, SPS and Yabloko netted their out-of-family converts from disparate pools. The biggest reservoir for SPS was former centrist voters, followed by former supporters of the 1995 government party, NDR. Yabloko, with its more leftish economic program, was strongest among former socialists, with former centrists in second place.[56]

Liberal politicians connected with the citizenry through the same ganglia as everyone else. In spite of Yabloko's fondness for person-to-person and print-age methods, our survey data show its voters to have ranked high in but one aspect of premodern campaign contact—home canvassing, where it was second to the KPRF (but with a measly contact rate of 1 percent, and 3 percent among Yabloko voters). Yabloko stood fourth among the six major parties in receipt of mailed materials, sixth in billboards, posters, and leaflets, and fourth in attendance at rallies. SPS was fifth in canvassing, mailings, and street advertising and third in rallies.[57] The liberals' purposive efforts in the modern media arena were not notably efficacious. Among survey respondents who said they strongly liked any party's televised advertising clips, 17 percent liked SPS's ads and 12 percent liked Yabloko's, leaving them fifth and sixth among the large parties. In the news realm (see appendix table C-6), our survey-based modeling shows exposure to NTV as slightly conducive to voting for both SPS and Yabloko (though not at a statistically significant level) and the two state networks working in opposite directions, with viewing of ORT exerting a negative effect on the Yabloko vote and viewing of RTR having a positive effect on the SPS vote. An exotic result is that membership in the fraction of the adult population that does not watch television at all was predictive of the Yabloko vote ($p \leq .10$), implying that divorce from the quotidian flow of information—being in a political time warp, perhaps—heightened receptivity to Yavlinskii's party.

Demographics and Current Conditions

Sociodemographic correlates of support for SPS and Yabloko go in parallel (see appendix table B-1). They also conform to the targeting decisions of these organizations' campaign planners. All things taken into account, the mass of voters for the liberals were more apt than other citizens to be younger, live in big cities, and have completed post-secondary schooling. The urbanization effect is larger for SPS, the education effect larger for Yabloko; SPS also took a hit from residency in Moscow, a by-product, one may assume, of the Kiriyenko-Luzhkov mayoral tilt. Only in their youthfulness were SPS and Yabloko voters much like the 1999 supporters of the party of power, Unity.

Between the two liberal formations, the one sharp difference—foretold, again, in their market research—concerns standard of living. The high social status of Yabloko voters was out of whack with their low-to-medium incomes and consumption levels. For SPS voters, material welfare was consonant with status. The total effect for our consumption variable is −.03 (minus 3 percentage points) on the probability of voting Yabloko and .23 (plus 23 percentage points) on the probability of voting SPS. The consumption effect for SPS dwarfs that for any other party.

Tracing the electoral consequences of perceptions of current conditions reinforces the point. SPS supporters were swayed more than any in the electorate by the sense of getting ahead in the 1990s and were second only to Unity voters in responsiveness to satisfaction with the economy as a whole. Yabloko voters displayed negligible positive effects for gain in the 1990s and assessment of the state of the economy, and for pocketbook welfare in the preceding year the effect was negative—the largest minus value on this indicator in the 1999 election.

The regional factor was of secondary import for the liberals. SPS and Yabloko were about average among parties and quasi parties in dispersal of their votes across the Russian landmass.[58] Save for Titov of SPS in Samara, the two had no steadfast allies among provincial governors and presidents. SPS took more than 22 percent of the vote in Samara—the only region where either liberal party exceeded 20 percent—but the communists took 4 percentage points more. OVR's and Luzhkov's strength depressed liberal voting in Moscow. In St. Petersburg, whose governor was also in the OVR camp, SPS came in a close second to Unity in the popular vote, and Yabloko finished a disappointing fifth (after Unity, SPS, OVR, and the KPRF).

Partisanship and Issue Opinions

Small minorities of the electorate in 1999—about 8 percent, all told—felt themselves partisans of the liberal parties. As with the other parties and quasi parties, they tended to vote for the political organization with which they identified. The total effect for the partisanship variable in our statistical model (appendix table B-1) is .66 for the SPS vote and .43 for the Yabloko vote. Not a few self-proclaimed Yabloko partisans (as ascertained in wave 1 of our 1999–2000 panel survey) voted for another party list on December 19; fewer of SPS's smaller contingent of partisans did.[59] In raw proportions, partisans were more plentiful in the Yabloko electorate (39 percent) than in the SPS electorate (22 percent).

Liberal partisans in 1999–2000 had a nontrivial chance of having had similar attachments in the mid-1990s. Seventeen percent of the SPS partisans in year 2000 among our 1995–2000 survey panel had been partisans of a precursor party in 1995, and 27 percent had been partisans of some liberal party or other. Twenty percent of Yabloko partisans in 2000 had been Yabloko partisans in 1995, and 35 percent partisans of a liberal party. Like communists, liberals who were strong partisans were more likely to have had continuity in partisan attachment.[60]

The liberal parties conceived of themselves as guardians of ideals and principles: SPS as the instrument of the Westernizers who had awakened Russia from its torpor and now proposed to give reform a second wind; Yabloko as the friend of reform and the foe of the heartless way it was perpetrated in the 1990s. Both SPS and Yabloko went to great lengths to systematize their policy ideas and to hang their 1999 campaigns on them. We would expect, therefore, that the vote for the liberals would correspond perceptibly to issue opinions, as was the case with the communist vote. At best, the survey data lend faint confirmation to this expectation.

On the SPS vote (see appendix table B-1), there are sizable total effects for right self-placement on the left-right scale (.17) and preference for a more democratic over a communistic regime (.08). On the Yabloko vote, there is a significant negative effect of −.09 for endorsement of rule by a strongman leader. These are not very strong associations. If we look at issue opinions in combination, as a bloc of explanatory variables (appendix table B-3), they are about one-sixth as potent predictors of the vote for both SPS and Yabloko as they are for the KPRF, and about one-third as potent for the liberals as they are for Unity. It is the latter comparison that is counterintuitive, given Unity's scorn for ideology and its mood- and symbol-centered campaign.

Why were the liberals not more proficient at mobilizing citizens on the issues? We suspect their plight owed something to popular cynicism toward any Moscow-based party that shared in the responsibility for the reform roller-coaster of the 1990s. Unity, the upstart from the provinces, may have seemed to many Russian voters more like a proponent of change than SPS or Yabloko, despite the fact that Unity never campaigned for accelerated economic reforms or democratization. In terms of electoral alignment, SPS and Yabloko did no worse than the other parties on three of the seven issue opinions for which we tested: economic reform, federalism, and Chechnya. On economic reform, mass incredulity might well have played a large part. On centralization versus decentralization of the federal system, no liberal party telegraphed a forthright position. On Chechnya, where there was a clear difference of approach between SPS and Yabloko, neither approach caught on with the voters—whatever the aspirations of Chubais, wanting to cast SPS as hawkish and patriotic, or the apprehension of Igrunov that Yavlinskii's dovishness was scaring away voters in the millions. The liberals' educational endeavor on the war misfired: the great majority of voters either had no idea what SPS's or Yabloko's stance on Chechnya was or thought it was hard-line.[61] On a fourth issue, presidential versus parliamentary rule, SPS was caught in a contradiction, in that it saluted expansion of parliamentary powers, yet was manufactured by politicians who had earned their spurs in the executive branch and who backed President Yeltsin's suppression of an elected parliament in 1993. The recruitment of former prime minister Stepashin may have lured Yabloko into the same trap. Stepashin had been a member of Yeltsin's circle for a decade, which dented the halo of moral scourge of the establishment so carefully constructed by Yavlinskii.

The issue position that actually worked for Yabloko—resistance to one-person rule—is the one most congruent with Yavlinskii's waspish style and allergy to cooperation with presidents and bureaucrats. As for SPS, its title probably aided citizens in locating it in the left-right space, as was intended by its makers when they chose it, and its linkage with the value of a democratic regime sits well with its forerunners' record of anticommunism and expressions of admiration for Western institutions.

Evaluations of Political Players

No matter what their strategists thought and wished, SPS and Yabloko felt no electoral impact from popular assessments of incumbents. None of the parties in 1999, SPS and Yabloko included, was directly affected by pro- or anti-Yeltsin sentiment. Yabloko had been critical of Yeltsin since its invention in 1993, and one by one the makers of SPS had incurred Yeltsin's wrath or otherwise broken with him. Unity benefited from pro-Putin sentiment and the KPRF suffered from it; SPS and Yabloko did not systematically experience either. The well-choreographed encounter with Kiriyenko in Putin's office did SPS not an ounce of good, so far as can be made out from the survey data. It cannot be excluded that the visitation prevented pro-Putin opinions from damaging SPS's cause.[62]

A second set of political evaluations whose influence we have probed in this volume concerns the character of leaders. Grigorii Yavlinskii was the more senior of the two liberal headmen, both in age (forty-seven) and political longevity (active since 1990). Sergei Kiriyenko was a decade younger and, as a former prime minister, had flown higher politically; he had never sat in parliament or run in an election before 1999. Public evaluations of the two were uncannily similar. On the summary 0-to-10 scale used in our 1999–2000 panel survey, citizens rated Yavlinskii fourth of the six main party leaders, with a mean score of 4.28; Kiriyenko was fifth at 4.13. Trait by trait, respondents put Yavlinskii and Kiriyenko in a virtual dead heat (see table 6-1). On balance, they gave both men firmly positive assessments for intelligence and knowledge and moderately positive assessments for integrity; on strength and empathy, unfavorable assessments had a slight edge over the favorable. Russians, in short, tended to see both Kiriyenko and Yavlinskii as very smart and passably honest leaders but also as wimpish and aloof. Kiriyenko was the fourth-ranking party leader on strength and fifth on

Table 6-1. *Evaluations of Character Traits of Sergei Kiriyenko and Grigorii Yavlinskii*[a]

	Rating (percent)			
Trait	Yes/ probably yes	No/ probably no	Net yes/probably yes over no/ probably no	Ranking of net rating
Sergei Kiriyenko				
Intelligent and knowledge-able person	73	13	60	5
Strong leader	38	43	−5	4
Honest and trustworthy person	44	28	16	5
Really cares about people like you	34	37	−3	5
Grigorii Yavlinskii				
Intelligent and knowledge-able person	74	13	61	4
Strong leader	37	43	−7	5
Honest and trustworthy person	45	27	19	4
Really cares about people like you	36	37	−1	4

a. From 1999–2000 panel, wave 2 (N = 1,846 weighted cases). "Don't know" responses included in the denominator but not shown here.

the remaining three criteria; Yavlinskii ranked fifth on strength, by a razor-thin margin, and fourth on the others.

Table 6-2 indicates the associations between leadership assessments and voting for the right-wing party lists. It is redolent of the picture we have already chalked out for Unity, OVR, and the communists. Whatever else was missing from the suite of determinants of the liberal vote in 1999, leaders were not. As for Yevgenii Primakov and Gennadii Zyuganov, and less definitively for Sergei Shoigu, the increment in the character ratings that counts most is the third one, separating "Probably has" from "Has" the positive personality trait. For SPS, such a shift in the evaluation of Kiriyenko improved the chances of voting for the bloc threefold; for Yabloko and Yavlinskii, there was about a sixfold improvement. The liberals' problem was not the conversion of leadership evaluations into votes but the fact that citizens so infrequently placed rightist leaders in the upper zone of the character scale. Twenty-eight percent of the voters gave Shoigu the most complimentary assessment, 24 percent did for Primakov, and 22 percent did for Zyuganov,

Table 6-2. *SPS and Yabloko Votes and Evaluations of Characters of Kiriyenko and Yavlinskii*

Mean evaluation of four traits	Citizen opinion (percent)[a]	Predicted probability of voting for SPS/Yabloko[b]
Kiriyenko (SPS)		
Does not have the positive trait	7	.00
Probably does not have the positive trait	26	.02
Probably has the positive trait	58	.08
Has the positive trait	9	.28
Yavlinskii (Yabloko)		
Does not have the positive trait	6	.00
Probably does not have the positive trait	27	.01
Probably has the positive trait	58	.08
Has the positive trait	9	.46

a. N = 1,846 weighted cases. Missing data coded at the mean of the distribution for the specific trait.

b. Computed from multistage statistical model, holding causally prior and simultaneous variables constant at their medians. Sample N = 1,414; $p \leq .01$ for all cells in the column.

whereas a mere 9 percent did so for Kiriyenko and Yavlinskii. Their parties' electoral prospects were penalized accordingly.

For the third bloc of political assessments in our analysis, prospective evaluations of the parties' issue competence, a similar pattern applies. At the end of the day, as can be spied in table 6-3, far fewer Russian citizens felt SPS and Yabloko well qualified to deal with the issues than they did the KPRF, Unity, and OVR. Neither was graded higher than fourth on any one issue (they tied for fourth on foreign policy). The liberals were trusted most to steer the economy, but even here their boosters totaled less than 10 percent of the electorate. On Chechnya, only 1 percent saw SPS and 2 percent saw Yabloko as most competent. Irrespective of its support of the military offensive and Chubais's denunciation of Yavlinskii, SPS in fact ranked seventh on Chechnya, behind every other party that cleared the 5 percent barrier and also the Movement in Support of the Army, a fringe group which got about one-half of one percent of the popular vote.

Perceived issue competence was about as compelling a motivation for voting liberal in 1999 as it was for siding with any contender (see table 6-4). Ceteris paribus, the predicted probability of someone voting SPS exceeded .50 when the voter gave it top grades on two of the six issues; for Yabloko, the threshold was three issues. The stumbling bloc was not the conveyance of these assessments into votes but the paucity of citizens who held the liberals to be capable of dealing with Russia's prob-

Table 6-3. *Prospective Evaluations of Issue Competence of SPS and Yabloko*[a]

Issue	Say SPS/Yabloko is best prepared		Ranking
	Percent	Percent of those who named a party	
SPS			
Social security	4	6	5
Economy	8	11	5
Human rights	5	8	5
Chechnya	1	2	7
Foreign policy	3	5	4 (tie)
Crime and corruption	2	3	6
Yabloko			
Social security	4	7	4
Economy	8	11	4
Human rights	6	10	4
Chechnya	2	3	5
Foreign policy	3	5	4 (tie)
Crime and corruption	3	4	5

a. From 1999–2000 panel, wave 2 (N = 1,846 weighted cases).

Table 6-4. *SPS and Yabloko Votes and Prospective Evaluations of Their Issue Competence*

Number of issues SPS/ Yabloko can handle best	Citizen opinion (percent)[a]	Predicted probability of voting for SPS/Yabloko[b]
SPS		
0	88	.08
1	7	.31
2	2	.64
3	1	.84
4	0.5	.93
5	0.3	.97
6	0.8	.98
Yabloko		
0	87	.06
1	8	.19
2	2	.43
3	0.9	.69
4	0.9	.85
5	0.5	.93
6	0.8	.97

a. N = 1,846 weighted cases.

b. Computed from multistage statistical model, holding causally prior and simultaneous variables constant at their medians. Sample N = 1,414; $p \leq .01$ for all cells in the column.

lems. Eighty-eight percent of our survey respondents gave SPS the nod on no issues and 87 percent did for Yabloko; for Unity, OVR, and the KPRF, the proportion was 58, 79, and 68 percent, respectively. Five percent of citizens thought SPS the best on two or more issues, and the same for Yabloko; Unity, OVR, and the KPRF were judged the cream of the crop on two or more issues by 29, 11, and 25 percent.

The District Vote

Liberal campaigning in the single-mandate districts was desultory and largely relegated to local players. The upshot was dreadful: 5 deputies returned out of 66 nominees for SPS (down from the 9 elected by Russia's Democratic Choice in 1995) and 4 out of 113 for Yabloko (down from 14 in 1995).[63] In almost every winning situation, personal and parochial circumstances were key. Two SPS winners, Irina Khakamada in St. Petersburg and Boris Nemtsov in Nizhnii Novgorod, were high-visibility nominees from the national slate, and Nemtsov was a former governor of the region; a third prevailed with Governor Titov's blessing in Samara; the fourth and fifth were incumbents elected for DVR in 1995.[64] Two of the four Yabloko winners were the celebrity candidates Stepashin in St. Petersburg and Zadornov in Moscow; the other two, Sergei Popov in St. Petersburg and Mikhail Yemel'yanov in Rostov, were incumbents.[65] The several attempts to yoke district candidates to local champions of the party were exercises in futility. Yabloko's candidate for governor in Yaroslavl was trounced, as were the nominees in the two Duma districts there. Luzhkov won the Moscow mayoralty in a landslide, getting five times as many votes as Kiriyenko and depriving him of political coattails. The St. Petersburg gubernatorial election was postponed until May 2000, when the Yabloko nominee finished a distant second.

In crossover from party-list to district voting, there was not much to distinguish SPS and Yabloko from the others. Twenty percent of SPS supporters and 23 percent of Yabloko supporters, or slightly above average, voted the straight ticket (see table 6-5), but the practice of selective nominations meant that oftentimes liberal voters had no opportunity to duplicate their party-list choice. When a candidate from the party was on offer, Yabloko voters supported that candidate 40 percent of the time (spot on the nationwide average) and SPS voters 33 percent of the time (see table 6-6). When a nominee from the party was

Table 6-5. *Electoral Consistency between District and Party-List Votes, SPS and Yabloko Voters and All Voters*

Percent

Candidate voted for in the district	All districts			Districts where a nominee registered		
	SPS voters[a]	Yabloko voters[b]	All voters[c]	SPS voters[d]	Yabloko voters[e]	All voters[f]
Nominee of party supported in the party-list vote	20	23	17	33	40	40
Nominee of a different party	18	27	24	21	30	26
Independent candidate	46	37	45	33	17	24
Votes against all candidates	16	13	14	17	13	10

a. N = 125 weighted cases.
b. N = 90 weighted cases.
c. Excluding persons who voted against all parties in the party-list vote. N = 1,318 weighted cases.
d. N = 75 weighted cases.
e. N = 53 weighted cases.
f. Excluding persons who voted against all parties in the party-list vote. N = 566 weighted cases.

Table 6-6. *Electoral Consistency and Voter Knowledge, SPS and Yabloko Voters and All Voters, in Districts Where a Nominee of the Party Supported in the Party-List Vote Is Registered*[a]

Position	Percent			Percent of category who vote straight ticket		
	SPS voters[b]	Yabloko voters[c]	All voters[d]	SPS voters[b]	Yabloko voters[c]	All voters[d]
Knows there is a nominee and can identify the nominee	45	50	41	74	88	80
Knows there is a nominee and cannot identify the nominee	6	11	10	0	0	10
Thinks there is no nominee	22	20	24	20	0	21
Does not know if there is a nominee	27	19	25	16	0	24

a. Excludes persons who voted against all candidates in the district.
b. N = 66 weighted cases.
c. N = 46 weighted cases.
d. N = 509 weighted cases.

present in the district, about half of SPS and Yabloko voters were correctly informed about it, and under those conditions about three-quarters of SPS supporters and almost 90 percent of Yabloko supporters voted the straight ticket.

It was not, then, any exceptional laxity in emitting information that shot down a host of liberal candidates. Rather, parties whose national support was in the single digits and that got hardly any succor from regional elites had too little to fall back on when the usual limp efforts to link the district contests to the nationwide struggle came up short.

Presidential Postscript

The liberals were too weak to weigh in with authority in the presidential election and too much at daggers drawn to agree on their plight. Most of the chieftains in SPS, gratified to make it in numbers into the Duma, were against a quixotic presidential candidacy. When Konstantin Titov, a founder of SPS, declared for president in January, the bloc abandoned one of its own, leaving Titov to run an expensive but wasted campaign with support from some business groups but few established politicians. Sergei Kiriyenko and Anatolii Chubais signed on early to the Putin cause, Chubais speaking for most in arguing that, "since Putin's election is inevitable, it is better to support him now, despite his mistakes, in the hope that after the election he will promote policies backed by the Union of Right Forces."[66] The SPS council—with Yegor Gaidar, Irina Khakamada, and Boris Nemtsov abstaining and Titov sniping from the flanks—formally endorsed Putin in mid-March.[67] A second and a third liberal figured peripherally in the election: Ella Pamfilova, a minister in Yeltsin's early governments and head of Civic Dignity, and Yevgenii Savast'yanov, a little-known former leader of Democratic Russia who worked later in the Federal Security Service and the Kremlin administration. Mostly, they joined Titov in the curiosity column of the newspapers. Savast'yanov withdrew five days before election day. Titov and Pamfilova were to rack up fewer than 2 million votes, one-third of Titov's coming from the Samara region.[68]

Grigorii Yavlinskii was the one liberal candidate to give the appearance of mattering. After some hesitation in early to mid-January, he stepped forward. He journeyed as he always had—alone—and deflected proposals for unification around a consensual right-wing nominee.[69] Although he would not rule victory out, he knew it was a long shot and saw his dogged campaign in 2000, like 1996's, as an investment in his political future.

A Campaign of Second Thoughts

Disgruntled by Yabloko's showing in December, Yavlinskii ditched its campaign maestro, Vyacheslav Igrunov, and hired consultants to work with him to plot a more vigorous presidential drive. He terminated Igrunov's reliance on regional branches of Yabloko and indeed involved party structures little in any facet of the campaign.[70] Going to the banks, oil companies, and other businesses, he is said to have amassed a war chest of about $15 million, twice what Yabloko had for its Duma campaign. Ironically, it was Putin's massive lead in the polls that gave Yavlinskii the entrée. After December, Russia's capitalist elite—including financiers who had pulled out their wallets for the Unity bloc—were unnerved by the specter of coexisting with a hugely popular president indebted politically to no one but his predecessor and the mass public. For Putin to lose the election was neither desirable nor feasible; putting him to the inconvenience of a runoff was both. Quietly, therefore, certain plutocrats made substantial payments to the Yavlinskii team, in the hopes that he would bleed away enough votes to deprive Putin of a majority and trigger a second round.[71] The money enabled Yavlinskii to about double his spending on direct mailings, handouts, and billboards. His posted materials were a close second to Zyuganov's in volume, and his leaflets and street propaganda were more in evidence than those of any candidate. In the big cities, he was far and away the most visible.[72]

Gusinskii's NTV network provided Yavlinskii with all the positive stories, interviews, and photo ops he could ask for. To a lesser extent, so did Luzhkov's TV-Tsentr. Even state-owned but Berezovskii-controlled ORT and the government's RTR got in on the act, though without the zest of the others. News stories pictured Yavlinskii shaking hands with shoppers, attending an Orthodox mass, donating blood at a clinic, and talking soccer with young athletes. Sometimes accompanied by his wife, he made the rounds of Oprah-like talk shows and lifestyle programs, jabbering about "health, cooking, and happy couples."[73] In the print media, Yavlinskii got judicious support from the weekly *Argumenty i fakty* and the daily *Komsomol'skaya pravda,* two of Russia's high-circulation newspapers, and the open endorsement of *Novaya gazeta,* a small paper with an elite readership. Only with the vote a few days off did

ORT, undoubtedly at the Kremlin's bidding, do a U-turn to attack mode. Reports tasked Yavlinskii with illegally accepting funds from Americans and Germans, bribing journalists, concealing ill health, and having cosmetic surgery to reclaim his youthful look. ORT broadcast a press conference supposedly organized by "Gays for Yavlinskii," insinuating that he was a homosexual. It refused to air a paid Yavlinskii ad, saying it showed "disrespect for representatives of state authorities," and canceled two interview programs on which he was to speak.[74]

Throughout, Yavlinskii pleaded with voters to keep an open mind. Some of his TV spots had ordinary voters saying they regretted not having voted for Yabloko in December. One video showed him comforting wounded veterans of Chechnya, panning to a young man exclaiming, "If they had listened to [Yavlinskii] maybe everything would have been better. There would not have been so many victims, so many crying mothers."[75] Heeding his media consultants, Yavlinskii cast himself less as a teacher and more as a doer. Ads detailed his practical experience in the Soviet bureaucracy and in various roles since 1991. He dropped in on an army garrison near Moscow and was filmed confiding that his father was a career officer and that military pay should be raised.

The Yavlinskii campaign was generally less condemnatory in tone than the Yabloko campaign for the Duma.[76] Although it duly reiterated economic themes from the fall, the burden was on politics. In his spiels on Chechnya, Yavlinskii did not tangle with Putin personally, laying responsibility for the conduct of the campaign on the cabinet and the generals. Talking about the inadequacies of the new Duma, he referred to the machinations of Putin's "allies in the communist party," that is, to the KPRF deputies who had signed an accord on parliamentary business with the Unity caucus.

Yavlinskii's essential message was that he was the only bona fide *demokrat* on offer and the one who would stand up for the individual against arbitrary state power. Playing off Putin's arias to a "strong state," he implored Russians not to relive historical tragedies:

What is it that makes a civilized state different from a barbarian [one]? It is a full observance and protection of human rights. Regrettably, this main rule of a democratic state has been broken in Russia millions of times in the past 1,000 years alone. . . . Can it be that today we are ready to repeat the mistakes of the past, and agree that the end justifies the means and that the image of a strong state is worth the lives of individual citizens? . . . The individual today is Russia's main and only asset that remains. A policy oriented towards the individual is the one that can lead Russia out of a political dead end.[77]

Without quite accusing the acting president, Yavlinskii fished for suspicions that Putin was hiding totalitarian ambitions. Against them, the best indemnity was a familiar and nonmenacing face like himself:

[One] commercial [mocked] Putin's reluctance to reveal himself while others enthusiastically endorse him. The opening camera angle is from the point of view of a patient on an operating table. A voice-over asks, "Would you entrust your health to a person you barely know?" One dubious-looking surgeon prepares to operate, as another doctor says, "He's an excellent specialist." The voice-over answers his own question: "I doubt it." Then the viewer sees a door opening to a stranger. The voice-over asks, "Would you loan a large sum of money to someone you barely know?" The man seeking money says nothing but his buddy assures the viewer, "It's literally for two days." The voice-over says, "I don't think so." Then the video cuts to Yavlinskii with a Russian flag in the background. The voice-over says, "Trust those you know well. Grigorii Yavlinskii. Reason. Will. Results."[78]

The Few Who Trusted

In the end, precious few trusted Yavlinskii come March 26. About two in four (37 percent) of his diminutive band of voters had supported Yabloko in the Duma election; one in five (23 percent) had supported OVR; one in eight (13 percent) had supported SPS; the balance hailed from every point on the compass. Most galling for Yavlinskii was the standoffish behavior of the liberal electorate from December. While 10 percent of SPS supporters swung to Yavlinskii in March, 79 percent, aping most of their leaders, threw in with Putin. Forty-five percent of Yabloko supporters from 1999 fled to Putin, 6 percentage points more than the devotees who stayed with Yavlinskii.[79]

Inspection of influences on the Yavlinskii vote from our statistical model of electoral behavior (see appendix tables B-2 and B-4) discloses a few differences from December. All in all, it was a recipe for also-ran

Table 6-7. *Evaluations of Yavlinskii's Character Traits, Presidential Campaign*[a]

Trait	Rating (percent)			Ranking of net rating
	Yes/ probably yes	No/ probably no	Net yes/probably yes over no/ probably no	
Intelligent and knowledge-able person	70	18	52	4
Strong leader	29	52	–22	4
Honest and trustworthy person	36	39	–3	4
Really cares about people like you	26	48	–22	4

a. From 1999–2000 panel, wave 3 (N = 1,755 weighted cases). "Don't know" responses included in the denominator but not shown here.

status. Yavlinskii voters were still better educated and more urban than others, but no longer younger than average. They were more likely to be well-heeled economically, on this item resembling SPS voters from December more than Yabloko voters from December. Perceptions of current conditions, issue opinions, and evaluations of incumbents had no ramifications on support for the Yabloko leader. Yabloko partisanship did matter, although, like affinities for most parties other than the KPRF, it itself was a work in progress.

Evaluations of Yavlinskii's persona and issue competence, toward the end of the causal skein, exerted considerable influence over electoral decisions, but it was tough sledding for the prime liberal candidate. While mass opinions of Zyuganov's character altered little between the two elections, for Yavlinskii they took a downward turn—we must assume, owing to some combination of counterproductive campaigning on his part and attacks on him from other quarters. On the summary leadership scale from 0 to 10, Yavlinskii's mean score dropped from 4.28 to 3.77. On the trait-specific items (see table 6-7), he finished fourth on each, behind Putin, Zyuganov, and Aman Tuleyev, who was to obtain less than 3 percent of the popular vote. More damaging, the balance between positive and negative assessments of Yavlinskii's intelligence, strength, integrity, and empathy had deteriorated and was in the red for every attribute except intelligence (compare table 6-7 with table 6-1). In terms of conversion of these evaluations into votes, the trend was also prejudicial, as is evident from a comparison of table 6-8 with

Table 6-8. Yavlinskii Vote and Evaluations of His Character

Mean evaluation of four traits	Citizen opinion (percent)[a]	Predicted probability of voting for Yavlinskii[b]
Does not have the positive trait	10	.00
Probably does not have the positive trait	37	.01
Probably has the positive trait	47	.04
Has the positive trait	50	.28

a. N = 1,846 weighted cases. Missing data coded at the mean of the distribution for the specific trait.

b. Computed from multistage statistical model, holding causally prior and simultaneous variables constant at their medians. Sample N = 1,481; $p \leq .01$ for all cells in the column.

Table 6-9. Prospective Evaluations of Yavlinskii's Issue Competence[a]

Issue	Say Yavlinskii is best prepared		
	Percent	Percent of those who named a candidate	Ranking
Social security	4	6	4
Economy	12	16	3
Human rights	6	9	3
Chechnya	1	2	4
Foreign policy	3	5	3
Crime and corruption	1	2	5

a. From 1999–2000 panel, wave 3 (N = 1,755 weighted cases).

table 6-2. We estimate that the median voter who thought worst of Yavlinskii's leadership qualities had no chance of voting for him; for the median voter who thought best of him, the probability of supporting Yavlinskii was still only .28, far below 50 percent.[80]

A similar trend comes to light on issue competence. Twelve percent of citizens in 2000 assessed Yavlinskii as the most competent to manage the economy (see table 6-9). On every other issue, less than 10 percent rated him as most proficient. He ranked lower than Putin and Zyuganov on all six issues. He also yielded to Tuleyev on social security, to Vladimir Zhirinovskii on Chechnya and on crime and corruption, and to the nuisance candidate Yurii Skuratov on crime and corruption. Even if every voter who assayed Yavlinskii as most competent on a single issue (16 percent of our survey sample) had voted for him, he still would have finished a country mile behind the leaders. As it happened (see table 6-10), the median voter would have needed to rate Yavlinskii as tops on five of six issues for the probability of supporting him to go over .50.[81] Ninety-nine percent of Russians in 2000 did not think that kindly of Yavlinskii's promise.

Table 6-10. *Yavlinskii Vote and Prospective Evaluations of His Issue Competence*

Number of issues Yavlinskii can handle best	Citizen opinion (percent)[a]	Predicted probability of voting for Yavlinskii[b]
0	84	.02
1	9	.05
2	4	.12
3	1	.27
4	0.8	.48
5	0.3	.68
6	0.6	.82

a. N = 1,755 weighted cases.

b. Computed from multistage statistical model, holding causally prior and simultaneous variables constant at their medians. Sample N = 1,481; $p \leq .01$ for all cells in the column.

Conclusions

The liberals exited the electoral cycle of 1999–2000 the way they entered, a house divided against itself. Although in agreement on overarching goals of individual freedom and repudiation of Russia's authoritarian and statist heritage, they went after them in contrary ways. The Union of Right Forces, having defied gloomy forecasts and made it into the Duma, pursued what its organizers instinctively prefer—informing and sharing in power. Yabloko, having fallen short of this target, went about its standard routine—chastising and checking the holders of power. SPS remained largely the voice of social engineering and modernization, Yabloko the voice of conscience.

The right-wing parties could not and did not claim after the event that they had been uniquely vilified or victimized during the campaign season. When it came to popular support, SPS organizers were quite happy with their showing, while Yabloko leaders were quite disappointed. Aggregate support for the liberals, however, remained static. In the parliamentary contest, at least, SPS, Yabloko, and two small-fry parties held their combined voting strength at roughly the plateau it had been at for a half-decade—15 to 20 percent of the electorate. They did not do worse because, for all the miseries that radical reform has brought, enough Russians still feel Westernization is the best or the only road for the country to travel and some are already benefiting from the course. They did not do appreciably better because they failed to enlarge the audience for whom their ideas, leadership, and capacity to govern inspired confidence and they did a wretched job of putting together district campaigns. It did not help, but it remains unclear how much it hurt, that they were unable to work civilly with one another. Rumors of the death of the Russian right have always been highly exaggerated.[82] Staying alive to fight another day may be an uninspiring outcome, but inasmuch as it amplifies the range of choice open to citizens, it is vastly preferable to the subtraction of the liberals from the scene.

7 *Putin*

By the time most of them went to bed on Sunday, March 26, 2000, Russians knew for sure that Vladimir Vladimirovich Putin was to be their second president. Putin had been a focal player in the election cycle from the day he was brought in as prime minister the previous August. What makes his ascent unusual in the annals of democracies and half-democracies is that this landslide winner in a presidential election, on the back of a parliamentary election in which his allies did astonishingly well, wanted to have nothing to do with the *campaign* process and was able to claim with a straight face that he did not participate foursquare in it.

Boris Yeltsin recollects that when he broached the promotion to premier, Putin immediately asked what he was supposed to do in the imminent Duma campaign. Yeltsin assured him the government would midwife a new pro-Kremlin party—the germ of the Unity project—and that his priority should be to earn respect by doing his duties conscientiously, whereupon Putin expressed antipathy to, as he phrased it, electoral "struggle" (*bor'ba*): "I do not like electoral struggle. I really do not. I do not know how to carry it out and I do not like it."[1]

Putin's past as KGB lieutenant, an intelligence agent in East Germany, and municipal functionary and deputy mayor in his hometown, St. Petersburg, was not ideal preparation for a parliamentary or a presidential election. In *First Person,* a volume of extended interviews with three journalists published before the 2000 vote, he recalled several episodes in the 1990s. He had helped his patron, the first-wave democrat Anatolii

Sobchak, get elected mayor of St. Petersburg in 1991, mainly by button-holing deputies to the city council to authorize the popular election of a mayor and back Sobchak's candidacy. When Sobchak was up for reelection in 1996, Putin says he warned him electoral amateurism was now passé: "It had become clear that to be victorious you needed professionals and technology for running a campaign and not just successful negotiations with some deputies."[2] *First Person* does not touch on Putin's role in the 1993 and 1995 Duma elections, but it is known that Sobchak assigned him to the Russia's Choice campaign in 1993[3] and in 1995 put him in charge of the local effort of Our Home Is Russia, in which capacity he "made all the mistakes a dilettante can make"—among them, plastering stern portraits of Viktor Chernomyrdin all over downtown.[4] Both parties of power had unsatisfactory results in St. Petersburg. Putin describes with palpable distaste his involvement in the 1996 mayoral campaign in which Sobchak was beaten by Vladimir Yakovlev, a former vice mayor of the city and a future co-leader of OVR. Yakovlev had allies in the Kremlin and entrusted his campaign to an up-and-coming consulting company, Aleksei Koshmarov's NOVOKOM. Although Putin says he did little besides fulminating at Yakovlev as a "Judas" and getting his city hall colleagues to threaten to resign en masse, other reports show him supervising the campaign staff, underestimating the Yakovlev threat, and engineering an ill-starred rescheduling of the vote (so as not to coincide with the presidential vote).[5] Putin despised campaign fundraising, concluding that it was an invitation to requests for corrupt deals.[6] The loss of this bitterly fought and dirty election led to Putin's move to Moscow and Sobchak's flight into exile in France.

It is telling that Putin's version of the Kremlin conversations with Yeltsin in 1999 dwells on national security and public policy, not elections. He relates his anxiety over the summertime incursion of Shamil Basayev's Chechen irregulars into Dagestan, which, he said, threatened Russia with a rerun of the disintegration of the Soviet Union. "My evaluation of the situation in August, when the bandits attacked Dagestan, was that if we did not stop it immediately Russia as a country in its current sense was finished."[7] There is no reason to question the earnestness of this statement (its wisdom is another matter). Combined with his appetite for power, Putin's conviction that Russia was lost unless someone stepped in to clean up and bolster its state overrode his temperamental aversion to mass politics and electioneering.

As we have argued, the 1999 Duma campaign was universally perceived as cognate to an American primary election that would prune the field of candidates for the presidency. Those plotting Putin's campaign could not have hoped for a more salutary outcome. The surprise showing of the Unity bloc had a domino effect on possible competitors and set him up as odds-on favorite in the pending battle. Gennadii Zyuganov, it soon transpired, was going to oppose him, but few of the KPRF faithful thought he would fare better than second (and fewer still that he could win a runoff). Victory for Grigorii Yavlinskii or Vladimir Zhirinovskii, whose parties had barely cleared the 5 percent barrier, was a pipe dream. The three electoral blocs to elect Duma representatives on the party lists were on board the Putin express: Unity, the party of power; SPS, where there was a rift over the question but that came around to an endorsement in March; and OVR, whose leaders (Yevgenii Primakov, Yurii Luzhkov, and the governors from All Russia) all registered their support, holding their noses as they did. For Putin and his confederates in Unity, the surrender of Fatherland–All Russia, after they and the KPRF left it out in the cold in the division of spoils in the Duma in January, was sweet revenge as well as good politics.[8] Most other parties and blocs with national networks—Our Home Is Russia, the Agrarian Party, and Women of Russia, principally—queued meekly behind the others. The widespread attitude, as Primakov put it glumly in February, was that holding out "is senseless, since the future head of state has already been defined."[9]

VTsIOM monitoring polls had tracked a relentlessly upward path for Putin's reputation from summer through winter. Approval of his work as prime minister and then acting president stood at 31 percent in the mid-August poll, 53 percent in September, 66 in October, 78 in November, and 79 percent in December and January. Two percent of citizens who intended to vote were Putin supporters in August 1999; by September that was 4 percent and by October it jumped to 21 percent, overtaking Primakov and Zyuganov. In November Putin's anticipated vote had doubled to 45 percent and in election week in December it stood at 51 percent. During the week of January 13–17, 2000, 61 percent were prepared to cast their ballots for Putin, almost exactly what wave 2 of our 1999–2000 panel survey showed.[10] He eventually was to receive 53.44 percent of the popular vote, under the January crest but more than augured in December.

So why bother with the presidential election at all? Wish as he might to dispense with it, Putin was bound to observe the form of submitting to approval from below, even if it was via a "noncampaign" and not a conventional campaign.

Besides procedural propriety, the unpredictability of the transitional environment militated in favor of taking notice of the electorate. The rampant uncertainty that had enabled Putin's ratings to fly into the stratosphere could, in theory, crash them to earth. The presidential prospects of Primakov and Luzhkov had gone through boom and bust in a matter of months in 1999, so why not his? A Yavlinskii staffer, Vladimir Braginskii, drew the comparison as nominations closed:

> It wouldn't hurt to remember that in the past year we already had [several] "invincible" claimants to the post of president of Russia. . . . We have two months until the next elections and everything can change before then. The political organization of Russian society is still unstructured and unstable. The political opinions of people are very volatile, diverse, and changeable. Putin appeared unexpectedly in Russian politics, where he did not participate before. That is why we should not treat the results as predetermined. . . . It is important to continue the fight.[11]

For the laggards, it was important to stay in the fight. For Putin, it was important to commence it.

If enough of a tailspin to erase Putin's lead was unlikely, there remained a third consideration, about the margin of victory. It was widely believed that the closeness of the qualifying round of the 1996 election, and the two-man runoff it precipitated, magnified Yeltsin's need for financial and organizational support from the Russian moguls and his indebtedness to them afterward.[12] Putin, mindful of that and of his difficulties raising money for Sobchak, was determined not to be put over the same barrel and not to owe favors to any vested interests.[13] Speaking of the inadvisability of a runoff in public, he adverted only to the cost to the treasury (about $30 million), saying the money would be better spent on pensions. Putin apologists speculated that a second round would inflate Zyuganov's prestige—as KPRF organizers counted on it doing—and that Chechen guerrillas would somehow exploit the three weeks between rounds.

The fourth and most remote hazard was of the victory ride being derailed by voter turnout below the legally required level of 50 percent or by extensive recourse to the "against all candidates" line on the ballot. A word-of-mouth "'No' Movement" concocted by one Vladimir Pribylovskii, a supporter of Yavlinskii, prodded citizens angry at the election's prearranged quality to vote against Putin in the first round and against both candidates in the second. Under Russian law, the election would have to be voided if straight negative votes exceeded the votes cast for the leader in the runoff. The state media condemned the possibility repeatedly, and Aleksandr Veshnyakov of the Central Electoral Commission pronounced attempts to suborn a boycott or negative voting illegal. It did not aid Pribylovskii's cause that he had a reputation as a political prankster.[14]

The Noncampaign

Putin chose, for reasons of personal style and tactical advantage, to frame his pursuit of victory as a noncampaign. It was, in truth, a lightly camouflaged campaign by other means, cleverly fashioned to exploit his de facto incumbency, the absence of viable alternatives, and the rapport he had established with the populace before December.

Hail to the Chief

Russia's first president lifted Putin from the inner sanctum of the bureaucracy to its summit in a chain of appointments in 1998 and 1999. His chief of staff at the time, Valentin Yumashev, sold Yeltsin on Putin's talents and promise in the summer of 1998, when Putin was deputy head of the presidential administration for relations with the regions.[15] Within a year, having run the FSB and the Security Council without a glitch, Putin was prime minister. Yeltsin shattered precedent on August 9, 1999, by saying he coveted Putin as his heir, presenting him as the man who could "consolidate society" and "ensure the continuation of reforms." He did Putin no less of a favor on December 31 by resigning six months ahead of term and effectively *making* him head of state with one stroke of the pen. Article 92 of the 1993 constitution says only that upon the president stepping down the prime minister "temporarily carries out the duties" of president until an election is held (within three months) and the winner sworn in. It matter-of-factly describes the prime minister in these circumstances as "acting president" (*ispolnyayushchii obyazannosti Prezidenta*). These clauses had not been tested since the constitution was promulgated. Russian officials after December 31 went miles beyond a minimalist interpretation, referring to Putin as acting president in a manner intimating this was an actual position held, not a cipher for supplementary responsibilities he would shoulder as premier. No court or legislative body challenged this expansive reading of Article 92. Still prime minister, and thus in daily control of the civil service and the budget, Putin now issued presidential decrees and, as commander-in-chief, orders to the armed services.[16]

Not only was Putin on an institutional pedestal, with his unloved predecessor out of sight, but the pesky electoral calendar had been moved forward by ninety days, pinching the time available to opponents to mobilize against him and available to him to make a revealing mistake. The media portion of the campaign was trimmed from four weeks, in the Duma campaign, to three. A seamless transfer of power let Putin cast himself as too busy attending to the public's welfare to be much distracted by the contest. His candidacy, he said in an "Open Letter to Russian Voters," forced him "to separate what I am obliged to do every day *as leader of the country* from what it is allotted to me to do as a participant in the election campaign." "As in all the months that have gone before," he continued, "I will go on exercising my usual official duties. There are no special campaign events on my working schedule." Implying that grubbing for votes would offend the dignity of his office and of the masses he already represented, he would go no further than offering to share his "stand" on the national political agenda.[17]

As leader of the country, Putin found his official duties now encompassed representing Russia in international relations. Without having to innovate in policy, something his campaign staff wanted left until after his inauguration, he was free to receive foreign statesmen and look reassuringly presidential in their company. He hosted Britain's prime minister, Tony Blair, in St. Petersburg and NATO's secretary general, George Robertson, in Moscow, telling Robertson Russia might some day apply to join the alliance. Domestically, Putin had the undivided attention of the governors and republic presidents who had tugged in so many directions during the Duma race. The air of inevitability about him convinced them almost to a man to scurry to declare their allegiance. One analyst compared their antics to the "socialist competition" for attainment of production targets common in Soviet days: "A peculiar sort of 'socialist competition' was provoked among the leaders of the regions—for who could support the acting president the best and the loudest. Any form of neutrality, to say nothing of opposition, was made out to threaten unpleasant postelection consequences."[18] The crusty Vasilii Starodubtsev of Tula, who endorsed Zyuganov, was the only member of the governors' club to refuse to play along. Eight joined the "initiative group" that placed Putin's name in nomination. Putin toured twelve regions between January and March and was regaled by leaders ranging from supporters of Unity to incorrigible communists and founders of the OVR bloc. In many places, he convened meetings of executives from the branch of the economy dominant in the region, underlining his attentiveness to national needs. Several sorties were timed to coincide with appropriate national holidays. For example, Putin visited Volgograd, formerly Stalingrad, for the Day of the Defender of the Fatherland (February 23). On International Women's Day (March 8) he traveled to Ivanovo, the capital of the Russian textile industry, whose mills employ mostly female workers.[19]

Sufficient Means to Communicate

Behind the statesmanlike facade, Putin nonetheless enlisted the "professionals and technology" he had told Sobchak were the requisites of electoral success. Until December 31 members of Yeltsin's team scoped out his presidential bid, including Aleksandr Voloshin (head of the Kremlin administration since April 1999), Igor Shabdurasulov (deputy to Voloshin and liaison with Unity), and Dmitrii Yakushkin (presidential press secretary). Working through the oil company Sibneft, they hired a New York public relations firm, Shandwick International, to work for the Putin cause. The contract lapsed at year's end once it was apparent Putin was not going to need a pricy campaign. In January Putin added new people more associated with him personally. He named a St. Petersburg friend, Dmitrii Medvedev, as chairman of campaign headquarters and deputy head of the administration for relations with the government apparatus, obscuring the line between public and private functions. Medvedev, who had little campaign experience, reached out to others who did. Aleksandr Abramov, holder of Putin's former job of deputy head of administration for regional relations, was number two in the campaign. Key operatives were Vladislav Surkov, another deputy head of the presidential administration; Ksenya Ponomarëva, a former executive director of ORT; Mikhail Margelov of the RIA-Novosti news agency, a onetime partner in Video International; and Sergei Popov, the deputy head of Unity's 1999 campaign. Two election gurus and advisers to Voloshin—Gleb Pavlovskii of the Foundation for Effective Politics and Aleksandr Oslon of the Public Opinion

Foundation—were instrumental in developing and debugging the Putin message.

Putin did not have to worry about how to afford this expertise. Most of Medvedev's crew were on the state payroll. The bread and butter of Pavlovskii and Oslon, formally in the private sector, was government contracts. Corporations fell over one another offering counsel and cash.[20] Almost 99 percent of the approximately $1.2 million officially collected for the Putin election fund—the unofficial total is anyone's guess—came from thirty-six unidentified organizations.[21]

The badge of the noncampaign was abstention from standard campaign activities. Putin released no written program, asserting, in Medvedev's words, that it "would not be right" to do so during an abbreviated election period.[22] He almost never attacked his rivals by name, and media surrogates like Sergei Dorenko, who were so instrumental in destroying OVR, were instructed to cool down their rhetoric.[23] Putin did not court endorsements from parties, trade unions, or celebrities.[24] There were no street rallies, town hall meetings, billboards, or rock concerts, and monumentally bland leaflets did not make an appearance until a few days before the vote. Fewer than 1 percent of our survey respondents were canvassed by the Putin organization, a mere 9 percent said they received mailings from it, and 14 percent encountered leaflets and posters on the streets—percentages smaller than those registered for Zyuganov and Yavlinskii.[25]

It was a point of pride for Putin that he had no paid clips on television or radio and waived the free time made available to all candidates. Campaign videos he denigrated as no better than advertisements about "what is more important, Tampax or Snickers."[26] He declined to debate the other candidates and made a show of returning one-sixth of his campaign budget, unspent, to the donors. Putin expounded on his recoil from campaigning in these words:

> I had never imagined myself taking part in an election campaign. You know, mostly and mainly [this is] because all the modern campaign technologies are rather unscrupulous things. They all boil down to the candidate looking in the eyes of millions of people and making all sorts of promises while knowing in advance that they are [unworkable]. I cannot force myself to cross this line. I am very glad that I have not had to do this so far. This is largely one of the reasons why I decided not to use the campaign television films, not to take part in the debates and so on.[27]

Although Putin's hostility to campaign hoopla seems to have been heartfelt, he was, after all, so very much in the lead at the outset that he did not *need* expensive means to grab the electorate's attention. The assertion that he was nobly refusing to pander to special interests was good electoral politics but also a false claim. Putin was not above using state resources to bribe supporters—and not with promises only but with delivery of the goods. Right after the January holidays, for instance, he said the government would add a 20 percent increase in old-age pensions to those increases he instituted in November. Subordinates followed up with commitments to hike veterans' allowances and repay all wage debts to budget-funded workers by April 15. Putin announced another multistep pension increase on March 2.[28]

Furthermore, Putin and his boosters freely admitted he was anything but starved for opportunities to link up with the electorate. In announcing on March 3 that he would forgo free airtime, campaign headquarters magnanimously explained that they were trying "to create equal conditions for all candidates" and noted that Putin possessed "sufficient" means "to communicate with voters and set forth his positions."[29] In his missive to voters, Putin urged them to judge him by his record as prime minister: "My state position is open and familiar to everyone. The last half-year gave people ample opportunity to see what I consider important and what I am doing about the nation's politics and economy."[30] The droll adjectives—"sufficient" and "ample"—were window dressing for the plain truths that Putin had in essence been governing Russia for months, that any Russian who was not a hermit had to be aware of him and his point of view, and that the terms of dialogue with the electorate were blatantly unequal.

The unlevel playing field puts the avoidance of canonic campaign techniques into perspective. Much was made of the unorthodoxy of Putin's methods for conversing with voters. On February 7 and 8 ORT broadcast a one-hour interview with him at home, lounging with his white toy poodle. On February 11 he did a telephone call-in show with readers of *Komsomol'skaya pravda*. In a gesture to the postmodern campaigning style, his open letter to the nation was deposited at an interactive Putin website, initiated on February 25; Russians could e-mail him questions, to which his staff gave brief answers once a week.[31] *First Person*, out in mid-March, provided blunt, folksy summaries of Putin's biography and personal views intended to appeal to the average Ivan Ivanovich.[32] In Moscow, the insipid leaflets put out on the eve of the election were pasted on walls and telephone poles above eye level, apparently in an effort to make Putin's face ubiquitous and downplay the text.[33]

All of this, and the studied abstemiousness about advertising, pale in significance before the communications tool that was his fundamental resource—news offerings in the state-run and state-influenced mass media that were one endless Putin infomercial. As Putin's open letter acknowledged, it had been playing for "the last half-year," since he became prime minister. The week of February 28 to March 5, for example, the main ORT evening news broadcast spent about three minutes reporting on Zyuganov, nine minutes on Yavlinskii, and fifty-one minutes on Putin. That same week on RTR Putin got twenty-seven minutes and Zyuganov and Yavlinskii about two minutes each. The commercial network NTV did not slant its coverage editorially in Putin's favor, but because it considered Putin newsworthy, it also gave him a big edge in minutes spent—sixty-one, versus thirteen for Zyuganov and twenty-five for Yavlinskii.[34]

Defender of the Homeland

Nowhere was there more wall-to-wall coverage of the provisional president than on the Chechnya issue. Beginning with a New Year's Day sojourn in the republic, he was incessantly shown praising the military's courage and manliness, meeting with decorated and wounded veterans, and inveighing against the Chechen "bandits." During an afternoon news bulletin on March 26, with the polling stations open, an ORT newsreader commented, "Today's reports from Chechnya yet again confirm that as soon as possible the country needs to elect an active president who can cope with the [Chechen] fighters and bring the antiterrorist operation to its conclusion." Any watcher would have recognized it as a plug for Putin. ORT and RTR almost always took a can-do attitude toward the military offensive, minimizing Russian casualties, portraying the rebels as on the brink of capitulation, and presenting critics of the war as disloyal crybabies. On the last day of campaigning, March 24, "Putin taped a three-minute address urging citizens to turn out to vote. That address was broadcast in full at the beginning of every ORT and RTR newscast. . . . Technically, Putin did not call on voters to support him, but the subtext of his address was clear. Among other things, he reminded viewers that in choosing a president they were also choosing a commander-in-chief."[35]

State Builder

While advisers cerebrated offstage about appropriate analogies in European and world history, Putin grounded his electoral message firmly in contemporary realities.[36] He asserted the irrelevance of ideological abstractions and enmities, sharpening a point made offhandedly by the Unity bloc (and OVR) in the Duma campaign:

> I am convinced that the defining feature of the new century will be not the battle of ideologies but an acute competition over the quality of life and over national wealth and progress. Speaking of progress, it is either there or it is not. The poverty of peoples cannot be justified by any references to the purity of party principles, be they "right" or "left" ones.[37]

Russia, he said, had fallen disgracefully behind and was spinning its wheels as "a rich country of poor people." The Soviet regime, shackled to an obsolete economic doctrine and burdened by imperial overreach, had smothered Russia's potential before 1991. Since then, the culprits were a continued lack of realism in foreign policy, "a shift in mentality that mistakes the absence of order for true democracy," and—Putin's visceral concern—a dysfunctional state. "The state machine has gotten out of hand and its motor, the executive branch, rattles and wheezes as soon as you try to get it to into motion. Clerks shuffle paper without getting things done and have almost forgotten the meaning of official discipline." Putin soberly singled out Portugal's standard of living as Russia's highest aspiration for the coming decade.

Putin's economic prescriptions generally had a liberal flavor, as he called for an end to privileges and subsidies and with as much fervor for entrenchment of property rights and relaxation of governmental control over enterprise: "You know, it is equally necessary to be rid of greenhouse favoritism and of deadly restrictions. Whoever wants and is able to live well will be helping out himself and his country." He accused the communists, for all their verbal moderation, of seeking to renationalize privatized property and proposed a referendum on land ownership to settle that question once and for all. Individual rights, in Putin's opinion, needed to be protected and enhanced and the postcommunist state needed to be made "effective and strong" and purged of "clan or group" interests. He maintained that under a "dictatorship of the law" there would be no contradiction between an iron-willed state and liberty because impersonal and transparent rules would be applied dispassionately to the citizenry, business, political leaders, and government: "In a state not bound by the laws, and therefore weak, the person is defenseless and unfree. The stronger the state, the freer the individual."

For Putin, the ultimate sellout of state interests had been in Chechnya, whose insurrection he typified as expressing not local anti-Russian nationalism or religious zeal but the twisted mores of "the criminal world."[38] Saying Russian federalism had become excessively decentralized, he vowed not to barter away the country's integrity and broached the idea of superimposing huge intermediate units, responsible to the Kremlin, on the eighty-nine administrative regions and making the governors removable by presidential decree.[39] It was a far cry from the stroking of the regional barons so common in the Duma campaign.

In making his pitch, Putin tiptoed around values and ideas, much as he abjured formal ideology. He spoke of society's "moral foundations" and patriotic cohesion, but cast them as part of the psychological endowment of all citizens and not as guides to political action.[40] His preference was to go on about "priorities," not values. A top priority for Putin was to tidy up the state's own backyard. He expressed puzzlement over the shared ignorance of the dimensions of things: the size of the population (there had been no census since 1989), the number of state employees, the budget deficit, and so on. Putin implicitly likened himself to a newly appointed factory manager: "When a new director takes over, the first thing he wants to see is how the books balance. Russia is also a firm (*khozyaistvo*), one that is enormous, complicated, and very diverse. It is senseless to argue about whether we are poor or rich as long as no one has toted up our successes and failures." As a good manager, he advocated patience and living within one's means. In foreign policy, say, if Russia were tempted to undertake a big initiative but had trouble meeting basic needs at home, then it "should above all weigh our abilities and maybe wait a bit."

New Time

"Who is Mr. Putin?" was the question asked in world capitals in 1999–2000. Obviously, Russians, too, could project different meanings onto him. Focus groups commissioned by the authors before the March election brought out a rainbow of reasons for liking or disliking Putin. In one discussion among Muscovites aged eighteen to thirty-five, a woman reported that she planned to vote for him because he would provide an adequate pension for her grandmother, someone else believed he would do the most thorough job of evicting ethnic non-Russians from the capital, and a third person was for Putin because he was the candidate most likely to pursue radical economic reforms and create job opportunities for young people. When asked what kind of leader Russia needed today, most Putin supporters named Peter the Great, although some also adduced such different role models as Lenin, Stalin, Pëtr Stolypin (the reformist prime minister of Russia from 1906 to 1911)—and Hitler![41]

Instead of historical parallels, the final ribbon on the noncampaign package was the conveying of Putin's newness to the scene and juxtaposing him with those who had governed Russia in the 1990s. One task was to uncouple him in the public's mind from Yeltsin, who had long since worn out his welcome. This required a delicate touch, since Putin had been recruited by him, signed an immunity decree for him on December 31, and retained many members of his circle. Putin made several token changes in personnel. As he had with Unity in 1999, Yeltsin—who said in his resignation speech Russia must "enter the new millennium with new faces"—cooperated by going underground. During the campaign the two were not photographed together, except fleetingly on Yeltsin's birthday (February 1), and Yeltsin refrained from commentary on his successor during the election campaign.

Another imperative was to deal with Putin's association with the epitome of the Soviet regime Yeltsin did so much to wreck, the KGB. He was unapologetic in *First Person* about his fifteen years in the agency, stressing that his specialty was foreign intelligence—which he laconically depicted as "information work"—and detailing his growing awareness in the 1980s that the regime had lost its élan and could not save itself. Putin image-makers hyped his spying career as a sign of his patriotism and competence, as so many of the best and the brightest in his generation had gone into the KGB. They also linked it to his fondness for things stereotypically German and his fluency in the language.

Putin's relative youth, good health, and athleticism all posed a convenient contrast to Yeltsin and to much of Russia's cohort of senior leaders. Media vignettes showed Putin as early to rise and late to leave the office, with the evening news cataloguing the numerous functions and meetings he had attended that day. *First Person* highlighted his devotion to judo and sports more generally and carried photos of him in a kimono and black belt, in skiing attire, and playing ping-pong wearing only a bathing suit.[42] Accompanying photographs showed him in domestic settings with his wife Lyudmila and two school-age daughters. Right after Anatolii Sobchak's death in February, an interview with him praising Putin's sobriety popped up in the press. The Putin team, by testimony of Sobchak, "go to the theater or to [art] exhibitions, not to the sauna to get drunk."[43] Six days before the election, in a stunt exhibiting his vigor and bravery, Putin was shown on the small screen behind the controls of a Sukhoi-27 jet fighter streaking off into the blue over Chechnya. Other materials documented that he was the first Russian leader since the Bolshevik Revolution to be a practicing Orthodox Christian.[44]

During the last days of the campaign, ORT and RTR television played advertisements reminding Russians to turn their clocks ahead one hour as the season changed that weekend. Against pictures of ice thawing, flowers blooming, and clocks ticking, a voice-over said, "March 26—a transition to a new time." "The commercials were not labeled political advertising . . . but their subtext was unmistakable. Russians normally refer to daylight-saving time as 'summer time,' not 'new time.' Putin evoked the same theme in his March 24 televised address, saying the resetting of the clocks was 'symbolic' of an old era ending and a new one beginning."[45] Left unspoken was that the new time was to be Putin's time.

The Voters

What did Russians see in Vladimir Putin? Which of the array of potential sources of electoral behavior considered in this book spurred them to vote in their millions for someone most had not heard of a year before?

Full Court Press

Putin had close to unanimous support from Russia's political and economic elites. So universal was the obeisance to the chief and the exhorting to do the right thing on March 26 that exposure to any one source of facts and advice did not always have much to do with popular behavior. In the media realm, the Putin vote, aping Unity, was influenced mainly by consumption of *some* television programming (see appendix tables C-6 and C-7). A citizen who watched any television was .18 (18 percentage points) more likely to vote for Putin than the rare person who did not watch television at all.[46] More specific viewing habits were not good predictors of a vote for Putin. As a sign of the less surly style of campaigning in 2000, tuning in to the Dorenko weekend show was unrelated to deciding in Putin's favor.

Another change from the parliamentary campaign was the wholesale co-option of subnational players into the Kremlin's full court press. Within the electorate, the Putin tide rolled with almost as much regularity across geographic boundaries as it did within the elite. Yeltsin in 1996 carried forty-six of Russia's eighty-nine regions in the first round, eleven of them with an absolute majority, and fifty-seven in the runoff, forty-nine of them with an absolute majority. Putin, with the governors and republic presidents in his hip pocket, carried eighty-four regions, fifty-six of them by absolute majority. He swept twenty of the twenty-four provinces where the KPRF took the most votes in the 1999 party-list contest, including Starodubtsev's Tula and Zyuganov's home region of Orël. Where the chief executive had subscribed to the Fatherland–All Russia alliance in 1999, anti-Kremlin animus was exchanged for pro-Putin ebullience, most likely because these politicos felt under more pressure to prove their loyalty. Putin took a plurality of the votes in all nine of these regions and an absolute majority in seven (excluding only Moscow and Moscow province). The citizens of Ingushetiya, having zigged on the advice of their president, Ruslan Aushev, and given more than 89 percent of their votes to OVR in December, zagged with him in March and gave more than 88 percent to Putin (the counting aided, one assumes, by Aushev-friendly returning officers). In every OVR bastion but Moscow and Ingushetiya, the Putin vote was substantially larger than the combined OVR and Unity votes in 1999.[47]

Putin's People

The die for victory was cast early. Although Putin's popularity receded slightly from its early winter peak, it was more than sufficient for a first-round victory. Sixty-four percent of our survey respondents who intended to vote in the presidential election said when interviewed in the weeks after the Duma election, in wave 2 of the survey, that they would vote for Putin. Reinterviewed in wave 3, 79 percent of those persons told us they had cast ballots for Putin on March 26. Putin had shed about a fifth of his intended supporters by election day but had simultaneously picked up enough followers to buffer their loss. Fourteen per-

Table 7-1. *Putin Vote and 1999 Party-List Vote*[a]

1999 party-list vote	Percent of citizens in that category who voted for Putin in 2000	Percent of Putin voters consisting of citizens in that category
KPRF	29	13
Unity	88	33
OVR	60	11
SPS	79	11
Yabloko	45	4
LDPR	66	4
Minor parties	65	9
Against all parties	63	2
Abstained	63	13

a. N = 1,459 weighted cases. Duma vote ascertained in wave 2 of 1999–2000 panel and presidential vote in wave 3.

cent of Putin voters had intended several months before to vote for another candidate, and 14 percent were unsure how they were going to vote or meant to vote against all candidates.

A more apposite comparison, made in table 7-1, is with actual voting conduct in the parliamentary election. Putin's appeal was remarkably ecumenical. Only among 1999 supporters of two major parties that fielded their own presidential candidates in 2000—the KPRF and Yabloko—was Putin limited to less than 50 percent of the votes, and with Yabloko it was a close call. Sixty-six percent of LDPR voters sided with Putin and not with the LDPR nominee, Zhirinovskii. Almost 90 percent of Unity voters supported Putin, as did almost 80 percent of the 1999 supporters of the liberal SPS. OVR supporters from 1999, whose party had been humiliated in the Duma election but came around to supporting Putin, voted for him at a rate of 60 percent. More than 60 percent of persons who voted for minor parties, voted against all the parties, or abstained in December 1999 supported Putin if they went to the polls in March. The composition of the Putin electorate was highly heterogeneous in terms of party orientation—which it would have had to be for him to prevail. Even with Unity's impressive showing in the Duma campaign and the Putin mania among its supporters, he could not have been elected president on the basis of their ballots alone. One-third of Putin's people were Unity voters from December. One-half had voted for other parties. Fifteen percent had either voted against all parties or abstained in the Duma election.

Putin's constituents were also a mixed bag sociologically. The total effects of all social characteristics on the Putin vote, as estimated in our multivariate model of the voting decision (see appendix table B-2), were small. Effects statistically different from zero are detectable for only women and citizens living at western longitudes; both are of minor magnitude (< .10). Putin's base of support in 2000 was uniform—uniformly high—across most subgroups. It was noticeably flatter than Unity's had been in 1999 on two points: age and community size.[48] On both, the greater symmetry in distribution of the Putin vote is the product of differential gains in social groups where Unity, which drew disproportionately among younger and rural voters, was relatively weak. Compared with Unity's vote in December (see table 3-1 for figures), support for Putin among voters under the age of thirty increased by 25 percentage points (from 37 percent to 62 percent), whereas among voters over the age of sixty-nine it increased by 45 points (from 15 percent to 59 percent). Among the least urbanized fifth of the population, the Putin vote was 20 points higher than the Unity vote had been (54 percent versus 34 percent); in the most urbanized fifth, Putin was 44 points stronger in 2000 than Unity had been in 1999 (57 percent versus 13 percent).

The Putin electorate had more structure when it came to attitudes toward current conditions in the country. Not surprisingly, it took a more positive view of economic and political trends than the men and women who voted for Zyuganov or other opposition candidates. Mass perceptions of current conditions had about two times the overall impact on the Putin vote that similar perceptions had on the Unity vote three months before. Pocketbook considerations were of marginal import, but assessments of the state of the economy as a whole and especially of political developments (the state of democratization) were much more influential. For the median voter, the probability of voting for Vladimir Putin was .24 (24 percentage points) higher if the individual had the most bullish assessment of the state of the Russian economy and .36 (36 percentage points) higher for the best assessment of the polity.

Partisanship

Partisanship was a secondary or tertiary factor in Putin's election. The party-like entity with which he consorted, Unity, remade itself from an electoral bloc into a registered political movement only in February 2000. Putin had himself nominated for president by a polyglot initiative group, not by Unity, although Unity's nomination would have been his at the drop of a hat had he asked. Sergei Shoigu and the official Unity hierarchy, such as it was, were next to invisible in the Putin campaign. Given Unity's newborn status and its dependency on Putin's star power in the Duma election, any attempt to draw a precise causal arrow between citizen affinities for Unity and their tendency to vote for Putin must rest on unverifiable assumptions. Our model (see appendix table B-2) estimates the total effect of Unity partisanship on the probability of voting for Putin to be .16—approximately one-quarter of the effect of KPRF partisanship on the Zyuganov vote. About every tenth Russian citizen in the spring of 2000 was a Unity partisan, to go by responses to our survey questions. These people were a lock to vote for Putin for president—97 percent of those who voted cast their ballots for him—but Unity partisans made up only 19 percent of the Putin electorate. There can be little question he would have won if Unity had not existed.

Issue Opinions

Normative opinions on the issues of the day cannot be dismissed as easily as partisanship. They did figure conspicuously in Putin's conquest of the electorate. Ideational influences on the Putin vote have certain things in common with influences on the Unity vote. Total effects of rightist self-placement on the left-right scale and rejection of a Soviet-type political regime were very similar for Putin to what they had been for the Unity vote. Also similar was the irrelevance of substantive preferences on federal-regional relations and the Chechen problem. Strange as it may seem, Russians' positions on the neuralgic Chechnya issue had no significant bearing on support for Putin, any more than they did on support for Unity before him.

The similarities aside, there were several notable differences between Putin and Unity in the area of issue effects. Issue opinions taken together had nearly twice as much influence on the choice of Putin as they had exerted on the choice of Unity (compare appendix tables B-3 and B-4). This time, citizen preference on the course of economic reform, which was unrelated to the tendency to vote for the party of power in 1999, was correlated with the Putin vote. All other things being equal, the person who wanted Russia to deepen and accelerate market reform was .12 (12 percentage points) more likely to vote for Putin than someone who advocated resurrection of the socialist economic model.

Most predictive of the future was the pronounced switch in the political opinions most contributory to the voting choice. The total effect in our model of the opinion testing preference for a Soviet-type regime, as opposed to reformed socialism, the current political system, or "democracy of the Western type," remained steady: we estimate it at .26 for influence on the Unity vote in 1999 and at .23 for influence on the Putin vote in 2000. What did not hold steady was the influence of two other political opinions: preference for presidential over parliamentary power (or, as a middle setting, a balanced regime) and agreement with the assertion that Russia needs a "strong leader who does not have to bother with parliament and elections." For the Unity vote, we estimate the total effect of the presidentialism variable to be .11 and of the personalism variable to be a statistically insignificant .07. For the Putin vote, the total effect of presidentialist sentiment has more than doubled, to .26, and for the preference for a political strongman it has risen to .12. Ceteris paribus, the total displacement in the probability of choosing Putin increased by .38 when a median voter went from having the most parliamentarist and the least personalist opinions to the most presidentialist and the most personalist. That is about one and a half times the effect of a change in preference from an unreformed Soviet regime to a Western democracy. The influence of presidentialism and personalism, moreover, was greatest on citizens who preferred a Soviet-type regime. For them, the combined total effect was .43; for individuals who preferred a Western-type democracy, the joint total effect was .29.

The implication is that Putin's transition within the transition was already affecting how Russians thought of their leaders. In December 1999 the biggest political cleavage was still over whether to embrace or repudiate the Soviet heritage. Predictions that Russia would surmount the polarized politics of the mid-1990s seemed to be disconfirmed by the 1999 Duma election.[49] By March 2000, however, the earth had indeed moved. Mass politics was still deeply divided between two principal alternatives, but the axis of division had evolved away from the stark advance-or-retreat alternative of a few years before. Putin did not promise to take Russia backward. It was Zyuganov, not Putin, who carried the votes of mostly older Russians who pined for the political practices of the former Soviet regime. It is what Putin wanted to take Russia forward *to* that must cause concern. His supporters were more responsive to notions of presidential supremacy than of Western-style democracy, and at least some of them were entranced by the possibility of a soft authoritarian regime—one in which the formal institutional setting incorporated in the 1993 constitution stays intact but one way or the other a commanding leader does what it takes to govern, whatever the letter of the law.[50]

Performance

The most powerful influence on Putin's people, bar none, was the brace of retrospective evaluations of the work of incumbents from atop the executive branch—Putin himself and Yeltsin, the president until he passed the torch to Putin on the last day of the millennium. Putin's work as prime minister and now as acting president continued to get rave reviews from the population. When we asked survey respondents about his record in office around the time of the presidential election, "Don't know" responses had dwindled from the first time we posed the question, around the time of the parliamentary election, from 10 percent to 1 percent, while responses commingling approval and disapproval had crept from about one-quarter of the total to about one-third (36 percent). Still, a comfortable majority of Russians, 59 percent, either approved or strongly approved of Putin's activities and a mere 4 percent registered strong or moderate disapproval. Net assessments of Yeltsin's record, on the other hand, were not much kinder than they had been in the earlier sampling. There was a bit of a shift toward the undecided category, but, as before, hardly anyone (5 percent) approved or strongly approved of Yeltsin's work, a majority (56 percent) disapproved or strongly disapproved, and about one citizen in three (32 percent) gave him a mixed grade.[51]

Russians had had an entire decade to see Yeltsin in action and disposed of little new information about him in March 2000.[52] Putin had been in the national spotlight for seven and a half months, for only three of which he had been interim head of state. What, then, went into citizens' judgment of him? In wave 3 of our 1999–2000 survey panel, we asked informants to say in their own words which of the decisions taken by Putin in the posts of prime minister and acting president "was, in your opinion, the very best for the country," and then to say which was "the very worst for the country." Interviewers were instructed to write down the answers verbatim and to record multiple responses if they were proffered.

The summary pattern of responses to the open-ended question is reproduced in table 7-2. Fifty-three percent of respondents were able to come up with at least one best decision and many fewer, 21 percent, with at least one worst decision.[53] The balance, without doubt, was pro-Putin, but there were subtleties. One-quarter of the subset of individuals who told us of a good Putin decision also mentioned a bad decision, and two-

Table 7-2. *Responses to Open-Ended Questions about Best and Worst Decisions Taken by Putin as Prime Minister and Acting President*[a]

Response	Percent
Best decisions	
Mention at least one	53
No good decisions	4
Don't know	44
Worst decisions	
Mention at least one	21
No bad decisions	16
Don't know	63

a. From 1999–2000 panel, wave 3 (N = 1,755 weighted cases).

Table 7-3. *Most Frequently Mentioned Best and Worst Decisions Taken by Putin*

Decisions	Percent
Best[a]	
Chechnya	51
Pensions	39
Higher wages	7
Worst[b]	
Chechnya	57
Yeltsin immunity decree	19
Inflation	5

a. N = 926 weighted cases.
b. N = 366 weighted cases.

thirds of those who described a bad decision also told of a good decision. Also, although the numbers who believed Putin had made either no good decisions (4 percent) or no bad decisions (16 percent) were small, much larger groups (44 percent for good decisions, 63 percent for bad decisions) were not able to give a definite answer. Russians who were able to name one or more good decisions were much more likely than others to approve of Putin's record in office in general, and those who ascribed a bad decision to him were much more likely to disapprove.[54]

Table 7-3 details which concrete decisions of Putin's earned him the public's support and disapproval. It lists those decisions cited by 5 percent of those respondents who indicated at least one good decision or at least one bad decision. Putin's decisionmaking on Chechnya has a slim majority of the positives, yet did not have the field to itself.[55] About 40 percent of Russians singled out his main initiative in social policy, the increases in pensions effected, to the drumbeat of government publicity, between November 1999 and March 2000. Seven percent referred to Putin decisions that increased their wages.[56] Putin's actions on the war in Chechnya and on pensions found audiences in very different social groups. His actions in Chechnya were most popular among the young: they were cited as very good for the country by 63 percent of respondents under the age of thirty but by 34 percent over the age of sixty-nine. His pension choices were most popular among the old: they were fingered by 26 percent of voters younger than thirty but by 59 percent in their sixties and seventies. Among Putin's incorrect decisions, the pace is set by the same one that tops the list of correct decisions—Chechnya, which was to some degree a two-edged sword in the politics of 1999–2000.[57] Also mentioned frequently were the decree indemnifying Boris Yeltsin against prosecution and, at a lower level, policies that fed inflation. When pressed in a separate closed-ended question to place a value on the immunity edict, about twice as many Russians expressed disapproval as approval of the Putin action.[58]

In the 1999 voting for the party lists, citizen evaluations of Yeltsin's record had no statistically reliable effect on the likelihood of voting for the Unity bloc—hence the Teflon metaphor we used in chapter 3—and evaluations of Putin's record had a total effect of .38. In popular decisions about the 2000 presidential candidates, appraisals of Yeltsin did have a significant effect on the Putin vote (the total effect was .25), and appraisals of Putin as incumbent exerted twice as much of a total effect on the Putin vote (.73) as on the Unity vote in 1999.

This reinforcement of accountability for both leaders is a logical outgrowth of changes in the electoral context. Putin after December 31 was more tied to Yeltsin than before: he had been inducted as Yeltsin's successor and had signed a decree on immunity of the former president, over the foreseeable objections of millions of Russians. Many voters clearly did see Putin as Yeltsin's boy. By the same token, Putin as acting president, and no longer Yeltsin's subaltern prime minister, also gave the electorate more to fasten on than before in terms of his own actions. The total effect for evaluation of Putin's record in office is very large—although less colossal than the analogous effect for Boris Yeltsin in the 1996 presidential election—and is highly robust when confounding effects are taken into account.[59]

Table 7-4. *Putin Vote, as Conditioned by Evaluations of Yeltsin's and Putin's Records*[a]

Predicted Probabilities

Evaluation of Putin's record	Evaluation of Yeltsin's record				
	Completely disapprove	Disapprove	Approve some, disapprove some	Approve	Completely approve
Completely disapprove	.11	.17	.26	.36	.47
Disapprove	.25	.36	.47	.59	.70
Approve some, disapprove some	.46	.59	.70	.79	.86
Approve	.69	.79	.86	.91	.94
Completely approve	.85	.90	.94	.96	.98

a. Computed from multistage statistical model, holding causally prior and simultaneous variables constant at their medians. Sample N = 1,481; $p \leq .01$ for all cells in the table.

Table 7-4 lets one see contingencies in the effects of citizen assessments of their past and future presidents. The median voter who approved or completely approved of the record of both Yeltsin and Putin (represented here in the bottom right of the table) was highly likely to support Putin's candidacy. His or her counterpart who disapproved or strongly disapproved of both (in the upper left of the table) would in all likelihood support another candidate. The interesting combinations are in the middle of the table. As the total-effect statistics indicate in summary, variation in evaluations of Putin's record (which can be followed by reading down the table rows) tended always to have bigger implications for the vote than variation in evaluations of Yeltsin's record (reading across the table columns). But there was also a tendency for these effects to offset one another, not compensate for one another. The more critical the citizen was of Yeltsin's legacy, the greater the impact of a positive opinion of Putin's record on the chances of voting for Putin. And the worse the person thought of Putin's activities, the greater the room for a positive evaluation of Yeltsin to tip the balance of probabilities toward a Putin vote.[60]

Character

Mass evaluations of the candidate's personal qualities were second in importance as drivers of the Putin vote, behind approval of incumbents' record in office and a whisker ahead of issue opinions. The measure of Russians' romance with Vladimir Putin can be taken from table 7-5. He

Table 7-5. *Evaluations of Putin's Character Traits*[a]

Trait	Rating (percent)			Ranking of net rating among 4 candidates
	Yes/ probably yes	No/ probably no	Net yes/probably yes over no/ probably no	
Intelligent and knowledge- able person	92	3	90	1
Strong leader	83	6	77	1
Honest and trustworthy person	70	7	63	1
Really cares about people like you	64	14	50	1

a. From 1999–2000 panel, wave 3 (N = 1,755 weighted cases). "Don't know" responses included in the denominator but not shown here.

had very favorable balances in assessments of his intelligence, strength, integrity, and empathy with ordinary people. On all four criteria, he was far ahead of the three other presidential candidates about whom we asked the questions of our survey panel (Zyuganov, Yavlinskii, and Aman Tuleyev). On every one, he was also better perceived than all of the party leaders concerning whom we posed the same questions around the time of the Duma election.[61] Popular soundings of Putin, it is true, were not without blemish. Opinions of his strength, honesty, and empathy were a shade less favorable than they were when we asked about Putin's character in the preceding wave of the election survey. There was also a gradation of enthusiasm, from consensus on his intelligence and knowledge on through to a more tentative judgment of his empathetic qualities. All things considered, though, this is an overwhelmingly appreciative report card. Putin's KGB background does not seem to have worked against him among the population, any more than it did with Yeltsin. Fifty-two percent of our survey respondents said that knowing a presidential candidate had experience in the organs of state security would make them more likely to vote for him; only 10 percent saw it as a detriment.[62]

The electoral consequences of these assessments are set forth in table 7-6. The median voter who thought that on average Putin did not have the positive character traits of intelligence, strength, integrity, and empathy had a slim chance of voting for him (.14), and still had a less than even chance of doing so if he thought Putin probably did not have those attributes. Once the citizen believed Putin probably had the desired traits or, all the more so, definitely had them, the likelihood of voting

Table 7-6. *Putin Vote and Evaluations of His Character*

Mean evaluation of four traits	Citizen opinion (percent)[a]	Predicted probability of voting for Putin[b]
Does not have the positive trait	1	.14
Probably does not have the positive trait	5	.39
Probably has the positive trait	58	.71
Has the positive trait	36	.90

a. N = 1,755 weighted cases. Missing data coded at the mean of the distribution for the specific trait.

b. Computed from multistage statistical model, holding causally prior and simultaneous variables constant at their medians. Sample N = 1,481; $p \leq .01$ for all cells in the column.

Table 7-7. *Prospective Evaluations of Putin's Issue Competence*[a]

Issue	Percent	Say Putin is best prepared Percent of those who named a candidate	Ranking
Social security	38	51	1
Economy	38	50	1
Human rights	37	52	1
Chechnya	62	77	1
Foreign policy	50	69	1
Crime and corruption	52	66	1

a. From 1999–2000 panel, wave 3 (N = 1,755 weighted cases).

for him zoomed. As 94 percent of Russians were convinced in 2000 that Putin had or probably had the stuff of leadership, it is easy to see a compelling link to his electoral success, despite the myriad other factors that entered into the voting decision.

Competence

The final bloc of mass-level variables we have used to explain electoral choice concerns apprehended competence to deal with issues in national policy. In this domain, Putin's advantage in popular opinion was still greater than on character issues (see table 7-7). On each of the six issues where we asked survey informants to indicate which of the candidates was best equipped to handle the issue, Putin led the field. In fact, on every particular issue Putin was adjudged the best-prepared politician by a *majority* of all who were able to name a candidate as best. Seventy-three percent felt Putin to be best qualified on at least one issue, and 23 percent thought him best on all half-dozen issues. Not unexpectedly, Chechnya was his biggest selling point, with three-quarters of all respondents saying he was best qualified. On foreign policy,

Table 7-8. *Putin Vote and Prospective Evaluations of His Issue Competence*

Number of issues Putin can handle best	Citizen opinion (percent)[a]	Predicted probability of voting for Putin[b]
0	27	.58
1	11	.70
2	13	.79
3	10	.86
4	10	.91
5	6	.94
6	23	.96

a. N = 1,755 weighted cases.

b. Computed from multistage statistical model, holding causally prior and simultaneous variables constant at their medians. Sample N = 1,481; $p \leq .01$ for all cells in the column.

he had been speaking for Russia since December 31, and a former KGB lieutenant colonel could have been thought by many to be the right person to suppress crime and corruption. On social policy, the several hikes in old-age pensions might perhaps have inspired confidence. It remains hard to fathom what would possess rational people to reckon Putin the surest bet for improving the Russian economy or safeguarding human rights. There surely was some agglutination across issue areas of sentiment about his competence.[63]

Impressions of Putin's problem-solving potential did tell on voting decisions (see table 7-8). The total effect for our additive issue-competency index, weighing the six policy spheres equally, is .38, which is far from a trivial value. The only reason it is not higher, as is plain from the table, is that the typical voter, even if he thought Putin to have nothing to offer in terms of handling hot issues, was already likely to cast a ballot for him. Our model predicts the probability of a Putin vote for the most skeptical median voter—a person who gave Putin a score of zero on the issue index—to have been .58, or 58 percent. The likelihood of that same person voting for Putin if he judged him best on all six issues was .96, or 96 percent. For the minority of citizens who were inimical to Putin's record or his personality, perceived issue competence tended to make more of an impact. The total effect of the issue-competence score on the probability of voting for Putin, .38 for the median voter, was .57 for the person who gave Putin's character the most negative evaluation and .61 for the person who most strongly disapproved of his job performance.

Conclusions

The making of the president of Russia in 2000 often resembled a coronation more than the "electoral struggle" Vladimir Putin disdained. Rather than ask the people for their support and engage opposing candidates, he shunned promises and ignored the opposition. Never having been elected to anything in his life, he ran for the highest office in the land as the quasi incumbent and as one who miraculously had no political past to answer for. The noncampaign Putin waged was, of course, not what it was made out to be: it inverted the campaigning style of propositioning the electorate while preserving its essence. "To refuse to advertise," the journalist Andrei Kolesnikov wrote of Putin in March 2000, "is also a form of advertising."[64] The noncampaign flooded the citizenry in a sea of politicized information masquerading as objective news reporting. As a holding operation, it was more than adequate, if less than infallible. Its job was easy because when presidential nominations opened in January Putin was already the choice of more than 60 percent of the intended voters—the result of the first phase of the campaign season, stretching back to August of 1999. He took his first-round majority without breaking a sweat, but with 8 to 10 points less of the popular vote than when he was at the acme of his popularity.

Putin and his campaign team put together and held together an unusually diverse electoral coalition. To the kernel of Unity voters who flocked to the lumbering Russian bear on its streamer in December 1999, he added citizens of nearly all political persuasions. He ran well in almost every major social stratum and segment. He attracted individuals who thought happy days, economic and political, were returning to the country. Partisan attachments mattered very little to Putin's drive. Approval of his and to a lesser extent Yeltsin's performance in office was the most potent influence on the Putin vote, followed by evaluations of his personal qualities, issue opinions, and faith in his competence to govern. Orientations toward Putin's public persona, and links to preexisting attitudes and perceptions of the election's dynamic surroundings—all had to be instilled by political communication. For better or for worse, the deed was done with cold-blooded dispatch.

8

Results, Consequences, and Implications for U.S. Policy

HAVING TRACED THE electoral cycle from start to finish, we are now in a position to review its results and to consider consequences for the Russian political system and implications for American foreign policy.

Balance Sheet

Throughout this volume, we have adduced many pieces of evidence about the factors that brought tens of millions of Russians to vote the way they did. The reader who wishes to see them neatly collated can turn to the total-effects tables in appendix table B-1 for the Duma election and table B-2 for the presidential election. Appendix tables B-3 and B-4 present group effects, the conjoint influence of the blocs of explanatory variables in our statistical model of the vote.

Table 8-1 is a digest of that information. It ranks whole blocs of explanatory variables in terms of their estimated impact on the political preferences of all voters in 1999–2000, regardless of party or presidential candidate favored.

Explaining the Vote

As table 8-1 shows, there are intriguing differences from election to election. Partisanship is the most potent influence on voting for the party lists, whereas leadership qualities not surprisingly are foremost in

Table 8-1. *Rank Ordering of Influence of Blocs of Explanatory Variables on Party-List and Presidential Votes, 1999 and 2000*[a]

Rank	Party-list vote, 1999	Presidential vote, 2000
1	Partisanship	Leadership qualities
2	Issue competence	Evaluations of incumbents
3	Leadership qualities	Issue opinions
4	Issue opinions	Partisanship
5	Evaluations of incumbents	Issue competence
6	Current conditions	Current conditions

a. Ranking is of weighted averages of absolute values of modified total effects (differences in predicted probabilities for simultaneous, moderately large changes in all variables in bloc). Methodology explained in appendix B.

the presidential voting. Leadership qualities, issue opinions, and evaluations of incumbents figure larger in the presidential than in the parliamentary election; partisanship and issue competence decline in importance; and current conditions have the same humble standing in the two elections.[1] The rank orderings are quite similar to the preceding pair of national elections, in 1995 and 1996.[2]

Instructive as table 8-1 and its elaborations may be, they have their limitations. As we have seen time after time, specific sources of influence varied in their effects on voting behavior, especially in the Duma election. Issue opinions, for example, had a more thorough impact on KPRF voters than any other factor but were far less weighty for the other parties. Unity voters were more affected than other citizens by evaluations of incumbents, while current conditions had the largest say on the Union of Right Forces (SPS) vote, and assessments of issue competence were the chief determinant of the Fatherland–All Russia (OVR) vote.

More to the point, table 8-1 does not transport us from understanding voters at the *micro* level to understanding the elections at the *macro* level, which was our principal target in undertaking the project. In thinking systemically about the twinned campaigns, we should reflect on the function of elections in the Russian polity, changes in the elite players, and overarching patterns in state-society relations.

Affirming Elections

Compared with elections in most of Europe, the parliamentary election of 1999 was messy. It was tarnished by media bias, infringements of spending limits, and some instances of ballot box stuffing. Compared with how leaders have been selected over Russia's thousand-year history, the third consecutive election of the State Duma, which has lasted longer than any other freely chosen legislative body there, looks rather democratic. Judging by their participation in 1999, all major political actors now accept elections as the one legitimate means for assuming power. By paying campaign consultants and not forming militias, leaders ranging from communist Gennadii Zyuganov to liberal Boris Nemtsov affirmed their belief in the electoral process.

The December vote was held on schedule and under law—a law ratified by elected legislators, with only superficial amendments from the 1993 and 1995 elections. Continuity in rules of the game stabilizes expectations and aids in institutional consolidation. Another plus was a turnout of over 60 percent; this for an election pundits declared would not much shape policy or Russia's future. The results were unknown before the vote, and many incumbents lost. Only 157 of the 441 deputies elected in December 1999 (9 more were chosen in special votes in 2000) were incumbents, 66 of them elected on the party lists and 91 in districts.[3] The turnover rate in the Duma in 1999 vastly outstrips that of the U.S. House of Representatives in 2002, when 99 percent of sitting members seeking reelection retained their districts. If Russia were a tyranny pure and simple, so many candidates, parties, and sponsors would not have competed so hard for positions. Nor would the progovernment media have needed to discredit the OVR leadership. It would have been less trouble simply to falsify the results or coerce citizens to vote correctly.

In the 2000 presidential election, power in the Kremlin changed hands for the first time ever through electoral means. The election took place as constitutionally prescribed. More than two-thirds of the eligible voters participated, and they appeared to make informed choices among candidates who offered a range of platforms, policies, and leadership styles. All this took place with the economic calamity of 1998 fresh in everyone's minds and with an internal war raging in the North Caucasus.

Further encouragement is to be taken from the eclipse of antisystem movements. Most by 1999 were either marginalized or had changed their ways. Vladimir Zhirinovskii's Liberal Democratic Party of Russia (LDPR) once looked like a Nazi clone. The latter-day LDPR that (in the guise of the Zhirinovskii Bloc) reaped about 6 percent of the party-list vote in 1999 operates primarily as a commercial operation, hawking its votes in the Duma to the highest bidder. The more militant nationalist groups that competed in the 1999 election performed miserably. The

Communist Party of the Russian Federation (KPRF) garnered its largest percentage yet of the party-list vote, but its mellower outlook has neutralized it as a threat to the post-Soviet regime. Marxist fundamentalists who reject capitalism and democracy fled to splinter movements of the left, almost all of which were shut out of the new Duma.[4] In the 2000 presidential election, none of the candidates was an extremist of the far left or the far right.

Rather than gravitating to the poles, the most successful of the parties in 1999 and of the presidential hopefuls in 2000 began to converge on the center of the political spectrum. The 1995–96 elections were distinguished by acrimonious debate about market reform, the first war in Chechnya, and foreign policy. In 1999 and 2000, a magnifying glass was sometimes needed to make out distinct positions on national issues. Unity, OVR, and Putin forsook formal ideology completely. Other players, such as the communists and the liberals, held fast to their principles but narrowed the range of overt disagreement with their competitors.[5] Citizens were repelled by bellicose groups and, as noted in chapter 2, wasted many fewer votes than in 1995–96 on parties that did not make it into the legislature and on crank presidential candidates.

Elite Players

Like all competitive elections, Russia's in 1999 and 2000 were won by political entrepreneurs. It may be read as a good omen for democracy that, although there was some abatement in numbers, the supply of electoral entrepreneurs remained robust. Onerous and capricious registration procedures were not enough to keep almost six thousand candidates from taking the field in the Duma campaign and eleven from running for president.[6] Contestants found ingenious ways to make their mark. The communists banked on informal networking and on enfolding their campaign in the mystique of the Great Patriotic War. Unity used anti-Moscow and pro-youth slogans and a television blitz giving the impression of a groundswell. SPS tried rock concerts and a referendum signature drive, while OVR traded on the reputations of its VIP nominees and Yabloko put its leader, Grigorii Yavlinskii, at the forefront. Vladimir Putin utilized a regal noncampaign in which he uttered no overt promises to the population. For some district candidates, the long suit was connections with the local governor or proficiency at lobbying for pork barrel projects.

In comparative perspective, a crucial question for Russia's political development is whether 1999–2000 witnessed a tendency toward the solidification of an orderly multiparty politics. The signs are mixed.

By Western standards, individuals in the electorate were still abnormally volatile. A mere one in four party-list voters in 1999, and one in three whose 1995 party was still in existence, voted the same as four years before. No more Russians had partisan attachments in 1999–2000 than in the mid-1990s. Their psychic bonds to parties were no less volatile than their voting behavior. For their part, many of the parties and quasi parties were rudderless and had a tenuous grasp on their own agents. And both campaigning and voting in the territorial districts were often meagerly connected to goings-on in the party-list portion of the Duma election.

There were indications, nonetheless, of emerging equilibria and of some aggregate-level staying power. Of the six parties and blocs that crossed the 5 percent threshold in 1999, four—the socialist KPRF, the liberal Yabloko and SPS, and the nationalist LDPR—shared attributes that suggest steps toward a structured multiparty system. Between them, they took almost one-half of the popular vote. Three earned representation in parliament for the third time and the core of the fourth, SPS, had taken party-list and district seats in 1993 as Russia's Choice and district seats in 1995 as Russia's Democratic Choice. All except the LDPR bagged roughly the same percentage of the PR vote in 1999 as they had in 1995.[7] These organizations have defined political profiles and styles, newsworthy leaders, and a nucleus of organizers, loyal supporters, and benefactors. Aside from the sniping between SPS and Yabloko, they put more effort in 1999 into maintaining their electorates than into competing with one another. Their objective was essentially to gain entry to the Duma.

Contrary to any notion of a bump-free glide toward party politics, the other two blocs that made 5 percent and that took almost 40 percent of the entire popular vote—the party of power, Unity, and the centrist Fatherland–All Russia—had none of these characteristics. Both were brand new organizations and both fixed their sights on the 2000 presidential race and not on the 1999 parliamentary race. Yurii Luzhkov created Fatherland, and Yevgenii Primakov joined Fatherland–All Russia, to promote their presidential aspirations. In response, the Kremlin conjured Unity to undermine Luzhkov and Primakov and advance the prospects of Boris Yeltsin's greenhorn prime minister, Putin. Being new, OVR and Unity had no pool of tested supporters and so needed to mount fierce efforts to enlist constituents from scratch. Much more than the entrenched parliamentary parties, the public ratings of these presidential-oriented coalitions fluctuated in the four months before election day. When the OVR project for electing a president collapsed, the alliance broke up.

Further bad tidings for the maturation of the parties is how little they counted in the election that really counted—the one for president. Party leaders Zyuganov and Yavlinskii did place second and third, yet neither had a serious chance of prevailing. Putin did not seek out Unity's nomination or draw it into his noncampaign. The parties did not set the menu of choices, define the cleavage issues, or, except for the KPRF, have much to do with mobilizing voters. The upshot is that the political parties continue to play their main role in constituting parliament, an institution with little power. The perception grows that they are bystanders to the high-stakes political game. As one Russian student of the parties noted in 2002, "The media have long since lost interest in party life, the reasoning being that real politics is carried out in the corridors of power [in the executive branch]."[8] Even in the Duma, the parties' reign is incomplete, as half of the deputies are elected in single-member districts where independents, not partisan nominees, took almost half of the district seats in 1999, about 15 percentage points more than they had in 1995. One indicator of the low repute afforded the Duma and the parties populating it is the caravan of party leaders who voted with their feet after the population voted with its ballot slips. Among the big six, only the LDPR had all three leading members of its slate, as approved by the electorate, take up their seats in the Duma. Sergei Shoigu, the cabinet minister who headed up the Unity list, renounced his and was promoted to deputy premier in the government. The St. Petersburg politician who chaired the Unity caucus in his place, Boris Gryzlov, was soon to depart for the Ministry of the Interior. The men listed third on the KPRF national list (Vasilii Starodubtsev), second and third by OVR (Yurii Luzhkov and Vladimir Yakovlev), first by SPS (Sergei Kiriyenko), and second by Yabloko (Sergei Stepashin) also found better things to do.[9]

State and Society

Broad patterns in state-society relations were laid bare in the 1999–2000 elections. Democratic elections are the main device whereby social forces influence the choice of leaders and make political actors account for their actions. In transitional Russia, things are not so straightforward. In its latest national elections, it was *those ensconced in the institutions of the state* who did the most to propel events at every phase.

Their involvement began with the definition of the cast of characters. Looking back on his years in power, Boris Yeltsin reveled in his ability to show them into the limelight: "Even a few years ago the political stage of the new Russia was empty and bare. By giving a politician the chance to occupy a premier's or vice-premier's chair, I immediately made his name well-known, his actions significant, and his personage note-worthy. . . . Gaidar, Chernomyrdin, Kiriyenko, Primakov, Stepashin, Chubais, and others got onto the political stage precisely because of those unexpected, from time to time vexing personnel decisions, which in their day incited so much criticism and controversy."[10] The fruits were there for all to see in 1999–2000. Unity, the party of power, was headed by a member of Yeltsin's government (Shoigu). Unity's antecedent, the moribund NDR, went into battle behind a former prime minister (Chernomyrdin). The troika atop OVR's list of candidates con-sisted of a former prime minister (Primakov) and two regional chief executives (Luzhkov and Yakovlev). A former prime minister (Kiri-yenko) was first on the SPS list and a former first deputy prime minister (Nemtsov) second, while another former state minister (Chubais) was chief organizer and fund-raiser, and Yeltsin's prime minister in 1992 (Gaidar) had a place on the list. Yet another former premier (Stepashin) was number two for Yabloko. The KPRF, though no longer in the sad-dle, put forward dozens of candidates who had held senior government office in the 1990s, were in comparable positions or had tenure in the apparatus of the ruling party before 1991, or were heads of regional governments.[11] The most eminent state official to enter the fray was, of course, Vladimir Putin in 2000. His presence deterred most other func-tionaries from contending for president.

The electoral contestants in 1999–2000, all and sundry, entered a playing field systematically tilted to the benefit of players who defended the interests of powerful officeholders in the executive wing of the fed-eral government. A businessman then close to the Kremlin, Boris Bere-zovskii, gave Unity its start, and the bloc was thereafter assisted in every conceivable way by state agencies. Yeltsin's timely resignation and anointing of Putin as his replacement and heir set all alternative candidates for the presidency back on their heels. Already referring to himself as "leader of the country," Putin could stage his election bid from a wood-paneled Kremlin office, bathed in the deference a national leader enjoys—the Russian equivalent of a U.S. Rose Garden strategy. Regional governments also got in on the act, supporting an assortment of parties in 1999 but closing ranks around Putin in the 2000 election.

The mass media were a key link in the chain of influence. Although there was one private television network (NTV) with a national audience, a station owned by the city of Moscow (TV-Tsentr), scores of independent radio stations, dozens of quasi-independent regional channels and fully private cable television networks, and hundreds of independent newspapers, Russians got the bulk of their political news from the first and second channels on the TV dial (ORT and RTR), both of them part of the government's web of influence. State television tirelessly valorized Unity and then Putin. In a candid moment on election night in March, Putin recognized Zyuganov's showing as stronger than expected, given the fact he "did not have many of the media resources, especially electronic," that Putin had.[12]

The flimsiness of most of the parties and of other associations autonomous of the state eased the way for state-based office seekers. Both the parliamentary and the presidential election "reflected the weakness and embryonic character of the structures of civil society" in Russia.[13] In an underorganized political space, newborn quasi parties nurtured by the bureaucracy—like Unity and OVR—had plenty of room for wildfire growth. Putin leveraged his position and command over state resources into an insurmountable lead before the presidential derby started. Without question, the lack of effective competition diluted the democratic quotient of the 2000 election, and worse than it had in the hard-fought Duma election. Not only did Putin win hands down, but he got away with evading articulation of a vision of the future. It is an oversimplification to say, as Russian critics allege, that the election of Putin was "the triumph of the psychology of state paternalism,"[14] but there is no denying that the transfer of power had many of the "delegative" qualities that Guillermo O'Donnell has shown are debilitating to democratic governance.[15]

A more even-handed election would also have been good for the integrity of the electoral process. In a tight race, as Floridians and other Americans learned in 2000, small mistakes, deceptions, and errors in counting procedures come out in the wash. In a landslide, these flaws go unexposed since divulging them will not change the electoral outcome.

Zyuganov and his aides claimed the morning after the presidential vote that KPRF monitors had uncovered 1,855 procedural abuses and that if the votes had been tallied fairly a runoff would have been necessary.[16] We cannot adjudicate these charges. We do know from transnational experience that the truth ought to have been ascertained and publicized by impartial investigators. Putin's margin of victory precluded that, and Russian democracy was the worse for it.[17]

Managed Democracy

Much ink has been spilled in recent years on betrayals of the promise of the "third wave" of global democratization that stretched from the 1970s into the 1990s, of which the fall of the Soviet dictatorship and of its satellites in Eastern Europe was a capstone. Although there have been democratic success stories in the former Soviet Union, there have been terrible failures and disappointments as well.[18] The Russian regime that put down roots under Boris Yeltsin in the 1990s had many of the features of an "electoral democracy," while not displaying the robust institutions and norms typical of a full-fledged "liberal democracy."[19] Especially after enactment of Yeltsin's presidentialist constitution in 1993, mass-based interest groups were consigned to the fringes, pluralist interest intermediation was feeble, individual liberties began to be abridged by arbitrary practices, and institutions that could help redress the imbalance—parliament, the party system, and the judiciary—lacked strength and independence.[20]

In consolidated democracies, electoral results can trigger policy changes. A new tone, new laws, new economic programs, and new foreign policies are normal spin-offs from elections, even if drastic changes are rare.[21] It is unusual for elections to bring forth modifications in the rules for doing the public's business. Were they to change every time the balance of power changed, institutions—democratic or otherwise—would have no causal significance.[22]

The unconsolidated nature of Russia's regime lowered the barriers to institutional change after the electoral cycle of 1999–2000. Vladimir Putin quickly put his imprint not only on policy but also on the rules of the game for making policy. He has not amended or radically trespassed on the 1993 constitution and has not upended the institutional configuration of Yeltsin's regime. Nor does he seem to have any coherent plan for doing so in the future. He has, however, initiated or tolerated a congeries of discrete changes that have chipped away at the democratic legacy of the reform years. Yeltsin, in recruiting Putin from the closed world of the security agencies and announcing him as the "steel core" of a revitalized government, undoubtedly expected a course correction in the direction of discipline and order. It is clear that he now thinks Putin has gone too far in certain respects.[23]

Putin's innovations coincide with a spate of revisionist thinking about democratization in the contemporary world. Some say autocracies have as often as not been replaced by hybrid regimes entwining democratic with authoritarian principles. Others go further to assert that Russia and a series of other countries are best thought of as "competitive authoritarian" systems, in which the authoritarian element has the upper hand.[24]

It is premature to pigeonhole Russia in any of these categories. The phrase "managed democracy" will do as a marker for the current condition of its polity. If it is too early to sign the death certificate for democracy, it is too late to ignore tokens of a backing away from the liberal and democratic ideals in whose name the Soviet regime was overthrown. Having begun on Yeltsin's watch, the retreat has gathered momentum on Putin's. Russia's present rulers are modernizers in the economic and socioeconomic sphere and pro-Western realists in foreign policy. In the political domain, they take the electoral mechanism and the formal institutions of democracy for granted. They accept that they must periodically renew their popular mandate and that when they do society must be afforded alternatives to the status quo. They do not speak openly about canceling elections or suspending the constitution. They also are reconciled to a limited diversity of opinion and interest within the state machinery. Without setting out to extinguish it, they do aim nonetheless to contain this diversity within boundaries fixed by them alone. For those at the rudder, democracy is neither good nor evil. It is an existential product of larger forces that, like gravity, cannot be switched off, yet with the appropriate engineering, can be canalized and harnessed to one's own purpose.

Breaking the Logjam in the Duma

Putin entered office bent on resuming the economic reforms that had been stymied by governmental disorganization and legislative resistance in Yeltsin's second term. Although he selected a known face from the

Yeltsin era, Mikhail Kas'yanov, to head his first cabinet, he inserted into the next tier a team of market liberals, most of them known to him from St. Petersburg days. Key players were the new first deputy prime minister and minister of finance, Aleksei Kudrin (a fellow vice mayor with Putin in Anatolii Sobchak's administration), the minister for economic development and trade, German Gref, and the president's personal adviser on economic affairs, the iconoclastic Andrei Illarionov. The team came in with an ambitious program encompassing tax reform, land privatization, deregulation, changes in labor and welfare policy, and incentives for foreign investors.

The 1999–2000 electoral cycle, by putting in place a Duma and a president with the same basic political orientation, enabled the government to make rapid strides on this reform agenda. The Unity bloc, partnering with the People's Deputy faction (consisting of pro-Kremlin deputies from the districts) and Regions of Russia (which peeled away from OVR after the Duma election), materialized as the pivotal force within the Duma.[25] It and its allies swung a deal with the KPRF to parcel out the chairs of major committees, cutting OVR, SPS, Yabloko, and the LDPR out of the spoils.[26] The pact made the KPRF's Gennadii Seleznëv speaker for a second term. It transpired, though, that Seleznëv's binding commitments were now to Putin and the Kremlin, as his subsequent exit from the communist hierarchy was to make apparent. Unity's alliance with the KPRF was purely tactical and unwound in the course of 2000 and 2001. Unity increasingly counted on rightist and centrist deputies to help it pursue its legislative agenda, leaving a jilted Zyuganov to huff that Putin was a "liberal dictator."[27]

For the first time since 1993, the balance of power in Russia's parliament after 1999 was decisively anticommunist. The Duma has not indulged in brinkmanship with the president by debating impeachment and nonconfidence resolutions. Pushed to act on the economy by Putin and his government, it has enacted new sections of the Russian tax code that had been in legislative limbo for years, putting in place a flat income tax of 13 percent and a lower profits tax.[28] It has gone along with a new labor code considered very friendly to business interests and a land code that allows for the ownership and sale of farms and urban land. Putin and the executive also have managed to work with the Duma to pass balanced and feasible budgets, a feat rarely accomplished in the Yeltsin years when parliament and president were so estranged.[29] Putin has only begun to tackle some of the most painful structural changes, such as those touching on pensions, social assistance, and housing. This said, much has been accomplished in the realm of economic reform since the polarization between executive and legislature was eased as a consequence of the 1999–2000 elections.[30]

To call this new relationship between the Duma and the president antidemocratic would be wrong. Every president around the world wants to have a pliant parliament to work with. The nondemocratic flavor to executive-legislative relations in Putin's Russia comes not from the desire to have a parliamentary majority but from the way the majority has been achieved, that is, as discussed in earlier chapters, through elections in which pro-executive candidates were given an unfair advantage.

Taming the Upper House

Putin's ability to assemble supermajorities in the Duma—majorities capable of overriding vetoes of bills handed down by the Federation Council, the upper house of parliament—permitted him to retool the very organization of the house and perforce of the federal system. To everyone's surprise, he made reform of the Federation Council one of his top political goals in his first months in office.

The Russian constitution states that, after an interim period (1993–95) during which members were directly elected, each region of the federation was to send two deputies to the Federation Council: one representing the province's legislative assembly and one representing its chief executive. The constitution does not specify how these representatives were to be selected. By the end of the interim period, the regional governments had secured agreement on a law mandating that all provincial leaders be popularly elected—until then, Yeltsin had appointed many governors—and that governors and legislative heads henceforth sit ex officio in the Federation Council. This formulation gave the governors and their legislative colleagues increased local legitimacy and greater autonomy from Yeltsin and Moscow. By granting the governors and republic presidents a direct voice in the national parliament, it also created a constitutional anomaly, as these individuals concurrently wore executive and legislative hats. The Federation Council functioned mostly as a lobby for regional interests.

Two weeks after being sworn into office, Putin proposed a new recipe for picking the upper house that replaced the regional leaders with persons designated by them under an intricate formula.[31] The members of the Federation Council resisted tenaciously, knowing they would lose their apartments and offices in Moscow, their parliamentary immunity, and much of their clout with the Russian government. After a heated battle in which the Duma warned it would override a Federation Council veto and the Kremlin allegedly threatened governors with criminal investigations if they did not support Putin's plan, the law was adopted in July 2000. As a sop, many governors and retired governors were appointed to a new body advisory to the president, the State Council.

The reform has sapped a significant institutional counterweight to the president. Its members, being unelected, do not have the same authority as previous members of the council. Many, in fact, are Muscovites with patronage ties to Putin who acquired their seats with his administration's backing and have put the Kremlin's interests ahead of their constituents.[32] The new setup also makes it more difficult for regional leaders to take collective action vis-à-vis the central government. As the Duma deputy Vladimir Lysenko stated in 2001, "The president . . . managed to get rid of one of the strongest and most authoritative state bodies in the country. It provided the function of check and balance on the other branches of power, especially the executive, which is fast evolving into an authoritarian regime."[33]

Again, Putin's changes to the Federation Council did not formally transgress the democratic rules of the game outlined in Russia's constitution.[34] Nor was the prior method of constituting the upper house perfect, as it fudged the lines between executive and legislative authority. Putin's correction to this odd formulation, however, was not the democratic move that many had proposed for years, that is, direct election of senators. Instead, he decreased the role of citizens in selecting their government representatives and enfeebled another check on the Kremlin's power.

Center-Regional Relations

In another aspect of managed democracy, the clipping of the governors' wings has extended to their home turf. In a decree on May 13, 2000, Putin overlaid seven super-regions ("federal districts"), accountable to Moscow, on the eighty-nine units of the federation. Each was to be headed by a plenipotentiary who would be appointed by the president personally and would sit on his Security Council. Five of the seven envoys named in 2000 were from the FSB, the army, or the police.[35]

They have writ over all federal agencies in the regions other than the military and thus have access to officials in the politically most sensitive and influential positions, such as those in the treasury, tax inspectorate, procuracy, FSB, and regular police. Their mission is to oversee the activities of the bureaucracy and to report to the president's office on any regional noncompliance with the constitution or laws of Russia.

Other changes accompanied the super-regions. First, a law passed in July 2000 authorizes the president to suspend elected governors accused of wrongdoing by the procurator-general's office. Inasmuch as criminal proceedings could drag out indefinitely (especially if that suits the president), the law is tantamount to a presidential right to fire governors. Putin has used the power only once, and indirectly at that (when he orchestrated the ouster of Governor Yevgenii Nazdratenko of Primor'e region in 2001), but the mere threat has had a chilling effect on gubernatorial initiative.[36] Putin can also dismiss any regional legislature that passes laws contravening federal laws or the constitution. Second, Putin's government has stopped signing the bilateral agreements with the provinces that were one of Yeltsin's favorite instruments for attaining their acquiescence. Beginning in 2003, the division of labor among the national and subnational governments is to be governed by an omnibus law, which in principle is to be applied uniformly across Russia's territory. Third, Moscow has pushed through a more centralized allotment of tax receipts. As of 1999, roughly 45 percent of the revenues collected in the regions were supposed to be transferred to the central government, although the amount that reached it was often less. Under a law signed by Putin in 2000, about 55 percent is to go to Moscow and 45 percent to the regions, and the balance is to be reviewed regularly. Regions like Bashkortostan that for years paid almost no federal taxes by virtue of bilateral agreements are once again contributing to the federal budget.

Parties and Elections

Changes within Russia's principal party groupings erupted soon after the 1999–2000 voting. The Fatherland–All Russia bloc, whose founding touched off the electoral struggle, spoke for current and recent officeholders who sought control of the national government on the assumption that Yeltsin and his entourage were a spent force. Unity, the response to OVR's challenge, was at the outset the creature of some pro-

Kremlin governors and of businessmen, particularly Boris Berezovskii, who were anxious about the dangers to them if OVR and Yevgenii Primakov came to power.

Both founding groups miscalculated. OVR leaders made the biggest blunder, as they fumbled the Duma election and then concluded they could not field a credible candidate for president. All Russia and the Regions of Russia caucus defected in January 2000 and mended fences with the Kremlin. In due course, the entire coalition followed them abjectly into Putin's camp.

The original masterminds of Unity miscalculated in a different way. Although Unity achieved electoral success and incorporation into the power structure, its architect, Berezovskii, did not survive as a political insider. Anticipating Putin's gratitude, Berezovskii got the back of his hand, as Putin was nervous that the "Family" group around Berezovskii and his business ventures had accumulated excessive influence. He first ostracized Berezovskii and then pushed him into exile in London in 2001. Berezovskii is currently fighting Russian attempts to extradite him from Britain to face criminal charges relating to alleged tax fraud in the mid-1990s.

Unity thrived without Berezovskii, upgrading its legal status from electoral bloc to civic movement and then, in 2002, into a political party named United Russia. OVR agreed in December 2001 to a phased-in merger with United Russia, which will be complete in time for the campaign for the 2003 parliamentary election. Whereas Yeltsin discarded two consecutive parties of power, Russia's Choice and Our Home Is Russia, Putin has favored Unity/United Russia's strengthening as an organization and seems ready to endorse and assist it in 2003–04. United Russia's staying power is far from certain. It has more resources, more support from ruling elites in Moscow and the regions, and better rapport with national television networks than any previous party of power going into a second parliamentary election. At the same time, its identity and orientation remain as ambiguous in 2003 as Unity's was in 1999, and its only strong trademark is Putin himself. It is heading into the next election season with the lackluster Boris Gryzlov, doing double duty as interior minister, as its chairman. And, after four years in office, United Russia candidates can no longer pretend to be the new, fresh faces from the periphery.

Within the main opposition party, the KPRF, a smoldering disagreement between the leader, Zyuganov, and the parliamentary speaker,

Seleznëv, burst into flame in 2002. Seleznëv resigned from the party and, with Kremlin support, kept his speaker's job. He has formed his own political organization, Russia (Rossiya), and vows to battle the KPRF for leftist votes in the next elections. There is much dissatisfaction with Zyuganov's inflexibility, and it is even possible that the KPRF will nominate a younger and less hidebound individual, such as Sergei Glaz'ev, as its presidential standard bearer in 2004. Despite battles at the top of the party, the KPRF's base remains loyal and unlikely to defect and support some new leftist organization.

On the right, SPS has made the transition from a coalition of parties and movements to a political party. The head of its 1999 slate, Sergei Kiriyenko, withdrew from its affairs when he accepted the job of Putin's plenipotentiary in the Volga super-region. This left Boris Nemtsov as parliamentary chairman, with Anatolii Chubais lurking in the wings. Having cooperated with the government and seen it institute a liberal economic policy, SPS worries that it will not have a distinctive platform to sell to the electorate in 2003 and will gain no credit for the country's relative prosperity. Several veterans of the Russian democratic movement, most prominently Sergei Kovalëv, have quit the party in disgust at its pro-war stance on Chechnya.[37] Ironically, since Kovalëv's departure, SPS has gradually crept back toward its pro-democratic roots as Putin's policies move in the opposite direction. SPS's liberal rival, Yabloko, suffered a number of defections after March 2000, including the manager of its 1999 campaign, Vyacheslav Igrunov, who left to form his own boutique political movement.[38] Yavlinskii remains at the helm and has firmed up his relationship with Mikhail Khodorkovskii, the CEO of Yukos. Sporadic negotiations with SPS over a common slate in 2003 or other forms of collaboration have been in vain.[39] After years of standoffishness toward government, Yavlinskii has edged closer to Putin, perhaps aware of how much the president's blessing could help him in the next election. Putin's attitude toward the liberals was apparently influenced by their conduct during the crisis sparked by Chechen fighters' seizure of hundreds of hostages in a Moscow theater in October 2002. He accused Nemtsov of exploiting the disaster for political gain and praised Yavlinskii for not doing so. His reaction fueled suspicion that Putin might back Yabloko as his liberal ally instead of SPS.[40]

Whatever comes of these partisan intrigues and squabbles, there are two other changes afoot that must be watched for their long-term effects. The first stems from the interest within the Russian leadership in revamping the rules for party formation and electing the State Duma. Addressing Unity's convention in February 2000, Putin spoke in favor of a "workable" party system containing "two, three, or four parties."[41] Streamlining was the main aim of a new law on parties passed in 2001, which stiffened the requirements for registration and stipulated that electoral blocs would now have to include one political party.[42] Unity in 1999 preached the need to eliminate proportional representation and for all deputies to be chosen in districts. Its motivations were not altruistic. Their poor showing in the districts in 1999 notwithstanding, Unity's founders calculated that a party of power would do better in a district-based system, especially if it could polarize the district races and then prevail in the runoff. Unity and its Duma allies have so far failed to institute such a change, but in 2002 they did succeed in raising the threshold for the party list from 5 to 7 percent, effective in 2007 (they originally proposed 12.5 percent), which will tend to decrease the number of parties that get into parliament. Ultimately, Putin's brain trust hopes to push all parties other than United Russia and the KPRF to the sidelines.[43] Were the KPRF and United Russia to collude to dispense with proportional representation altogether, Russia's proto-multiparty system could become a hegemonic party system dominated by United Russia.[44]

The second and more alarming trend is toward arbitrary interference by the central authorities in regional elections, usually with the connivance of local politicos, electoral commissions, and courts. The tone was set in November 2000 when, instigated by Kremlin officials, a judge removed the incumbent, Aleksandr Rutskoi, from the ballot for the governor's election in Kursk region on the eve of the voting. Rutskoi, a supporter of Unity in 1999 and Russia's vice president from 1991 to 1993, had among other things offended Putin during the controversy over the sinking of the nuclear submarine *Kursk* several months before.[45] In April 2002 the scenario was repeated with the front-runner for election of president of Ingushetiya, a republic bordering Chechnya.[46] The same year, Moscow intervened on behalf of clients in gubernatorial elections in Krasnoyarsk and Nizhnii Novgorod, and charges flew of fraud in the vote counting.[47] New legislation may confine such practices, but any trace of them, whether or not they spread to the national level, compromises Russia's functioning even as an electoral democracy.[48] Andreas Schedler has compared the assessment of electoral democracies to multiplication by zero, not addition: "Partial compliance to democratic norms does not add up to partial democracy. Gross violation of any one condition invalidates the fulfillment of all the others. If the chain of democratic choice is broken anywhere, elections become not less democratic but undemocratic."[49]

Chechnya and Civil Liberties

Putin's rise to power dovetailed with a cruel war in Chechnya, the second Russia has fought there in a half decade. As we have mentioned, Unity and then Putin were seen by the electorate as the political players who could best handle an issue that has tormented Russia more than any other. Russia had the sovereign right to deal with the lawlessness that enveloped the republic after the Khasavyurt accord ended the first Chechen war in 1996, a plague whose most barbarous manifestation was a wave of kidnappings and of sale and execution of hostages. The initial limited use of force against the Chechen fighters who marauded in Dagestan in 1999 was also justified. The response the Russian government then chose—a full-scale military reoccupation, bombardment by heavy weaponry, and oppressive patrols and filtration camps—has not brought about the promised result. Putin has pledged military reform, as Yeltsin pledged before him, and appointed a civilian, Sergei Ivanov of the FSB, as defense minister in 2000, but this objective has taken a back seat to prosecution of the war by an archaic military manned by a Soviet-era officer corps and sullen conscripts.[50] Wars are always brutal. Neither that nor the violence of the guerrillas and of terrorists linked to them exonerates Russia's routinely inhumane acts in Chechnya. The monitoring organization Human Rights Watch has documented atrocities that take in summary shootings, the torching of villages, the rape of Chechen women, and the mistreatment of prisoners of war.[51] Experts reckon that 400,000 refugees have been displaced by the fighting.[52] Moscow has no strategy for either withdrawal or a negotiated settlement, claiming there is no one to negotiate with. To staunch the flow of information about human rights violations, it has expelled the Organization for Security and Cooperation in Europe's (OSCE's) observer mission from the republic.

Since Putin's inauguration, the leash on the FSB, which he headed in 1998–99 and is now directed by his close associate Nikolai Patrushev, has been loosened. The agency has stepped up the harassment of targeted human rights activists and environmentalists, Western nongovernmental organizations (NGOs), and religious groups affiliated with out-side organizations.[53] New guidelines on foreign contacts for academics have been issued. Several researchers and environmentalists have been prosecuted for espionage, although conspicuous cases have ended in acquittal or pardon.[54] At the end of 2002, the FSB became more aggressive in limiting contacts between Russian citizens and foreigners. Visa invitations must now be screened by the police. In addition to evicting the OSCE from Chechnya, the Russian government canceled its agreement with the U.S. Peace Corps and refused reentry to Irene Stevenson, the long-time director of the AFL-CIO's Solidarity Center in Moscow.

The Media

Putin has also tightened the state's grip on the mass media, assigning priority to national television.[55] The commercial network NTV supported OVR in the Duma campaign and, though less warmly, Yavlinskii in the presidential campaign and provided the most candid coverage of the second Chechen war, as it had of the first. Putin moved to settle scores in the spring of 2000. His Kremlin administration leaned on prosecutors to investigate reputed past misdeeds of Vladimir Gusinskii, president of the Media-Most company that owned NTV, and Gazprom called in a large loan to NTV. In the space of several months, Gazprom's media holding company took over NTV, Gusinskii fled abroad, the staff of the weekend newsmagazine "Itogi" was fired, and the daily newspaper owned by Media-Most, *Segodnya,* was shut down. Gazprom was to purge NTV a second time in January 2003, removing Boris Jordan, the Russian-American director it had appointed in 2000. Yevgenii Kiselëv and many of NTV's best journalists and producers migrated to TV-6, a much smaller station owned by Berezovskii, only to have the government close it down. The original NTV team headed by Kiselëv got back on the air a third time on a channel called TVS in 2002, but it drew a limited fraction of the national audience and had recurrent financial problems. The board of TVS included such unlikely partners as Kiselëv, Chubais, Arkadii Vol'skii, and Yevgenii Primakov, who "called on editorial staff to exercise 'internal censorship' in order to keep the network 'responsible.'"[56] In June 2003 the Media Ministry, ignoring the legal requirement for a court order, declared TVS bankrupt, took it off the air, and announced it would transfer the frequency to a government-backed sports channel. By the time Berezovskii relinquished TV-6, he had already ceded his large minority stake and editorial control in ORT, and Sergei Dorenko, the acid-tongued anchorman who was his and the Kremlin's battering ram against OVR in 1999, had been sent packing. Independent media are not flourishing in the regions, either, as local heads of administration usually keep a tight reign on editorial policy. The flow of information is most limited in Chechnya, where governmental agencies have severely restricted access to the territory by Russian and foreign correspondents and have arrested and intimidated several print journalists whose war stories they found inconvenient.[57]

The struggle over the media involves business and personality issues as well as questions of free speech. The losers to date are not blameless. Gusinskii's financial practices were risky, and NTV can be faulted for not offering equal access to all comers during the 1999–2000 elections.[58] Nevertheless, the pluralism that comes from multiple owners and multiple biases is preferable to the monotone that would result from a total state monopoly over provision of the news. In nationwide television broadcasting, Russia is closer today to such a monopoly than any time since the establishment of NTV in 1993. As the 2003–04 round of elections approaches, even moderate opponents of Putin have many fewer outlets for delivering their message than they had in 1999–2000.[59]

What Is Putin After?

We have seen enough of Putin to realize that he and his statecraft cannot be appraised on one level or by one criterion. We have not seen enough yet to allow us to sort through the ellipses and contradictions in the thinking of the public man. The private man remains behind many veils.

Some of the handiwork we label managed democracy is a pragmatic response to the trying circumstances his country found itself in at the end of the 1990s. Boris Yeltsin, capable of flashes of imagination and boldness, was bored with the minutiae of government and preferred changing officials to rethinking policies. To buy support and stability in tumultuous times, he made numerous concessions to groups like the provincial governors and the new business elite, barely considering the costs. Putin inherited these arrangements, found many of them lacking, and set out to enforce or negotiate better terms. The particulars often reflect common sense more than they do ideology and might very well have been implemented no matter who succeeded Yeltsin. We and most

Russians see nothing objectionable in Putin's having ended the polarization between executive and legislature, removed the anomaly of governors sitting in the upper house of parliament, squeezed more tax revenues out of the provinces, tinkered with the electoral system, put one or two of the most arrogant oligarchs in their place, or retaliated against the Chechen incursion into Dagestan. In economic policy, Putin has listened to liberal advice and converted it into legislation more consistently and effectively than Yeltsin did. His reforms, along with the 1998 devaluation and the rise in world oil prices, have helped sustain an economic recovery now in its fifth year, a welcome respite after being so long in the doldrums.

Prolonged economic growth should be conducive to democracy, for it will give rise to a middle class that will demand freedoms and accountable government.[60] This could end up being Putin's most benign legacy to Russia. Nor should we be blind to the institutional and political projects Putin supports that may strengthen democratic governance in the long run. To his credit, for example, he favors legal reforms that will pare the powers of prosecutors, introduce jury trials nationwide, and lessen the incarceration rate.[61] In 2002 he vetoed restrictive amendments to the law on the mass media passed by parliament after the Moscow hostage crisis. And Putin on occasion says the right things about democracy and human rights. In November 2001 he attended a Civic Forum sponsored by his administration with the purpose of bridging the chasm between state officials and grass-roots activists. The sight of a former KGB agent, Putin, sitting at the same table as a former Soviet dissident and the head of the Moscow Helsinki Group, Lyudmilla Alekseyeva, was a stirring one, although some fretted it was all a ploy to co-opt the activists.[62] A year later Putin met with a similar group on International Human Rights Day and proclaimed that his heart was with them: "Protecting civil rights and freedoms is a highly relevant issue for Russia. You know that next year will see the tenth anniversary of our constitution. It declares the basic human rights and freedoms to be the highest value and it enshrines them as self-implementing standards. I must say that this is of course a great achievement."[63]

Unfortunately, Putin's actions all too frequently are at variance with his words. He has worked assiduously to weaken the ramshackle checks and balances built up during Yeltsin's tenure and to impose the tidy logic of the rationalizer and controller and not, as a rule, the logic of the democrat. Yeltsin loved adding pawns to the political chessboard. Putin is happier subtracting them, as he has with Fatherland–All Russia, the oligarchs who got too close to the throne (including, in 2003, Khodorkovskii), the governors who rashly meddled in Moscow politics, the parties he wants to limit to "two, three, or four," and the elected government of Chechnya. When the chips are down, he has shown himself to be, if not actively antagonistic to democratic values, indifferent to their application. In his pursuit of a strong state that can solve Russia's problems, he tends to forget what he said in his open letter to the electorate in February 2000—that a strong state, capable of promoting popular freedom and welfare, must itself be "bound by the laws." A presidential administration that schemes to have candidates whisked off the ballot hours before a gubernatorial election is not bound by the laws. Neither is a government that invokes phony legal excuses to seize control of an NTV or a TV-6 or that lets ill-trained troops run amok in the North Caucasus.

It is not the trees we wish to dwell on here but the forest. Putin's managed democracy is partly about practical problem solving, but it is also about eliminating external checks on the power of the state and the leader, without scrapping the constitutional framework bequeathed by Yeltsin. We reiterate that Russia's political institutions were never more than partly democratic and were not properly consolidated during the Yeltsin period. This makes it all the more deplorable that Putin has applied himself to diverting the country further away from democratic governance. After the completion of the critical set of elections in 1999–2000 and the first several years in office of the talented leader who triumphed in them, the future of Russian democracy is *more uncertain* than before.

Popular Attitudes

One sometimes hears it said that the decline in democratic practices and institutions in Russia conforms to the will of the people. At some level of abstraction this obviously must be the case, for it was the Russian electorate, and not the Ethiopian or the Portuguese, that voted Putin into office and seems very likely to do so again in 2004.

Our inquiry into the elections shows, though, that authoritarian attitudes can at a maximum be considered one of a multitude of factors that drove support for Putin in March 2000. The median voter who wanted the president to be stronger than parliament and who found rule by a strongman tempting was perceptibly more inclined to vote for Putin than others. But even in the realm of political values, pro-Putin citizens were not unambiguously authoritarian. They were much less apt than Zyuganov voters to favor a revival of the unreformed Soviet regime. On Chechnya, they were no more hawkish than the rest.

Russians, admittedly, did not flock to politicians with more liberal views than Putin and his Unity allies. But demagogues openly espousing dictatorship fared more miserably at the polls than the liberals. The LDPR, which led the party-list voting in 1993, scraped over the 5 percent barrier in 1999. In 2000 its leader, Zhirinovskii, received fewer than 3 percent of the votes.

Do Russians want democracy? We asked this question repeatedly in our citizen surveys in 1999–2000, using a variety of question wordings. Invariably, we found a majority answering in the affirmative. When asked if they "in general support the idea of democracy," roughly two respondents in three said they did while fewer than one in five said they did not. Asked if democracy is an appropriate way to govern Russia, 60 percent said it was a very good or fairly good model for the country, with far fewer, 24 percent, portraying it as fairly bad or very bad. When disaggregated into components, endorsement of democratic institutions and practices is higher in Russia than the already considerable support for democracy as a universal concept. Eighty-seven percent of respondents to our surveys answered that it was important to them that the country's leaders be popularly elected. More than 85 percent of those polled felt that the freedoms of conscience, expression, and the mass media were important to them. Seventy to 75 percent found free choice of place of residence and religious freedom to be important.[64]

There is a yawning gap between Russians' opinion of democracy as an ideal and their assessment of realities in their own country. Almost 80 percent of respondents questioned after the presidential election said Russia should be a democratic country (see table 8-2). Only about 20 percent thought it is a democratic country today. A majority of citizens, therefore, find practice to jar with preference.

Popular assessments of electoral procedures in 1999 and 2000 reveal further incongruities (see table 8-3). On a five-point scale measuring fairness, about 40 percent rated the Duma election on the fair side of the midpoint and about 55 percent rated the presidential election fair. A substantial majority in 1999 and a substantial minority in 2000 either thought the election unfair, gave it an equivocal rating, or could not say. Notice that this puts confidence in the fairness of elections approxi-

Table 8-2. *Attitudes toward Democracy as an Ideal and a Reality*[a]

Question and response	Percent
Do you agree Russia should be a democratic country?	
Yes	78
No	10
Don't know	12
Do you think Russia is a democratic country today?	
Yes	21
No	62
Don't know	18

a. From 1999–2000 panel, wave 3 (N = 1,755 weighted cases).

Table 8-3. *Attitudes toward Fairness of the 1999 and 2000 Elections*[a]

Percent

Fairness scale	Duma election[b]	Presidential election[c]
1 – Fair	22	39
2	16	17
3	24	15
4	11	7
5 – Unfair	11	9
Don't know	16	12

a. Question reads, "In some countries, people believe their elections are conducted fairly. In other countries, people believe that their elections are conducted unfairly. Speaking of the recent election of [the State Duma or the president], how fair was this election? Please use a 5-point scale where 1 means that the election . . . was conducted fairly and 5 means that the election . . . was conducted unfairly."

b. From 1999–2000 panel, wave 2 (N = 1,846 weighted cases).

c. From 1999–2000 panel, wave 3 (N = 1,755 weighted cases).

mately halfway between the normative and descriptive positions Russians took on democracy. Elections were lacking, as compared with people's view of what governance in Russia should be like, but they were less bemoaned than the political system as a whole. Notice also the discrepancy between the parliamentary and the presidential elections. More Russians thought the Duma campaign unfairly waged, although the detached observer might just as easily call it the other way around. In our estimation, both campaigns were less than fair, but in different ways. The Duma election was marred by bare-knuckled tactics and the war of words against OVR. The presidential election gave the appearance of greater evenhandedness because most of the publicity stream of the victor, Putin, that flowed through daily news bulletins suddenly became placid and reverential of the new chief.

In Russia's transitional environment, the toughest questions about democratic values concern trade-offs between them and other prized

Table 8-4. *Attitudes toward Trade-Off between Democracy and a Strong State*[a]

Question and response	Percent
Is it possible for Russia at the present time to be simultaneously a democratic country and a country with a strong state or must we choose one or the other—either a strong state or democracy?	
We can have both	56
We must choose	34
Don't know	10
What is more important for Russia right now— to have a strong state or to be a democratic country?	
A strong state	46
Democracy	6
Equally important (volunteered response)	41
Don't know	7

a. From 1999–2000 panel, wave 3 (N = 1,755 weighted cases).

ends. Table 8-4 sets forth responses to a pair of questions we put to survey respondents in 2000 about the relationships between democratic government and the strong state. Table 8-5 probes the tension between democracy and economic growth. In both cases, we asked first if it was necessary to choose between democracy and the other value, or if Russia could find a way to achieve both. For a strong state and economic development alike, a majority of Russians (56 percent for the strong state and 63 percent for economic growth) were inclined to say those worthy objectives *could be reconciled* with democracy. These results come as a mild relief. Not so the responses to questions about which of each pair of objectives they found most important—in other words, what they would do *if forced to choose*. Here democracy gets the short end of the stick, preferred over a strong state by a mere 6 percent of individuals and over economic growth by a mere 2 percent. The only consolation is that a large subset of respondents—41 percent for the strong state and 38 percent for economic growth—insisted that the interviewer write down as a volunteered response that the two objectives were equally important.

So far as Putin's electorate is concerned, the fascinating thing is how he tapped into the desire of so many Russians to avoid having to make these wrenching choices, as opposed to opting unreservedly for democracy (which very few were willing to do) or choosing autocracy (which most Zyuganov voters did not flinch at). Sixty-one percent of Putin voters in 2000 believed Russia could combine democracy and a strong state

Table 8-5. *Attitudes toward Trade-Off between Democracy and Economic Growth*[a]

Question and response	Percent
Is it possible for there to be in Russia at the present time both democracy and economic growth, or must we choose one or the other—either economic growth or democracy?	
We can have both	63
We must choose	27
Don't know	10
What is more important for Russia right now—economic growth or democracy?	
Economic growth	55
Democracy	2
Equally important (volunteered response)	38
Don't know	5

a. From 1999–2000 panel, wave 3 (N = 1,755 weighted cases).

and 69 percent believed it could experience both democracy and economic growth. If presented with the forced choice of one objective or the other, 47 percent of Putin voters held out for giving democracy and a strong state equal priority and 43 percent said democracy and economic growth were equally important.[65]

Extrapolating to the future, public reactions to Putin's leadership will be affected by how he perceives the choices the country faces and how believable he is in communicating his preferred option. Most Russians— and more than the average among those who voted for him in March 2000—want to buy into order, prosperity, *and* democracy. To gain their consent for a dramatically different basket of goods would require framing the alternatives differently. A heavier club than managed democracy might be needed to get the solution across.

Implications for American Policy

The 1999–2000 electoral cycle did not serve to consolidate democracy in Russia. The process was flawed, if not out-and-out disastrous. Voting brought to power leaders whose prescription for what ails Russia includes a dose of measures to lessen checks and balances within the polity and heighten the state's control over political activity. Some of their changes in economic policy, and their attempts to shore up state capacity and political stability after a decade of turmoil, are positive developments. But the general trend toward managed democracy is negative.

At a time when democratic principles are beleaguered in Russia, American policymakers have other things on their mind. President George W. Bush and his administration are for well-known reasons occupied with more immediate national security issues. As this book goes to press, Washington is in the midst of an occupation of Iraq and is confronting North Korea and Iran over their nuclear weapons programs. Moreover, in the war on terror that has consumed the United States since September 11, 2001, Putin's Russia has become a prized ally.[66] An unlikely friendship between Presidents Bush and Putin, which began to form before September 11, bloomed after that dark day. Bush has gone along with Putin's proposition that the United States and Russia are in essence fighting a common enemy—Islamic radicals supported by the Al Qaeda network, be they in Afghanistan or Chechnya. For the sake of solidarity and of obtaining Putin's cooperation, the U.S. government seems prepared to ignore Russia's political backsliding.

This Faustian bargain is a shortsighted one. Our country has every reason to want Russian cooperation against terrorists and rogue regimes, but it also has a valid national security interest in the consolidation of democracy in Russia. A democratic Russia will continue to integrate into Western institutions and will in time develop into a stable strategic partner of the United States. An autocratic Russia will not succeed in integrating into the West and can only be an erratic partner. In the short term, American national security has benefited from cooperation with autocratic regimes. In times of war, such as World War II, such alliances are necessary. Over the long run, however, the most reliable partners of the United States have always been democracies. Not infrequently, ostensible gains from partnerships with autocratic governments and movements—such as the Shah in Iran, Suharto in Indonesia, the mujaheddin in Afghanistan, and the apartheid system in South Africa— were more than offset by setbacks to American security and embarrassments to American ideals. As the theory of the "democratic peace" predicts, almost every democracy in the world at present has cordial relations with the United States.[67] No democracies are enemies of the United States. Not all dictatorships in the world are foes of the United States, but every foe of the United States—Saddam Hussein's Iraq, the Taliban's Afghanistan, Iran, Libya, North Korea, Cuba, and, possibly in the future, China—has been a dictatorship.

With Russia, the relationship between domestic governance and foreign policy has been clear. When a communist regime ruled Russia during the Soviet era, it pursued foreign policies that countered and threatened the United States. When this regime collapsed and a democratic regime began to take hold in an independent Russia, the cold war ended and a new, more cooperative era in U.S.-Russian relations began.[68] A democratizing Russia and a democratic United States endured rough spots in their bilateral relations, including disputes over Chechnya, NATO expansion, the Balkans, and Iraq, but none of these crises threatened war and the overall trend in the relationship was positive.[69] Had fascists seized control in 1993, or communists in 1995, or a military junta in 1996, the momentum would have been in a different direction.

Regime change is not the sole reason for the sea change in Russian behavior. Russia today is much diminished—geographically, demographically, militarily, and economically—from the vanished Soviet superpower. Even if it wanted to underwrite anti-American movements in third countries or construct anti-NATO alliances, it would not easily find the means to do so. And yet, power capabilities are not the only variable behind the absence of balancing against the West, any more than the military equation was the only reason for Soviet-American enmity during the cold war. Russian foreign-policy intentions have changed more substantially than Russian capabilities. Were Russia ever to revert to hostility toward the West, its population, geographic location, advanced military technology, and immense storehouse of weapons of mass destruction would allow it to imperil world peace and Western priorities once again. The return of dictatorship would trigger a more confrontational relationship with the West. To stay in power without the support of the people, a despot in the Kremlin would have to rely on the very groups—the military, the FSB, and the military industrial complex—that are most suspicious of American intentions, most opposed to Russian integration into the West, and most uncooperative on third-party issues like Iran's nuclear program.

If the United States has a great stake in the consolidation of democracy, and if Russia's regime is currently sliding in an antidemocratic direction, what can the United States do to brake and reverse the trend? The honest answer is not much. Russia is a far-flung, well-endowed society that does not depend on the United States or the West for its survival. In the post–cold war era, no American administration has devoted serious policy time or resources to democratization in Russia or anywhere else. Even in the 1990s, when the trajectory in Russia was in a democratic direction, the makers of American foreign policy achieved limited results in bolstering Russian democracy.[70] Progress will be harder now, especially if policy is implemented with fewer resources, as has been proposed by the Bush administration, and without strategic input from the highest level of the U.S. government.

The elections of 1999–2000 and the advent of Putin do not imply that the struggle over Russia's domestic regime is over and done. In truth, the regime is still in flux and the man who personifies its managed democracy seems of two minds when it comes to democracy. Although Putin has shown no proclivity to promote democracy, he speaks regularly of its importance and without doubt he sees Russia's integration into the West as a high priority. Putin has weakened checks on his power but has not destroyed them. The actors and institutions that constitute a liberal democracy are in a worse position than before, but they have not disappeared. Human rights activists still challenge the authority of the state, independent journalists still publish uncensored stories, and opposition parties still hold seats in parliament. Elections, even if not conducted on a level playing field, are still the only accepted way to assume political power in Russia today.

If Russia's political system were either a dictatorship or a consolidated democracy, then American assistance for democratization would be irrelevant—in the former case because it would have little impact and in the latter because it was not needed. Russia, though, is a place where a strategic intervention for democracy might make the difference.

As a start on a forward-leaning and realistic approach to Russia's regime, President Bush and his team should state that they see its democratization as a national interest of the United States. They must speak bluntly about the condition and prospects of democracy. They cannot pretend not to see the trends sketched in this chapter and the fact that Russia's participation in the international system is, as Lilia Shevtsova puts it, "prolonging the life of the traditional Russian system" at home.[71]

To maintain American credibility on issues of democracy and to encourage those within Russia willing to make sacrifices in its name, Bush and his team must speak honestly about abuses of democracy in Russia. No issue demands straight talk more than Chechnya. The Bush administration was right to call upon the Chechen leadership to sever its ties with international terrorist organizations and to classify three Chechen organizations, including the instigators of the 2002 hostage incident in Moscow, as terrorist. At the same time, it must emphasize that not all Chechens—not even all Chechen fighters—are terrorists, that pursuing a just cause by unjust means has been a disaster for Russia, and that only negotiations with responsible Chechen leaders will avert more devastation. Another point on which frankness is necessary is elections in Russia. We should not conceal our concern with the transgressions against civilized electoral procedures that were visible in 1999–2000 and with the cynical abrogation of norms in some regions of the country, and we should be vigilant against any worsening in 2003–04 and beyond.

Bush can engage Putin in a dialogue about democracy without sounding preachy or superior. Rather, Bush can talk to Putin as a friend with a problem. Friends do not let friends drive their country into dictatorship. Although Putin's understanding of democracy may be patchy, he has stated clearly his desire to build capitalism in Russia and integrate it into international institutions. Bush should explain to Putin that capitalism will not thrive and integration will not happen without democratic consolidation. After a decade of postcommunist transition, one of the striking outcomes across the board is the correlation between democracy and economic growth.[72] Democratization also will facilitate integration into the Western community of states. Putin wants to make Russia a great European power once again. Bush can remind Putin that all great European powers today are democracies.

Bush can make credible his commitment to fostering Russian democracy by providing concrete rewards for steps in the democratic direction. If Russian leaders show leadership in undertaking reforms that qualify Russia as a member of the club of democratic states, then it is up to Bush to foster Russia's entry into it. Bush should remove unfair trade restrictions on Russian goods imported into the United States and encourage his counterparts in the European Union to do the same. Many lingering legacies of the cold war that impede Russian integration must also be on the table.[73] With democratic consolidation as a precondition, the United States could offer tangible benefits, including the end of the ban on Russian weapons in NATO armies, cooperation on missile defense, and at a certain point membership in a redesigned NATO.

It is not enough to try to persuade Putin and his government to adhere to democratic practices for reasons of self-interest. In addition, top officials must do more to defend and assist those individuals and organizations fighting for democracy within Russia. President Ronald Reagan never went to Moscow to meet with Soviet leaders without holding separate meetings with societal leaders. It is time for this practice to return. Independent journalists, human rights activists, civic organizers, business leaders, and trade union officials should be approached, celebrated, and defended—especially when the Russian state abuses their rights.

In parallel to renewed emphasis on state-to-state interactions, democratization must also receive greater attention in American assistance programs to Russia. In the last decade, American assistance has concentrated on denuclearization, economic reform, and humanitarian projects, not democracy.[74] These priorities, perhaps appropriate in the past, today need to change. While denuclearization programs should be continued and expanded, economic and humanitarian assistance programs are no longer necessary or even desired by Russians. By contrast, democracy aid programs are more necessary today than at any time in Russia's post-Soviet history. The Bush administration has slashed funding for this assistance at a time that Russia's grades on democracies are declining, not improving. American policymakers have to remain committed for the long haul, just as their predecessors were in democratizing and integrating Germany and Japan after World War II.

Resources for democracy assistance should also be channeled differently. We believe recent history and Russian attitudes toward democracy suggest that democratization is best achieved by supporting society from below rather than the state from above. The old formula for democracy was, "Get the institutions right, and the people will follow." The new formula should be, "Represent the will of the people within the state, and the institutions will follow." For years, democracy assistance programs have provided technical help for the crafting of democratic institutions, be they electoral laws, constitutions, courts, or political parties. The approach was top-down. If the rules, laws, and procedures were democratic, then society eventually would be remade by these "right" rules into the "right" kind of citizens—democrats. Current Russian society is more transformed—more democratic—than the political structures governing it. The problem of undemocratic institutions remains. In thinking of new ways to promote democracy, program managers would be well advised to consider projects that empower society and to realize that society-centered programs require much more resources than technical assistance to state institutions.

The experience of the 1990s also suggests that the propagation of ideas and information about democracy represents the most cost-effective way to promote democratization within Russia. When compared with Poland, South Africa, or even the United States in its day, the Russian transition from dictatorship to democracy was sudden and unexpected, outpacing the intellectual development of democratic ideas and norms. Therefore programs that facilitate the flow or stimulate the discussion of democratic ideas in Russia should urgently be supported. Among the vehicles are education, exchanges, and support of NGOs and nonstate communications media—which will gain in centrality if Putin's government continues to crack down on independent associations and news media. Remote and on-site electoral monitoring, and follow-up reporting, should be taken more seriously than they have been in the past. American foundations, NGOs, and academic groups will have more to offer on this issue than government agencies.

The Bush administration has been preoccupied with arms control and the war on terror in its dealings with Russia. Both are massively important agenda items. But the U.S. government has the capacity to pursue multiple objectives at once. Previous administrations, Republican and Democratic, have mastered multitrack diplomacy, pressing issues of human rights and religious freedom at the same time as they negotiated on security issues.[75] Many of the coalition partners in the fight against terrorism will be temporary allies. Our relationship with Russia has the potential to blossom into something deeper and more lasting. The key condition for such an outcome is the deepening of Russian democratization at home and Russia's integration into Western and international institutions abroad. President Bush has stated emphatically and on numerous occasions that democracy promotion must be a focus of American foreign policy. With Russia, he needs to follow up this rhetoric with real policy actions.

A

The Survey Work

Our analysis of voting behavior in the 1999 and 2000 elections rests mainly on a large-scale panel survey of the Russian electorate. The survey was performed under contract by the Demoscope group at the Institute of Sociology of the Russian Academy of Sciences. It was done in three waves. All interviews were carried out face-to-face in the Russian language at the respondents' homes. We interviewed 1,919 voters between November 13 and December 13, 1999, before the Duma election. Of them, 1,842 were reinterviewed after the Duma election, between December 25, 1999, and January 25, 2000. The questionnaire for wave 2 included the entire electoral-survey module of the Comparative Study of Electoral Systems (CSES), coordinated by the Institute for Social Research at the University of Michigan.[1] Wave 3 occurred after the presidential election, between April 9 and June 10, 2000, and involved reinterviews of 1,748 first-wave respondents, all but 22 of whom had also been interviewed in wave 2. Panel mortality was 4.0 percent between waves 1 and 2 and 8.9 percent between waves 1 and 3. Median dates of interview were November 22 for wave 1, January 8 for wave 2, and April 24 for wave 3.

Respondents were selected in a multistage area-probability sample of the voting-age population (eighteen and older), with primary and secondary sampling units in thirty-three regions of the Russian Federation. Sampling procedures and exclusions were similar to those described in other work.[2] A total of 2,954 persons were drawn into the sample.[3] The proportion who were questioned in wave 1 was thus 65.0 percent. This is considerably lower than the response rates obtained in Russia in the mid-1990s, a result of the greater mobility of the population and of growing resistance to submitting to interviews for commercial or research purposes. About 55 percent of failures to interview in wave 1 were caused by potential respondents' refusal to be interviewed or to open the door. In about 30 percent of the cases, no one was at home during three visits by the interviewer or the respondent selected was away. Interviewers were forbidden to make substitutions for designated respondents who were unavailable for an interview.

A second source of individual-level information that we used mainly to understand trends in the electorate was an effort to reinterview the surviving members of an analogous three-wave survey panel constructed by Colton and William Zimmerman to study the Russian parliamentary and presidential elections of 1995–96. That panel was originally much larger than the 1999–2000 panel, with 2,841 members in wave 1 (which was in the field in November–December 1995) and 2,456 in wave 3 (July–September 1996). Targeting mostly persons who had been interviewed all three times in 1995–96, we reinterviewed 1,565 of them in 2,447 attempts between April 9 and June 26, 2000, that is, after the presidential election of 2000 (median date of interview April 24). This yields a retention rate of 64.0 percent over a hiatus of four years.[4] Only about 15 percent of the nonresponses can be attributed to outright refusal to interview. More than a third of nonrespondents had moved and a sixth are known to have died.

Multistage sampling procedures that end in selection of one person within a dwelling unit overrepresent individuals who live alone or in small households, such as young, single persons or widows. To correct this bias, sample weights based on the number of eligible adults in each household were applied to all descriptive statistics and all bivariate analysis in the book.

B

A Statistical Model
of the Vote

AT MANY POINTS in the book we use results from a multistage statistical model of the voting decisions of individual Russian citizens in 1999–2000. It contains the same independent variables (or their logical equivalents) in both elections but is applied separately to yield separate estimates for the two events.

Method

The method we have used is multinomial logit regression, a maximum likelihood algorithm well suited to the analysis of a dependent variable—in this case choice among multiple party lists or presidential candidates—consisting of discrete, nonordered categories.[1] The parameters we cite in the text are not the raw regression coefficients, which are without substantive interest and are hard to interpret for a variety of reasons, but quantities of interest derived from them and applied in simulations in which the analyst can counterfactually manipulate conditions.[2] These quantities are of two related kinds: predicted probabilities of given outcomes obtaining; and differences in predicted probabilities, which represent the shift in the predicted probability of the citizen voting for the party list or presidential candidate in question that is associated with a specified shift in the value of the independent variable, holding control variables constant at their medians. When, for any independent variable, the shift in the value of that variable is from its minimum to its maximum value and the control variables encompass all explanatory variables causally prior and equivalent to the variable under scrutiny, we refer to the difference in predicted probabilities as the "total effect" of the independent variable. The total effect may be thought of as "an approximation of the overall extent to which differences between voters on that variable were in fact responsible for 'producing' differences between them in their vote."[3] We characterize total effects with magnitudes of at least .10 as major effects and ones with smaller magnitudes as minor effects.

To construct a multistage model, the analyst must posit the sequence in which explanatory factors exert their influence. Following Warren E. Miller and J. Merrill Shanks, we use a "bloc recursive" approach. That is, we introduce variables hierarchically in thematic blocs and assume that causality is unidirectional.[4] Explanatory variables at all stages are assumed to have direct effects on the voting decision and indirect effects mediated by variables downstream from them in the causal progression. We envision six causal stages: a first stage reserved for citizens' background social characteristics; a second for popular perceptions of current economic and political conditions in the country; a third for partisanship and issue opinions; a fourth for retrospective evaluations of the record of incumbents; a fifth for assessments of the leadership qualities of politicians; and a sixth stage for prospective evaluations of the competence of parties and candidates to govern after the election.

Dependent Variables in Logit Regressions

Our dependent variables are party-list vote for the State Duma and choice of a presidential candidate.

PARTY-LIST VOTE FOR STATE DUMA. Electoral choice here was ascertained in wave 2 interview, with seven nonordered categories for vote for the KPRF, Unity, OVR, SPS, Yabloko, and the LDPR, and for any other party or against all the parties (an allowable choice in a Russian election).

PRESIDENTIAL ELECTION. Electoral choice here was ascertained in wave 3, with categories for vote for Putin, Zyuganov, and Yavlinskii, and for any other candidate or against all the candidates.

Independent Variables in Logit Regressions

Our independent variables are social characteristics, current conditions, partisanship, issue opinions, and evaluations of incumbents, leadership qualities, and issue competence.

SOCIAL CHARACTERISTICS. Information was used on ten social characteristics. (a) *Community size:* five-point measure (by quintile within the survey sample). (b) *Education:* six-point index (none or elementary education, incomplete secondary, secondary, secondary specialized, incomplete higher, higher). (c) *Ethnic non-Russian:* dummy variable. (d) *Age group:* six-point index (eighteen to twenty-nine years, thirties, forties, fifties, sixties, and seventies and older as of December 1999). (e) *Former member of Communist Party of the Soviet Union:* dummy variable. (f) *Consumption:* nine-point index (count of ownership by respondent or a member of his or her family of an automatic washing machine, a personal computer, an automobile, a dacha or second dwelling, and a telephone, and also access to the Internet, past travel abroad, past travel to a "capitalist country"). (g) *Woman:* dummy variable. (h) *Moscow:* dummy variable for residence in Moscow. *(i) South:* dummy variable for location at latitude less than 54 degrees. *(j) East:* dummy variable for location in Siberia or the Far East. All this information was gathered in wave 1.

CURRENT CONDITIONS. Variables measured perceptions of four basic conditions. (a) *Gained in 1990s:* "In general, did you win or lose as a result of the reforms carried out in the country in the 1990s?" Responses are that respondent lost, mostly lost, mostly won, or won, with "Won some and lost some" as a volunteered response. (b) *Pocketbook economic assessments:* change in the "material situation" of the respondent's family over the past twelve months (worsened a lot, worsened a little, no change, improved a little, improved a lot). (c) *Sociotropic economic assessments:* changes in the national economy over the past twelve months (same categories as for pocketbook). (d) *Assessments of democratization:* "On the whole, are you fully satisfied, satisfied, dissatisfied, or completely dissatisfied with how democracy is developing in Russia?" All these questions were asked in wave 1, before the Duma election, and then repeated in wave 3, after the presidential election.

PARTISANSHIP. We used seven dummy variables for professed partisan attachment to the KPRF, Unity, OVR, SPS, Yabloko, the LDPR, and any other party. Partisans either named a party or quasi party as "my party, my movement, my association" or named one "which more than the others reflects [my] interests, views, and concerns." Questions asked in wave 1 and repeated in wave 3.

ISSUE OPINIONS. We used seven variables here. (a) *Left-right:* self-placement on an eleven-point left-right scale. (b) *Market reform:* after a preamble on economic reforms, respondent asked preference among "(1) We should return completely to the socialist economy, (2) We should for the time being retain important elements of the socialist economy, (3) We should continue market reforms, but less painfully, (4) We should deepen and accelerate market reforms." (c) *Independent Chechnya:* position on a five-point scale where 1 denotes that "Russia should keep Chechnya at all costs" and 5 that "it is necessary to let Chechnya leave Russia." (d) *Democratic regime:* "What kind of political system, in your opinion, would be most appropriate for Russia? (1) The Soviet system we had in our country before perestroika, (2) The Soviet system, but in a different, more democratic form, (3) The political system that exists today, (4) Democracy of the Western type." (e) *Presidentialism:* "Some people believe that, regardless of who is president of Russia, he should have more powers than the parliament. Others want the parliament to have more powers than the president. What is your point of view? Please use a scale from 1 to 5, where 1 denotes that the president should have much more power than parliament and 5 denotes that parliament should have much more power than the president." Coded in reverse order from question wording. (f) *Centralization:* preference for federal arrangements: "(1) Everything should be decided in Moscow, (2) Most questions should be decided in Moscow, (3) Some questions should be decided in Moscow and some in the regions, (4) Most questions should be decided in the regions, (5) Everything should be decided in the regions." Coded in reverse order from question wording. (g) *Strongman leader:* thinks it would be very good, fairly good, fairly bad, or very bad thing for Russia to have "a strong leader who does not have to bother with parliament and elections." Questions on market reform, Chechnya, presidentialism, and centralization were asked in wave 1, and on left-right scale, democratic regime, and strongman leader in wave 2. All questions were repeated in wave 3.

EVALUATIONS OF INCUMBENTS. We used approval of activity in office of Boris Yeltsin and Vladimir Putin on a five-point scale (fully approve, approve, approve some and disapprove some, disapprove, completely disapprove). Both questions were asked in wave 2 and repeated in wave 3 and were coded in reverse order.

LEADERSHIP QUALITIES. A four-point index was constructed as the mean of the scores assigned to each politician (no, probably no, probably yes, yes) for intelligence ("an intelligent and knowledgeable person"), strength ("a strong leader"), integrity ("an honest and trustworthy person"), and empathy ("really cares about people like you"), rounded to the nearest integer. For Duma election (questions asked in wave 2), the model includes indicators for the top leaders of each of the six leading parties (Gennadii Zyuganov, Sergei Shoigu, Yevgenii Primakov, Sergei Kiriyenko, Grigorii Yavlinskii, and Vladimir Zhirinovskii). For presidential election (questions in wave 3), the model has indicators for the four top-finishing candidates (Putin, Zyuganov, Yavlinskii, and Aman Tuleyev).

ISSUE COMPETENCE. An additive index was formulated from six items. Respondents were told they will be given a list of problems facing Russia and will be asked to indicate which party or bloc (Duma election) or presidential candidate (presidential election) "would do the best job of pursuing that objective . . . or would there be no particular difference between the parties [candidates]." Concrete problems mentioned were providing social guarantees to the population, improving the Russian economy, safeguarding human rights and democratic freedoms, Chechnya, promoting Russia's international interests, and combating crime and corruption. For Duma election, the model includes indices for the six main parties and a single indicator for all other parties. For presidential election, includes indices for the three top candidates and a single indicator for all other candidates. Questions asked in waves 2 and 3.

MISSING VALUES. A number of tables in the book refer to nonresponses to attitudinal questions as "Don't know" responses. These include two situations noted by interviewers on the questionnaire form: "finds it hard to say" and, less frequently encountered, "refusal to answer." In the multivariate analysis, we substitute the weighted mean of the distribution for missing values, except in cases where a nonresponse can obviously be construed as a negative response (for example, in the questions about partisanship).

Total Effects

Table B-1 gives the total effects computed for each explanatory variable in our model upon the likelihood of voting in the party-list component of the 1999 Duma election for the five parties and quasi parties studied in this book, that is, excluding the LDPR. Table B-2 repeats the exercise for the three leading candidates for president in 2000.

For three blocs of political attitudes—partisanship, leadership qualities, and prospective evaluations—we also estimated total effects of attitudes toward political players other than the organization or individual

Table B-1. *Total Effects on the Party-List Vote, 1999*[a]

Explanatory variables	KPRF	Unity	OVR	SPS	Yabloko
Social characteristics					
Community size	−.14**	−.13**	.01	.12**	.08**
Education	−.16**	−.01	.07*	.05	.09**
Ethnic non-Russian	.04	−.05	.07*	.01	−.03
Age group	.25**	−.14**	.02	−.07**	−.07*
Former member CPSU	.17**	−.05	−.01	−.05*	−.00
Consumption	−.20**	.08	−.01	.23**	−.03
Woman	−.04	.01	.03	−.01	.01
Moscow	−.07	−.21**	.44**	−.05*	−.00
South	.10**	.02	−.03	−.03	−.05**
East	.06	−.00	−.05*	.00	.02
Current conditions					
Gained in 1990s	−.10*	−.05	−.00	.14**	.05
Pocketbook economic assessments	−.00	.06	−.02	.03	−.08**
Sociotropic economic assessments	−.16**	.18**	−.08*	.12**	.03
Assessments of democratization	−.21**	.08	−.01	.05	.08
Partisanship	.45**	.37**	.50**	.66**	.43**
Issue opinions					
Left-right	−.34**	.30**	−.10*	.17**	.05
Market reform	−.04	.00	−.08	.05	.02
Independent Chechnya	.02	−.03	−.02	.01	.00
Democratic regime	−.35**	.26**	−.04	.08**	.01
Presidentialism	−.12**	.11*	.05	.02	−.02
Centralization	−.01	−.10	.08	−.06	.04
Strongman leader	.03	.07	.03	−.00	−.09**
Evaluations of incumbents					
Yeltsin	−.04	.05	.03	.05	.01
Putin	−.25**	.38**	−.07	.02	−.04
Leadership qualities	.50**	.56**	.42**	.28**	.46**
Issue competence	.83**	.72**	.86**	.91**	.91**

** $p \leq .01$
* $p \leq .05$

a. Differences in predicted probabilities. Computed from multistage statistical model, holding causally prior and simultaneous variables constant at their medians. Sample N = 1,414.

politician mentioned in the table row. For example, for the KPRF vote in 1999, we calculated not only the effect of KPRF partisanship (large and positive) but the effects of partisanship for other parties and blocs such as Yabloko or the LDPR (these values are small and negative). We also estimated the effects of evaluations of non-KPRF leaders, such as Yavlinskii or Zhirinovskii, as well as the total effect of evaluations of Zyuganov's leadership traits. These corollary measures are omitted from tables B-1 and B-2 for parsimony's sake.

Table B-2. *Total Effects on the Presidential Vote, 2000*[a]

Explanatory variables	Putin	Zyuganov	Yavlinskii
Social characteristics			
Community size	.03	–.10**	.05*
Education	.03	–.16**	.10**
Ethnic non-Russian	.06	–.02	–.01
Age group	–.08	.15**	–.02
Former member CPSU	–.08	.11**	–.04**
Consumption	–.08	–.13**	.16**
Woman	.06**	–.01	–.02
Moscow	–.05	–.02	.03
South	–.00	.03	–.02*
East	–.08*	.06*	–.00
Current conditions			
Gained in 1990s	.06	–.09	.02
Pocketbook economic assessments	.09	–.12*	–.02
Sociotropic economic assessments	.24**	–.15**	–.00
Assessments of democratization	.36**	–.25**	–.03
Partisanship	.16**	.55**	.41**
Issue opinions			
Left-right	.35**	–.41**	.03
Market reform	.12*	–.03	–.04
Independent Chechnya	–.06	.02	.03
Democratic regime	.23**	–.23**	–.01
Presidentialism	.26**	–.14**	–.02
Centralization	–.01	–.01	.01
Strongman leader	.12**	–.02	–.03
Evaluations of incumbents			
Yeltsin	.25**	–.14**	–.03*
Putin	.73**	–.39**	–.10*
Leadership qualities	.75**	.52**	.28**
Issue competence	.38**	.52**	.80**

** $p \leq .01$

* $p \leq .05$

a. Differences in predicted probabilities. Computed from multistage statistical model, holding causally prior and simultaneous variables constant at their medians. Sample N = 1,481.

Group Effects

In thinking about influences on the vote, it is helpful to know what might be the electoral contributions of entire blocs of explanatory variables, such as issue opinions or evaluations of leadership qualities, as opposed to the single variables laid out in the total-effect tables. Group effects could in principle be obtained through extension of the same procedure used for the single-variable effects, namely, by computing differ-

Table B-3. *Modified Total Effects of Blocs of Explanatory Variables on the Party-List Vote, 1999*[a]

Bloc of variables	KPRF	Unity	OVR	SPS	Yabloko	Weighted average of absolute values
Current conditions	−.16**	.11*	−.06*	.18**	−.00	.12
Partisanship	.45**	.37**	.50**	.66**	.43**	.45
Issue opinions	.52**	−.26**	−.02	−.08**	−.09**	.28[b]
Evaluations of incumbents	−.15*	.22**	−.02	.04	−.02	.12[b]
Leadership qualities	.40**	.50**	.18**	.30**	.31**	.35
Issue competence	.34**	.32**	.55**	.44**	.38**	.38

**p ≤ .01
*p ≤ .05

a. Differences in predicted probabilities for simultaneous, moderately large changes in all variables in bloc. Estimates control for effects of all causally prior and simultaneous variables. Sample N = 1,414.

b. Counting effects where *p* > .05 as 0.

Table B-4. *Modified Total Effects of Blocs of Explanatory Variables on the Presidential Vote, 2000*[a]

Bloc of variables	Putin	Zyuganov	Yavlinskii	Weighted average of absolute values
Current conditions	.23**	−.17**	−.02	.20[b]
Partisanship	.16**	.55**	.41**	.30
Issue opinions	−.47**	.47**	−.00	.43[b]
Evaluations of incumbents	.56**	−.31**	−.07**	.45
Leadership qualities	.48**	.45**	.24**	.45
Issue competence	.34**	.23**	.19**	.30

**p ≤ .01

a. Differences in predicted probabilities for simultaneous, moderately large changes in all variables in bloc. Estimates control for effects of all causally antecedent and simultaneous variables. Sample N = 1,481.

b. Counting effects where *p* > .05 as 0.

ences in predicted probabilities that accompany shifts in the values of all explanatory variables in the class from their minimum to their maximum levels. Because such antipodal shifts would be artificially extreme, it is more useful to estimate the consequences of simultaneous but moderately large changes in the values of all terms within blocs of variables. We calculate these group effects only for the political variables in our model, exempting the social characteristics that in the real world cannot change much in the short run.

Tables B-3 and B-4 present the modified total effects of blocs of explanatory variables for the six main parties and the three main presidential candidates. The column at the extreme right in each table is the average group effect for all parties and candidates, weighted by their share of the popular vote.

Judgments as to what constitutes a "moderately large" difference in an explanatory variable are somewhat arbitrary. These are the criteria we have employed:

—Current conditions: *Gained in 1990s* from "lost" to "mostly lost." *Pocketbook economic assessments* and *Sociotropic economic assessments* from "slightly worse" to "slightly better." *Assessments of democratization* from "dissatisfied" to "satisfied."

—Partisanship: from nonpartisanship to partisanship for given party.

—Issue opinions: *Left-right* from position 7 to position 3 on scale. *Market reform* from continue reforms, but less painfully, to retain important elements of socialism. *Independent Chechnya* from position 2 to position 4 on scale. *Democratic regime* from reformed socialism to unreformed Soviet system. *Presidentialism* from position 4 to position 2 on scale. *Centralization* from deciding most questions in the regions to deciding most questions in Moscow. *Strongman leader* from strongman being "fairly bad" to "fairly good."

—Evaluations of incumbents: from "disapprove" to "approve."

—Leadership qualities: from average score of "probably no" to "probably yes" for the leader in question and from "probably yes" to "probably no" for other leaders.

—Issue competence: in Duma election, from score of 0 to 2 for the given party and from .64 to .31 for each of the other parties (calculated from mean number of positive responses = 3.85). In presidential election, from score of 0 to 2 for the given candidate and from 1.51 to .84 for each of the others (calculated from mean number of positive responses = 4.52).

C The Mass Media and the Elections

Campaigning in russia in 1999 and 2000 was by and large modern campaigning, conducted, as in other industrial countries, through the mass communication media. Russia inherited from the Soviet Union well-ramified systems of print and broadcast communication. Campaign organizers quickly realized, as competitive countrywide campaigns became regular events in the 1990s, that the mass media were their best and for some almost their only bet for getting their political message through to potential voters.

Sixty-three percent of the voting-age individuals interviewed in our 1999–2000 panel survey read newspapers, and those who did reported spending about a half-hour a day perusing them (see table C-1). Radio usage touched a slightly thinner slice of the population (60 percent) but occupied considerably more time per day for the listeners (almost two hours). Television viewing is almost universal in contemporary Russia, and it fills many more hours than either radio or television. Among our survey respondents, 96 percent watched television, for an average of three and a half hours a day. Saturation of the media market and average time spent understate television's hold on the Russian electorate. When asked which medium was their "basic source of information about political events," an overwhelming 89 percent of those in our survey panel replied it was television, far ahead of the 8 percent for radio and the 3 percent for newspapers.

In the dominant medium, television, signals from the 51 percent state-owned ORT channel (controlled de facto in 1999 by Boris Bere-

Table C-1. *Media Markets and Political Information in Russia*

Medium	Percent who use it[a]	Average hours per day among users[a]	Percent for whom it is the basic source of political information[b]
Newspapers	63	0.58	3
Radio	60	1.87	8
Television	96	3.50	89

a. From 1999–2000 panel, wave 1 (N = 1,919 weighted cases).
b. From 1999–2000 panel, wave 2 (N = 1,808 weighted cases). Omits 38 respondents who were unable to respond to the question.

zovskii) and the 100 percent state-owned RTR reached almost all television sets in Russia. NTV, the commercial network, had about 75 percent coverage by 1999, while TV-Tsentr, owned by the city of Moscow, and TV-6, an entertainment-oriented channel controlled by Berezovskii and associates, got through to about half of the national market.

In Russia, as in most places, the routine form in which political information is consumed is the daily news program. Ninety percent of all our survey respondents and 93 percent of all television viewers reported watching the daily news. Forty-nine percent said they had watched the daily news every day in the preceding week, 24 percent almost every day, 14 percent several times, and 1 percent once.[1] News programs are broadcast six or seven times a day by the major national channels and last on average twenty to twenty-five minutes. The most often watched are the main evening news events, aired at 9 P.M. on ORT (the program is called "Vremya," or "Time"), at 8 P.M. on RTR ("Vesti," or "News"), and at 10 P.M. on NTV ("Segodnya," or "Today"). The "Sobytiya" ("Events") program on TV-Tsentr, "Novosti" ("News") on TV-6, and various news programs on local and cable channels figured far less prominently in viewing habits in 1999–2000. These programs tended to last for thirty to forty minutes.

Table C-2 shows frequency of viewing of daily news programs in the week preceding the wave 1 interview in our survey (wave 1 occurred in November–December 1999). "Vremya" on ORT leads the field, with more than half of all respondents saying they had watched it practically every day in the past week. A bit more than one-third had watched "Vesti" on RTR as frequently, and about one-quarter had watched "Segodnya" on NTV practically every day. For TV-Tsentr and TV-6, the daily audience was below 10 percent, and combined viewing of local and cable news was about 20 percent daily.

As the raw proportions on viewing suggest, Russians frequently take

Table C-2. *Daily News Programs Watched in Past Week*[a]

Percent

Frequency	"Vremya" (ORT)	"Vesti" (RTR)	"Segodnya" (NTV)	"Sobytiya" (TV-Tsentr)	"Novosti" (TV-6)	Local or cable
Practically every day	55	37	28	5	7	19
Sometimes	29	41	25	16	19	27
Never	15	22	46	78	74	54
Proportion who do not receive the channel[b]	1	2	24	50	47	29

a. From 1999–2000 panel, wave 1 (N = 1,919 weighted cases).

b. As volunteered by the respondent. These ratios do not correspond exactly to those in table C-4.

Table C-3. *Cross-Channel Viewing among Persons Who Watch National Daily News Programs Practically Every Day*[a]

Percent

Number of other programs watched practically every day	"Vremya" (ORT)	"Vesti" (RTR)	"Segodnya" (NTV)	"Sobytiya" (TV-Tsentr)	"Novosti" (TV-6)
None	29	5	22	4	7
One	41	52	25	13	19
Two	20	30	36	14	20
Three or four	9	14	18	68	54

a. From 1999–2000 panel, wave 1 (same respondents as in row 1 of table C-2).

in news from more than one television source. In fact, channel-switching, now made easy by handheld devices, is the norm rather than the exception. Twenty-nine percent of frequent viewers of "Vremya," and 22 percent of "Segodnya" fans, did not watch any other national news program on a daily basis (see table C-3). For all the other daily news programs on the main channels, the proportion of exclusive regular viewers was less than 10 percent. Of the most frequent viewers, between 9 percent ("Vremya") and 68 percent ("Sobytiya") watched the news daily or almost daily on three or more additional national channels.

A sizable majority of Russians in 1999–2000 were also frequent viewers of the *telezhurnaly,* the newsmagazines broadcast on Saturday and Sunday evenings and lasting from one to two hours each. All the newsmagazines were anchored by a celebrated correspondent who had passed through an apprenticeship in evening news work. Seventy-nine percent of the citizens we interviewed, and 82 percent of the television viewers, said they watched the newsmagazines. As on nightly television, the ORT flagship, in this case the Sergei Dorenko show, reached the

Table C-4. *Weekend Newsmagazines Watched in Past Month*[a]

Percent

Frequency	Sergei Dorenko (ORT)	Nikolai Svanidze (RTR)	Yevgenii Kiselëv (NTV)	Vladislav Flyarkovskii (TV-Tsentr)	Stanislav Kucher (TV-6)
Three or four times	33	16	19	1	2
One or two times	37	36	24	8	10
Never	30	48	57	90	88
Proportion who do not receive the channel[b]	1	2	21	44	42

a. From 1999–2000 panel, wave 1 (N = 1,919 weighted cases).
b. As volunteered by the respondent. These ratios do not correspond exactly to those in table C-2.

Table C-5. *Cross-Channel Viewing among Persons Who Watch Weekend Newsmagazines Three or Four Times a Month*[a]

Percent

Number of other newsmagazines watched three or four times	Sergei Dorenko (ORT)	Nikolai Svanidze (RTR)	Yevgenii Kiselëv (NTV)	Vladislav Flyarkovskii (TV-Tsentr)	Stanislav Kucher (TV-6)
None	49	14	37	8	13
One	31	48	29	19	28
Two	16	32	27	15	23
Three or four	3	7	6	58	36

a. From 1999–2000 panel, wave 1 (same respondents as in row 1 of table C-4).

widest audience, with 33 percent tuning in three or four times in the month before the survey interview and another 37 percent watching one or two times (see table C-4). The "Zerkalo" ("Mirror") program hosted on RTR by Nikolai Svanidze was second in total viewership, although the "Itogi" ("Summing Up") program on NTV, anchored by Yevgenii Kiselëv, had slightly more who watched it weekly or almost weekly. Vladislav Flyarkovskii's "Nedelya" ("Week") program on TV-Tsentr and Stanislav Kucher's "Obozrevatel'" ("Observer") on TV-6 had extremely small audiences.

For most of the weekend programs, regular viewers took in one or several newsmagazines on other channels, as was the norm with the daily news (see table C-5). But two of the newsmagazines stood out from the rest in this connection. Half of the most frequent viewers of the Dorenko show did not watch any other weekend show. Almost 40 percent of Kiselëv's frequent viewers also stuck exclusively with him.[2]

Svanidze, Flyarkovskii, and Kucher, by contrast, shared even their most attentive viewers with rival programs.

Russian media markets are differentiated to some extent by demographics. ORT has been popular with older viewers, the poorly educated, and residents of villages and small towns. NTV has been more popular with younger, better-educated, and more urbanized people. The education gradient is the steepest. TV-Tsentr has had its audience mostly in Moscow, Moscow province, and a patchwork of a few other regions. The TV-6 news audience had no particular shape in 1999–2000.

Did exposure to the hegemonic news medium, television, influence voting in 1999 and 2000? In appendix B we show the results of a multistage statistical model that includes a great many political variables but no indicators of media consumption. That model is already very complex and would be made even more so if we tried to incorporate media variables. We also felt the present state of the art gave us no basis for knowing where in the multistage model to insert the media indicators. The model in appendix B is the one relied on in most of the book. When we discuss the role of the media, however, we occasionally refer to a separate model of the vote that contains only media variables, plus a few other indicators introduced as controls. We assume that the media have an impact on voting behavior, if at all, through attitudinal variables. The attitudinal variables in the main model of the vote, as encapsulated in appendix B, have already been influenced by exposure to the media. The media-based model summarized here is formulated without reference to those variables and is not a representation of the whole range of processes that determine voting choice.

As with our main model of the vote, the effects given in tables C-6 and C-7 are derived from multinomial logit regression, processed in this case in a single stage. The independent variables include measures of exposure to the daily newsbroadcasts and the weekend newsmagazines on the four main television channels, omitting TV-6, which was largely devoted to entertainment. The model includes a dummy variable for watching some television (effects for which are reported here), two other dummies for watching some daily news and watching some newsmagazines (effects omitted here in the interests of concision), and five sociodemographic variables correlated with patterns of television viewing (effects also omitted here).

Table C-6. Media Influences on the Party-List Vote, 1999[a]

Explanatory variable	KPRF	Unity	OVR	SPS	Yabloko
Watches some television	−.05	.17*	−.04	−.02	−.16
Exposure to daily news[b]					
"Vremya" (ORT)	.11	.02	−.07*	−.04	−.01
"Vesti" (RTR)	.03	.03	.01	−.01	−.01
"Segodnya" (NTV)	.05	−.04	.01	.01	.02
"Sobytiya" (TV-Tsentr)	.03	.04	.01	−.04	.01
Exposure to weekend newsmagazines[c]					
Sergei Dorenko (ORT)	−.04	.16**	−.02	−.01	−.06*
Nikolai Svanidze (RTR)	−.04	−.11**	.01	.06*	.04
Yevgenii Kiselëv (NTV)	−.11*	−.08*	.06*	.03	.04
Vladislav Flyarkovskii (TV-Tsentr)	−.00	−.05	−.02	−.04	−.00

** $p \leq .01$.

* $p \leq .05$.

a. Differences in predicted probabilities. Computed from multinomial logit model, holding other explanatory variables constant at their medians. Sample N = 1,414. Model includes dummy variables for watching some daily news and some newsmagazines and five sociodemographic indicators (for community size, education, age group, consumption, and Moscow residency, all as defined in appendix B). Measures of media variables ascertained in 1999–2000 panel, wave 1.

b. Three-point index for frequency in the past week (never, sometimes, practically every day).

c. Three-point index for frequency in the past month (never, once or twice, three or four times).

Table C-7. Media Influences on the Presidential Vote, 2000[a]

Explanatory variable	Putin	Zyuganov	Yavlinskii
Watches some television	.18	.01	−.11
Exposure to daily news			
"Vremya" (ORT)	.10	−.05	−.03
"Vesti" (RTR)	−.03	.05	−.04
"Segodnya" (NTV)	−.09	.07	.05*
"Sobytiya" (TV-Tsentr)	.04	−.08	−.00
Exposure to weekend newsmagazines			
Sergei Dorenko (ORT)	−.01	.06	−.02
Nikolai Svanidze (RTR)	.05	−.07	.01
Yevgenii Kiselëv (NTV)	.00	−.08	.02
Vladislav Flyarkovskii (TV-Tsentr)	−.12	.10	.02

* $p \leq .05$.

a. Differences in predicted probabilities Computed from multinomial logit model, holding other explanatory variables constant at their medians. Sample N = 1,481. Measures of media variables ascertained in 1999–2000 panel, wave 3. Definition of explanatory and control variables same as in table C-6.

D   *Tracing the Flow of the Vote*

GRASPING TRENDS IN voting behavior is a high priority for analysts of a transitional polity like Russia's, where institutions are fragile and civic activity is not yet routinized. Persistence in the support extended to political parties is of special relevance to the consolidation of the new political system. Parties have been the principal organizing factor in Russian parliamentary elections, as in almost all countries where political competition is allowed, and have carved out a lesser role in presidential elections.

The official results of any one election, if truthfully rendered by the authorities, will sum up the array of choices arrived at by the electorate as a whole. A comparison of vote columns across elections should give an equally unambiguous measure of the macro-trend. If, however, the aim is to disaggregate the voting public into its individual members, the totals will say nothing directly about their actions. Citizens can be far more changeable than electorates.[1] Election-to-election differences in votes received capture only the net transfer of votes from one party or politician to another, as distinct from the underlying micro-dynamics of the human beings who make up the electorate.

The only sure way around aggregation bias is to approach individual citizens and obtain firsthand information about their actions at different points in time. The usual tool for doing so is, of course, survey research. Besides pinning down voting choice in the election just concluded, national election surveys typically administer some questions about the respondent's prior voting history. Were this recall information to be

Table D-1. *Missing Information in Recall of 1995 and 1999 Party-List Voting Behavior among Respondents Eligible to Vote in 1995*[a]

Percent

Unable to recall	1999–2000 panel[b]	1995–2000 panel[c]
1995 election		
Participation	2	6
Vote choice	21	22
1999 election		
Participation	1	1
Vote choice	2	6
Total with some missing information	24	31

a. All respondents in the 1995–2000 panel were eligible to vote in December 1995 (that is, were no younger than eighteen at the time), but some in the 1999–2000 panel had not been of voting age in 1995.

b. Includes all qualifying respondents interviewed in waves 1 and 2 (N = 1,744 weighted cases). Questions about 1995 behavior asked in wave 1 and about 1999 behavior in wave 2.

complete and trustworthy, gauging continuity and change would be an easy task.

A problem with recall information is that it is often anything but complete. Generally speaking, the longer the time lapse between the event at issue and the survey interview, the shakier the recall. As table D-1 shows, this is very much so with Russian elections. Column 1 draws on the three-wave panel survey done in 1999–2000 on which this book mostly relies; column 2 refers to the four-wave survey carried out in 1995–96 and again in 2000 (see appendix A for details). About one in four of our 1999–2000 respondents blanked out on at least one piece of their behavior in the party-list portions of the 1999 and 1995 Duma elections. Memory gaps were much more frequent in connection with the distant 1995 campaign than with the just concluded 1999 election. For the 1995–2000 panel, the asymmetry between the two elections was similar but the leakage of information worse: almost one in three could not recall a key fact.

Table D-2 lays out the 1995 behavior recalled by those in our two panels whose actions are most worth tracing: persons who by their own account voted for one of the national party lists in 1999. Again, a good deal of information is missing. The informed members of both panels, consistent with the aggregate returns, testified in far larger numbers to having voted for a party in 1995 than to abstaining or voting against all the parties. As to which party 1999 voters favored in 1995, the two panels diverge. Individuals in the 1999–2000 sample were 13 percentage points more likely to recall switching parties between elections than

Table D-2. *Recall of 1995 Party-List Voting Behavior among 1999 Party-List Voters Eligible to Vote in 1995*[a]
Percent

Recalled behavior in 1995	1999–2000 panel[b]	1995–2000 panel[c]
Voted for a party		
Same as party reported for 1999	25	39
Different from party reported for 1999	38	34
Cannot recall which party	20	19
Voted against all parties	2	1
Abstained	12	3
Cannot recall if participated	2	3

a. Includes only respondents who reported voting in the 1999 election and voting for one of the party lists (that is, excluding voters who opted to vote against all the parties).

b. N = 1,333 weighted cases.

c. N = 1,085 weighted cases.

staying put; in the 1995–2000 panel, there was a 5-point gap in the opposite direction. Also, more people recalled abstaining in 1995 in the 1999–2000 panel than in the 1995–2000 panel. The discrepancies aside, one has to wonder how much of the recall information from either bloc of informants is to be believed. Studies in established democracies have discovered that one-quarter or more of survey respondents err in their portrayal of past voting behavior one election removed from the present. The most widespread mistake is "to make the past choice consistent with present choice," yielding an inflated image of voter consistency.[2] In Russia, the ever-changing jumble of political parties and quasi parties might breed extra confusion and wishful thinking. Perhaps, then, both columns in table D-2 distort the facts.

Fortunately, we are able to check on the veracity of citizen recall for one of the two Russian panels: that for 1995–2000, which was initially struck to study the election cycle of the mid-1990s and so contains information about the 1995 Duma election garnered *at the time*. To be sure, this panel was interrogated about the 1999 Duma election in the spring of 2000, several months after the standard postelection interview undertaken for the 1999–2000 panel.[3] The delay gave rise to the somewhat higher incidence of inability to recall 1999 decisions (see table D-1) and must have spawned some minor errors in the testimony of the large majority who did stipulate their 1999 voting behavior. The 1995–2000 panel remains, nonetheless, an invaluable diagnostic.

Tables D-3 and D-4 juxtapose actual and recalled tendencies in the party-list voting behavior of individual citizens, based on the 1995–2000 survey data. Table D-3 groups the information by respon-

Table D-3. *Actual versus Recalled Party-List Voting Behavior, 1995 and 1999, by 2000 Recollection of 1995 Behavior*[a]

Percent

Actual behavior in 1995	Recall voting for a party in 1995			Recall voting against all parties in 1995	Recall abstaining in 1995	Cannot recall if participated in 1995 election
	Same as party reported for 1999	Different from party reported for 1999	Cannot recall which party			
Voted for a party						
Same as party reported for 1999	51	6	6	0	22	25
Different from party reported for 1999	40	83	79	58	38	66
Voted against all parties	1	1	2	25	3	0
Abstained	8	10	13	17	38	9

a. From 1995–2000 panel. Same respondents as in table D-2, column 2, minus individuals who did not report 1995 behavior at the time. N = 1,049 weighted cases.

Table D-4. *Actual versus Recalled Party-List Voting Behavior, 1995 and 1999, by Actual Behavior in 1995*[a]

Percent

2000 recollection of 1995 behavior	Voted for a party in 1995		Voted against all parties in 1998	Abstained in 1995
	Same as party reported for 1999	Different from party reported for 1999		
Voted for a party				
Same as party reported for 1999	81	25	31	28
Different from party reported for 1999	9	45	19	32
Cannot recall which party	5	23	25	23
Voted against all parties	0	1	19	2
Abstained	3	2	6	12
Cannot recall if participated in election	3	3	0	3

a. From 1995–2000 panel. Same respondents as in table D-3.

dents' recall, in 2000, of what they had done in the 1995 Duma election; table D-4 rotates the axis to group the same information by actual conduct in the 1995 election. Both tables have much less missing information, in relation to the survey sample, than would any attempt to reconstruct what happened by exploiting only latter-day recall. As can be seen in table D-3, a strong majority (83 percent) of those respondents who recalled having voted for a different party in 1995 than they supported in 1999 had indeed switched their votes—but so had majorities of the persons who could not recall whether they had participated in the election, who could not recall which party they had voted for in 1995, and who thought they had voted against all parties in 1995.[4] Most interesting, 40 percent of respondents who told interviewers they had voted for the same party in 1995 as in 1999 had in fact switched parties (versus a bare majority of these respondents, 51 percent, who got it right). Self-identified electoral loyalists, in other words, had quite fallible recall, while self-identified electoral defectors had much better recall. The result, as is evident from table D-4, is sharply different rates of accuracy of recall within the several behavioral subsets of the electorate. The bulk (81 percent) of the individuals who voted for the same party in 1995 and 1999 could correctly recall what they had done. But accurate recall was displayed by fewer than half (45 percent) of those who voted for different parties in the two elections; the remaining 55 percent of this subset are submerged in other recall categories. Of 1999 party-list voters who had voted against all the parties or abstained in 1995, recall is an even more flawed guide, on target in 19 percent and 12 percent of the cases, respectively.

Two broad conclusions about Russian and post-Soviet electoral politics emerge. One is that recall of past behavior cannot be counted on for insights into consistency in citizen choice across elections. Of the survey respondents who were the source for tables D-3 and D-4, spot on *one-half* of them (525 out of 1,049 weighted cases) did not get the story straight. Either they could not retrieve their 1995 behavior from memory or the recall made was false. The recall problems that plague political surveys everywhere are exacerbated in Russia, so much so that any statement about continuity based on recall alone deserves to be taken with a grain of salt.[5] More than anything, these difficulties would seem to reflect the inchoateness of the transitional political environment. Indicative is that Russian presidential elections, which feature simpler choices involving fewer players, evoke less confusion about past behavior than parliamentary elections. In our 1995–2000 panel, for example, 56 percent of respondents correctly recalled their performance in the first round of the 1996 presidential election. For the second round, pitting Boris Yeltsin head to head against Gennadii Zyuganov, that figure rose to 67 percent.[6]

A second conclusion is that selective and erroneous recall systematically exaggerates the impression given of consistency over time in Russians' voting behavior. This, again, is a universal pattern in such research, present in magnified form in contemporary Russia. Every second member of our 1995–2000 panel who claimed to have voted for the same party in 1995 and 1999 had not done so. Respondents who recalled voting for two different parties were by and large on the mark but are overshadowed numerically by the time-inconsistent voters who reported their behavior otherwise. The degree of exaggeration of voter continuity will depend on the circumstances under which the survey information is collected. One plausible reason our 1999–2000 panelists gave less skewed a picture of their voting consistency in the successive Duma elections is that the questions about the vote were posed in separate interviews: about 1995 in wave 1 of the survey, well before any of them entered the voting booth on December 19, 1999, and about 1999 in wave 2, after December 19.[7] Our 1995–2000 panelists were debriefed retrospectively about the 1995 and 1999 Duma elections in one and the

Table D-5. *Party-List Voting Behavior in 1999 versus 1995 among 1999 Party-List Voters*[a]

How voted	Percent
For same party in 1999 and 1995	23
For different parties in 1999 and 1995	60
For a party in 1999 and against all parties in 1995	1
For a party in 1999 and abstained in 1995	10
For a party in 1999 and not of voting age in 1995	5

a. From augmented 1995–2000 panel. Same respondents as in tables D-3 and D-4, plus all members of the 1999–2000 panel born after December 1977. Imported observations assigned special weight in proportion to the size of the two panels (1,612/1,846). N = 1,110 weighted cases.

same interview, and in almost consecutive questions to boot. It would have been entirely natural for them to feel more pressure for cognitive consistency than their counterparts in the 1999–2000 panel.[8]

Since we are lucky enough to have at our fingertips the 1995–2000 panel, containing close to real-time data from 1995, we need not bog down in methodological speculations about the psychology of recall. Table D-5 is our best estimate of actual individual-level trends in the Russian electorate spanning the State Duma elections of December 1995 and December 1999. To compensate for the 1995–2000 panel's lack of younger voters (persons not of voting age when the panel was constituted in 1995), we have supplemented it with data for those age cohorts from the 1999–2000 panel, weighting the imported observations in keeping with the relative size of the panel of origin (see table D-5, note a). The augmented panel is subject to sampling error and to a modicum of near-term recall error surrounding behavior in the two elections. It in all probability understates the number of 1995 abstainers and "against all" voters in the 1999 electorate.[9] All things considered, though, it ought to be a fair approximation of the distribution of the behaviors of concern in the Russian electorate.

The chief lesson of table D-5 is that instability still trumped stability in the ranks of the Russian electorate as the country's first decade of independence drew to a close. Fewer than one in four 1999 party-list voters selected the same party they had chosen four years previous. Repeat voters who switched parties outnumbered them by a ratio of 2.58:1. Clearly both of the recall exercises recapped in table D-2 exaggerated continuity in the vote. The same citizens whose behavior is encapsulated in table D-5, when asked to recite their 1995 behavior from memory, yield an analogous ratio of .89:1—which is a severe warping of the truth. Among our 1999–2000 panel, the ratio was a less fallacious 1.55:1. Even if rather closer to reality overall, this information is doubtless riddled with errors.

Table D-5 is thus the foundation for the flow-of-the-vote discussion that runs through various sections of the book.

Notes

Chapter One

1. On the causes and consequences of the 1998 crisis, see Anders Åslund, *Building Capitalism: The Transformation of the Former Soviet Bloc* (Cambridge University Press, 2002); Chrystia Freeland, *Sale of the Century: Russia's Wild Ride from Communism to Capitalism* (New York: Crown Books, 2000); David E. Hoffman, *The Oligarchs: Wealth and Power in the New Russia* (New York: PublicAffairs, 2002); Juliet Johnson, *A Fistful of Rubles: The Rise and Fall of the Russian Banking System* (Cornell University Press, 2000); and Randall Stone, *Lending Credibility: The International Monetary Fund and the Post-Communist Transition* (Princeton University Press, 2002). For international context, see Paul Bluestein, *The Chastening: Inside the Crisis that Rocked the Global Financial System and Humbled the IMF* (New York: PublicAffairs, 2001).

2. Boris Yel'tsin, *Prezidentskii marafon* (Presidential marathon) (Moscow: AST, 2000), p. 232.

3. The Russian economy—after shrinking steadily through 1996, growing in 1997, and then hitting the skids in 1998—started to register expansion in March 1999. Growth has continued until the present day.

4. *RFE/RL Newsline,* August 9, 1999. This very useful chronicle of current information prepared by Radio Free Europe/Radio Liberty staff is archived at www.rferl.org.

5. The immunity decree applied to all former presidents, but there was only one such person, and it obviously was crafted for Yeltsin's benefit. Analysts of the period have blown the decree out of proportion. Yeltsin was much more worried about his political legacy than about the far-fetched possibility of criminal charges, and all knew that the rescript could be revoked or overridden by

legislation. As any functionary in Putin's position would have signed it, it does little to explain why Yeltsin chose him.

6. Yel'tsin, *Prezidentskii marafon,* p. 254.

7. The false starts included Generals Aleksandr Rutskoi (Yeltsin's vice president from 1991 to 1993), Aleksandr Lebed (head of national security in 1996), Nikolai Bordyuzha (chief of the presidential staff in 1998–99), and Andrei Nikolayev (a former commander of the border guards whom Yeltsin considered making prime minister in 1998). The two prime ministers before Putin (Yevgenii Primakov and Sergei Stepashin) were civilians with years of seasoning in security-related posts.

8. The phrase could also be translated "manageable democracy" or "guided democracy."

9. Sergei Markov, writing in April 2000, in Henry E. Hale, ed., *Russia's Electoral War of 1999–2000: The Russian Election Watch Compendium* (Strengthening Democratic Institutions Project, John F. Kennedy School of Government, Harvard University, 2000), p. 196.

10. Residents of Chechnya did not vote for the national party lists in December either. With most of the republic back under Russian control, they did cast votes in the presidential election in March 2000. A special election in the Duma district was held in August 2000.

11. Zhirinovskii had also run in Russia's first presidential election in 1991, as had another 2000 candidate, Aman Tuleyev. Tuleyev campaigned for president in 1996 but withdrew three days before the vote. It is a matter of judgment whether to include as a repeat performer in 1999 the liberal Union of Right Forces (SPS), an amalgam of forerunner groups, several of which had run in the 1995 Duma election. It is counted as a new organization here. Later in the study we qualify that decision by classifying 1999 SPS voters who had supported an antecedent party in 1995 as party "loyalists" with consistent preferences over time.

12. Grigorii Golosov in Hale, *Russia's Electoral War,* p. 39.

13. Ibid., p. 26.

14. Boris Makarenko, "Fatherland–All Russia (OVR)," in Michael McFaul, Nikolai Petrov, Andrei Ryabov, and Elizabeth Reisch, eds., *Primer on Russia's 1999 Duma Elections* (Washington: Carnegie Endowment for International Peace, 1999), p. 74.

15. Hale, *Russia's Electoral War,* p. 28.

16. Press conference at the National Press Institute (transcript translated and distributed by the Federal News Service), October 6, 1999.

17. Boris Makarenko and Sergei Markov in Hale, *Russia's Electoral War,* pp. 53, 57. Cf. Nikolai Petrov and Alexey Makarkin, "Unity (Medved)," in McFaul and others, *Primer on Russia's 1999 Duma Elections,* p. 124, which allowed that Unity might get 5 percent of the vote but said, "disgust with the current regime is so high that a bloc openly affiliated with the Yeltsin regime is unlikely to perform well in the upcoming vote."

18. Vladimir Boxer in Hale, *Russia's Electoral War*, p. 68.

19. *Nezavisimaya gazeta,* December 8, 1999, p. 12.

20. See the discussion in chapter 7.

21. Both of the authors took part in a symposium on heirs to Yeltsin at George Washington University on March 25–26, 1999. Colton wrote the paper on Yurii Luzhkov, the mayor of Moscow. There was no essay on Putin, and he was not mentioned in the discussion. The papers were published in *Problems of Post-Communism,* vol. 46 (September–October 1999). McFaul did speculate at the meeting that whoever was sitting in the prime minister's chair at the time of the election would be a strong contender.

22. Hale, *Russia's Electoral War,* p. 26. The article went on to say that Yeltsin's decision "has given Putin a chance to prove himself as a leader, and if he justifies his reputation as a skilled administrator, his authority may begin to rise," as it had with the last prime minister, Sergei Stepashin.

23. Aleksandr Rar, *Vladimir Putin: "Nemets" v Kremle* (Vladimir Putin: "German" in the Kremlin) (Moscow: OLMA-PRESS, 2002), p. 252.

24. Peter Rutland, "Putin's Path to Power," *Post-Soviet Affairs,* vol. 16 (November–December 2000), p. 313.

25. One of us wrote in the summer of 1999 that the formation of OVR "might be the most important development in Russian politics since the 1996 presidential elections" and that OVR "has the potential to dominate the post-Yeltsin era." Michael McFaul, "Russia's Political Forces Realign," *Wall Street Journal* (European edition), August 26, 1999, p. 6. The second author said much the same to students and colleagues well into the autumn.

26. Compare table 1-1 with the classification by the Russian Central Electoral Commission: Tsentral'naya izbiratel'naya komissiya Rossiiskoi Federatsii, *Vybory deputatov Gosudarstvennoi Dumy Federal'nogo Sobraniya Rossiiskoi Federatsii 1999: elektoral'naya statistika* (The 1999 election of deputies to the State Duma of the Russian Federation: electoral statistics) (Moscow: Ves' Mir, 2000), p. 213. It refers to liberal parties as "democratic" parties and amalgamates government, centrist, and miscellaneous parties into one centrist group. It classifies one of our small nationalist parties (the Conservative Movement of Russia) and one socialist party (the All-Russian Party of the People) as centrist, but otherwise concurs in our choices.

27. Unity's share of votes in 1999 exceeded the KPRF's in 1995 (22.73 percent). The next fattest share was the 22.92 percent received by the LDPR in the 1993 election, when the communists were held to 12.40 percent.

28. By July 2001 the Unity faction totaled eighty-three deputies. Another eighty-eight, almost all of them independents from the districts, were members of the Regions of Russia and People's Deputy groups in the Duma, which voted most of the time in lockstep with Unity. On the whole, OVR's forty-five deputies (down from the sixty-eight elected in 1999) also sided with the government. See Thomas F. Remington, "Putin and the Duma," *Post-Soviet Affairs,* vol. 17

(October–December 2001), pp. 285–308. Exact numbers of deputies affiliated with party fractions in the Russian Duma have always fluctuated and are affected by elaborate intergroup bargaining. See Thomas F. Remington, *The Russian Parliament: Institutional Evolution in a Transitional Regime, 1989–1999* (Yale University Press, 2001), chap. 7.

29. The LDPR finished a hair ahead of Yabloko in the popular vote but was sixth in deputies because it elected no candidates in the districts.

30. Of SPS and NDR, Igor Bunin and Boris Makarenko said, "Only a miracle could bring one of these parties into the Duma." In Hale, *Russia's Electoral War,* p. 34. They were right about NDR but wrong about SPS.

31. From the *Moscow Times,* August 27, 2002, as carried in Johnson's Russia List of that day.

32. Of the hundreds of books in this lineage that could be cited for the United States alone, it would be hard to improve on Theodore H. White's classic *The Making of the President, 1960* (New York: Atheneum, 1961).

33. One excellent review says this body of work "may well be the largest literature in all of political science." Morris P. Fiorina, "Voting Behavior," in Dennis C. Mueller, ed., *Perspectives on Public Choice* (Cambridge University Press, 1997), p. 391. One of us has already published a book in this vein: Timothy J. Colton, *Transitional Citizens: Voters and What Influences Them in the New Russia* (Harvard University Press, 2000). Political scientists have recently become more interested in the environment in which citizens make voting decisions, and this has spawned new research on political strategies, campaigning, and the news media.

34. As in its first national campaign in 1993, the LDPR's core message remains that the West and internal minorities have conspired to "bring Russia to its knees": Evelyn Davidheiser, "Right and Left in the Hard Opposition," in Timothy J. Colton and Jerry F. Hough, eds., *Growing Pains: Russian Democracy and the Election of 1993* (Brookings, 1998), p. 191. The party's share of the popular vote in 1999 was not much more than one-quarter of that in its peak year, 1993, and it did not elect candidates in the districts. Zhirinovskii got less than 3 percent of the presidential vote in 2000.

Chapter Two

1. See especially Thomas Carothers, "The End of the Transition Paradigm," *Journal of Democracy,* vol. 13 (January 2002), pp. 5–21. For contrary views, see the essays by Guillermo O'Donnell and Ghia Nodia in the July 2002 edition of this same journal.

2. See www.freedomhouse.org/research/freeworld/2002. In the area of economic reform, surveys of the former Soviet Union and Eastern Europe invariably give Russia a similarly middling grade. Economic evaluations are ably

pulled together in Anders Åslund, *Building Capitalism: The Transformation of the Former Soviet Bloc* (Cambridge University Press, 2002).

3. The uncertainty motif permeates the literature on regime change. One of the earliest and most authoritative works emphasizes "the extraordinary uncertainty of the transition, with its numerous surprises and difficult dilemmas." Guillermo O'Donnell and Philippe C. Schmitter, *Transitions from Authoritarian Rule: Tentative Conclusions about Uncertain Democracies* (Johns Hopkins University Press, 1986), p. 3.

4. Archie Brown, "Evaluating Russia's Democratization," in Brown, ed., *Contemporary Russian Politics: A Reader* (Oxford University Press, 2001), p. 568.

5. See Michael McFaul, *Russia's Unfinished Revolution: Political Change from Gorbachev to Putin* (Cornell University Press, 2001).

6. Adam Przeworski, *Democracy and the Market: Political and Economic Reforms in Eastern Europe and Latin America* (Cambridge University Press, 1991), p. 13.

7. Our Home Is Russia and several pro-Kremlin factions, with some support from Yeltsin's office, tried several times to increase the share of the 450 Duma seats filled in districts, apparently thinking they would elect more deputies that way.

8. Yeltsin's account is in Boris Yel'tsin, *Prezidentskii marafon* (Presidential marathon) (Moscow: AST, 2000), pp. 28–33. In an interview with Colton on January 28, 2001, Chubais confirmed its main lines.

9. Some observers think Yeltsin schemed in 1999–2000 to have himself declared president of the confederal "union" with Belarus, the Slavic republic wedged between Russia and Poland. We do not find this speculation credible, given Yeltsin's preference for real and not symbolic power. Under the 1993 constitution, the president of Russia was popularly elected, and he would have been a much more formidable figure than the head of a joint venture with a small country.

10. It was widely and accurately expected that the fighting in Chechnya would intensify after the Caucasus mountain snows melted in April and May.

11. Three other slates requested registration but did not submit verified lists of candidates. One of the five applicants denied was the fascistic Spas (Savior) movement headed by Aleksandr Barkashov, whose 1998 registration by the Ministry of Justice was retroactively annulled by a court ruling in November 1999, for inadequate documentation of its regional membership. The CEC then expunged Spas from the ballot. Many Russian liberals, although contemptuous of Spas and its aims (Barkashov's followers wear swastika-like insignia and greet him with a gesture that resembles a Nazi salute), felt that the grounds for its removal from the ballot were trumped up. Russian law could have been used to ban a group as extreme as Spas, "but the grounds for revoking its registration

had nothing to do with laws against stirring up ethnic hatred." *RFE/RL Russian Election Report,* no. 4 (November 26, 1999), p. 4. This extremely valuable source of information about the elections of 1999–2000 was and is available online at www.rferl.org/elections.

12. In Henry E. Hale, ed., *Russia's Electoral War of 1999–2000: The Russian Election Watch Compendium* (Strengthening Democratic Institutions Project, John F. Kennedy School of Government, Harvard University, 2000), p. 79. Nikonov was active in the OVR campaign in 1999, but that did not cloud his judgment on this point.

13. Yitzhak M. Brudny, "Continuity or Change in Russian Electoral Patterns? The December 1999–March 2000 Election Cycle," in Brown, *Contemporary Russian Politics,* p. 169, identifies five regions (Bashkortostan, Ingushetiya, Kemerovo, Komi, and Samara) where "prominent political figures disliked by the regional authorities were either refused registration or removed from the ballot by district electoral committees during the campaign."

14. A third person withdrew when his signatures were challenged. The CEC initially denied registration to Vladimir Zhirinovski of the LDPR, finding he had not declared an apartment belonging to his son, but a court reinstated him on appeal. One of twelve registered candidates, Yevgenii Savast'yanov, withdrew of his own accord in the final week of the campaign.

15. Tsentral'naya izbiratel'naya komissiya Rossiiskoi Federatsii, *Vybory prezidenta Rossiiskoi Federatsii 2000: elektoral'naya statistika* (The 2000 election of the president of the Russian Federation: electoral statistics) (Moscow: Ves' Mir, 2000), pp. 62–63.

16. SPS's reported campaign spending was 43.7 million rubles, or about $1.7 million. The Yabloko and SPS officials, interviewed by McFaul well after the election (in December 2002 and March 2003), provided this information on the condition they not be identified.

17. Sergei Markov in Hale, *Russia's Electoral War,* p. 75. For background, see Vladimir Gelman, "The Iceberg of Russian Political Finance," in Brown, *Contemporary Russian Politics,* pp. 179–94.

18. The candidates sent the CEC financial reports by the suitcase. Putin alone submitted forty-nine volumes—12,825 pages! Tsentral'naya izbiratel'naya komissiya, *Vybory prezidenta,* p. 147. The CEC postmortem on the Duma registration process referred with satisfaction to 12,680 documents (not pages) given in, in quadruplicate. Tsentral'naya izbiratel'naya komissiya Rossiiskoi Federatsii, *Vybory deputatov Gosudarstvennoi Dumy Federal'nogo Sobraniya Rossiiskoi Federatsii 1999: elektoral'naya statistika* (The 1999 election of deputies to the State Duma of the Russian Federation: electoral statistics) (Moscow: Ves' Mir, 2000), p. 65.

19. We owe the phrase "party substitute" and much clear thinking on Russian parties to Henry E. Hale of Indiana University. His findings are presented in "The Political Economy of Machine Politics in Russia's Regions," *Post-Soviet*

Affairs, vol. 19 (July–October 2003), forthcoming, and *Crashing Parties: Electoral Markets, Party Substitutes, and Stalled Democratization in Russia* (book manuscript). Elections of legislators and chief executives in Russia's regions and municipalities have also been open to parties and nonparty players on an equal footing, with the result that in most places the parties' role has been minor.

20. Robert G. Moser, "The Impact of Parliamentary Electoral Systems in Russia," in Brown, *Contemporary Russian Politics,* p. 204.

21. The designers of the election rules thought Russia's Choice, the pro-Kremlin party of the day, would do better than it did in the 1993 election. They also knew that parties developed through PR were going to be strongest in exactly the institution—parliament—that under the new Russian constitution was going to be weakest. See Michael McFaul, "Explaining Party Emergence and Non-Emergence in Post-Soviet Russia: Institutions, Agents, and Chance," *Comparative Political Studies,* vol. 34 (December 2001), pp. 1159–87.

22. See Robert G. Moser, *Unexpected Outcomes: Electoral Systems, Political Parties, and Representation in Russia* (University of Pittsburgh Press, 2001); and Michael McFaul, "Institutional Design, Uncertainty, and Path Dependency during Transitions: Cases from Russia," *Constitutional Political Economy,* vol. 10 (March 1999), pp. 27–52.

23. Russian survey respondents were asked after the 1996 presidential election how many parties they thought the country should have. The average given was 2.8. Timothy J. Colton, *Transitional Citizens: Voters and What Influences Them in the New Russia* (Harvard University Press, 2000), p. 107.

24. Nine of the thirteen contenders in the Duma election of December 1993 had come into being that year, and six of them sprang up after President Yeltsin liquidated the Supreme Soviet in September and called the snap election.

25. Twenty of twenty-six parties in 1999 came in under 3 percent of the votes and eighteen under 2 percent. In the presidential election, candidates had to refund the small subsidy the CEC forwarded for their campaigns if they did not make 3 percent. Eight of the eleven candidates were required in the end to do so.

26. The index originated in the 1970s from Markku Laakso and Rein Taagepera. For overviews of it and related measures, see Arend Lijphart, *Electoral Systems and Party Systems: A Study of Twenty-Seven Democracies, 1945–1990* (Oxford University Press, 1994); and Gary W. Cox, *Making Votes Count: Strategic Coordination in the World's Electoral Systems* (Cambridge University Press, 1997).

27. As one careful analyst has pointed out (Moser, "The Impact of Parliamentary Electoral Systems in Russia," p. 200), the 6.40 score for effective legislative parties in 1993 was higher than any found in the definitive study on the subject (Lijphart, *Electoral Systems and Party Systems,* pp. 160–62). Russia's index of 4.57 after the 1999 Duma election is surpassed by thirteen of the seventy electoral arrangements in Lijphart's book—still on the high side but no longer off the charts.

28. The appellation was derived from the last names of the group's founders (Yavlinskii, Yurii Boldyrev, and Vladimir Lukin). Boldyrev broke with his comrades years ago and in 1999 ran a slate jointly with the nationalistic Congress of Russian Communities.

29. *Nezavisimaya gazeta,* December 8, 1999, p. 9.

30. For example, in chapter 3 we quote Sergei Shoigu, the leader of the Unity bloc, as saying his group was not rightist, leftist, or centrist but was "a party of consolidation of all healthy forces in society." It was more common for politicians to signal their moderation by criticizing left and right extremes but not centrism.

31. The terminology varied. The most common formulation was "social and political movement" (*obshchestvenno-politicheskoye dvizheniye*), but phrases such as "political and social movement" and "political and social organization" were also employed. Civic movements that become immersed in Russian elections often recharter themselves eventually as official parties. Some party leaders dream of doing the reverse. After the Pensioners Party picked up 2 percent of the PR votes in the 1999 election, its press secretary "said the party's ultimate goal is to become a major lobbying force, akin to the powerful American Association for Retired Persons in the U.S." *RFE/RL Russian Election Report,* no. 8 (January 7, 2000), p. 4. By early 2000, as presidential nominations opened, the number of eligible parties and civic movements was up to 147. The new players included the Party of People's Capitalism, the Fellowship of Wives of Russian Soldiers, and the All-Russian Patriotic and Political Movement for the Study of the Legacy of Joseph Stalin.

32. Nikolai Petrov and Aleksei Titkov, "Nachalo kampanii" (The start of the campaign), in Michael McFaul, Nikolai Petrov, and Andrei Ryabov, eds., *Rossiya nakanune Dumskikh vyborov 1999 goda* (Russia on the eve of the 1999 Duma election) (Moscow Carnegie Center, 1999), p. 16.

33. In a farcical follow-up, the CEC reinstated the LDPR list in early December—without Zhirinovskii at its head—then reversed this decision, leaving the Zhirinovskii Bloc as the only "LDPR" in the race. Zhirinovskii milked it for all it was worth. As one observer put it the next week, "In all likelihood the twists and turns surrounding the LDPR's registration have helped Zhirinovsky's campaign. Not only have they generated a tremendous amount of free publicity, they have helped Zhirinovsky cultivate an image as an outsider. Newscasts on December 2 featured the LDPR [leader] ranting and raving at [CEC] Chairman Aleksandr Veshnyakov." *RFE/RL Russian Election Report,* no. 6 (December 10, 1999), p. 2. The CEC rulings did not prevent the LDPR from nominating candidates in a small number of single-member districts, none of whom was to win election.

34. Petrov and Titkov, "Nachalo kampanii," p. 16.

35. Moser, "The Impact of Parliamentary Electoral Systems in Russia," p. 196. For comparative analysis, see Matthew Shugart and Martin Wattenberg,

eds., *Mixed-Member Electoral Systems: The Best of Both Worlds?* (Oxford University Press, 2001).

36. Article 55 of the 1999 election law forbade candidates on federal party lists who were concurrently running in districts to appear on national TV or radio broadcasts on behalf of their parties. But they could still be freely mentioned in such broadcasts, and were. Five heads of slates that fell short of the 5 percent barrier took seats in districts: Viktor Chernomyrdin (Our Home Is Russia), Dmitrii Rogozin (Congress of Russian Communities), Viktor Ilyukhin (Movement in Support of the Army), Andrei Nikolayev (Nikolayev and Fedorov Bloc), and Vladimir Bryntsalov (Russian Socialist Party). Vladimir Ryzhkov, the number two on the NDR list, also won in a district. In 1995 about twenty-five leading members of tiny electoral slates made it into the Duma through districts. See Laura Belin in *RFE/RL Russian Election Report*, no. 8 (January 7, 2000), pp. 8–9.

37. One hundred and five nonparty deputies were among the 216 elected on December 19. All 9 seats filled in 2000 (1 in Chechnya and 8 in repeat voting elsewhere) were carried by independents, elevating their percentage of the take to 50.67.

38. In wave 3 of our 1999–2000 panel, survey respondents were asked to rate all eleven candidates on a ten-point scale. For only Podberëzkin and Dzhabrailov were majorities unable to rate the candidate (55 percent could not for Podberëzkin and 52 percent could not for Dzhabrailov). Neither attracted 100,000 votes. Eighty-one percent were able to rate Pamfilova, who received about 750,000 votes.

39. Because the election is for one chief executive, and not a multimember assembly, there is no equivalent to the effective number of legislative parties.

40. Pippa Norris, *A Virtuous Circle: Political Communications in Postindustrial Societies* (Cambridge University Press, 2000), pp. 137, 139, 149.

41. Four percent of our survey respondents said they had access to the Internet in 1999. The ratio was less than 1 percent in villages and small towns and in people over the age of sixty, but 8 percent in the top quintile by population and 8 percent among persons under thirty. Access among persons with an incomplete higher education (many of them college students) was almost 20 percent. More than 40 percent of informants in their sixties, seventies, and eighties could not answer the question about the Internet—plainly, they had never heard of it.

42. Sixty percent of our survey respondents received mailings from district candidates in 1999 and 63 percent saw street materials.

43. Forty-two percent of our respondents received materials in their mailboxes in 2000, and 46 percent came across leaflets and posters.

44. Information gathered in waves 2 and 3 of the 1999–2000 panel survey (N = 1,846 and 1,755 weighted cases). Compare to figures for 1995–96 in Colton, *Transitional Citizens,* pp. 52–54. Making allowance for question wording, reported participation levels are similar to those in EU countries (Norris, *A*

Virtuous Circle, p. 157). Interestingly, Russians seem more inclined than West Europeans to give individual political advice to others.

45. ROMIR, "Vtoroi reiting Rossiiskikh PR-agenstv (po initsiative zhurnala *Sovetnik*)" (The second rating of Russian PR agencies [on assignment from the magazine *Sovetnik*]), mimeo, 2000. See also the extensive descriptions in Ol'ga Blinova, *Sovetniki: issledovatel'skiye i konsaltingovyye struktury Rossii* (Advisers: research and consulting structures in Russia) (Moscow: GNOM I D, 2002). For general background on the industry, see also Julie Corwin, "The Business of Elections: Russian Races and the Consultants Who Manage Them," paper delivered at the convention of the American Association for the Advancement of Slavic Studies, Pittsburgh, November 22, 2002.

46. Nikkolo M, Gleb Pavlovskii, and the Gruppa IMA firm, for example, were active in the Ukrainian parliamentary campaign of 2002.

47. Rusova's role in the Unity campaign is described in chapter 3. She died in an automobile accident in 2002.

48. In the early days, they acquired this expertise through technical assistance programs provided by U.S. party-promoting organizations such as the National Democratic Institute and the International Republican Institute. At the time, many were members of or closely aligned with Russia's nascent political parties. They observed American campaigns, participated in workshops in Russia organized by Western campaign experts, and received thousands of pages of translated documents from the United States on how to run successful campaigns. In the early 1990s *How to Win Elections,* a multivolume set of Republican Party materials printed and distributed by the INDEM organization, could be spotted on the desk of every major party leader.

49. See the informative but highly critical account in Avtandil Tsuladze, *Bol'shaya manipulyativnaya igra: tekhnologii politicheskikh manipulyatsii v period vyborov 1999–2000 gg.* (The big manipulative game: technologies of political manipulation during the elections of 1999–2000) (Moscow: Algoritm, 2000).

50. Some of these themes, as well as broader issues, have been taken up in Nikkolo M's book series "Politics and Psychology," initiated in 1993.

51. We do not deal in detail with Zhirinovskii's LDPR. Its funding sources are mysterious and may include support from business groups loyal to the Kremlin.

52. Source: interviews with political consultants involved in this work who prefer not to be named.

53. Nikolai Petrov and Aleksei Titkov, "Vybory-99 v regional'nom izmerenii" (The election of 1999 on the regional dimension), in Nikolai Petrov, ed., *Regiony Rossii v 1999 g.* (The regions of Russia in 1999) (Moscow Carnegie Center, 2001), p. 199.

54. The questions about the state of the Russian economy and economic trends were asked in wave 2 of the 1999–2000 panel survey (N = 1,846

weighted cases). The question about August 1998 was asked in wave 1 (N = 1,919 weighted cases). In an election-related survey supervised by Colton and William Zimmerman during the 1995 Duma campaign (see Colton, *Transitional Citizens*), 88 percent of respondents described the economy as bad or very bad.

55. These questions were asked in wave 1 of our 1999–2000 survey. For more on Russian attitudes toward democracy, see Timothy J. Colton and Michael McFaul, "Are Russians Democratic?" *Post-Soviet Affairs,* vol. 18 (April–June 2002), pp. 91–121; and Theodore P. Gerber and Sarah E. Mendelson, "Russian Public Opinion on Human Rights and the War in Chechnya," *Post-Soviet Affairs*, vol. 18 (October–December 2002), pp. 271–305.

56. Sixty-five percent of Russians questioned after the 1995 Duma election (see Colton, *Transitional Citizens,* p. 92) said they were dissatisfied or completely dissatisfied with how democracy was developing (versus 79 percent later). Surveyed after the 1996 presidential election, 34 percent agreed with the statement that Russia was a democracy and 29 percent disagreed (versus the much more pessimistic 19 percent and 51 percent in 1999).

57. The question about approval of Yeltsin was asked in wave 2 of the panel survey (N = 1,846 weighted cases). One percent strongly approved of Yeltsin's work, 5 percent approved, 33 percent gave a mixed assessment, 37 percent disapproved, and 22 percent strongly disapproved.

58. All these questions were asked in wave 2 of the 1999–2000 panel. Comparisons are with responses given in wave 2 of the 1995–96 election survey.

59. Announced turnout was 61.69 percent in the Duma election (about 3 percentage points lower than in 1995) and 68.74 percent in the presidential election (about 1 point lower than in 1996). We include spoiled ballots in the denominator in calculating voting turnout.

60. For discussion, see Timothy J. Colton, "Parties, Citizens, and Democratic Consolidation in Russia," in Michael McFaul and Kathryn Stoner-Weiss, eds., *After the Collapse: The Comparative Lessons of Post-Communist Transitions* (Cambridge University Press, forthcoming 2004). For a somewhat different view concentrating on the early years, see Ted Brader and Joshua A. Tucker, "The Emergence of Mass Partisanship in Russia, 1993–1996," *American Journal of Political Science,* vol. 45 (January 2001), pp. 69–83.

61. Strong partisans said there was a party or quasi party they thought of as "my" party, recalled its name, and said it was fully reflective of their "interests, views, and concerns." Moderate partisans were the same but said their favored party fulfilled their needs only partially. Weak partisans named a party that reflected their interests "more than the others." Nonpartisans offered straight negative responses or could not answer.

62. In analogous questioning in 1995, 49 percent of Russians surveyed proved to be strong, moderate, or weak partisans. In 1996 the total was 31 percent.

63. As with voting, in 1995 some partisans identified with a party that had gone out of business by four or five years later. Of 1995 partisans for a party

that survived, 24 percent remained attached to it in 2000 and 27 percent had defected to another party. Of those whose favored party had disappeared, 44 percent were partisans of another party in 2000.

64. For the scholarly debate over opinion change and governmental responsiveness to it in the United States, see Lawrence R. Jacobs and Robert Y. Shapiro, *Politicians Don't Pander: Political Manipulation and the Loss of Democratic Responsiveness* (University of Chicago Press, 2000); and Robert S. Erikson, Michael McKuen, and James A. Stimson, *The Macro Polity* (Cambridge University Press, 2002).

65. John R. Zaller, *The Nature and Origins of Mass Opinion* (Cambridge University Press, 1992), p. 266.

Chapter Three

1. See Adam Przeworski, *Democracy and the Market: Political and Economic Reforms in Eastern Europe and Latin America* (Cambridge University Press, 1991); Guillermo O'Donnell and Philippe Schmiter, *Transitions from Authoritarian Rule: Tentative Conclusions about Uncertain Democracies* (Johns Hopkins University Press, 1986), p. 62; and Herbert Kitschelt, Zdenka Mansfeldova, Radoslaw Markowski, and Gabor Toka, *Post-Communist Party Systems: Competition, Representation, and Inter-Party Competition* (Cambridge University Press, 1999).

2. See Andrei Ryabov, "'Partiya vlasti' v politcheskoi sisteme sovremmenoi Rossii" (The "party of power" in the political system of contemporary Russia), in Michael McFaul and Andrei Ryabov, eds., *Formirovaniye partiino-politicheskoi sistemy v Rossii* (The formation of Russia's system of political parties) (Moscow Carnegie Center, 1997), pp. 80–96; A. V. Likhtenshtein, "'Partii vlasti': elektoral'nyye strategii rossiiskikh elit" (The "parties of power": electoral strategies of the Russian elites), in V. Ya. Gel'man, G. V. Golosov, and Ye. Yu. Meleshkina, eds., *Vtoroi elektoral'nyi tsikl v Rossii* 1999–2000 g. (Russia's second electoral cycle in 1999–2000) (Moscow: Ves' Mir, 2002); and Regina Smyth, "Building State Capacity from the Inside Out: Parties of Power and the Success of the President's Reform Agenda in Russia," *Politics and Society,* vol. 30 (December 2002), pp. 555–78.

3. Yeltsin in May 1995 demanded the creation of two parties friendly to the government, one he described as "left-center" and one "right-center." The leftish Ivan Rybkin Bloc (headed by the then speaker of the Duma) was an electoral bust and soon vanished. The right-center player was Our Home Is Russia. Russia's Choice, renamed Russia's Democratic Choice, ran as a self-styled opposition party of liberal orientation in the 1995 Duma election, taking 3.94 percent of the party-list vote.

4. Boris Yel'tsin, *Prezidentskii marafon* (Presidential marathon) (Moscow: AST, 2000), p. 113.

5. See Richard Rose and Evgeny Tikhomirov, "Russia's Forced-Choice Presidential Election," *Post-Soviet Affairs*, vol. 12 (October-December 1996), pp. 351–79; Michael McFaul, *Russia's 1996 Presidential Election: The End of Polarized Politics* (Stanford, Calif.: Hoover Institution Press, 1997); and Timothy J. Colton, *Transitional Citizens: Voters and What Influences Them in the New Russia* (Harvard University Press, 2000).

6. Vladimir Ryzhkov, interview with McFaul, September 21, 1999.

7. Aleksei Makarkin, "Gubernatorskiye partii" (The governors' parties), in Michael McFaul, Nikolai Petrov, and Andrei Ryabov, eds., *Rossiya nakanune Dumskikh vyborov 1999 goda* (Russia on the eve of the 1999 Duma election) (Moscow Carnegie Center, 1999), p. 179.

8. See his comments on NDR in *Prezidentskii marafon*, pp. 384–85. Chernomyrdin attributed this change in attitude to members of Yeltsin's "Family" political circle, including Boris Berezovskii. Chernomyrdin, interview with Colton, September 15, 2000.

9. Valerii Khomyakov, chairman of the executive committee of Voice of Russia, interview with McFaul, September 23, 1999. The only governors to participate actively in the group were Titov and Leonid Roketskii of Tyumen region (Likhtenshtein, "'Partii vlasti,'" p. 95). For lists of governors who endorsed Voice of Russia and other political organizations in 1999, see McFaul and others, *Rossiya nakanune Dumskikh vyborov*, pp. 304–06.

10. Disagreements among them were evident a day or two after the letter was released. Some governors did not seem to realize it was inspired by pro-Kremlin forces. Others claimed it was a mere moral statement and did not presage creation of an electoral bloc. See Pëtr Akopov in *Nezavisimaya gazeta*, September 22, 1999, pp. 1, 3.

11. About one-quarter of the regional chiefs were still members of NDR in 1999, but almost all found excuses for not campaigning for their positions on its behalf and for favoring clientelistic relations with local supporters. See Mikhail Afanas'ev, "Politicheskiye partii v rossiiskikh regionakh" (Political parties in the Russian regions), *Pro et contra* (Fall 2000), pp. 164–83.

12. The impression that Unity was a "governors' party" lingered long after. See Makarkin, "Gubernatorskiye partii," pp. 184–85.

13. General Lebed's campaign platform in 1996, of which Golovkov was the main author, has been described as one of "liberal nationalism" and resembled in general tone the Unity approach in 1999. After the 1996 election, though, Lebed signed a provisional peace deal with the Chechen rebels. On Chechnya, Unity was to take a hardline position. Aleksandr Rar, *Vladimir Putin: "Nemets" v Kremle* (Vladimir Putin: "German" in the Kremlin) (Moscow: OLMA-PRESS, 2002), p. 139.

14. Shoigu's department changed name several times in the 1990s. It had been the Ministry of Civil Defense, Emergency Situations, and Liquidation of the Consequences of Natural Disasters since 1994.

15. Shoigu blamed Vladimir Ryzhkov for the failure to join with NDR (interview in *Kommersant'*, October 2, 1999). But Unity organizers resisted unification from the beginning, thinking that NDR would add baggage without attracting new voters. NDR's demands in negotiations included renaming the bloc, giving Ryzhkov one of the top three spots on the candidates' list, and acceptance of its overtly "conservative" ideology. See Makarkin, "Gubernatorskiye partii," p. 182.

16. Likhtenshtein, "'Partii vlasti,'" p. 100. The others included the Movement in Support of Independent Deputies, the All-Russian Union for Supporting Small and Medium Business, My Family, Generation of Freedom, the Moslem organization "Refakh," and the Russian Christian Democratic Party.

17. This was the figure given by Yuliya Rusova, campaign manager for Unity, in an interview with McFaul on February 25, 2000.

18. *Nezavisimaya gazeta,* December 8, 1999, p. 9.

19. Sergei Popov, interview with McFaul, December 16, 1999; presentation by Aleksei Chesnakov at Moscow Carnegie Center, February 14, 2000.

20. *Itar-Tass,* September 27, 1999.

21. *Nezavisimaya gazeta,* December 8, 1999, pp. 9, 12.

22. Aleksei Makarkin, "Partii vlasti" (The parties of power), in Michael McFaul, Nikolai Petrov, and Andrei Ryabov, eds., *Rossiya v izbiratel'nom tsikle 1999–2000 godov* (Russia in the electoral cycle of 1999–2000) (Moscow Carnegie Center, 2000), p. 146. Shoigu had a flair for gestures like this. He also proposed depriving citizens who missed three federal elections in a row of their Russian citizenship.

23. Quoted at www.nupi.no/cgi-win/Russland (campaign website of NUPI Centre for Russian Studies, Oslo).

24. *Segodnya,* October 26, 1999, p. 4.

25. "Tezisy platformy izbiratel'nogo bloka 'Yedinstvo'" (Theses for a platform for the Unity electoral bloc), in *Nezavisimaya gazeta,* December 8, 1999 (insert NG-Stsenarii), p. 12.

26. Makarkin, "Partii vlasti," p. 148. Lukoil also made large donations to OVR until midway in the campaign.

27. Tsentral'naya izbiratel'naya komissiya Rossiiskoi Federatsii, *Vybory deputatov Gosudarstvennoi Dumy Federal'nogo Sobraniya Rossiiskoi Federatsii 1999: elektoral'naya statistika* (The 1999 election of deputies to the State Duma of the Russian Federation: electoral statistics) (Moscow: Ves' Mir, 2000), p. 104.

28. *RFE/RL Russian Election Report,* no. 6 (December 10, 1999), pp. 7–8. Treading the same fine line, Unity materials railed at venal bureaucrats and showed pictures of well-fed officials driving foreign cars.

29. Analytical report by the Russian Center for Political Marketing: Tsentr Politicheskoi Kon'yunktury Rossii, *Parlamentskiye vybory 1999 goda v Rossii: analiticheskii doklad* (The 1999 parliamentary election in Russia: an analytical

report) (Moscow: TsPKR, February 11, 2000). The center's director, Aleksei Chesnakov, was principal campaign adviser to Shoigu in the election.

30. *RFE/RL Russian Election Report,* no. 3 (November 19, 1999), p. 10. In Putin's statement endorsing Unity on November 24, he threw cold water on the notion that "Shoigu . . . needs to be punished for his trips around the country." *Segodnya,* November 25, 1999, p. 1.

31. Sarah Oates, "The 1999 Russian Duma Elections: The Dirty Road to the Duma," *Problems of Post-Communism,* vol. 47 (May/June 2000), p. 12.

32. Aleksei Chesnakov, interview with McFaul, February 25, 2000.

33. As mentioned in chapter 2, the state owned 51 percent of the shares in ORT, while Berezovskii and a number of other businessmen owned the other 49 percent. In 1999, however, Berezovskii controlled the channel through a combination of off-budget emoluments paid to employees like Dorenko and the selection of management personnel loyal to him. Dorenko spent the closing days of the campaign in the North Caucasus republic of Karachayevo-Cherkessiya, making speeches in favor of Berezovskii, a candidate for the republic's Duma district. Berezovskii won the seat by a close margin. See *RFE/RL Russian Election Report,* no. 8 (January 7, 2000), p. 17.

34. Sergei Popov, interview with McFaul, December 16, 1999.

35. Aleksei Glubotskii, "Kemerovskaya oblast'" (Kemerovo region), in Nikolai Petrov, ed., *Regiony Rossii v 1999 g.* (The regions of Russia in 1999) (Moscow Carnegie Center, 2001), p. 435.

36. Putin address to the State Duma, November 24, 1999, translated and distributed by the Federal News Service.

37. See Yedinstvo: voprosy i otvety (Unity: questions and answers), campaign brochure (Moscow, 1999); "Tezisy platformy"; and Tatyana Krasnopevtseva, "Comparing Party Platforms," Russia's 1999 Duma Elections, Bulletin no. 1 (Moscow Carnegie Center, December 2, 1999), pp. 1–9. Denis Myuller wrote that these texts consisted of "scraps" of ideas hastily glued together. "They also economized by not inviting a professional editor. They decided they would take care of it themselves. And so they did—quickly, angrily, and clumsily." *Nezavisimaya gazeta,* December 8, 1999, p. 13.

38. *Nezavisimaya gazeta,* December 8, 1999, p. 9; "Tezisy platformy."

39. *Nezavisimaya gazeta,* December 8, 1999, p. 9.

40. Andrei Kolesnikov in *Kommersant'-Vlast',* December 7, 1999, p. 9.

41. Laura Belin in *RFE/RL Russian Election Report,* no. 6 (December 10, 1999), pp. 10–11. In the original fairy tale, the bear accidentally wrecks the cottage. The Russian bear's slowness to respond to provocation differentiates it from the dominant animals in other national myths—the African lion, for example, or the Indian tiger.

42. He also had a reputation for incorruptibility. One unfriendly press report noted that in his declaration with the Central Electoral Commission Shoigu mentioned ownership of a large dacha and swimming pool outside of Moscow

and a BMW 540, on 1998 earnings of about $4,000 (Svetlana Ofitova and Vitalii Romanov in *Segodnya,* November 25, 1999, p. 2). There is no response from Shoigu on the record.

43. Quotations from *RFE/RL Russian Election Report,* no. 5 (December 5, 1999), p. 9, and *Itar-Tass,* December 1, 1999. Putin was perfectly entitled to endorse a party as prime minister and not only "as a citizen." All of his predecessors, going back to 1991, were involved in the 1999 election, and the communists were demanding formation after the election of a "government of the parliamentary majority" chaired by the head of the party that took the most seats.

44. Yuliya Rusova, interview with McFaul, February 25, 2000. Tracking polls by survey organizations such as VTsIOM, FOM, and ROMIR all showed a ratings bounce for Unity at the end of November.

45. Yel'tsin, *Prezidentskii marafon,* pp. 387–88.

46. *Nezavisimaya gazeta,* December 8, 1999, p. 12.

47. "Tezisy platformy."

48. On the NDR campaign, see Michael McFaul, *Russia between Elections: What the December 1995 Results Really Mean* (Moscow Carnegie Center, 1996), p. 28.

49. There were Unity nominees in the one district in Kaliningrad, Kalmykiya, and Tuva; in one of two districts in Kursk and in Tver; in one of three in Omsk region; in two of Primor'e's three districts; and in two of Kemerovo's four. In Chukotka's one district, there was no Unity candidate, although a pro-Kremlin businessman (Roman Abramovich) did run and win.

50. Rostislav Turovskii, "Vybory v odnomandatnykh okrugakh" (The election in the single-mandate districts), in McFaul and others, *Rossiya nakanune Dumskikh vyborov,* p. 85. On Platov's travails, see Sergei Glushkov and Boris Ovchinnikov, "Tverskaya oblast'" (Tver region), in Petrov, *Regiony Rossii v 1999 g.,* pp. 399–408.

51. Seven 1995 parties and quasi parties made up more than 5 percent apiece of the defectors to Unity: the socialistic KPRF (23 percent) and Agrarian Party (6 percent), the pro-government NDR (16 percent), the centrist Women of Russia (11 percent), the nationalistic Congress of Russian Communities (9 percent) and LDPR (7 percent), and the liberal Yabloko (7 percent). More 1995 voters for NDR, Women of Russia, and the Congress of Russian Communities turned out for Unity in 1999 than repeated a vote for those parties.

52. These questions were asked in wave 2 of the 1999–2000 panel survey. The ads mentioned with the second greatest frequency were those of the LDPR (23 percent), followed by the KPRF and OVR (20 percent each). The number of respondents who said there were advertisements they especially liked was 361.

53. Unity's 7.07 percent of the Moscow popular vote put it in fifth place, behind OVR, the KPRF, SPS, and Yabloko.

54. In our sample, the liberal parties had a combined 23 percent support among voters aged eighteen to twenty-nine and 8 percent among voters older than sixty-nine. Socialist parties took 40 percent of the votes in the smallest communities and 13 percent in the largest communities, where the biggest draw was centrist parties (mostly Fatherland–All Russia).

55. For purposes of comparing across elections, voters may also be grouped by decade of birth. The variable used here and in the statistical modeling is derived from annualized age (see appendix B). The estimated effects are practically identical.

56. The questions about printed materials asked respondents to mention whose propaganda they had encountered "most often" (*chashche vsego*). They were allowed to mention more than one party or quasi party. The question about canvassing asked whose representatives had contacted the respondent (without the "most often" caveat); again, multiple positive responses were possible.

57. Unity got just under 30 percent in the Tver region, about 28 percent in Primor'e, and 19 percent in Omsk.

58. The distinction between pocketbook and sociotropic economic assessments is clearly laid out in Donald R. Kinder and D. Roderick Kiewiet, "Sociotropic Politics: The American Case," *British Journal of Political Science,* vol. 11 (April 1981), pp. 129–61. As Kinder and Kiewiet put it (p. 132), sociotropic citizens "vote according to the country's pocketbook, not their own."

59. The total effect is .25 for citizens in the least urbanized communities and .12 for those in the most urbanized. For living in Moscow, it is .04.

60. The questions about partisanship were asked in wave 1 of the 1999–2000 panel survey, before the Duma vote. Sixty-eight percent of Unity voters qualified as nonpartisan and 19 percent as partisans of other parties.

61. Among participating voters in our survey sample, the rate of support for the Unity list was 26 percent for persons who adopted the most hawkish position on Chechnya (keeping it in Russia at all costs) and 24 percent for those who took the most dovish position (allowing Chechnya to leave the federation).

62. The predicted probabilities here are all relatively high because approval of Putin is being held constant at its median and relatively high value ("approve"). If the approval rating of Putin is lowered to "disapprove," the predicted probabilities of voting for Unity fall in the range .11 to .14.

63. The evidence here is reinforced by a question asked of participating voters in the postelection interview. Eighteen percent of all voters said the opinion of Prime Minister Putin was "very important" to them in making up their mind on how to vote. This was much more than the 4 percent attributing importance to President Yeltsin's opinion and the 7 percent to the provincial governor. Sixty-six percent of the citizens who cited Putin's advice voted for Unity, and they came to 47 percent of all Unity voters in our sample. We have doubts about how far self-analysis like this can be counted on to explain citizen motivation. Fifteen

percent of respondents who said Putin's opinion was of great importance to them voted for the KPRF.

64. Because more people considered Unity competent on Chechnya and crime, they were better represented in the final set of Unity voters. Seventy-seven percent of Unity voters thought it the best party on Chechnya and 64 percent thought it best on crime and corruption. For the other issues, those proportions were in the range of 55 to 60 percent.

65. In the other regions with pro-Unity governors, candidates lost in Kaliningrad, Kursk, Omsk, and Tver. In Kemerovo, all four district winners were in the thrall of Governor Tuleyev. Two were formally Unity nominees, one was a KPRF nominee, and one was an independent.

66. See N. B. Yargomskaya, "Effekty izbiratel'noi sistemy i elektoral'nyye strategii na dumskikh vyborakh" (The effects of the electoral system and electoral strategies in the Duma election), in Gel'man and others, *Vtoroi elektoral'nyi tsikl,* pp. 76–78.

67. Rostislav Turovskii, "Osnovnyye itogi vyborov v odnomandatnykh okrugakh" (Key results of the election in the single-mandate districts), in McFaul and others, *Rossiya v izbiratel'nom tsikle 1999–2000 godov,* p. 266.

68. Vadim Boiko, former official in the presidential administration, interview with McFaul, September 24, 2002.

69. Rogozin was the incumbent in the district but had been elected in a by-election and was thought by many to have been inattentive to his constituents and vulnerable to defeat. His margin of victory in 1999 over the communist candidate was about 7 percent.

Chapter Four

1. Sergei Markov in Henry E. Hale, ed., *Russia's Electoral War of 1999–2000: The Russian Election Watch Compendium* (Strengthening Democratic Institutions Project, John F. Kennedy School of Government, Harvard University, 2000), p. 40.

2. Boris Makarenko, "Blok 'Otechestvo-Vsya Rossiya'" (The Fatherland–All Russia Bloc), in Michael McFaul, Nikolai Petrov, and Andrei Ryabov, eds., *Rossiya nakanune Dumskikh vyborov 1999 goda* (Russia on the eve of the 1999 Duma election) (Moscow Carnegie Center, 1999), p. 120.

3. Polling numbers in *Vlast',* no. 31 (August 10, 1999), p. 2; Leontii Byzov, "Elektorat osnovnykh politicheskikh sil" (The electorates of the main political forces), in McFaul and others, *Rossiya nakanune Dumskikh vyborov,* pp. 42–45; and ARPI, *Regional'nyi sotsiologicheskii monitoring,* no. 39 (December 10–12, 1999), p. 6.

4. Yelena Yegorova in *Moskovskii komsomolets,* August 5, 1999, pp. 1–2 (translated in *Izvestia Press Digest,* August 5, 1999).

5. For profiles, see Timothy J. Colton, "Understanding Iurii Luzhkov," *Problems of Post-Communism,* vol. 46 (September–October 1999), pp. 14–26; and David E. Hoffman, *The Oligarchs: Wealth and Power in the New Russia* (New York: PublicAffairs, 2002), chaps. 3 and 10.

6. Boris Yel'tsin, *Prezidentskii marafon* (Presidential marathon) (Moscow: AST, 2000), p. 320. Numerous corruption stories, accompanied by transcripts of telephone conversations taped by Gusinskii's security service, were published in the newspaper *Moskovskii komsomolets.* Luzhkov also infuriated Yeltsin in 1999 by voting in the Federation Council against the president's attempt to dismiss Procurator-General Yurii Skuratov, who had accused the head of the Kremlin business office, Pavel Borodin, of taking kickbacks on government contracts.

7. *Novyye izvestiya,* December 22, 1998, p. 2.

8. Isayev, born in 1964, is one of a handful of principals in Fatherland who started in the anticommunist "informal" movement of the 1980s. He was active in anarchist and green groups.

9. Four governors had been members of the board of Our Home Is Russia, one signed the Voice of Russia appeal earlier in 1999, and two affiliated themselves with both organizations.

10. See Makarenko, "Blok 'Otechestvo-Vsya Rossiya,'" pp. 122–24.

11. The members of the council are given in "Otechestvo-Vsya Rossiya" (Fatherland–All Russia), in *Arkhiv izbiratel'nykh kampanii 1999–2000* (Archive of the electoral campaigns of 1999–2000), at www.elections.ru/duma/ovr (July 2002).

12. See Sergei Mulin on the issues this posed for Shaimiyev, who wanted steady relations with the Kremlin, in *Segodnya,* July 29, 1999, p. 2.

13. Robert V. Daniels, "Evgenii Primakov: The Reluctant Candidate," *Problems of Post-Communism,* vol. 46 (September–October 1999), p. 31.

14. *Segodnya,* August 18, 1999, pp. 1–2.

15. Hale, *Russia's Electoral War,* p. 25.

16. Sergei Mndoyants, Primakov adviser and representative at OVR headquarters, interview with McFaul, September 22, 1999. Mndoyants asserted that the only reason he was working on the OVR campaign was to advance Primakov's presidential prospects.

17. Primakov's age encouraged Luzhkov to think he would serve only one term in high office, clearing the stage for Luzhkov in 2003–04.

18. Lapshin press conference, National Press Institute, August 20, 1999, translated and distributed by Federal News Service.

19. The expression is used in G. V. Golosov, "Politicheskiye partii i nezavisimyye kandidaty na dumskikh vyborakh" (Political parties and independent candidates in the Duma election), in V. Ya. Gel'man, G. V. Golosov, and Ye. Yu. Meleshkina, eds., *Vtoroi elektoral'nyi tsikl v Rossii 1999–2000 g.* (Russia's second electoral cycle in 1999–2000) (Moscow: Ves' Mir, 2002), p. 46.

20. Makarenko, "Blok 'Otechestvo-Vsya Rossiya,'" p. 129.

21. *RFE/RL Newsline,* August 19, 1999.

22. See Avtandil Tsuladze, *Bol'shaya manipulyativnaya igra: tekhnologii politicheskikh manipulyatsii v period vyborov 1999–2000 gg.* (The big manipulative game: technologies of political manipulation during the elections of 1999–2000) (Moscow: Algoritm, 2000), p. 129; and *RFE/RL Newsline,* September 24, 1999. The Agrarian leadership had decided in July to compete as an independent bloc. Lapshin and Kulik were elected to the Duma on the OVR's national list. The district deputy to run for OVR was Nikolai Sukhoi in Saratov region, who successfully defended his seat. He was first elected in a by-election as an independent.

23. Aleksandr Vladislavlev, secretary of the Fatherland political council, interview with McFaul, September 20, 1999.

24. We were told that the companies Missiya-L, Novyi PR-Konsortium, Business League, and International Press Club worked with the All Russia group before the alliance with Fatherland. There were reports early on that Jacques Seguela, a former press attaché to François Mitterand, was also advising Luzhkov and OVR. See Yelena Danilova in *Nezavisimaya gazeta,* September 18, 1999, p. 3.

25. The fact that OVR kept most of its business in-house meant, of course, that these outside critics could not sell their services to one of 1999's richest contestants.

26. The Central Electoral Commission reported OVR's campaign spending at 44.7 million rubles, in third place behind the LDPR and Unity, but as always these figures are gross understatements. Tsentral'naya izbiratel'naya komissiya Rossiiskoi Federatsii, *Vybory deputatov Gosudarstvennoi Dumy Federal'nogo Sobraniya Rossiiskoi Federatsii 1999: elektoral'naya statistika* (The 1999 election of deputies to the State Duma of the Russian Federation: electoral statistics) (Moscow: Ves' Mir, 2000), p. 104.

27. "Otechestvo-Vsya Rossiya" (Fatherland–All Russia), in *Arkhiv izbiratel'nykh kampanii 1999–2000,* at www.elections.ru/duma/ovr.

28. Gusinskii and Berezovskii teamed up in 1997 in the auction to privatize the Svyazinvest telecommunications company, losing to a rival bidder. Their relations then deteriorated, and in 1999 they were on opposite sides of the fence. Having gone into foreign exile after Putin became president, they are now allies again. For details, see Hoffman, *The Oligarchs.*

29. A good example of a city-regional split is Krasnodar, where Mayor Vladimir Samoilenko fought for OVR against the pro-communist governor, Nikolai Kondratenko. See Rodion Mikhailov, "Krasnodarskii krai v 1999–nachale 2000 g." (Krasnodar region in 1999 and early 2000), in Nikolai Petrov, ed., *Regiony Rossii v 1999 g.* (The regions of Russia in 1999) (Moscow Carnegie Center, 2001), pp. 384–98. Other big cities whose mayors supported OVR included Arkhangel'sk, Astrakhan, Chita, Volgograd, and Yekaterinburg.

30. *Izvestiya,* January 30, 1999, p. 2.

31. Sergei Mndoyants, interview with McFaul, September 22, 1999.

32. Vladimir Zharikin, campaign consultant then employed by Nikonov's Politika Foundation, interview with McFaul, December 11, 2002.

33. Aleksandr Boreiko in *Segodnya,* November 23, 1999, p. 2.

34. Boos statement on NTV talk show "Glas naroda," December 14, 1999 (program viewed by the authors).

35. We follow here the translation by Laura Belin in *RFE/RL Russian Election Report,* no. 2 (November 12, 1999), pp. 11–12. The original is available in *Nezavisimaya gazeta,* November 6, 1999. Fatherland published some brochures of its own, including "My verim v sebya i v Rossiyu" (We believe in ourselves and in Russia), at www.luzhkov-otechestvo.ru/program/parts/intro.html. All Russia also put out the rather nondescript "Znakom'tes': voprosy i otvety" (Get acquainted: questions and answers).

36. *RFE/RL Russian Election Report,* no. 6 (December 10, 1999), pp. 9–10.

37. Vladislavlev continued to serve as executive head of Vol'skii's Union of Industrialists and Entrepreneurs, and Vol'skii himself was on the OVR candidates' list. In an interview with McFaul (September 20, 1999), Vladislavlev insisted he was economically more liberal than Anatolii Chubais, Russia's arch privatizer under Yeltsin. After the election, the union broadened its membership to include the leading oligarchs, most of whom made their fortunes through financial manipulations before moving into petroleum and other export industries.

38. Hale, *Russia's Electoral War,* p. 92.

39. *Nezavisimaya gazeta,* December 8, 1999, p. 9.

40. Laura Belin in *RFE/RL Russian Election Report,* no. 7 (December 17, 1999), p. 8. See also Tsuladze, *Bol'shaya manipulyativnaya igra,* pp. 213–68.

41. *RFE/RL Russian Election Report,* no. 7 (December 17, 1999), p. 12.

42. ARPI, *Regional'nyi sotsiologicheskii monitoring,* no. 39 (December 10–12, 1999), p. 19. See also Igor' Zadorin, "Sredstva massovoi informatsii i elektoral'noye povedeniye rossiyan" (The mass media and the electoral behavior of Russians), in Michael McFaul, Nikolai Petrov, and Andrei Ryabov, eds., *Rossiya v izbiratel'nom tsikle 1999–2000 godov* (Russia in the electoral cycle of 1999–2000) (Moscow Carnegie Center, 2000), pp. 208–21.

43. Interviews with several members of the analytical division of the OVR campaign group by McFaul, December 15, 1999.

44. For some of these charges, see *What the Papers Say,* December 6, 1999, and *RFE/RL Newsline,* December 3, 1999. It was widely reported in the press in August that FSB officers interviewed Yelena Baturina, Luzhkov's wife, on allegations that her firm had illicitly received a lucrative contract from Moscow city hall. In St. Petersburg, the police started a criminal investigation into the financing of All Russia's founding congress in May 1999. See Tat'yana Drabkina, "Sankt-Peterburg" (St. Petersburg), in Petrov, *Regiony Rossii v 1999 g.,* pp. 411–13.

45. Yevgenii Primakov, *Vosem' mesyatsev plyus* . . . (Eight months plus . . .) (Moscow: Mysl', 2001), p. 217.

46. Andrei Kolesnikov in *Kommersant'-Vlast'*, December 7, 1999, p. 9. Unity took more than 17 percent of the popular vote in the republic.

47. Sergei Mndoyants, interview with McFaul, December 14, 1999. Mndoyants described the decision as a mistake.

48. Igor Bunin and Boris Makarenko in Hale, *Russia's Electoral War*, pp. 89–90.

49. *RFE/RL Newsline*, October 18, 1999, and Primakov, *Vosem' mesyatsev plyus*, p. 216.

50. Interviews with OVR campaign staff by McFaul, December 15, 1999.

51. As with other parties, some celebrity candidates affiliated with OVR also chose to run unattached. An example would be the singer Iosif Kobzon, who was on the national OVR list but won district 215 (Angiiskii-Buryatskii) as an independent.

52. Vladimir Kozlov, "Vybory glav ispolnitel'noi vlasti regionov" (The elections of chief executives of the regions), in Petrov, *Regiony Rossii v 1999 g.*, pp. 132, 137–39. The Tver candidates lost. In Moscow province one OVR man, General Boris Gromov, was the winner, defeating the incumbent, also supported by OVR, Anatolii Tyazhlov (a member of OVR's national list in the Duma election). Gromov's opponent in the runoff was Gennadii Seleznëv, the communist speaker of the State Duma. In a scintillating case of opportunism, the Kremlin supported Seleznëv.

53. Rostislav Turovskii, "Vybory v odnomandatnykh okrugakh" (The election in the single-mandate districts), in McFaul and others, *Rossiya nakanune Dumskikh vyborov*, p. 83. One symptom of the problem was the unusually large number of districts in which an OVR nominee withdrew before the election. Candidates were proposed in 118 districts but were not on the ballot at campaign's end in 27 of them.

54. Makarenko, "Blok 'Otechestvo-Vsya Rossiya,'" p. 131.

55. Questions about the campaign effort were asked in wave 2 of our 1999–2000 panel survey (N = 1,846 weighted cases).

56. Eighteen percent of our survey respondents, questioned before the election, had read one of the four main pro-OVR dailies (*Segodnya, Izvestiya, Moskovskii komsomolets*, and *Komsomol'skaya pravda*) in the preceding week. Of those readers who voted in the Duma election, 17 percent sided with OVR, 5 percentage points more than persons who did not read those newspapers.

57. The leading liberal parties, SPS and Yabloko, were next highest in spatial concentration, with 31.03 percent and 31.99 percent, respectively, from their five most productive regions. Determinants of the vote for these groups are discussed in chapter 6.

58. The OVR vote also topped 30 percent in two regions where the role of

the local leader was not clear: the republic of Kabardino-Balkariya and the Aginskii-Buryatskii autonomous district.

59. There are suspicious though oblique signs of some falsification in Tatarstan and Bashkortostan. In Ingushetiya, where Aushev had engineered similarly lopsided victories for other parties in the past, it seems not to have been important. See Boris Ovchinnikov, "Parlamentskiye vybory-1999: statisticheskiye anomalii" (The 1999 parliamentary election: statistical anomalies), in Petrov, *Regiony Rossii v 1999 g.,* pp. 225–37.

60. The situation was not much better in Kareliya, where the local chief executive, Sergei Katanandov, was on the OVR list but the bloc received 8.99 percent of the popular vote.

61. In Tatarstan's five electoral districts, for example, the OVR vote ranged from about 20 percent to almost 60 percent. In Bashkortostan's six districts, it ranged from about 15 percent to almost 50 percent. OVR trailed Unity in Kazan and Ufa, the capital cities of the two republics. In Moscow region, the OVR vote was more than 30 percent in districts near Moscow but less than 15 percent toward the periphery. See Tsentral'naya izbiratel'naya komissiya, *Vybory deputatov Gosudarstvennoi Dumy,* pp. 210–13.

62. Eight percent of OVR supporters told our interviewers the opinion of the governor or president of their region was "very important" to their voting decision. The average for the supporters of other parties was 7 percent. Nineteen percent of OVR voters attributed some influence to family and friends, 28 percent to information obtained from television, and 24 percent to information from newspapers. The one guide to decision on which OVR voters differed sharply from the average was influence by Prime Minister Putin's opinion, which was cited by 4 percent of OVR voters but 21 percent of others. These question items were asked in wave 2 of the 1999–2000 panel survey (N = 1,403 weighted cases; persons who voted against all parties were not asked).

63. We interviewed 136 people in Moscow and 47 in Tatarstan, but none in Bashkortostan. Among active voters, 55 percent of our Muscovites and 31 percent of our Tatarstan residents voted for OVR.

64. The source here is the 1995–2000 survey panel.

65. Fifty-two percent of all OVR voters tested out as nonpartisan and 19 percent as the partisans of other parties.

66. Zhirinovskii's net ratings were 11 for intelligence, –8 for strength, –54 for integrity, and –54 for empathy. On the summary evaluation index, ranging from 0 to 10, Luzhkov's mean was 3.71. This was lower than any party leader except Vladimir Zhirinovskii (at 2.23)

67. As with several other party and bloc leaders in 1999, the estimated total effect from the multivariate analysis is larger than the bivariate effect. In other words, we would underestimate the true relationship between the leadership variable and voting choice if we looked at leadership in isolation from other

explanatory factors. If we incorporate a term for Luzhkov into the model, its total effect is .24, while the total effect for Primakov shrinks slightly to .40. For the median voter, the probability of voting OVR is .02 when the person has the lowest opinion of Luzhkov; it rises to .26 when he or she has the highest opinion. For voters with the most positive opinion of Primakov, the effect of the Luzhkov variable is much higher: the probability of voting OVR is .09 for citizens with the worst opinion of Luzhkov and .64 for those with the best opinion of Luzhkov.

68. Two candidates ran and lost in the OVR core region of Kirov. There was no candidate from the bloc in Ingushetiya or Kareliya. Oleg Morozov, the peacemaker between Shaimiyev and Luzhkov, was reelected as an OVR nominee in district 23 in Tatarstan; he had been elected in 1995 as an independent.

69. Boris Makarenko, "Otechestvo-Vsya Rossiya" (Fatherland–All Russia), in McFaul and others, *Rossiya v izbiratel'nom tsikle 1999–2000 godov,* p. 162. Another analyst counts six seats (in Arkhangel'sk, Buryatiya, Penza, Perm, Saratov, and Ul'yanovsk regions) where OVR candidates had some support from the regional leadership as well as significant electoral resources of their own, and only two OVR winners (Artur Chilingarov in the Nenetskii region and Vitalii Shuba in Irkutsk) who prevailed against strong opposition from the regional authorities. Rostislav Turovskii, "Osnovnyye itogi vyborov v odnomandatnykh okrugakh" (Key results of the election in the single-mandate districts), in ibid., p. 264.

70. OVR had no nominee in 133 of 224 districts. Of our survey respondents who voted for the OVR party list, 48 percent did not have the option of voting for an OVR nominee in the district.

71. These were the LDPR and Russia's Choice in 1993 (when there were only thirteen parties in the race) and the KPRF in 1995.

72. Makarenko, "Otechestvo-Vsya Rossiya," p. 157.

Chapter Five

1. Yevgenii Primakov, *Vosem' mesyatsev plyus* . . . (Eight months plus . . .) (Moscow: Mysl', 2001), pp. 8–11. The conversation took place the morning of September 10, 1998. A description of an exploratory conversation with Maslyukov, if not an offer, is in Boris Yel'tsin, *Prezidentskii marafon* (Presidential marathon) (Moscow: AST, 2000), p. 229.

2. This is the total as of the tallying of the votes in December. The official KPRF caucus as of February 2000 numbered eighty-nine. Several dozen KPRF deputies sat in other leftist fractions, notably the Agroindustrial group.

3. Underpinning these activities was a notion of "state patriotism," to be realized through a "national front" in which the KPRF "would be the nucleus around which Russian nationalists and left-wing statists would unite." Joan Barth Urban and Valerii D. Solovei, *Russia's Communists at the Crossroads*

(Boulder, Colo.: Westview Press, 1997), p. 74. For more on this symbiosis of leftism and nationalism, see John T. Ishiyama, "Red Phoenix? The Communist Party in Post-Soviet Russian Politics," *Party Politics,* vol. 2 (April 1996), pp. 147–75; Veljko Vujacic, "Between the Soviet Left and the Russian Right: Russian Nationalism, Gennadii Ziuganov, and the Third Road," *Post-Soviet Affairs,* vol. 12 (April–June 1996), pp. 118–54; Richard Sakwa, "Left or Right? CPRF and the Problems of Democratic Consolidation in Russia," *Journal of Communist Studies and Transition Politics,* vol. 14 (January–June 1998), pp. 128–58; and Geir Flikke, "Patriotic Left-Centrism: The Zigzags of the Communist Party of the Russian Federation," *Europe-Asia Studies,* vol. 52 (March 1999), pp. 275–98.

4. Aleksandr Lebedev, deputy chairman of Spiritual Heritage, interview with McFaul, September 22, 1999; Urban and Solovei, *Russia's Communists at the Crossroads,* pp. 184–86. One issue on which Zyuganov did not hesitate was the formation of multiple "platforms" within the KPRF. In May 1998 he squelched an attempt by a "Leninist-Stalinist" group to draw up an alternative program while remaining in the party. *RFE/RL Newsline,* May 25, 1998.

5. Zyuganov and most KPRF deputies opposed a Duma motion reprimanding Makashov in November, and Zyuganov issued a statement charging that the "haters of Russia are trying to force the so-called Jewish question on us." *RFE/RL Newsline,* November 12, 1998.

6. Ilyukhin took over the movement when its less radical founder, General Lev Rokhlin, was murdered in July 1998. Zyuganov offered him no more than inclusion in the KPRF list, at the party's discretion, of several members. This rigidity "served for the [KPRF] leadership as a guarantee that undesirable allies would not wind up in its ranks" for the campaign. Sergei Chernyakhovskii, "Kommunisticheskiye ob"edineniya" (Communist associations), in Michael McFaul, Nikolai Petrov, and Andrei Ryabov, eds., *Rossiya nakanune Dumskikh vyborov 1999 goda* (Russia on the eve of the 1999 Duma election) (Moscow Carnegie Center, 1999), p. 100. A similar line was taken with hard-core Marxist groups.

7. Primakov, *Vosem' mesyatsev plyus,* p. 216.

8. *Vlast',* no. 31 (August 10, 1999), p. 20; and Boris Makarenko, "Otechestvo-Vsya Rossiya" (Fatherland–All Russia), in Michael McFaul, Nikolai Petrov, and Andrei Ryabov, eds., *Rossiya v izbiratel'nom tsikle 1999–2000 godov* (Russia in the electoral cycle of 1999–2000) (Moscow Carnegie Center, 2000), p. 156.

9. Interview with McFaul, September 23, 1999.

10. Fifty-two KPRF deputies voted against the nomination, thirty-two voted for, four abstained, and forty-one did not participate. Putin received 233 votes, only 7 more than necessary for confirmation. Had the communists who supported him voted nay, the motion would have failed. Roll call information kindly communicated by Thomas F. Remington of Emory University.

11. The KPRF reported campaign expenditures of 39.5 million rubles (fifth among the parties and blocs), about one-quarter of them raised from individual donors (the highest ratio). Tsentral'naya izbiratel'naya komissiya Rossiiskoi Federatsii, *Vybory deputatov Gosudarstvennoi Dumy Federal'nogo Sobraniya Rossiiskoi Federatsii 1999: elektoral'naya statistika* (The 1999 election of deputies to the State Duma of the Russian Federation: electoral statistics) (Moscow: Ves' Mir, 2000), p. 104. The KPRF likely received fewer funds under the table than other leading parties did.

12. Sixteen self-described KPRF members were interviewed in our panel survey, or 0.8 percent of the sample. If the party's claims were accurate, its members would have been about 0.5 percent of the entire electorate in 1999.

13. This point was stressed by Ivan Mel'nikov, a member of the KPRF leadership, in an interview with McFaul on November 17, 1999.

14. Chernyakhovskii, "Kommunisticheskiye ob"edineniya," p. 106; McFaul interviews with Viktor Peshkov, November 16, 1999, and campaign consultant Maksim D'yanov, February 24, 2000.

15. *RFE/RL Russian Federation Report*, November 10, 1999.

16. Aleksei Glubotskii, "Kemerovskaya oblast'" (Kemerovo region), in Nikolai Petrov, ed., *Regiony Rossii v 1999 g.* (The regions of Russia in 1999) (Moscow Carnegie Center, 2001), p. 435; *RFE/RL Russian Federation Report*, November 17, 1999. A contributing factor seems to have been a grudge Tuleyev bore for being placed on the KPRF candidates' list below Starodubtsev, who had precedence owing to his status in the APR. Some communist leaders were afraid beforehand that Tuleyev might withdraw from the list during the campaign. Under the election law, if any of the top three candidates on a national party list resigned, the entire list was to be disqualified.

17. See Aleksei Makarkin, "Kampaniya A. Tuleyeva" (The campaign of Aman Tuleyev), in McFaul and others, *Rossiya v izbiratel'nom tsikle 1999–2000 godov*, pp. 469–70.

18. Chernyakhovskii, "Kommunisticheskiye ob"edineniya," p. 107.

19. Viktor Peshkov, interview with McFaul, November 16, 1999. The party also had a crude website at which it parked documents: www.kprf.ru.

20. *RFE/RL Russian Election Report*, no. 2 (November 12, 1999), p. 10.

21. Ivan Mel'nikov and Viktor Peshkov, interviews with McFaul, November 17 and December 16, 1999. OVR officials believed, though, that the Kremlin downplayed the communists so as to increase their chances of finishing high in the Duma vote, thinking Zyuganov would be easier than Primakov to defeat in a presidential campaign. Sergei Mndoyants, interview with McFaul, September 22, 1999.

22. Mikhail Dmitriev, "Party Economic Programs and Implications," in Michael McFaul, Nikolai Petrov, Andrei Ryabov, and Elizabeth Reisch, eds., *Primer on Russia's 1999 Duma Elections* (Washington: Carnegie Endowment

for International Peace, 1999), pp. 38–39. Dmitriev is a liberal economist and staunch anticommunist.

23. Tatyana Krasnopevtseva, "Comparing Party Platforms," *Russia's 1999 Duma Elections,* Bulletin no. 1 (Moscow Carnegie Center, December 2, 1999), p. 5.

24. Examples are Valentin Chikin (editor of *Sovetskaya Rossiya*), Anatolii Luk'yanov (erstwhile speaker of the Soviet parliament), Igor Rodionov (a former Russian defense minister), Valerii Saikin (a former mayor of Moscow), Vasilii Shandybin (a desk-thumping orator in the Duma), and Vasilii Starodubtsev (governor of the Tula region).

25. KPRF, *Vstavai, strana ogromnaya!* (Stand up, giant land!) (Moscow: ITRK, 1999), p. 12; Krasnopevtseva, "Comparing Party Platforms," p. 5.

26. KPRF, *Vstavai, strana ogromnaya!,* p. 4; Krasnopevtseva, "Comparing Party Platforms," p. 4.

27. Quoted in Sergei Chernyakhovskii, "The Communist Party of the Russian Federation," in McFaul and others, *Primer on Russia's 1999 Duma Elections,* p. 79.

28. Quoted in Krasnopevtseva, "Comparing Party Platforms," p. 5.

29. KPRF, *Programma vosstanovleniya i razvitiya ekonomiki agropromyshlennogo kompleksa Rossii* (Program for reviving and developing the economy of Russia's agroindustrial complex) (Moscow: ITRK, 1999), pp. 4–5.

30. *RFE/RL Russian Election Report,* no. 3 (November 19, 1999), p. 11.

31. In one interview, Zyuganov said the KPRF had a "businesslike political partnership" with Ilyukhin's movement, which would help both to breach the 5 percent threshold "and unite our efforts inside the Duma." "Let the patriots Ilyukhin and Makashov work among that seething, radical section of the population, for whom the [ethnic] Russian question is extremely acute. . . . Let them use their ethnic philosophy and propaganda to take away a sizable stratum of the electorate from all false patriotic alliances and lead their own deputies into the Duma." *RFE/RL Russian Election Report,* no. 2 (November 12, 1999), p. 10.

32. Summaries of the district nominations by the Central Electoral Commission (and secondary sources based on them) refer to 127 KPRF nominees, but the breakdown in Tsentral'naya izbiratel'naya komissiya, *Vybory deputatov Gosudarstvennoi Dumy,* pp. 182–208, shows 129. The party nominated 130 district candidates in 1995.

33. Viktor Akimov, election consultant to the KPRF in 1999, interview with McFaul, December 11, 2002.

34. We were told by persons close to the communist campaign that Vol'skii made donations to a dozen KPRF or KPRF-allied candidates. One of them was Nikolai Ryzhkov, the former prime minister of the USSR who is one of the leaders of Vol'skii's Union of Industrialists and Entrepreneurs. Ryzhkov ran as an independent candidate in district 62 in Belgorod region.

282 / Notes to pages 118–23

35. See Rodion Mikhailov, "Krasnodarskii krai v 1999–nachale 2000 g." (Krasnodar region in 1999 and early 2000), in Petrov, *Regiony Rossii v 1999 g.*, pp. 389–91, and Glubotskii, "Kemerovskaya oblast'," pp. 434–35.

36. The exact numbers are 69 percent (90 of 130) in districts where there was a candidate in 1995 and 41 percent (39 of 94) in districts where there was not. As throughout this discussion, the one Duma district in Chechnya, where there was no election activity in 1999, is excluded from the calculation. Most KPRF candidates who lost in 1995 were replaced by others in 1999. In some districts, the party backed an independent. In district 28 in Udmurtiya, for example, Yurii Maslyukov, elected on the KPRF national list in 1995, ran as an independent and defeated the incumbent.

37. Source: 1999–2000 panel, wave 2 (1,403 weighted cases). In chapter 2 we cited average participation levels for all citizens, which are slightly lower than for individuals who voted in the election.

38. The KPRF list finished first in six of the nine regions and second to Unity in three (Kemerovo, Stavropol, and Vladimir). The party's share of the vote increased between 1995 and 1999 in six of the nine and declined in three (Kemerovo, Ryazan, and Smolensk). The region of the nine where the KPRF performed best was Altai (37.42 percent of the valid votes cast). Altai ranked seventh in Russia in turnout for the KPRF.

39. The fifth region was Rostov.

40. Nineteen percent of the persons who had read one of the three newspapers did vote for the KPRF. The average exposure to these papers for all participating voters was 2 percent.

41. Oddly, regular viewing of "Vremya," the daily 9 P.M. news offering on state-owned ORT, was positively tied to the KPRF vote ($p \leq .10$, that is, at less than our normal threshold of statistical significance). The correlation may be a spurious product of preexisting habits. Or it may point to some subliminal effect of the style of reporting on the main public channel. Conceivably, some viewers associated deference toward the Russian government and the party of power with deference to the KPRF, the relic of the party of power of an earlier age.

42. Source: 1995–2000 survey panel. Most nationalist defectors had voted for the LDPR in 1995. Twenty percent of the KPRF's converts voted in 1995 for a centrist party (usually Women of Russia), 18 percent for the government party (Our Home Is Russia), and, rather unexpectedly, 25 percent for a liberal party.

43. From the 1999–2000 survey panel, waves 1 and 2. Eighty percent of respondents who gave a KPRF voting preference in wave 1 voted for the party. Fifteen percent of KPRF voters, half of the average, said after the election they thought at one time they would vote differently.

44. Compare with the values in Timothy J. Colton, *Transitional Citizens: Voters and What Influences Them in the New Russia* (Harvard University Press, 2000), p. 80. Several of the 1995 indicators are defined somewhat differently.

The only significant predictor of the KPRF vote in 1999 for which no association existed in 1995 is easterly geographic location.

45. Citizens tended to ascribe a hawkish position to the KPRF, but almost 40 percent of our survey respondents in wave 1 of the 1999–2000 panel could not say what the party's position was on the war.

46. The average summary evaluation given to Zyuganov, scored 0 to 10, was 4.59, roughly midway between Primakov (4.94) and Yavlinskii (4.28).

47. The total effect of the Zyuganov variable, controlling for other relevant causal variables, is about .20 less than the bivariate effect. This is because other political attitudes, such as partisanship and issue opinions, shaded evaluations of Zyuganov in 1999, much more than those of Shoigu, Primakov, and other party leaders. Introducing controls for these attitudes diminishes the observed impact of leadership assessments on the KPRF vote.

48. The regression summarized in table 5-6 holds the values of all variables other than the Zyuganov factor constant at their median values. The median value on all the dummy variables we use to measure partisan attachments is the nonpartisan setting.

49. The KPRF is said to have extended some support to twenty-three candidates elected as independents. Five sat in the KPRF caucus after the election and ten in the Agroindustrial group. Rostislav Turovskii, "Osnovnyye itogi vyborov v odnomandatnykh okrugakh" (Key results of the election in the single-mandate districts), in McFaul and others, *Rossiya v izbiratel'nom tsikle 1999–2000 godov,* p. 269.

50. N = 1,511 weighted cases for the six-candidate question, 1,576 for the Putin-Zyuganov runoff, and 1,554 for the Putin-Primakov runoff. Contemporary Russian polls by agencies such as VTsIOM, ROMIR, and the Public Opinion Foundation came up with similar results.

51. The Unity-KPRF deal left OVR with no committee chairs. OVR and several other parties walked out of Duma proceedings for three weeks in protest.

52. Sergei Chernyakhovskii, "Kampaniya G. Zyuganova" (The campaign of Gennadii Zyuganov), in McFaul and others, *Rossiya v izbiratel'nom tsikle 1999–2000 godov,* p. 442; Viktor Peshkov and Viktor Zorkal'tsev, interviews with McFaul, March 22 and 26, 2000.

53. Zyuganov did not come out and say that he had no hope of winning, but spokesmen did concede the defensiveness of the campaign in interviews and semipublic settings—for example, in a presentation by Vladimir Akimov at the Moscow Carnegie Center on February 22, 2000.

54. See Amelia Gentleman, "Communists Defect as Putin Heads for Triumph," *The Observer*, March 19, 2000. The faction within the APR that sided with the KPRF in 1999 endorsed Zyuganov.

55. *RFE/RL Russian Election Report,* no. 11 (March 17, 2000), p. 6, and no. 12 (March 24, 2000), p. 10.

56. The five candidates received more than 5 million votes, the bulk of them going to Tuleyev and Zhirinovskii. Some of these votes would otherwise have gone to Zyuganov, but a fair number, we suspect, would have been cast for Putin.

57. Rostislav Turovskii, "Regional'nyye strategii kandidatov" (The regional strategies of the candidates), in McFaul and others, *Rossiya v izbiratel'nom tsikle 1999–2000 godov,* p. 503. In none of the four regions where Zyuganov led in the popular vote (Altai republic, Lipetsk, Omsk, and Bryansk) had the governor endorsed him or the KPRF in 1999. Tuleyev led the polls in his own Kemerovo region, collecting one-third of all his votes Russia-wide there.

58. In Henry E. Hale, ed., *Russia's Electoral War of 1999–2000: The Russian Election Watch Compendium* (Strengthening Democratic Institutions Project, John F. Kennedy School of Government, Harvard University, 2000), p. 152.

59. *RFE/RL Russian Election Report,* no. 9 (March 3, 2000), p. 9.

60. In our survey sample, 22 percent of Zyuganov voters in 2000 received his campaign materials in their mailboxes, up 10 points from 1999. Canvassing by a party representative was up from 1 percent to 3 percent. Exposure to leaflets and posters was down slightly, from 17 percent of KPRF voters in 1999 to 15 percent of Zyuganov voters in 2000.

61. Zyuganov press conference at the Moscow Carnegie Center, February 28, 2000 (staff summary circulated as mimeo).

62. *RFE/RL Russian Election Report,* no. 10 (March 10, 2000), p. 6.

63. In Hale, *Russia's Electoral War of 1999–2000,* p. 154. "More often than not," Peshkov added dryly, "this interest is positive."

64. Quotations from *RFE/RL Russian Election Report,* no. 10 (March 10, 2000), p. 7.

65. See *RFE/RL Russian Election Report,* no. 11 (March 17, 2000), pp. 2–3. In the summary of his views submitted to the CEC, Zyuganov complained of the mistreatment of Russians by "petty princes" in the minority republics. Tsentral'-naya izbiratel'naya komissiya Rossiiskoi Federatsii, *Vybory prezidenta Rossiiskoi Federatsii 2000: elektoral'naya statistika* (The 2000 election of the president of the Russian Federation: electoral statistics) (Moscow: Ves' Mir, 2000), p. 98.

66. Seventy-three percent of the survey respondents in this category intended to vote for Putin and 21 percent for Primakov.

67. There was also great continuity stretching back to earlier elections. Of the persons in our 1995–2000 panel survey who voted for Zyuganov in 2000 and had participated in the 1996 presidential election, 66 percent supported him in the first round in 1996, and 77 percent in the second round.

68. The global evaluation on the scale of 0 to 10 went up marginally, from 4.59 to 4.61. On specific traits there was a mildly negative trend. Sixty-six percent of citizens on average considered Zyuganov to have or probably to have the desirable character traits, versus 70 percent at the time of the Duma election.

Among the four candidates about whom we asked the character questions, he was rated second on all the traits (behind Putin, ahead of Yavlinskii and Tuleyev).

69. These quantities are sensitive to evaluations of issue competence of other candidates—in particular, Putin. The simulations hold the values of other variables constant at their median. For Putin in 2000, the median competence score was three issues (for every other candidate it was zero issues). If the simulation is run with issue competence for Putin set at zero, the range of predicted probabilities for voting for Zyuganov goes up from .26 to .83, and crosses .50 at three issues.

Chapter Six

1. M. Steven Fish, "The Travails of Liberalism," *Journal of Democracy,* vol. 7 (April 1996), pp. 114–15. See also Fish, "The Predicament of Russian Liberalism: Evidence from the December 1995 Parliamentary Elections," *Europe-Asia Studies,* vol. 49 (March 1997), pp. 191–200.

2. In *RFE/RL Russian Election Report,* no. 3 (November 19, 1999), pp. 4–5.

3. Henry E. Hale, ed., *Russia's Electoral War of 1999–2000: The Russian Election Watch Compendium* (Strengthening Democratic Institutions Project, John F. Kennedy School of Government, Harvard University, 2000), pp. 43, 103.

4. Grigorii Yavlinskii, interview with Colton, September 6, 1999.

5. Sergei Mulin in *Segodnya,* August 30, 1999, p. 1. See the results of VTsIOM's tracking polls in Richard Rose and Neil Munro, *Elections without Order: Russia's Challenge to Vladimir Putin* (Cambridge University Press, 2002), p. 112.

6. Alexey Zudin, "Union of Right Forces (SPS)," in Michael McFaul, Nikolai Petrov, Andrei Ryabov, and Elizabeth Reisch, eds., *Primer on Russia's 1999 Duma Elections* (Washington: Carnegie Endowment for International Peace, 1999), p. 105.

7. See Yitzhak Brudny, "The Dynamics of 'Democratic Russia,' 1990–1993," *Post-Soviet Affairs,* vol. 9 (April–June 1993), pp. 141–70.

8. For a detailed portrait, see Michael McFaul, "Russia's Choice: The Perils of Revolutionary Democracy," in Timothy J. Colton and Jerry F. Hough, eds., *Growing Pains: Russian Democracy and the Election of 1993* (Brookings, 1998), pp. 115–39.

9. Eight of the parties competing for the liberal vote in 1995 were offshoots of Russia's Choice, and twenty had leaders once affiliated with Democratic Russia.

10. This was widely reported in the press. See the articles by Ol'ga Tropkina in *Nezavisimaya gazeta,* July 6, 1999, p. 3, and July 14, 1999, p. 3.

11. The leader of the faction was Vladimir Ryzhkov, the chairman of NDR's caucus in the Duma. Chubais and the DVR group much preferred to have Ryzhkov as NDR point man in any coalition with them, but Ryzhkov had ideo-

logical objections to his potential partners: "They are liberals, we are conservatives" (interview with McFaul, September 21, 1999).

12. *RFE/RL Newsline,* August 23, 1999.

13. "Chubais . . . literally forced the Right politicians of the old and new waves to accept each other. He effectively used his own authority, influence, and control of financial resources to solve the problems that arose in the process of building the coalition." Zudin, "Union of Right Forces," pp. 108–09.

14. Of 183 candidates on the national list, 42 were members of DVR and there were 17 each from New Force and Young Russia. Ten other organizations were represented. G. V. Golosov, "Politicheskiye partii i nezavisimyye kandidaty na dumskikh vyborakh" (Political parties and independent candidates in the Duma election), in V. Ya. Gel'man, G. V. Golosov, and Ye. Yu. Meleshkina, eds., *Vtoroi elektoral'nyi tsikl v Rossii 1999–2000 g.* (Russia's second electoral cycle in 1999–2000) (Moscow: Ves' Mir, 2002), pp. 44–45.

15. Gaidar explained (interview with McFaul, December 14, 1999) that he considered it more important to have a united front than for DVR to have proportionality on the list.

16. The most significant loss was the Forward Russia movement, which received 1.98 percent of the popular vote in 1995. Its leader, Boris Fëdorov, brought it into an electoral coalition with Our Home Is Russia and ran himself, unsuccessfully, for governor of Moscow region.

17. Leonid Gozman, interview with McFaul, April 24, 2003.

18. Kiriyenko's political organization was brand new and therefore members had little campaign experience. Instead of workers in the new organization, he invited two political consultants, Pëtr Shchedrovitskii and Yefim Ostrovskii, to represent his interests at campaign headquarters. They did not get along well with the rest of the SPS campaign team.

19. See Aleksei Makarkin in *Segodnya,* October 2, 1999, p. 1. Siberian Aluminum has a large smelter in Samara region, home base of Voice of Russia's founder, Konstantin Titov. A former mayor of Samara, Oleg Sysuyev, is vice president of Alpha. Our main source of information on fund-raising is McFaul's and also Colton's interviews with SPS campaign personnel. Transneft's support petered out after its president, the Chubais loyalist Dmitrii Savel'ëv, was removed from the company in late September.

20. Murat Gel'man served as head of Kiriyenko's mayoral campaign.

21. Mikhail Shneider, interview with McFaul, December 15, 1999. Shneider was responsible in the SPS staff for voter contact. We also benefited on this issue from interviews with Viktor Pokhmelkin (September 22, 1999) and Leonid Gozman (December 16, 1999). Gozman, a psychology professor and aide to Chubais at Unified Energy System, supervised the research program, which was carried out mostly by VTsIOM.

22. For changing meanings of "right" and "left" in Russian political discourse, see Timothy J. Colton, "Ideology and Russian Mass Politics: Uses of the

Left-Right Continuum," in Matthew Wyman, Stephen White, and Sarah Oates, eds., *Elections and Voters in Post-Communist Russia* (Cheltenham: Edward Elgar, 1998), pp. 161–83, and the sources given therein.

23. "Iz 'pravogo manifesta'" (From the "right-wing manifesto"), in *Nezavisimaya gazeta*, September 8, 1999 (insert *NG-Stsenarii*), p. 12. Similar statements were posted at www.prav.ru.

24. *Obrashcheniye Soyuza pravykh sil, "K tem, kto khochet zhit' kak v Yevrope"* (Appeal of the Union of Right Forces, "To those who want to live as they do in Europe") (leaflet, distributed fall 1999).

25. Tatyana Krasnopevtseva, "Comparing Party Platforms," *Russia's 1999 Duma Elections*, Bulletin no. 1 (Moscow Carnegie Center, December 2, 1999), pp. 2–3.

26. Gaidar and Nemtsov interviews with McFaul. The significance of this change of heart on Chechnya should not be underestimated. Gaidar's relations with Yeltsin were ruined by the row over the first war, and Nemtsov in 1996 spearheaded a mass signature campaign that put pressure on Yeltsin to negotiate with the rebels.

27. The question that received the most publicity was on deputies' immunity, where SPS candidates sparred over the details. "At the very least," as one correspondent wrote in November, "the campaign suggests to voters that the bloc's candidates are not running for the Duma in order to evade criminal prosecution." Laura Belin in *RFE/RL Russian Election Report*, no. 3 (November 19, 1999), p. 7.

28. *Golos Rossii: nezavisimyi regional'nyi zhurnal*, no. 7 (November 1999), p. 2. Television clips underscoring SPS's youthfulness often put words to this effect in the mouths of older people. In one ad, "an elderly man says he knows how people work 'when they get to be my age' and says young, smart people should be in government." *RFE/RL Russian Election Report*, no. 6 (December 10, 1999), p. 12.

29. *Nashe delo pravoye* (Our cause is correct) (leaflet, distributed fall 1999), pp. 2, 4.

30. According to an SPS staffer who asked not to be identified, the film of the meeting was originally played on ORT at 3 P.M. Its quality and length did not please SPS, so Chubais called Berezovskii and prevailed on him to have the ORT crew reshoot the event. The new clip was shown at 5 P.M. and on the evening news.

31. Vladimir Boxer, SPS official responsible for the districts, interview with McFaul, December 15, 1999.

32. Valerii Khomyakov, SPS coordinator for regional projects, interview with McFaul, February 19, 2002.

33. They continued to head policy-oriented think tanks after they went into politics—Epitsentr in Yavlinskii's case and the Institute for Transitional Economics in Gaidar's case.

34. Yavlinskii's views on economic reform are more comprehensive than space permits us to discuss here. For his most detailed statement, see Serguey Braguinsky and Grigory Yavlinsky, *Incentives and Institutions: The Transition to a Market Economy in Russia* (Princeton University Press, 2000). This book went through the same blind review process as any academic book at a leading university press.

35. Aleksei Kuz'min and Boris Ovchinnikov, "Yabloko," in Michael McFaul, Nikolai Petrov, and Andrei Ryabov, eds., *Rossiya nakanune Dumskikh vyborov 1999 goda* (Russia on the eve of the 1999 Duma election) (Moscow Carnegie Center, 1999), p. 141.

36. During the 1996 presidential race, for example, Yeltsin offered him the position of first deputy prime minister, in exchange for his withdrawal in Yeltsin's favor. Yavlinskii publicly demanded numerous concessions, including the removal of Prime Minister Chernomyrdin, which the president refused to grant.

37. Yurii Boldyrev, one of the three cofounders, left before the 1995 election, and in 1999 was high on another slate. Other defectors included Ivan Grachëv, Igor Lukashëv, and Vladimir Lysenko.

38. Vladimir Putin did meet with Yavlinskii in August 1999 to sell him on the grand right-center coalition, but got nowhere. Svetlana Sukhanova in *Segodnya,* August 19, 1999, pp. 1–2.

39. The Central Electoral Commission disqualified Mikhailov for failing to declare some personal property (see chapter 2). Travkin's party had existed only on paper for years. He was elected to the Duma on the NDR slate in 1995.

40. Seven of twelve names on its central sublist had been there in 1995, versus four of twelve for the KPRF and LDPR. Of the 175 candidates on the national list, 127 were members of the party. Kuz'min and Ovchinnikov, "Yabloko," p. 148, and Golosov, "Politicheskiye partii i nezavisimyye kandidaty," p. 45.

41. Source for the $7 million: a senior Yabloko campaign manager who prefers not to be identified. The figure may be an understatement of the true amount. See chapter 2, n. 16. Khodorkovskii publicly endorsed the party in July 1999.

42. From the Yabloko electoral program, "Budushcheye, Doveriye, Bezopasnost'" (The future, trust, security), at www.yabloko.ru/Union/Program/prog-99.html, p. 4. Beside this document, the party put out several dozen brochures on particular issues.

43. We learned about Igrunov's plan from McFaul's interview with him, December 10, 2002. For more on the films, see Sergei Pravosudov in *Nezavisimaya gazeta,* December 8, 1999, p. 3; and *RFE/RL Newsline,* December 7, 1999.

44. *RFE/RL Russian Election Report,* no. 7 (December 17, 1999), pp. 7–8.

45. See Boris Ovchinnikov, "Yabloko," in Michael McFaul, Nikolai Petrov, and Andrei Ryabov, eds., *Rossiya v izbiratel'nom tsikle 1999–2000 godov* (Rus-

sia in the electoral cycle of 1999–2000) (Moscow Carnegie Center, 2000), p. 168.

46. "Budushcheye, Doveriye, Bezopasnost'," p. 3. Against OVR, Yabloko's main charge was that it was the puppet of "feudal" elites in the provinces.

47. Interview in *Moskovskoye Yabloko,* no. 13 (December 11–17, 1999), p. 1.

48. "Putin chairs the government which I recently chaired. About 90 percent of the members of the government were appointed when I was prime minister, and I worked with those people." *Russian Political Monitor,* September 27, 1999, quoted here from *ISI Emerging Markets* of that day.

49. For a complete text, see www.chubais.ru/current/991125.html.

50. Vyacheslav Igrunov, interview with McFaul, December 19, 1999.

51. Source: a campaign consultant who urged Stepashin to change focus, interview with McFaul, February 23, 2000.

52. Highly unflattering statements about Yavlinskii's meddling by Igor Lukashëv, a member of the 1995–99 Yabloko caucus, are in "Russia: Yabloko Ex-Member Accuses Movement's Leader of Authoritarianism," *BBC Worldwide Monitoring,* July 22, 1999; and *Segodnya,* July 23, 1999.

53. Igrunov also negotiated with NDR. Their relations lost currency as the former party of power sank in the polls, although it was a factor in some district races and did win seven seats.

54. Rostislav Turovskii, "Osnovnyye itogi vyborov v odnomandatnykh okrugakh" (Key results of the election in the single-mandate districts), in McFaul and others, *Rossiya v izbiratel'nom tsikle 1999–2000 godov,* p. 268.

55. Source: 1999–2000 panel survey, waves 1 and 2.

56. Of 1999 Yabloko voters who had voted for a party in 1995, 29 percent had voted for the KPRF, 2 percent for the Agrarians, and 4 percent for Power to the People.

57. Yabloko claimed to produce and circulate more printed material than any other party (Ovchinnikov, "Yabloko," p. 169). Our survey data show this statement to have been either false or misguided.

58. SPS received 31.03 percent of its party-list votes in its top five regions and Yabloko 31.99 percent. This was approximately halfway between the regionally most concentrated party (OVR, 52.72 percent) and the least (Unity, 16.31 percent). Both parties' most productive regions included Moscow, Moscow province, and St. Petersburg. SPS's included Samara and Nizhnii Novgorod (the home region of Kiriyenko and Nemtsov), and Yabloko's included the Urals regions of Chelyabinsk and Sverdlovsk.

59. Forty-eight percent of Yabloko partisans voted for Yabloko, while 85 percent of SPS partisans voted for SPS. The largest group of defectors among the Yabloko partisans was the subset (22 percent) that voted for SPS.

60. Source: 1995–2000 panel. Twenty-one percent of weak SPS partisans in 2000, 26 percent of moderate SPS partisans, and 45 percent of strong SPS parti-

sans had been analogous partisans in 1995. For Yabloko, the figures were 13, 14, and 33 percent, respectively.

61. Our questions about preferred outcome in Chechnya were asked in wave 1 of the 1999–2000 panel (N = 1,919 weighted cases). Respondents were asked to locate seven parties, including SPS and Yabloko, on a five-point scale, with position 1 standing for commitment to keep Chechnya in the federation "at all costs" and 5 for allowing it to leave. Fifty-seven percent could not impute any position to SPS; those putting it at the hawkish end (scores 1 and 2) outnumbered those putting it at the dovish end (scores 4 and 5) by 29 percent to 6 percent. The number unable to say Yabloko's position was rather lower, 45 percent, but despite Yavlinskii's demand for a cease-fire and negotiated settlement, the distribution of positions attributed was not dissimilar to that for SPS, with 32 percent thinking Yabloko hawkish and 14 percent thinking it dovish.

62. The total effect for evaluations of Putin's work on the Yabloko vote is negatively signed but is not different from zero at the .05 level of significance.

63. Yabloko candidates finished first in three other districts but were not elected because the most votes were cast against all the candidates. When repeat elections were held in March 2000, independent candidates won all these districts.

64. The Samara victor, Vera Lekareva, took General Makashov's former seat in district 152. The incumbents are Viktor Pokhmelkin in Perm region and Yulii Rybakov in St. Petersburg's district 206.

65. Zadornov had been elected to the Duma in 1995 as a Yabloko candidate in the remote Kamchatka region but resigned his seat to become Yeltsin's finance minister. SPS tacitly supported Zadornov in the district by not funding its own candidate, the writer Mariya Arbatova.

66. Paraphrased by Laura Belin in *RFE/RL Russian Election Report*, no. 9 (March 3, 2000), p. 4.

67. Several SPS leaders endorsed Titov. Sergei Kovalëv, the former dissident, endorsed Yavlinskii. Titov said that the people in the bloc who supported him are those "for whom principles are more important than [government] posts." *RFE/RL Russian Election Report*, no. 12 (March 24, 2000), p. 11.

68. Although his home region was the only place Titov displayed any strength, he in fact finished third there, behind Putin and Zyuganov, and collected fewer than half as many votes as Putin. Titov resigned the governor's position in April only to run in the July election and win his old job back. His presidential campaign was well funded. Some say he raised about $10 million from his business sponsors, mostly from Samara region. Dmitrii Badovskii, "Kampaniya K. Titova" (The campaign of Konstantin Titov), in McFaul and others, *Rossiya v izbiratel'nom tsikle 1999–2000 godov*, p. 479.

69. Titov suggested in March that Yavlinskii withdraw in his favor, but phrased it in ways that Yavlinskii was sure to find objectionable. Yavlinskii, Titov said, was "ready to sit in opposition for not just 500 days but 500 years."

RFE/RL Russian Election Report, no. 10 (March 10, 2000), p. 4. When the marginal candidate Savast'yanov withdrew, he asked his supporters to vote for Yavlinskii.

70. Vyacheslav Igrunov and Sergei Mitrokhin, interviews with McFaul, March 23, 2000. Mitrokhin, a Yabloko member of the Duma, participated actively in the 2000 campaign but conceded it did not much involve the party's members or organization.

71. Source: interviews with political analysts close to Boris Berezovskii, Anatolii Chubais, and Vladimir Putin, by McFaul and Colton, March 2000. For public commentary, see Vladimir Boxer in Hale, *Russia's Electoral War,* pp. 144–45, and *RFE/RL Russian Election Report,* no. 9 (March 3, 2000), pp. 10–11.

72. In our survey panel, 19 percent received Yavlinskii mailings and 21 percent frequently encountered his street materials, as opposed to 11 percent and 12 percent, respectively, for the Yabloko campaign in 1999. Eight percent in communities in the lowest quintile by population size, but 35 percent in the highest quintile, saw Yavlinskii leaflets and posters; for Zyuganov, the figures were 17 percent and 20 percent.

73. Laura Belin in *RFE/RL Russian Election Report,* no. 11 (March 17, 2000), pp. 7–9.

74. Laura Belin in *RFE/RL Russian Election Report,* no. 12 (March 24, 2000), pp. 1–5.

75. Laura Belin in *RFE/RL Russian Election Report,* no. 10 (March 10, 2000), p. 10.

76. See Lee Sigelman and Eric Shiraev, "The Rational Attacker in Russia? Negative Campaigning in Russian Presidential Elections," *Journal of Politics,* vol. 64 (February 2002), p. 54.

77. "Russian Presidential Election Broadcast by Grigory Yavlinsky," *BBC Monitoring,* March 14, 2000. The passage was read out by a narrator.

78. *RFE/RL Russian Election Report,* no. 11 (March 17, 2000), p. 3.

79. These comparisons come from waves 2 and 3 of our 1999–2000 panel survey. With the 1996 presidential election, in which Yavlinskii ran fourth, continuity was less. Twenty-six percent of 1996 Yavlinskii voters who participated in the 2000 election voted for him a second time (according to waves 3 and 4 of our 1995–2000 panel).

80. Two analysts who have followed his career write correctly that "Yavlinskii, with the political image he had accumulated in previous years, was not perceived by voters as a politician who could successfully handle the duties of president." Il'ya Kudryavtsev and Boris Ovchinnikov, "Kampaniya G. Yavlinskogo" (The campaign of Grigorii Yavlinskii), in McFaul and others, *Rossiya v izbiratel'nom tsikle 1999–2000 godov,* p. 460. What this analysis omits is that Yavlinskii's image further deteriorated during the 2000 campaign.

81. As with the Zyuganov vote, the predicted probabilities in table 6-10 are sensitive to assessments of the other candidates, especially of the winner, Putin.

Putin's median score was for competence on three issues. If the simulation is repeated with the term for Putin set at zero, the probability of voting for Yavlinskii exceeds .50 at four issues.

82. A leading commentator called Yabloko's performance in the 2000 election his "true Waterloo." Leonid Radzikhovskii in *Segodyna*, March 28, 2000, p. 1. For a similar assessment, see Vladimir Korsunskii at www.Vesti.ru, March 26, 2000, p. 4.

Chapter Seven

1. Boris Yel'tsin, *Prezidentskii marafon* (Presidential marathon) (Moscow: AST, 2000), p. 358.

2. Quotation from Russian original, *Ot pervogo litsa: razgovory s Vladimirom Putinym* (From the first person: conversations with Vladimir Putin) (Moscow: VAGRIUS, 2000), p. 105. The book was published in English as Vladimir Putin, *First Person: An Astonishingly Frank Self-Portrait by Russia's President*, trans. Catherine Fitzpatrick (New York: PublicAffairs, 2000).

3. Sobchak did so in order to please the Yeltsin government, but in a marvelous example of political inconsistency he ran for the Duma himself on the list of the soon-to-be forgotten Russian Movement for Democratic Reforms.

4. Aleksandr Rar, *Vladimir Putin: "Nemets" v Kremle* (Vladimir Putin: "German" in the Kremlin) (Moscow: OLMA-PRESS, 2002), p. 104.

5. Compare ibid., pp. 106–10, with *Ot pervogo litsa*, pp. 105–09.

6. "The president of the firm Russian Video offered to do a broad advertising drive for Sobchak on local television, but demanded in return that the city administration help him get a loan for $300,000." The Russian tax police, apparently on Putin's initiative, searched the offices of the firm, after which the proposal was dropped. Enemies of Putin then spread false rumors that Putin owned shares in the company. Rar, *Vladimir Putin*, p. 110. Rar also writes (p. 109) that Putin refused all contributions from businesses associated with organized crime but was so nervous about them that during the campaign he slept with a loaded pistol beside his bed.

7. *Ot pervogo litsa*, p. 133.

8. The revenge was against Yakovlev, number three on the OVR list. Acrimony between Putin and him went back to Yakovlev's unseating of Sobchak in St. Petersburg and what Putin regarded as the subsequent persecution of his friend. Sobchak returned to Russia in 1999 under Putin's aegis, ran unsuccessfully for the State Duma, and died of a heart attack in February 2000. The Kremlin put up a candidate (Valentina Matviyenko) against Yakovlev in the May 2000 governor's election, but she made no headway and withdrew from the race, which Yakovlev won easily.

9. Paraphrase of Primakov statement by Marina Volkova, in *Nezavisimaya gazeta*, February 5, 2000, p. 3.

10. Figures posted at www.wciom.ru and www.russiavotes.org (a British website superintended by Richard Rose of Strathclyde University). Other leading polling firms showed the same trend, with small differences on the details. The ROMIR agency's numbers were available at www.romir.ru and the Public Opinion Foundation's at www.fom.ru. Wave 2 of our voters' survey, with a median date of interview of January 8, had 64 percent intending to vote for Putin.

11. In Henry E. Hale, ed., *Russia's Electoral War of 1999–2000: The Russian Election Watch Compendium* (Strengthening Democratic Institutions Project, John F. Kennedy School of Government, Harvard University, 2000), p. 143.

12. See Chrystia Freeland, *Sale of the Century: Russia's Wild Ride from Communism to Capitalism* (New York: Crown Books, 2000); and David E. Hoffman, *The Oligarchs: Wealth and Power in the New Russia* (New York: PublicAffairs, 2002).

13. Mikhail Margelov, deputy chairman of Putin campaign committee, interviews with McFaul, February 24, 2000, and Colton, April 15, 2000. For discussion by a perceptive journalist, see Yelena Tregubova in *Kommersant'-Vlast'*, March 28, 2000, p. 23.

14. *RFE/RL Russian Election Report*, no. 9 (March 3, 2000), p. 7, and no. 12 (March 24, 2000), pp. 5–6. Pribylovskii's position was explicated on the site www.deadline.ru. He is a serious person, but sometimes chooses light-hearted ways of expressing his views. In 1993, in a spoof of irresponsible politicians, he ran for the Duma in a Moscow district on a platform he named Subtropical Russia, in which he pledged to introduce legislation to outlaw cold winters in Russia and lower the boiling temperature of water.

15. Valentin Yumashev, interview with Colton, June 14, 2001.

16. Article 92 did explicitly deny him three presidential powers—to dissolve the Duma, initiate a referendum, and propose constitutional amendments.

17. "Otkrytoye pis'mo Vladimira Putina k rossiiskim izbiratelyam" (Open letter of Vladimir Putin to Russian voters), *Izvestiya*, February 25, 2000, p. 4, emphasis added.

18. Rostislav Turovskii, "Regional'nyye strategii kandidatov" (The regional strategies of the candidates), in Michael McFaul, Nikolai Petrov, and Andrei Ryabov, eds., *Rossiya v izbiratel'nom tsikle 1999–2000 godov* (Russia in the electoral cycle of 1999–2000) (Moscow Carnegie Center, 2000), p. 498.

19. Ibid., p. 500.

20. Vladislav Surkov went directly into the campaign from an executive position at Alpha Bank. Anatolii Chubais of Unified Energy System participated in brainstorming sessions.

21. Tsentral'naya izbiratel'naya komissiya Rossiiskoi Federatsii, *Vybory prezidenta Rossiiskoi Federatsii 2000: elektoral'naya statistika* (The 2000 election of the president of the Russian Federation: electoral statistics) (Moscow: Ves' Mir, 2000), pp. 125–32.

22. Statement at a symposium at Moscow Carnegie Center, March 14, 2000

(staff summary circulated as mimeo). In the same appearance, Medvedev defended Putin's refusal to say whom he would select as his prime minister.

23. Lee Sigelman and Eric Shiraev, "The Rational Attacker in Russia? Negative Campaigning in Russian Presidential Elections," *Journal of Politics*, vol. 64 (February 2002), p. 55.

24. Dozens of athletes, cultural figures, scientists, university presidents, heads of ethnic associations, businessmen, factory directors, and even military commanders signed Putin's official nomination papers in February but were not put on display during the campaign.

25. Our 1999–2000 panel survey, wave 3 (N = 1,755 weighted cases).

26. *RFE/RL Russian Election Report*, no. 10 (March 10, 2000), p. 5. Three minor candidates (Dzhabrailov, Pamfilova, and Podberëzkin) also had no paid TV advertisements, but they did use their unpaid time.

27. Interview on Radio Mayak with Andrei Bystritskii, March 19, 2000, transcript distributed by Federal News Service.

28. "Initiative Group Nominated Putin for President," *Jamestown Foundation Monitor*, vol. 6 (January 13, 2000), p. 3; *RFE/RL Russian Election Report*, no. 11 (March 17, 2000), p. 2; *RFE/RL Newsline*, March 3, 2000.

29. *RFE/RL Russian Election Report*, no. 9 (March 3, 2000), p. 8.

30. "Otkrytoye pis'mo."

31. The address was www.putin.ru. Putin's staff had shown awareness of the Internet when they created a government site in late December (www.pravitelstvo.gov.ru), at which an essay signed by Putin on "Russia at the Turn of the Millennium" was posted. It seems to have been aimed more at foreigners than at Russian voters.

32. The Central Electoral Commission demanded that Putin's headquarters distribute free copies, saying it was campaign propaganda, but enforcement was uneven. Putin headquarters claimed to have purchased 50,000 copies from the publisher. Some were given out without charge, but the book was easy to find for a price on the street and in bookstores.

33. On this last point, see Boris Makarenko, "Kampaniya V. Putina" (The campaign of Vladimir Putin), in McFaul and others, *Rossiya v izbiratel'nom tsikle 1999–2000 godov*, p. 433.

34. Sergei Chernyakhovskii, "Kampaniya G. Zyuganova" (The campaign of Gennadii Zyuganov), in McFaul and others, *Rossiya v izbiratel'nom tsikle 1999–2000 godov*, p. 449.

35. Both quotations from Laura Belin in *RFE/RL Russian Election Report*, no. 13 (April 7, 2000), pp. 9–10.

36. See Sergei Golovkov of Unity (in Hale, *Russia's Electoral War*, p. 186) on comparisons with Napoleon III, Bismarck, and de Gaulle.

37. All quotations here from "Otkrytoye pis'mo."

38. The theme of the strong state is a central one in "Russia at the Turn of the Millennium": "Russia will not soon become, if it ever becomes, a second copy of,

say, the U.S. or England, where liberal values have deep historic roots. A strong state for Russians is not an anomaly, not something that must be fought against, but on the contrary is the source and guarantor of order, the initiator and main driving force of all change." Quoted in Hale, *Russia's Electoral War,* p. 115.

39. On the origins of the super-region idea and its implementation after the election, see Eugene Huskey, "Political Leadership and the Center-Periphery Struggle: Putin's Administrative Reforms," in Archie Brown and Lilia Shevtsova, eds., *Gorbachev, Yeltsin, and Putin: Political Leadership in Russia's Transition* (Washington: Carnegie Endowment for International Peace, 2001), pp. 113–42. During the campaign, Putin also replaced many presidential representatives in the regions and addressed a meeting of the Union of Russian Cities, traditionally a counterweight to the governors.

40. Quotations again from "Otkrytoye pis'mo."

41. The groups were conducted just before or immediately after voting day by sociologist Leontii Byzov and his company, the Russian Independent Institute on Social and National Problems. Six met in Moscow, two in the provincial center of Tambov, and one in Pereyaslav'-Zalesskii, a small town. In his extended interviews with journalists, Putin mentioned de Gaulle and Ludwig Erhardt, the postwar chancellor of West Germany ("a very pragmatic person"), as his role models. *Ot pervogo litsa,* p. 175.

42. The skiing and ping-pong pictures were left out of the English-language edition of the book. For Putin's infatuation with fitness and sport, see Oleg Blotskii, *Vladimir Putin: istoriya zhizni* (Vladimir Putin: a history of his life), vol. 1 (Moscow: Mezhdunarodnyye otnosheniya, 2001). In 1976, the year after he joined the KGB, Putin was the judo champion of Leningrad, as St. Petersburg was then called.

43. Quoted in Hale, *Russia's Electoral War,* p. 163.

44. His religious awakening is said to date from 1993, when his wife was in a serious car crash, and was deepened by another family event, a fire that burned down their dacha several years later. There is a good description in www.pravda.ru, January 15, 2003. Several sources note that Putin's father was a "militant atheist," whereas his mother was a believer who gave him the crucifix he now wears around his neck.

45. *RFE/RL Russian Election Report,* no. 13 (April 7, 2000), p. 11.

46. Although the magnitude of this effect is large, the large standard errors in the estimate do not render it statistically significant from the zero at the level of confidence generally employed in our analysis. In this case, $p \leq .15$.

47. See Boris Makarenko, "Otechestvo-Vsya Rossiya" (Fatherland–All Russia), in McFaul and others, *Rossiya v izbiratel'nom tsikle 1999–2000 godov,* pp. 165–66. The difference in Putin's favor went from about 7 percent (in Bashkortostan) to about 29 percent (in St. Petersburg).

48. In the highly urbanized population, the special negative effect for Moscow residency also evaporates in 2000.

49. See Michael McFaul, *Russia's 1996 Presidential Election: The End of Polarized Politics* (Stanford, Calif.: Hoover Institution Press, 1997).

50. We repeat that the quantitative effects on the vote discussed here are estimated from a multistage model of the vote, with statistical controls for the confounding effects of other variables. For these particular explanatory variables, bivariate associations, which lack those controls, betray weaker associations. Forty-three percent of all our survey respondents who voted in March 2000 and who expressed an opinion on the president versus parliament question favored some sort of presidential primacy over parliament; for Putin voters, it was 52 percent. Thirty percent of all voters who answered the question thought rule by a strong leader unrestrained by parliament or elections would be fairly good for Russia, and 21 percent said it would be very good. Among Putin voters, these proportions were 32 and 22 percent, or almost the same.

51. Source: 1999–2000 panel, wave 3 (N = 1,755 weighted cases). Compare with table 3-3.

52. Yeltsin first came to general notice in the mid-1980s, when he was communist party boss of the city of Moscow, and especially in 1987, when he was the first party leader to break openly with Mikhail Gorbachev. He was elected to the Soviet parliament in 1989, became chairman of the Russian parliament in 1990, and was elected president of the Russian republic of the USSR in June 1991.

53. Within the 53 percent who mentioned at least one good decision, 10 percent mentioned two decisions and 2 percent mentioned three. Multiple answers for bad decisions were less frequent, coming to about one-half of 1 percent.

54. Seventy-five percent of respondents who approved completely of Putin's work described a good decision; 12 percent of those who disapproved strongly did so. Forty-two percent of persons who strongly disapproved of Putin's work volunteered a bad decision, while 20 percent of those who strongly approved of his work did so. This suggests that both admirers and detractors had a multivalent image of Putin.

55. Respondents often spoke interrelatedly of Chechnya and terrorism. A few referred only to terrorism. We have coded those responses as referring to Chechnya.

56. These responses are hard to interpret, since many if not most decisions about wages in contemporary Russia are made by private firms. Some respondents were probably thinking of public policies that stimulated economic growth and improved their pay indirectly. Others may have had in mind government decisions that lessened wage arrears in the state sector. Responses referring unambiguously to wage arrears were coded separately. They came to 3 percent of all references to good Putin decisions.

57. Although the issue cut both ways, more than twice as many citizens saw Putin's decisions on Chechnya in a positive light as saw them in a negative light. Chechnya had a roughly equal role in positive and negative thinking about Putin

as a decisionmaker, but many more Russians in 2000 thought Putin had made good decisions than thought he had made bad decisions.

58. Fifty-seven percent said they disapproved of the decision and 30 percent approved. The balance could not say.

59. Using the same methodology, the total effect of evaluations of Yeltsin's record as president on the Yeltsin vote was .82 in the first round of the 1996 election and .76 in the second round. See Timothy J. Colton, *Transitional Citizens: Voters and What Influences Them in the New Russia* (Harvard University Press, 2000), p. 183.

60. This second tendency does not apply smoothly across all conditions. For successive levels of approval of Putin, the total effect of evaluations of Yeltsin (the statistic in column 5 minus the statistic in column 1) goes from .36 for citizens holding the most negative evaluation of Putin to .45, .40, .25, and then .13.

61. The closest to Putin's margins would be Sergei Shoigu's +41 net score on empathy.

62. Our 1999–2000 panel, wave 3 (N = 1,755 weighted cases). Fifty-eight percent of Putin voters saw experience in state security as a plus, but this proportion was about 10 points higher among supporters of other candidates. Seventy-four percent of Zyuganov voters said they would be more likely to vote for a candidate who had worked in the security apparatus.

63. And yet, differences in assessments remain. For example, just over half of persons who thought Putin most competent on Chechnya thought he would be best on human rights and economic policy, whereas about three-quarters of them thought he would be best on foreign policy and on crime and corruption.

64. *Izvestiya,* March 4, 2000, p. 3.

Chapter Eight

1. The top-ranking bloc of variables in the parliamentary voting (partisanship) leads the others by a wide margin. In the presidential voting, the three leading influences (leadership qualities, evaluations of incumbents, and issue opinions) are closely bunched together.

2. Compare Timothy J. Colton, *Transitional Citizens: Voters and What Influences Them in the New Russia* (Harvard University Press, 2000), p. 222. The comparison is complicated by the fact that the 1996 presidential election had two rounds. The 2000 presidential election is closer to the runoff in the 1996 election than to the first round. In the party-list voting, partisanship ranked first in both 1995 and 1999; evaluations of leadership qualities were second in 1995 and third in 1999. In the presidential voting, issue opinions were first in the 1996 runoff and third in 2000; evaluations of incumbents were second in 1996 and first in 2000.

3. See www.nns.ru/Elect-99/chron99/1999/12/23.html.

4. The exception is the Movement in Support of the Army, which took two district seats.

5. On convergence of the party's platforms, see Tatyana Krasnopevtseva, "Comparing Party Platforms," *Russia's 1999 Duma Elections*, Bulletin no. 1 (Moscow Carnegie Center, December 2, 1999).

6. In the Duma election, there were 3,494 candidates on the party lists and 2,226 in the single-member districts.

7. For SPS to meet this criterion, it is necessary to factor in the votes cast in 1995 for several splinter groups other than Russia's Democratic Choice.

8. Avtandil Tsuladze in www.gazeta.ru, December 23, 2002.

9. Some of these individuals sat in the Duma for a month or two before exiting.

10. Boris Yel' tsin, *Prezidentskii marafon* (Presidential marathon) (Moscow: AST, 2000), p. 118.

11. Yurii Maslyukov, first deputy premier in 1998–99, and Igor Rodionov, minister of defense in 1996–97, are the best examples in the first category. Zyuganov, Valentin Kuptsov, and many others had been party apparatchiks under Soviet rule. Other former dignitaries had been prime minister of the Soviet Union (Nikolai Ryzhkov, who ran as an independent in 1999 with KPRF support), chairman of the Soviet parliament (Anatolii Luk'yanov), and minister of culture of the USSR (Nikolai Gubenko). Governors Vasilii Starodubtsev of Tula and Aman Tuleyev of Kemerovo ranked third and fourth on the KPRF's 1999 list.

12. Statement on ORT on election night, viewed by the authors.

13. Viktor Sheinis, "Vybory prezidenta: itogi i perspektivy" (The presidential election: results and perspectives), in Michael McFaul, Nikolai Petrov, and Andrei Ryabov, eds., *Rossiya v izbiratel' nom tsikle 1999–2000 godov* (Russia in the electoral cycle of 1999–2000) (Moscow Carnegie Center, 2000), p. 535.

14. Nikolai Petrov, "Vybory i obshchestvo" (The elections and society), in McFaul and others, *Rossiya v izbiratel'nom tsikle 1999–2000 godov,* p. 400.

15. Guillermo O' Donnell, "Delegative Democracy," *Journal of Democracy,* vol. 5 (January 1994), pp. 56–69.

16. Sergei Potapov, secretary of the KPRF central committee, quoted by Svetlana Sukhova in *Segodnya*, March 28, 2000, p. 2.

17. The communists at first demanded an inquiry, then quietly dropped the request. "One gets the impression that the KPRF leadership . . . feared getting into conflict with the authorities." Sergei Chernyakhovskii, "Kampaniya G. Zyuganova" (The campaign of Gennadii Zyuganov), in McFaul and others, *Rossiya v izbiratel' nom tsikle 1999–2000 godov,* p. 452.

18. Michael McFaul, "The Fourth Wave of Democracy *and* Dictatorship: Noncooperative Transitions in the Postcommunist World," *World Politics,* vol. 54 (January 2002), pp. 212–44.

19. On the differences between electoral and liberal democracies, see Larry Diamond, *Developing Democracy: Toward Consolidation* (Johns Hopkins University Press, 1999).

20. For elaboration, see Michael McFaul, *Russia's Unfinished Revolution: Political Change from Gorbachev to Putin* (Cornell University Press, 2001), chap. 9.

21. David Brady, *Critical Elections and Congressional Policy Making* (Stanford University Press, 1988).

22. See Adam Przeworski, *Democracy and the Market: Political and Economic Reforms in Eastern Europe and Latin America* (Cambridge University Press, 1991), esp. pp. 82–88.

23. Yeltsin continues to express general support for Putin but has criticized a number of specific decisions—for example, those to reinstate the melody of the Soviet national anthem and to renegotiate the confederal union with Belarus—and has hinted at doubts about others.

24. See Larry Diamond, "Thinking about Hybrid Regimes," *Journal of Democracy*, vol. 13 (July 2002), pp. 21–35; Steven Levitsky and Lucan Way, "The Rise of Competitive Authoritarianism," *Journal of Democracy*, vol. 13 (July 2002), pp. 51–65; Larry Diamond and Marc F. Plattner, eds., *Democracy after Communism* (Johns Hopkins University Press, 2002); and Marina Ottaway, *Democracy Challenged: The Rise of Semi-Authoritarianism* (Carnegie Endowment for International Peace, 2003). Some analysts have consistently labeled Russia's postcommunist regime a dictatorship. See in particular Peter Reddaway and Dmitri Glinski, *The Tragedy of Russia's Reforms: Market Bolshevism against Democracy* (Washington: U.S. Institute of Peace, 2001).

25. See Thomas F. Remington, "Putin, the Duma, and Political Parties," in Dale R. Herspring, ed., *Putin's Russia: Past Imperfect, Future Uncertain* (Boston: Rowman and Littlefield, 2003), pp. 39–62.

26. The pact scrapped a rule of thumb that assigned committee chairs in proportion to the size of the respective fractions. OVR and the two liberal groups, SPS and Yabloko, boycotted Duma sessions for several weeks, to no end.

27. Quoted by Susan Glasser in *Washington Post,* June 8, 2002, p. A14.

28. For details on the package, see Erika Weinthal and Pauline Jones Luong, "Resource Wealth and Institutional Change: The Political Economy of Tax Reform in Russia," unpublished paper, Tel Aviv University and Yale University (December 2002).

29. See Alexander Sokolowski, "Bankrupt Government: The Politics of Budgetary Irresponsibility in Yeltsin's Russia," Ph.D. dissertation, Princeton University, 2002.

30. Political polarization generally results in bad economic policy. Polarization between institutions produces especially bad policy, as the 1998 financial crisis in Russia starkly demonstrated. On the first issue, see Timothy Frye, "The Perils of Polarization: Economic Performance in the Postcommunist World," *World Politics*, vol. 54 (April 2002), pp. 308–37. On the second issue, see Sokolowski, "Bankrupt Government"; and Vladimir Mau, *Ekonomicheskaya reforma: skvoz' prizmu konstitutsii i politiki* (Economic reform:

through the prism of the constitution and politics) (Moscow: ad Marginem, 1999).

31. One representative is selected by the speaker of the regional assembly and confirmed by the assembly as a whole. The governor selects the second representative, but the assembly can veto the nominee with a two-thirds majority. Representatives serve at the pleasure of those who select them.

32. Aleksei Makarkin, "Sovet Federatsii: novyi sostav, novyye problemy" (The Federation Council: new composition, new problems), in Rostislav Turovskii, ed., *Politika v regionakh: gubernatory i gruppy vliyaniya* (Politics in the regions: governors and interest groups) (Moscow: Tsentr politicheskikh tekhnologii, 2002), pp. 53–75.

33. Vladimir Lysenko, "The Federation Council Fails to Become a House of Lords," in Yuri Senokosov and John Lloyd, eds., *Russia on Russia: Administrative and State Reform in Russia,* no. 5 (Moscow School of Political Studies, June 2002), p. 20.

34. The wording of the Russian constitution of 1993 allows such dramatic changes to occur in the way politics is organized without amending or changing the formal rules. For a strong statement to this effect, see Vladimir Ryzhkov in the *Moscow Times,* December 11, 2002, p. 10.

35. Many of the "federal inspectors" reporting to them from the administrative regions also have backgrounds in the FSB/KGB and uniformed police. Natal'ya Zubarevich, Nikolai Petrov, and Aleksei Titkov, "Federal'nyye okruga-2000" (The federal districts, 2000 version), in Nikolai Petrov, ed., *Regiony Rossii v 1999 g.* (The regions of Russia in 1999) (Moscow Carnegie Center, 2001), p. 190.

36. Nazdratenko, who supported the Unity bloc in 1999, was removed mainly because his government was incapable of dealing with power outages in the region. He was allowed to resign and was given the cushy Moscow post of head of the national fisheries agency, transferring later to the president's security apparatus. A variation on the formula was used to induce Governor Yakovlev of St. Petersburg to resign ahead of term in June 2003. Putin did not openly threaten to dismiss him but got Yakovlev to accept a senior position in Moscow (deputy prime minister) in exchange for early departure from his regional post.

37. Viktor Pokhmelkin and Sergei Yushenkov also quit SPS, ostensibly for the same reason. They joined forces with Berezovskii in 2002 to form a new movement, Liberal Russia, then broke ties with him some months later. Yushenkov was murdered in Moscow in April 2003.

38. Other defectors included well-known Duma deputies Nikolai Travkin and Yelena Mizulina.

39. In January 2003 SPS offered to support Yavlinskii as presidential candidate and to sever its ties to Anatolii Chubais, whom Yavlinskii abhors, but Yavlinskii rejected the proposition.

40. There were reports after the hostage crisis that Yavlinskii was considering taking a senior position in Putin's government. See Boris Sapozhnikov at www.gazeta.ru, December 23, 2002.

41. *RFE/RL Newsline,* February 28, 2000.

42. To register for the party-list half of the Duma election, a party must have at least 10,000 members and branches of no fewer than 100 members in forty-five regions. Parties that receive 3 percent of the party-list or presidential vote will be provided annual funding from the state budget.

43. This perception was widely discussed in the Russian press during the winter of 2002–03.

44. Pointing in a more positive direction is the 2002 federal law mandating proportional representation for determining 50 percent of the seats in local and regional legislatures, starting in July 2003. It creates incentives for party building at the subnational level, where it has gone at a snail's pace for the past decade. See the statement by Aleksandr Veshnyakov of the Central Electoral Commission at www.cikrf.ru/_1_en/doc_2_1.

45. The incident was widely reported at the time. See, for example, *Novosti Rossii* for November 9, 2000, at www.newsru.com/russia. Rutskoi confirmed the main elements of the story, without blaming Putin personally, in an interview with Colton in Moscow on June 5, 2001.

46. See *Novosti Rossii* for April 29, 2002.

47. See Anatolii Kostukov in *Nezavisimaya gazeta,* October 1, 2002, p. 1.

48. Revisions to the federal law on "basic guarantees of voter rights," adopted in June 2002, specify that only a court can remove a candidate for most violations of election law and can do so no later than five days prior to the election. We thank Henry Hale for this clarification.

49. Andreas Schedler, "The Menu of Manipulation," *Journal of Democracy,* vol. 13 (April 2002), p. 41.

50. Some Russian observers go so far as to speak of the militarization of civil government, the reverse of what Putin promised. See Olga Kryshtanovskaya, "Rezhim Putina: liberal'naya militokratiya?" (The Putin regime: liberal military rule?), unpublished manuscript (December 2002); and "KGB vo vlasti," *Kommersant-Vlast'*, December 23, 2002, posted at www.compromat.ru/main/fsb/kgbvovlasti1.

51. See, for instance, their publications: "Now Happiness Remains: Civilian Killings, Pillage, and Rape in Alkhan-Yurt," *Russia/Chechnya,* vol. 12 (April 2000), pp. 1–33; "February 5: A Day of Slaughter in Novye Aldi," *Russia/Chechnya,* vol. 12 (June 2000), pp. 1–43; "The 'Dirty War' in Chechnya: Forced Disappearances, Torture, and Summary Executions," *Russia/Chechnya,* vol. 13 (March 2001), pp. 1–42; and "Burying the Evidence: The Botched Investigation into a Mass Grave in Chechnya," *Russia/Chechnya,* vol. 13 (May 2001), pp. 1–26. *Chechnya Weekly,* published by the Jamestown Foundation, also provides

full coverage of the war, including human rights violations. There is extensive discussion of the first and second wars in Matthew Evangelista, *The Chechen Wars: Will Russia Go the Way of the Soviet Union?* (Brookings, 2002). Evangelista writes (p. 140) of "incontrovertible evidence that the Russian armed forces have committed systematic atrocities and war crimes" in both Chechen wars.

52. This figure is cited in Sarah E. Mendelson, "Russia, Chechnya, and International Norms: The Power and Paucity of Human Rights?" Working Paper (Washington: National Council for Eurasian and East European Research, July 17, 2001), p. 11.

53. Details may be found in the two issues on civil society in Russia in *Demokratizatsiya*, vol. 10 (Spring and Summer 2002); and in Sarah E. Mendelson, "Russians' Rights Imperiled: Has Anybody Noticed?" *International Security*, vol. 26 (Spring 2002), pp. 39–69.

54. Those involve Aleksandr Nikitin and Grigorii Pas'ko, who were accused of leaking classified information on the Russian navy's mismanagement of nuclear waste. Both were arrested while Yeltsin was still president. However, researcher Igor Sutyagin of the United States and Canada Institute of the Russian Academy of Sciences remains in jail, charged with treason for his collaboration with Western research organizations.

55. For details, see Misha Lipman and Michael McFaul, "Putin and the Media," in Herspring, *Putin's Russia*, pp. 63–84.

56. *RFE/RL Russian Political Weekly*, April 2, 2002.

57. Criminal prosecution by the national and regional authorities has also been widely utilized. Oleg Panfilov, the director of the Center for Journalism in Extreme Situations, has reported that the number of criminal cases opened against journalists under Putin already exceeds the total under Yeltsin. Quoted in *RFE/RL Russian Political Weekly*, January 11, 2003.

58. For details, see David E. Hoffman, *The Oligarchs: Wealth and Power in the New Russia* (New York: PublicAffairs, 2002).

59. The parties are thus devising new information strategies. These include expensive means for distributing programming to regional and cable stations.

60. See the argument in Adam Przeworski, Michael Alvarez, José Antonio Cheibub, and Fernando Limongi, *Democracy and Development: Political Institutions and Well-Being in the World, 1950–1990* (Cambridge University Press, 2000).

61. For overviews, see Leon Aron, "Russia Reinvents the Rule of Law," *AEI Russian Outlook*, March 20, 2002; and Richard Conn, "Challenges of Implementing a New Legal System," *Russia Business Watch*, vol. 10 (Winter 2002-03), pp. 13–19.

62. Alexander Nikitin and Jane Buchanan, "The Kremlin's Civic Forum: Cooperation or Cooptation for Civil Society in Russia?" *Demokratizatsiya*, vol. 10 (Spring 2002), pp. 147–65.

63. Remarks translated and circulated by Federal News Service, December 10, 2002.

64. The question about the idea of democracy was asked in wave 1 of the 1999–2000 panel and the other questions in wave 2.

65. Forty-six percent of Zyuganov voters felt the country could have both democracy and a strong state and 46 percent that it could have both democracy and economic growth. In the forced-choice questions, 62 percent of Zyuganov supporters preferred a strong state to democracy and 68 percent preferred economic growth to democracy.

66. See James Goldgeier and Michael McFaul, "George W. Bush and Russia," *Current History*, vol. 101 (October 2002), pp. 313–24.

67. On the theory and its critics, see Michael Brown, Sean Lynn-Jones, and Steven Miller, eds., *Debating the Democratic Peace* (Cambridge, Mass.: MIT Press, 1996).

68. For elaboration, see Michael McFaul, "The Precarious Peace: Domestic Politics in the Making of Russian Foreign Policy," *International Security*, vol. 22 (Winter 1997–98), pp. 5–35.

69. James Goldgeier and Michael McFaul, *Power and Purpose: U.S. Policy toward Russia after the Cold War* (Brookings, 2003).

70. Ibid.

71. In *Moscow Times*, November 25, 2002, p. 4.

72. Joel S. Hellman, "Winners Take All: The Politics of Partial Reform in Postcommunist Transitions," *World Politics*, vol. 50 (January 1998), pp. 203–34; Valerie Bunce, "The Political Economy of Postsocialism," *Slavic Review*, vol. 58 (Winter 1999), pp. 756–93; Anders Åslund, *Building Capitalism: The Transformation of the Former Soviet Bloc* (Cambridge University Press, 2002), chap. 9.

73. Examples of legislation Congress could review are restrictions on high-technology exports, severe dumping laws regarding Russian goods (especially steel), and the Jackson-Vanik Amendment to the 1974 Trade Act, the purpose of which was to enable the free emigration of Jews from the Soviet Union. Some executive policies, such as the requirement that Russian diplomats report their travel plans beyond a twenty-five-mile radius from Washington, also should be abolished. The most harmful holdover from the cold war era is the American visa regime still in place that impedes and complicates legitimate Russian travel in the United States. Russia also still has many laws on the books that are left-overs from the cold war era. For instance, Russia still refuses the use of Russian airspace for the commercial Global Positioning System. Russia also still has in place an outdated visa regime and registration system for American travelers to and residents in Russia, which if anything has become more restrictive in recent years.

74. For details, see Goldgeier and McFaul, *Power and Purpose*.

75. See on this point George P. Shultz, *Turmoil and Triumph: Diplomacy, Power, and the Victory of the American Ideal* (New York: Simon and Shuster, 1993).

Appendix A

1. See www.umich.edu/~cses. The data from this module and other core questions were archived in late 2002. The entire data set is being archived with the Inter-University Consortium for Political and Social Research in the fall of 2003.

2. See Timothy J. Colton, *Transitional Citizens: Voters and What Influences Them in the New Russia* (Harvard University Press, 2000), pp. 236–38, 317, which gives practice for an analogous three-wave survey done in 1995–96. The main difference is that in 1999–2000 we substituted the Siberian region of Novosibirsk for the less accessible Khanty-Mansiiskii district.

3. To be precise, the sampling procedure results in the selection of dwellings, within which one adult is selected for questioning using the procedure developed by Leslie Kish. A total of 3,074 dwellings were selected, 120 of which were found to be permanently or temporarily unoccupied as a residence.

4. The 2,447 attempts to interview included the 2,427 persons who had been interviewed in all three waves in 1995–96, as well as 20 who had participated in two of the three rounds.

Appendix B

1. For a description of multinomial logit, see J. Scott Long, *Regression Models for Categorical and Limited Dependent Variables* (Thousand Oaks, Calif.: Sage, 1997), chap. 6; and G. S. Maddala, *Limited-Dependent and Qualitative Variables in Econometrics* (Cambridge University Press, 1986), chap. 2.

2. One thousand Monte Carlo simulations were done for each estimation, using Michael Tomz, Jason Wittenberg, and Gary King, CLARIFY: Software for Interpreting Statistical Results, Version 2.1 (Harvard University, January 5, 2003, at www.king.harvard.edu). CLARIFY is used in conjunction with the STATA package.

3. Warren E. Miller and J. Merrill Shanks, *The New American Voter* (Harvard University Press, 1996), p. 196. Miller and Shanks use linear regression to estimate their total effects.

4. Ibid., pp. 205–09.

Appendix C

1. A fraction of 1 percent could not say. Of those who did not watch the news even once, some watched no television, some watched television but not

the daily news, and 1 percent said they did watch the news but had not done so in the preceding week.

2. This is partly an artifact of scheduling. For most of the period under review, Dorenko and Kiselëv shared the same time slot, 9 P.M. Sundays.

Appendix D

1. In principle, total macro-stability could coexist with total micro-instability. Imagine a hypothetical electorate in which two parties fight two elections four years apart and get an exactly equal number of votes in both elections. This could be the case even if 100 percent of the supporters of each party, and hence 100 percent of the active electorate, switched parties between elections.

2. See especially Hilde T. Himmelweit, Marianne Jaeger Biberian, and Janet Stockdale, "Memory for Past Vote: Implications of a Study of Bias in Recall," *British Journal of Political Science*, vol. 8 (July 1978), pp. 365–76. Cf. Hilde T. Himmelweit, Patrick Humphreys, and Marianne Jaeger, *How Voters Decide*, 2d ed. (Milton Keynes, U.K.: Open University Press, 1985); Bo Särvik and Ivor Crewe, *Decade of Dealignment: The Conservative Victory of 1979 and Electoral Trends in the 1970s* (Cambridge University Press, 1983); and Donald Granberg and Sören Holmberg, *The Political System Matters: Social Psychology and Voting Behavior in Sweden and the United States* (Cambridge University Press, 1988).

3. The median date for the 1999–2000 panel's wave 2 (post-Duma election) interview was January 8, 2000. For the 1995–2000 panel, the median date of the wave 4 interview was April 24, 2000.

4. Strictly speaking, respondents were asked for which party, if any, they had voted. Inferences about the flow of the vote were made post hoc, by the researchers.

5. Most students of Russian elections issue caveats about the reliability of recall information, then proceed to use it as if it were authentic. For an example of such carelessness by one of the authors of the present volume, see Timothy J. Colton, *Transitional Citizens: Voters and What Influences Them in the New Russia* (Harvard University Press, 2000), pp. 8–9.

6. For comparability, this counts only respondents who participated in the March 2000 presidential election and whose behavior in 1996 could be confirmed. N = 1,197 weighted cases for the first round in 1996 and 1,178 weighted cases for the second round.

7. The median date for wave 1 interviews was November 22, 1999, or forty-seven days before the median date for wave 2 interviews.

8. The questions about the 1995 Duma election were numbers 21 and 22 in wave 4 of the 1995–2000 panel. Questions about the 1999 Duma elections were numbers 27 and 28. The intervening questions were about the two rounds of the 1996 presidential election.

9. Part of the reason is accelerated attrition in the panel among 1995 nonvoters. Fifty-nine percent of known participants in the 1995 party-list vote were reinterviewed in 2000, whereas the reinterview rate for 1995 abstainers was 51 percent. A more serious problem has to do with the underrepresentation of 1995 abstainers in the panel from the outset (a phenomenon found in almost all election surveys), which has echo effects in the 2000 wave of the panel.

Index